THE YEAR BOOK OF WORLD AFFAIRS 1982

VOLUME 36

To
GEORGE W. KEETON
President
of
The London Institute of World Affairs
on his
Eightieth Birthday
May 22, 1982

THE YEAR BOOK

OF

WORLD AFFAIRS

1982

Published under the auspices of
THE LONDON INSTITUTE OF WORLD AFFAIRS

WESTVIEW PRESS

Boulder, Colorado

All editorial communications should be addressed to the
Managing Editor, 9 Boswell Drive, Ickleford,
Hitchin, Hertfordshire, SG5 3YB, England

Published in Great Britain in 1982 by
Stevens & Sons Limited of
11 New Fetter Lane, London
Photoset by
Promenade Graphics Ltd., Cheltenham
Printed in Great Britain by
Page Bros. (Norwich) Ltd.

Published in the United States of America in 1982 by
Westview Press
5500 Central Avenue
Boulder, Colorado 80301
Frederick A. Praeger, Publisher

Library of Congress Catalog Card Number 47–29156

ISBN 0 86531–392–X

CONTENTS

v

TRENDS AND EVENTS

This annual survey is intended to serve three purposes:

(1) With every additional volume of this *Year Book* it becomes increasingly difficult for new readers to derive the fullest benefit from the material available in earlier volumes. This survey brings together references to themes examined in the past which have particular current relevance.

(2) The specific object of an annual publication is to make possible analyses in a wider perspective and on the basis of more mature reflection than may be possible in a quarterly or monthly journal. Thus it is not the object of this *Year Book* to provide instant information on current issues of world affairs. Yet, international affairs have a stereotyped and, largely, repetitive character, so that, frequently, a "new" happening or "modern" development has been anticipated in one or more of the earlier volumes of the *Year Book*. "Trends and Events" provides evidence of some such community as may be traced over a span of years.

(3) References to earlier contributions also offer readers an opportunity to judge for themselves the adequacy of the conceptual and systematic frameworks chosen or taken for granted in the papers selected:

(A) SUPER-POWER POLITICS

1. *Relations between the Super-Powers*
Buchan, A.: *An Expedition to the Poles* (29 Y.B.W.A. 1975)
Geusau, F.A.M. Alting von: *Détente After Helsinki* (32 *ibid.*)
Home, The Rt. Hon. Lord: *The Scope and Limits of Détente* (34 *ibid.* 1980)
Nussbaumer, A.: *Industrial Co-operation and East-West Trade* (32 *ibid.* 1978)
Schwarzenberger, G.: *An Inter-Camp Agenda* (18 *ibid.* 1964)
———: *From Bipolarity to Multipolarity?* (21 *ibid.* 1967)
———: *Détente and International Law* (35 *ibid.* 1981)

2. *Super-Power Hegemony*
Ball, M.M.: *Recent Developments in Inter-American Relations* (3 *ibid.* 1949)
Berner, M.F.C.: *The Panama Canal and Future United States Hemisphere Policy* (34 *ibid.* 1980)
Bettany, A.G.: *Czechoslovakia Between East and West* (1 *ibid.* 1947)

1

Blakemore, H.: *Chile: Continuity and Change* (27 *ibid.* 1973)
Burnham, C.G.: *Czechoslovakia: Thirty Years After Munich* (23 *ibid.* 1969)
Falk, R.A.: *The Logic of State Sovereignty Versus the Requirements of World Order* (27 *ibid.* 1973)
Ginsburgs, G.: *Socialist Internationalism and State Sovereignty* (25 *ibid.* 1971)
———: *The Constitutional Foundations of the "Socialist Commonwealth"* (27 *ibid.* 1973)
Graber, D.A.: *United States Intervention in Latin America* (16 *ibid.* 1962)
Hilton, R.: *Castrophobia in the United States* (18 *ibid.* 1964)
Hutchinson, G.W.: *The Coup in Chile* (29 *ibid.* 1975)
Kaplan, M.A.: *Theoretical Inquiry and the Balance of Power* (14 *ibid.* 1960)
Katona, P. and Jotischky, L.: *New Patterns in Inter-Communist Relations* (17 *ibid.* 1963)
Lapenna, I.: *International Law Viewed Through Soviet Eyes* (15 *ibid.* 1961)
———: *The Soviet Concept of Socialist International Law* (29 *ibid.* 1975)
Nussbaumer, A.: *The Economic Systems of Socialist Eastern Europe: Principles Development and Operation* (29 *ibid.* 1975)
Parkinson, F.: *The Alliance for Progress* (18 *ibid.* 1964)
———: *Santo Domingo and After* (20 *ibid.* 1966)
Pettman, R.: *Pluralist America in a Hierarchic World* (34 *ibid.* 1980)
Remington, R.A.: *The Warsaw Pact: Communist Coalition Politics in Action* (27 *ibid.* 1973)
Rubin, A.P.: *The Panama Canal Treaties: Locks on the Barn Door* (35 *ibid.* 1981)
Salera, V.: *Economic Relations between the United States and Latin America* (14 *ibid.* 1960)
Seara Vazquez, M.: *Zones of Influence* (27 *ibid.* 1973)
Seton-Watson, H.: *Eastern Europe* (3 *ibid.* 1949)
Schwarzenberger, G.: *Hegemonial Intervention* (13 *ibid.* 1959)
———: *Civitas Maxima?* (29 *ibid.* 1975)
Strange, S.: *Cuba and After* (17 *ibid.* 1963)
Whitaker, A.P.: *The Organisation of American States* (13 *ibid.* 1959)
Wood, B.: *The Organisation of American States* (33 *ibid.* 1979)
Yalem, R.J.: *Regional Security Communities and World Order* (33 *ibid.* 1979)

3. *China*
Adie, W.A.C.: *China and the Developed Countries* (20 *ibid.* 1966)
Bell, C.: *The Containment of China* (22 *ibid.* 1968)

Boardman, R.: *China's Rise as a Nuclear Power* (25 *ibid.* 1971)
———: *Chinese Foreign Policy: Options for the 1980s* (34 *ibid.* 1980)
Buchan, A.: *An Expedition to the Poles* (29 *ibid.* 1975)
Erickson, J.: *The World Strategic Balance* (23 *ibid.* 1969)
Fitzmaurice, G.B.: *Chinese Representation in the United Nations* (6 *ibid.* 1952)
Frankel, J.: *The Balance of Power in the Far East* (7 *ibid.* 1953)
Katona, P.: *Sino-Soviet Relations* (26 *ibid.* 1976)
Keeton, G.W.: *Nationalism in Eastern Asia* (1 *ibid.* 1947)
Lindsay, Lord: *Chinese Foreign Policy* (15 *ibid.* 1961)
Lewisohn, W.: *Basic Problems in Modern China* (3 *ibid.* 1949)
Meissner, B.: *The Political Treaties of China and the Soviet Union in East Asia*
Schwarzenberger, G.: *Beyond Power Politics?* (19 *ibid.* 1965)
———: *From Bipolarity to Multipolarity?* (21 *ibid.* 1967)
Wittfogel, K.A.: *The Russian and Chinese Revolutions: A Socio-Historical Comparison* (15 *ibid.* 1961)
Yahuda, M.B.: *China's Nuclear Policy* (23 *ibid.* 1969)
Yalem, R.J.: *Tripolarity and World Politics* (28 *ibid.* 1974)
Yu, G.T.: *China in Africa* (24 *ibid.* 1970)

4. *In-between Areas*

(a) *Western Europe*
Burmeister, W.: *Brandt's Opening to the East* (27 *ibid.* 1973)
Clawson, R.W.: *EEC-CMEA Relations* (34 *ibid.* 1980)
Friedlander, R.A.: *Problems of the Mediterranean: A Geopolitical Perspective* (32 *ibid.* 1978)
Morgan, R.P.: *The Scope of German Foreign Policy* (20 *ibid.* 1966)
Northedge, F.S.: *American, Russia and Europe* (28 *ibid.* 1974)
Richardson, J.L.: *Two Theories of West European Defence* (15 *ibid.* 1961)
Scheuner, V.: *The Future of the European Community* (33 *ibid.* 1979)
Schmidt, H.: *New Tasks for the Atlantic Alliance* (29 *ibid.* 1975)
Smith, M.H.: *Britain and the United States in the Eighties* (35 *ibid.* 1981)
Strange, S.: *Strains on Nato* (10 *ibid.* 1956)
Williams, G.: *European Defence in the 1970s* (27 *ibid.* 1973)

(b) *Middle East*
Frankel, J.: *The Middle East in Turmoil* (10 *ibid.* 1956)
Friedlander, R.A.: *Problems of the Mediterranean: A Geopolitical Perspective* (32 *ibid.* 1978)

James, A.: *Recent Development in United Nations Peace-keeping* (31 *ibid.* 1977)

Kirk, G.: *The Middle Eastern Scene* (14 *ibid.* 1960)

Mitchell, C.R.: *Peace-keeping: The Police Function* (30 *ibid.* 1976)

Neumann, R.G.: *The Near East After the Syrian Coup* (16 *ibid.* 1962)

Parkinson, F.: *Bandung and the Underdeveloped Countries* (10 *ibid.* 1956)

Rodinson, M.: *Israel: The Arab Options* (22 *ibid.* 1968)

Roth, S.J.: *World Jewry and Israel* (28 *ibid.* 1974)

Spiegel, S.L.: *The Carter Administration and the Arab-Israeli Dispute* (34 *ibid.* 1980)

Strange, S.: *Palestine and the United Nations* (3 *ibid.* 1949)

———: *Suez and After* (11 *ibid.* 1957)

Troutbeck, Sir John: *Stresses Within the Arab World* (12 *ibid.* 1958)

(c) *Africa*

Berridge, G.: *Apartheid and the West* (35 *ibid.* 1981)

Bissell, R.E.: *The Ostracism of South Africa* (32 *ibid.* 1978)

Butterworth, R.: *The Future of South Africa* (31 *ibid.* 1977)

Doxey, G.V. & M.: *The Prospects of Change in South Africa* (19 *ibid.* 1965)

Doxey, M.: *The Rhodesian Sanctions Experiment* (25 *ibid.* 1971)

Legum, C.: *Foreign Intervention in Africa* (I-34 *ibid.* 1980; II-35 *ibid.* 1981)

———: *South Africa: The Politics of Detente (30 ibid.* 1976)

———: *The Future of Ethopia* (28 *ibid.* 1974)

Longmore, L.: *The South African Dilemma* (8 *ibid.* 1954)

Shaw, T.M.: *Southern Africa: From Detente to Deluge* (32 *ibid.* 1978)

Taylor, T.: *President Nixon's Arms Supply Policy* (26 *ibid.* 1972)

(d) *South-East Asia*

Burton, J.W.: *Western Intervention in South-East Asia* (20 *ibid.* 1966)

Caldwell, J.A.M.: *The United States Empire in the Far East* (21 *ibid.* 1967)

Houghton, N.D.: *Social Structure and Foreign Policy of the United Nations* (15 *ibid.* 1961)

Johnson, J.T.: *Just War, the Nixon Doctrine and the Future Shape of American Military Policy* (29 *ibid.* 1975)

Livingston, G.S.: *The Indo-China War and American Values* (25 *ibid.* 1971)

Mahajano, U.: *Sino-American Rapprochement and the New Configurations in South-East Asia* (29 *ibid.* 1975)

———: *Sino-Soviet Conflict and Rivalry in South-East Asia in the Post-Vietnam Phase* (32 *ibid.* 1978)

Meissner, B.: *The Political Treaties of China and the Soviet Union in East Asia* (27 *ibid*. 1973)

Morgenthau, H.J.: *United States Foreign Policy* (9 *ibid*. 1955)

Nicholas, H.G.: *The New Administration and United States Foreign Policy* (11 *ibid*. 1957)

Purcell, V.: *Indo-China and the Prospect in South East Asia* (9 *ibid*. 1955)

Rosenau, J.N. and Holsti, O.R.: *The United States In (and Out of) Vietnam* (34 *ibid*. 1980)

Smith, M.H. and Carey, R.: *The Nixon Legacy and American Foreign Policy* (32 *ibid*. 1978)

Vincent, R.: *Kissinger's System of Foreign Policy* (31 *ibid*. 1977)

(B) AUTHORITY AND DISSENT

1. *Dissent*

Glazov, Y.: *Dissent in Post-Stalinist Russia* (35 Y.B.W.A. 1981)

Roberts, A.: *Civil Resistance as a Technique in International Relations* (24 *ibid*. 1970

Szamuely, T.: *Student Revolt in East West* (24 *ibid*. 1970)

2. *Human Rights*

Franck, T.: *"Congressional Imperialism" and Human-Rights Policy* (35 *ibid*. 1981)

Hermens, F.A.: *Return to Democratic Government* (32 *ibid*. 1978)

Honig, F.: *Criminal Justice in Germany Today* (5 *ibid*. 1951)

Loescher, G.D.: *Human Rights and the Helsinki-Belgrade Process* (35 *ibid*. 1981)

Martin, A.: *Human Rights and World Politics* (5 *ibid*. 1951)

3. *Civil Strife*

Duncanson, D.: *Dilemmas of Defence Against National Liberation* (34 *ibid*. 1980)

Foot, M.R.D.: *Resistance, War and Revolution* (31 *ibid*. 1977)

Mitchell, C.R.: *External Involvement in Civil Strife: The Case of Chad* (26 *ibid*. 1972)

Roberts, A.: *Civil Resistance as a Technique in International Relations* (23 *ibid*. 1970)

Shearman, H.: *Conflict in Northern Ireland* (24 *ibid*. 1970)

4. *Terrorism*

Kittrie, N.N.: *Reconciling the Irreconcilable: The Quest for International Agreement over Political Crime and Terrorism* (32 *ibid*. 1978)

(C) Control of the Arms Race

1. *The Arms Race*

Barnaby, F.: *The Strategic Balance* (34 Y.B.W.A. 1980)

Bellany, I.: *The Acquisition of Arms by Poor States* (30 *ibid.* 1976)

Burns, A.L.: *Military Technology and International Politics* (15 *ibid.* 1961)

Cowley, Sir John: *Future Trends in Warfare* (14 *ibid.* 1960)

Douglas-Home, C.: *The Arms Sales Race* (23 *ibid.* 1969)

Erickson, J.: *The World Strategic Balance* (23 *ibid.* 1969)

Joynt, C.B.: *Arms Races and the Problem of Equilibrium* (18 *ibid.* 1964)

Martin, L.W.: *Ballistic Missile Defence and the Strategic Balance* (21 *ibid.* 1967)

Millar, T.B.: *On Nuclear Proliferation* (21 *ibid.* 1967)

Radojkovic, M.: *Les Armes Nucleaires et le Droit International* (16 *ibid.* 1962)

Smart, I.: *Alliance, Deterrence and Defence* (26 *ibid.* 1972)

Smith, H.A.: *Modern Weapons and Modern War* (9 *ibid.* 1955)

Williams, G.: *The Strategic Nuclear Balance and the Defence of Europe* (27 *ibid.* 1973)

2. *Attempts at Control*

Boyle, Sir Dermott: *Thoughts on the Nuclear Deterrent* (16 *ibid.* 1962)

Bull, H.: *Two Kinds of Arms Control* (17 *ibid.* 1963)

Coffey, J.I.: *The Limitation of Strategic Armaments* (26 *ibid.* 1972)

Curle, A.: *Peace Studies* (30 *ibid.* 1976)

Dinstein, Y.: *Another Step in Codifying the Laws of War* (28 *ibid.* 1974)

Garnett, J.C.: *The Concept of War* (30 *ibid.* 1976)

James, A.: *Recent Developments in United Nations Peace-keeping* (31 *ibid.* 1977)

Keohane, D.: *Hegemony and Nuclear Non-proliferation* (35 *ibid.* 1981)

Lee, R.: *Safeguards Against Nuclear Proliferation* (23 *ibid.* 1969)

Mitchell, C.R.: *Peace-keeping: The Police Function* (30 *ibid.* 1976)

Ranger, R.: *Arms Control in Theory and in Practice* (31 *ibid.* 1977)

Schwarzenberger, G.: *The Law of Armed Conflict: A Civilised Interlude?* (28 *ibid.* 1974)

(D) The World Economy

1. *Growth, Employment, Inflation and Oil*

Friedlander, R.A.: *Problems of the Mediterranean: A Geopolitical Perspective* (32 Y.B.W.A. 1978)

Odell, P.R.: *The International Oil Companies in the New World Oil Market* (32 *ibid.* 1978)

Scamell, W.M.: *International Economic Co-operation and the Problem of Full Employment* (6 *ibid.* 1952)
Shaw, C.A.: *Dilemmas of Super-Growth* (30 *ibid.* 1976)
Vaizey, J.: *International Inflation* (30 *ibid.* 1976)

2. *Monetary Systems*

Cohen, P.M.: *The Future of Gold* (31 *ibid.* 1977)
Desai, R.R.: *World Monetary Reform* (20 *ibid.* 1966)
Ross, L.W.: *The Washington Monetary Agreement* (26 *ibid.* 1972)
——: *Flexible Exchange Rates* (30 *ibid.* 1976)
Seidl-Hohenveldern, I.: *Multinational Enterprises and the International Law of the Future* (29 *ibid.* 1975)

3. *Trade and Payments*

Paenson, I.: *The Problems of East-West Trade* (10 *ibid.* 1956)
Ramcharan, B.G.: *Equality and Discrimination in International Economic Law* (III): *The Commonwealth Preferential System* (26 *ibid.* 1969)
Robertson, D.: *Proposals for a North Atlantic Free Trade Area* (23 *ibid.* 1969)
Strange, S.: *The Commonwealth and the Sterling Area* (13 *ibid.* 1969)
——: *Changing Trends in World Trade* (16 *ibid.* 1962)
Wells, S.J.: *The Kennedy Round* (20 *ibid.* 1966)

4. *The Third World*

Harrod, J.: *Non-Governmental Organisations and the Third World* (24 *ibid.* 1970)
Heeger, G.: *Turmoil and the Polities of the Third World* (35 *ibid.* 1981)
Levi, W.: *Are Developing States More Equal than Others?* (32 *ibid.* 1978)
Mahajani, U.: *Foreign Aid at the Operational Level in South-East Asia* (19 *ibid.* 1965)
Mugomba, A.T.: *Small Developing States and the External Operational Environment* (33 *ibid.* 1979)
O'Neill, H.: *UNCTAD V: Lessons Unlearned* (35 *ibid.* 1981)
Wionczek, M.S.: *External Indebtedness of Less Developed Countries* (35 *ibid.* 1981)

5. *Economic International Institutions*

Fisher, A.G.B.: *The Future of International Economic Institutions* (1 *ibid.* 1947)
Goldsmith, P. and Sonderkotter, F.: *Equality and Discrimination in International Economic Law* (IV): *The European Communities* (28 *ibid.* 1974)

——: *Equality and Discrimination in International Economic Law* (V): *The European Communities and the Wider World* (29 *ibid*. 1975)

Goodwin, G.L.: *GATT and the Organisation for Trade Co-operation* (10 *ibid*. 1956)

——: *United Nations Conference on Trade and Development* (19 *ibid*. 1965)

James, A.M.: *The UN Economic Commission for Asia and the Far East* (13 *ibid*. 1959)

Kaplan, G.G.: *Equality and Discrimination in International Economic Law* (II): *The UNCTAD Scheme for Generalised Preferences* (26 *ibid*. 1972)

O'Keefe, P.J.: *International Centre for Investment Disputes* (34 *ibid*. 1980)

Sutton, A.: *Equality and Discrimination in International Economic Law* (IV): *Trends in Regulations of International Trade in Textiles* (31 *ibid*. 1977)

6. *Private Enterprise*

Modelski, G.: *The Corporation in World Society* (22 *ibid*. 1968)

Penrose, E.: *Monopoly and Competition in the International Petroleum Industry* (18 *ibid*. 1964)

Schwarzenberger, G.: *An International Investment Insurance Agency?* (23 *ibid*. 1969)

Stoiber, C.: *Equality and Discrimination in International Economic Law* (VIII): *The Multinational Enterprise* (31 *ibid*. 1977)

(E) INTERNATIONAL STUDIES

Alexandrowicz, Ch.: *The Study of International Economics* (4 Y.B.W.A. 1950)

Banks, M.H.: *Two Meanings of Theory in the Study of International Relations* (20 *ibid*. 1966)

Boardman, R.: *Comparative Method and Foreign Policy* (27 *ibid*. 1973)

Burton, J.W.: *Recent Developments in the Theory of International Relations* (18 *ibid*. 1964)

——: *The Analysis of Conflict by Casework* (21 *ibid*. 1967)

Curle, A.: *Peace Studies* (30 *ibid*. 1976)

Fawcett, C.B.: *Maps in the Study of International Relations* (6 *ibid*. 1952)

Goodwin, G.: *International Relations and International Studies* (27 *ibid*. 1973)

Goormaghtigh, J.: *International Relations as a Field of Study in the Soviet Union* (28 *ibid*. 1974)

Joynt, C.B.: *Behavioural Science in International Relations* (33 *ibid*. 1979)

Kaplan, M.A.: *New Approaches to International Relations: Progress or Retrogression* (22 *ibid.* 1968)

Kimminich, O.: *International Relations and International Law* (27 *ibid.* 1973)

Lasswell, H.D.: *The Scientific Study of International Relations* (12 *ibid.* 1958)

Midgley, B.: *National Law and the Renewal of the Philosophy of International Relations* (29 *ibid.* 1975)

——: *The Crisis of Modernity and International Relations (35 ibid.* 1981)

Nicholas, M.B.: *Mathematical Models in the Study of International Relations* (22 *ibid.* 1968)

——: *Catastrophe Theory and International Relations* (35 *ibid.* 1981)

Pentland, C.C.: *Neofunctionalism* (27 *ibid.* 1973)

Rosecrance, R.N. & Mueller, J.E.: *Decision-Making and the Quantitative Analysis of International Relations* (21 *ibid.* 1967)

Rosenau, J.N.: *International Studies in the United States* (27 *ibid.* 1973)

Schwarzenberger, G.: *The Study of International Relations* (3 *ibid.* 1949)

Siotis, J.: *Social Science and the Study of International Relations* (24 *ibid.* 1970)

Vincent, R.J.: *The Functions of Functionalism in International Relations* (27 *ibid.* 1973)

Yalem, R.J.: *The Decline of International Relations Theory* (30 *ibid.* 1976)

——: *The Level-of-Analysis Problem Reconsidered* (31 *ibid.* 1977)

It may also be helpful to remind readers of the Cumulative Index to Volumes 1 to 25 in the 1971 Volume of the *Year Book of World Affairs — Managing Ed.,* Y.B.W.A.

THE DECLINE
OF INTERNATIONAL ORDER:

NORMATIVE REGRESSION
AND GEOPOLITICAL MAELSTROM

By

RICHARD FALK

THE notion of "decline" is elusive. My usage implies three dimensions: the risk of general war; the degree to which statecraft is militarised; and the diminishing extent to which world order values are realised. The first two seem reasonably clear, although criteria of risk and of militarisation are difficult to make precise. The third dimension involving world order values is of little significance without specification. In brief, world order values as used here refers to peace (violence-avoidance), economic well-being, human rights, and ecological balance.[1]

The central thesis of this analysis of international order is that international order is declining in quality with respect to each of these dimensions. The attempt here will be to provide a reasoned basis for reaching such a conclusion. It would be useful, in addition, to reinforce such reasoning with a careful compilation of evidence, a process that would move an interpretative argument of this sort closer to a demonstration.

Underlying this inquiry into the downward drift of international order is a hopeful posture towards the longer term political future. There is nothing inevitable about the course of politics on a global scale. If the proper climate of concern can be created, a new type of survival-oriented political leadership could emerge on the State level.[2] One way of expressing this prospect is to project a leadership for vital international actors oriented around the promotion of human interests rather than national interests.[3] Another way is to anticipate a citizenry that gradually complemented a statist orientation with a globalist orientation, one in our terms, concerned about the fuller realisation of world order values for all peoples.[4]

---

[1] Such a specification has been elaborated by the World Order Models Project (of the Institute for World Order) in various settings. See, e.g. S. H. Mendlovitz (ed.), *On the Creation of a Just World Order* (1975); my own elaboration can be found in *A Study of Future Worlds* (1975), pp. 11–48.

[2] See important, innovative discussion in R. C. Tucker, *On Political Leadership* (1981), esp. Chap. IV entitled "Leadership and Man's Survival."

[3] This distinction is developed in comprehensive and clear fashion in R. C. Johansen, *The National Interest and the Human Interest* (1980), esp. pp. 3–37.

[4] For creative consideration of this prospect see H. Lasswell, "Future Systems of Identity in the World Community," in C. E. Black and R. Falk (eds.), *The Future of the International Legal Order* (1972), pp. 3–31.

10

Such reorientations are not imminent. Whether their prospect is several decades away, or more, perhaps much more, is impossible to predict even in loose terms. We can, however, take account of a multi-dimensional process of globalisation that has itself been going on since the close of the last century, if not longer.[5] The completion and content of this great transition will depend upon many variables, including especially the avoidance of large-scale catastrophe.[6] The current decline of international order can also be expressed as a growing receptivity to catastrophic modes of transition, involving rising public expectations of nuclear war.

Also, it should be evident that globalisation is not necessarily positive from the viewpoint of world order values. In fact, considering the evidence at our disposal, the most probable forms of globalisation are likely to represent a further deterioration in the quality of societal life on the planet. More hopeful futures, to be realistic, cannot be derived by projection from the existing world.[7] Hopeful futures that are credible tend to posit "a mutation," whether in the form of axial upheaval or spiritual awakening.[8]

Finally, with respect to orientation, this interpretation of what might be ahead takes comfort from "a hypothesis of latent discontent."[9] In

---

[5] Culminating this process has been identified by some seminal figures as the great challenge of our time. See, *e.g.* P. A. Sorokin, *The Crisis of Our Age* (New York, 1941); K. Boulding, *The Meaning of the Twentieth Century* (1964); A. Bergeson, "From Utilitarianism to Globology: The Shift from the Individual to the World as the Primordial Unit of Analysis," in A. Bergeson (ed.), *Studies of the Modern World-System* (1980), pp. 1–12; P. Teilhard de Chardin. *The Future of Man* (1964).

[6] For instance, Sorokin (*op. cit.* in note 5, above) writes, note 5, p. 4, that "the final outcome of this epochal struggle will largely depend upon whether mankind can avoid a new world war. If the forces of the decaying sensate order start such a war, then, dissipating their remaining energy, these forces can end or greatly impede the creative progress of mankind." See also Sorokin's final statement in the book along similar lines, p. 326. Such apprehensions are quite typical for those authors who perceive our age as a time of "great transition." For an excellent overall assessment see R. J. Barnet, *The Lean Years* (1980).

[7] Trend projections that suppose the crisis to be on the plane of *things* rather than on the plane of *values* do not respond to the deeper forms of malaise, do not raise hopes, and, despite their optimism, are but another manifestation of despair. Along these lines see F. M. Esfandiary, *Optimism One* (1970); F. M. Esfandiary, *Up-Wingers* (1973); H. Kahn and others, *The Next 200 Years* (1976); at this stage, even the most institutionally optimistic auspices, that is, governments, are beginning to acknowledge the deteriorating situation. See, *e.g. Global Report 2000* (1980) issued by the United States Government.

[8] See conceptual and historical assessments in L. Mumford, *The Transformations of Man* (1956).

[9] In addition to a negation of dominant trends, there are diverse indications of newly emergent values, beliefs, and life styles that could provide the cultural foundation for a post-materialist, even a post-militarist civilisation. See, *e.g.* M. Ferguson, *The Acquarian Conspiracy* (1979); R. Inglehart, *The Silent Revolution: Changing Values and Political Styles Among Western Publics* (1977).

effect, this hypothesis posits that beneath the surface of the old, obsolescent, yet still predominant affinities, is a growing alienation from the conventional and receptivity to new, adaptive outlooks.[10] The distribution of power currently favours old ways to an overwhelming extent, but their security of tenure may be deceptive. Suppressed is a radical challenge, especially in the developed countries, that is waiting to be activated on a mass scale. To illustrate, the notion, but not the context of latent discontent, let us consider the surprising course of recent Iranian politics. As late as 1976, perhaps 99 per cent. of Iranians, or more, considered the Shah's rule impregnable for the remainder of the century. Two years later over 90 per cent. of the Iranian people were united, according to knowledgeable observers, in an unarmed struggle that successfully toppled the Shah. What was overlooked in the 1976 setting that erupted in 1978? To say, retrospectively, that certain elements of Iranian political culture were at the pre-eruption stage in 1976 is to explain nothing, but it does express the earlier reality of revolutionary potential.

There are obviously no facile analogies to be drawn here. The simple argument is that the conventional international order is in serious decline, that the experience of decline has been registering on human consciousness in a variety of ways for several decades, and that out of such an encounter come new possibilities, some awful, some hopeful.

My analysis of the decline of international order is divided into two parts. First, some consideration of the normative manifestations of the latest phase of this decline. Secondly, some discussion of the specific danger that arises from normative deterioration in a setting of intensifying militarism.

I—NORMATIVE REGRESSION

The image of "normative regression" implies a base point in the past. The analysis here proceeds from the general context of the post-Second World War world, say 1945–1960. Also, the inference of "regression" is an aggregate, or net inference, assessing a balance sheet of developments with varying normative weights. It is, in a sense, necessarily subjective. For instance, how do we appraise the weight of a continuing arms race as against a generally successful decolonialisation process? To some extent, the appraisal process is inevitably perspectival, reflecting

---

[10] See, *e.g.* T. Roszak, *Person/Planet* (1978); there is also an equivalent emphasis on mutation by the recovery of lost wisdom, *e.g.* in G. Snyder, *Myths and Texts* (1960); W. Berry, *The Unsettling of America* (1977).

priorities and preoccupations especially characteristic of the advanced industrial countries in the early 1980s.[11] Since part of the position, however, avows a human interest conceived from a global perspective, the overall content of the normative outlook adopted here is not easily classified. Perhaps, it is useful to acknowledge that the agenda is shaped by provincial consideration of time, place, and class, whereas the envisioning of lines of positive response, although not entirely separable, aspires to greater universality.

(a) *Erosion of legal inhibitions on aggressive war*

A major normative enterprise initiated after the First World War has been devoted to the effective outlawry of aggressive (that is, nondefensive) war. The Pact of Paris ("Kellogg-Briand Pact") of 1928 engaged the major governments of the world in a renunciation by treaty of aggressive war. The condemnation of the Axis Powers proceeded on this basis, as did the prosecution of the defeated leaders of Germany and Japan as war criminals.[12] The United Nations Charter carried forward this normative idea, although with admitted ambiguity, prohibiting recourse to force (Article 2(4)) except in instances of self-defence (Article 51, and only then, to the extent authorised by the Security Council. Throughout this period a major effort was made to achieve an agreed definition of aggression so as to specify more carefully the orbit of prohibition.[13]

This normative enterprise was from the beginning subject to sharp criticisms. It was attacked as vague, subject to gigantic loopholes, self-justifying.[14] Furthermore, its major punitive applications were widely criticised as "victors' justice," as hypocritical and unpersuasive.[15] Finally, international practice was alleged frequently to depart from these restraints without any reliable method to secure compliance. Peacekeeping based on normative propriety has never been consistently undertaken by the organs of the United Nations, or otherwise. The main

---

[11] The appraisal process here endorsed is based on world order values as a mechanism for identifying the content of the human interest. As such, it contrasts with geopolitical calculations seeking to maximise the national interest of a given actor or those associated with managing intra-imperial and inter-imperial rivalries.

[12] The essential material is intelligently collected in L. Friedman (ed.), *The Law of War* (2 Vols., 1972).

[13] For comprehensive presentation see B. B. Ferencz, *Defining International Aggression* (2 Vols., 1975).

[14] A comprehensive attack along these lines is to be found in J. Stone, *Aggression and World Order* (1958).

[15] For fundamental criticism see R. H. Minear, *Victors' Justice: The Tokyo War Crimes Trial* (1971); E. Davidson, *The Nuremberg Fallacy: Wars and War Crimes Since World War II* (1973).

international effort under United Nations auspices has been all along, at best, to prevent war and, then, if possible, restore peace, rather than to render effective the central normative idea that aggression must be resisted, regardless of political consequences by the collective strength of international society. The eruption of the Cold War in the late 1940s decisively weakened the prospects for collective security at the global level, and made it almost impossible, aside from exceptional cases, for collective machinery to operate in conflict-resolving, war-peace settings.[16]

At the same time, there has generally been "lip service" given by governments using force or relating to international conflicts to these normative notions. India was widely criticised in the West in the Security Council because it broke with these contentions when it forcibly took over the enclave of Goa from the Portuguese in 1962. The United States, in particular, has been a leader until recently in these efforts to present its own uses of force as "defensive" and those it opposes as "aggressive." Its diplomacy in justification of involvement in the Korean War and the Vietnam War was centrally keyed to the basic claim that its adversaries were aggressors.[17] In 1956 the United States Government even lined up with Nasser's Egypt to protect against the military attack initiated by England and France, its principal allies at the time. Part of the motivation appeared to be the importance the United States Government continued to attach to the prohibition, however imperfectly implemented, on aggressive war.

Thus, it is notable that there has been a falling away of this tradition in recent years. True, uses of force by adversaries are attacked in normative terms as vigorously as ever; for instance, consider the normative outrage directed against the Soviet Union for its use of military force in Afghanistan since the end of 1978. However, if only *adversary* uses of force are condemned then normative discourse in international affairs is properly located in the domain of propaganda rather than that of law and morality, or even a mixture of the three.

Armed attacks on unpopular or isolated governments have been tolerated without any effort either to demonstrate "defensive" intentions. The most obvious instances are China's attack on Vietnam (1979), Tanzania's 1978 attack on Amin's Uganda, and most recently, Iraq's attack on Iran.

The normative silence in the United Nations, and elsewhere, has been

---

[16] For an excellent conceptual and historical survey of recent international relations in light of the low disposition towards collective diplomacy see I. Clark, *Reform and Resistance in the International Order* (1980), esp. pp. 133–168.

[17] See, *e.g.* W. L. Standard, *Aggression: Our Asian Disaster* (1971); R. H. Hull and J. C. Novogrod, *Law and Vietnam* (1968); R. Falk, *The Vietnam War and International Law*, esp. Vol. 1 (of 4) (1968).

deafening. The Iraq/Iran War is a spectacular confirmation of this new trend towards geopolitical primacy. Iraq's large-scale attack was militarily unprovoked, and the Iraqi pretension that its use of force sought only satisfaction of a border claim was manifestly false. Of course, Khomeini's Iran (as was Vietnam and Amin's Uganda) was isolated and unpopular, and the attack occurred during the midst of the hostage-taking incident pitting Iran against the United States. As well, Iran's Islamic Revolution was feared by most governments in the region, as well as opposed by both super-Powers. The original expectation of governments was evidently that Iraq would sweep Iran clean of the Khomeini movement, or at the very least detach the Arab-populated oil-producing province of Khuzistan. The main point relevant here is that Iraq's undisguised war of aggression failed to engender any kind of normative condemnation in the United Nations or elsewhere on behalf of the victim State: the United States and the Soviet Union both declared themselves uninvolved and adopted a posture of neutrality. It should be clear that neutrality as a mode of response is incompatible with aggression/self-defence views about the propriety of military power that form the cornerstone of the normative assault on the discretionary status of recourse to war.

The United States diplomacy is especially significant in these regards. It was after all the United States that had championed the normative approach in the first instance. Without United States support there seemed little strength behind the basic Charter claim of prohibition, and a lapse into cynicism and undisguised *Realpolitik* is bound to occur.

This normative retreat by the United States (and others) is part of a broader pattern, one that relates to shifting geopolitical circumstances. Some comments on this shift will be made in Section II, but for now it can be summarily said that the United States, its allies and even its principal Northern rival, are increasingly convinced that military options are needed for security purposes, especially in connection with protecting the resource base in the Persian Gulf that underlies Western economic ascendency.[18]

(b) *The nuclear weapons challenge in international law*

Even before atomic bombs were developed and used, weapons innovations earlier in this century put great pressure on the law of war as a moderating force. The submarine and the bomber were powerful weapons whose optimal use defied the traditional limiting notions of international law as applied to wartime uses of force. These problems have become so acute, however, as a result of nuclear weaponry as to

---

[18] Persuasively spelled out along these lines by R. W. Tucker, "The Purposes of American Power," 59 *Foreign Affairs*, Winter 1980/81, pp. 241–274.

draw the entire enterprise of the law of war into doubt.[19] As is generally known, the classical legal tradition codified to a great extent at the Hague Conventions of 1899 and 1907 rested on the central idea that warfare could be conducted within a framework of restraint, and that the permissible range of means to injure a belligerent enemy were not unlimited. The main legal restraint, derived from far earlier just-war notions, insisted that legitimate uses of force be directed against military targets in a discriminate manner that generally avoids civilian and non-military damage. Even discounting for hypocricy and battlefield pressures, a restraining effect seemed to arise from these endeavours of international law. At least, the pretension of adhering to the law of war enabled a reconciliation of sorts between war as a social institution and ideas of civilisational concerns for ethical standards of behaviour.

Nuclear weapons challenge such a reconciliation in fundamental ways. The prospect of millions of casualties, devastated cities, and the dissemination of cancer-producing radiation in epidemic proportions suggests a weapon that is, *in its essence*, indiscriminate and cruel.[20] The seriousness of the normative damage is heightened by the central role played by nuclear weapons in the security policy of the super-Powers and their alliances. Nuclear weapons are not solely weapons of last resort, retained as a way to discourage others from ever making use of such weapons or to stave off the destruction of a country's sovereign reality. For the super-Powers, and this is plainer in the United States case, nuclear weapons are contemplated for a variety of contexts, both to deter "provocations" of an unspecified character and to achieve battlefield results by way of "limited nuclear warfare." Deterrence doctrine, made credible by actual weapons deployments, continuously threatens massive indiscriminate damage. This threat endorsed through alliance arrangements by powerful governments flaunts, in the most fundamental ways, the minimum claims of the law of war.

Such a condition has existed in some form ever since 1945. Its seriousness has grown evident recently as the numbers of nuclear-weapons States and range of weaponry increases, and their contemplated roles become more provocative. Such trends cumulatively increase the prospect of nuclear warfare. In that sense, the normative vacuum created by the unwillingness of the relevant governments to renounce the legitimacy of even first uses of nuclear weapons against non-nuclear adversaries is notable. If there is no normative inhibition on

---

[19] So discussed in M. Walzer, *Just and Unjust Wars* (1977), pp. 269–283.

[20] A powerful indictment developed out of the just war tradition can be found in J. W. Douglass, *The Non-Violent Cross* (1968); for later development and radicalisation of Douglass' response to the nuclear weapons challenge see *Lightning East to West* (1980).

such holocaustal violence directed at civilians and their surroundings, then lesser normative undertakings seem meaningless at best, at worst, diversionary.

(c) *Lowering the nuclear threshold*

Another central tenet of the normative environment has been the informal prohibition upon recourse to nuclear weaponry except as a matter of ultimate resort.[21] True, nuclear threats had been made from time to time by the super-Powers, and during the Dulles era of American foreign policy, the doctrine of massive retaliation seemed to indicate a willingness to use nuclear weapons in response to a whole, unspecified series of Soviet challenges to American interests around the world. In actuality, the American doctrine was never tested, and in 1960 was abandoned in favour of a policy that de-emphasised nuclear weapons except as ultimate weapons. The expansion of the role of nuclear weapons in the geopolitical strategy of the United States commenced after the Vietnam defeat in 1975, and was especially associated with the statements made about American defence policy by James Schlesinger during his tenure as Secretary of Defense.

A mixture of changing circumstances and new technical capabilities continue to lower the nuclear threshold. As with other aspects of this analysis, the main testing-ground is the Persian Gulf, although concerns are mounting about Europe as well, especially connected with the prospective deployment of Pershing II and Cruise Missiles on the American side and MIRVed SS-20 (intermediate range missiles) and backfire bombers on the Soviet side.[22] Increasingly, the United States position seems to be one of threatening to unleash nuclear war in the event that its hegemonial relationship to the oil-producers is any further weakened. Presidential Directive 59 and the enunciation of the Carter Doctrine in the aftermath of the Afghanistan intervention by Soviet troops tended to codify this expanded role for nuclear weapons in the security policy of the United States. Early Reagan defence policy goes even further in these directions. In this central Persian Gulf application of military policy, there is an appreciation that sub-nuclear capabilities cannot assure Western interests against either a large-scale internal challenge in a key producing country or an external attack. Conventional forces in the region are, at most, a tripwire.

This lowering of the nuclear threshold is augmented by popular

---

[21] R. Falk, L. Meyrowitz and J. Sanderson, "Nuclear Weapons and International Law," unpublished paper (1981).

[22] A discussion of European implications and response in this evolving strategic context can be found in E. P. Thompson, "The END of the Line," 37 *Bulletin of the Atomic Scientists* (1981), pp. 6–12, esp. pp. 10–13.

discussions of nuclear-war scenarios, especially if constructed by "specialists" in military matters, that reinforce anxieties about plausible nuclear-war prospects.[23] Especially in an international atmosphere of raised tensions and pervasive uncertainty, there is some disposition to increase the role of nuclear weapons as a way of imposing a kind of order upon the chaos of international relations. Also relevant is the spread of nuclear-weapons capabilities to additional countries; many States are near-nuclear Powers by virtue of their access to nuclear technology in addition to the seven States that are accepted as nuclear-weapons States (all save Israel having exploded a device).

Finally, the nuclear-arms race contains a new anxiety about surprise attacks, retaliatory credibility, and first-strike options. As a result, there seems to be a diminishing confidence that a crisis confrontation could be handled without unleashing a cycle of escalation, resulting in widespread mutual destruction, possibly on a scale of societal annihilation.

(d) *Disappearance of disarmament, and lately, even arms control from the active international agenda*

As with the campaign to outlaw aggression, so until recently there has been support, at least at the rhetorical level, for disarmament as a negotiating goal for all countries.[24] Such a disarmament campaign has never, true enough, got very far, but it was on the international agenda since the First World War, and really before that. What happened in the 1970s was the removal of disarmament from the serious negotiating agenda of the super-Powers, a conclusion only slightly qualified by the 1978 United Nations Special Session on Disarmament, an occasion that made few ripples and was virtually boycotted by leading States.

In the 1970s the Strategic Arms Limitation Talks (SALT) process of bipolar arms control displaced the headier objectives of disarmanent.[25] The arms control argument was based on attainable objectives, placing ceilings on some categories of weapons systems, cutting down on incentives to do wasteful and destabilising things (for instance, the ABM), building confidence for further steps including arms reduction. The central case, however, was built around stabilising the United States/Soviet relationship.[26]

---

[23] *e.g.* General Sir J. Hacket, *The Third World War: August 1985* (1979); see also S. Bidwell, *World War 3* (1978).

[24] See, *e.g.* Joint Statement of Agreed Principles for Disarmament Negotiations ("McCloy-Zorin Agreement"), text in B. Weston, R. Falk and A. D'Amato (eds.), *International Law and World Order* (1980), pp. 404–406; but note scepticism about disarmament in officially sponsored study A. Wolfers (*et al.*), *The United States in a Disarmed World* (1966).

[25] See, along these lines, various contributions to the Summer 1975 issue of *Daedalus* magazine on the theme "Arms, Defense Policy, and Arms Control."

[26] See contributions by J. J. Kruzel and R. Burt to the Winter 1981 issue of *Daedalus* pp. 137–158, 159–178; see also C. Bertram, "Rethinking Arms Control," 59 *Foreign Affairs* Winter 1980/1981, pp. 352–365.

The American failure to ratify the SALT II Treaty and the election of an anti-SALT president in 1980, has effectively removed arms control, as well as disarmament, from the international agenda. Such a development directly violates the pledge made by the nuclear-weapons States in the Non-Proliferation Treaty to pursue in good faith arms control and disarmament negotiations.[27] It also creates a normative vacuum with respect to the arms race at a time when budgetary outlays for defence are rising in absolute and relative terms, a trend with broad social and political implications in a context of reduced public service spending and concern. To sustain support for this militarist drift requires an atmosphere of international tension, including even a heightened fear of nuclear attack in the event that our side's guard is let down.

(e) *The falling stature of the United Nations*

The United Nations, as successor to the League of Nations, was established to sustain human hopes in normative progress, especially with regard to the issue of war and peace.[28] Again it was the West, particularly the United States, that viewed the United Nations as the chrysalis of a new statecraft, one that renounced pure unilateralism and balance of power approaches in favour of collective action and peaceful settlement procedures. As of 1945, and through the first decade of its existence, the United Nations was a compliant arena for the pursuit of United States-led Western foreign policy. Subsequent to the Korean War, however, the Cold War split the Organisation in immobilising directions as the Soviet bloc battled more effectively to prevent the United Nations from being used against its interests. More serious, perhaps, was the effect of the decolonialising movement on the composition of membership of the United Nations. As non-Western ex-colonial States began to dominate the General Assembly, the agenda changed and the perception of the Organisation shifted. For one thing the United Nations became an arena for Third-World economic demands often stridently stated. For another, from 1967 onwards the United Nations took an increasingly tough anti-Israeli line, a development that considerably reshaped its image in liberal eyes,[29] especially in the United States, earlier the main bastion of financial and ideological support.

In effect, then, the United Nations has receded from view; its normative character has been compromised in some critical quarters, and there

---

[27] The pledge is contained in Article VI of the Non-Proliferation Treaty: "Each of the Parties to the Treaty undertakes to pursue negotiations in good faith on effective measures relating to cessation of the nuclear arms race at an early date and to nuclear disarmament, and on a treaty on general and complete disarmament under strict and effective international control."

[28] But see I. Clark, note 16, pp. 133 *et seq.* for a view that the collective impulses underlying the United Nations were weak, or even absent, from the outset of its existence in 1945.

[29] See generalised attack so derived, A. Yesselson and A. Gaglione, *A Dangerous Place: The United Nations as a Weapon in World Politics* (1974).

is almost no disposition by important State actors to endow the Organisation with important missions. The United Nations has become distinctly a sideshow in the global political stage, and even public pressure to enhance its role is almost never evident any longer. Such a diminished stature for the United Nations could be rapidly reversed in the event that the super-Powers decide to entrust the Organisation with the resolution of a prominent issue.

(f) *The decline of idealistic elements in the foreign policy process*
In the earlier years of the post-war period, important idealistic and humanitarian undertakings seemed to form a genuine part of the foreign-policy process, especially as assessed in relation to the United States, leader of the Western alliance. To some extent, the pattern has oscillated back and forth over the years, varying considerably with the condition of the world economy, with the climate of domestic politics, including the orientations towards internationalism of the most prominent political leaders of the day. Nevertheless, since the mid-1970s, there has been a dramatic decline in support for redistributive approaches to poverty and inequality among States. This decline can be understood by comparison with earlier achievements. First of all, there was the effort to help Europe and Japan recover from the ravages of war. Secondly, there was the foreign aid programmes designed to give poorer countries help in achieving developmental goals, including self-sustaining growth. Thirdly, there were attempts, especially popular in the United States during the Kennedy presidency, to send young people to Third-World countries as sources of help with practical problems of health, education, and food production. Fourthly, there were varying attempts, including the recent one, especially by the United States Government early in the Carter Administration, to insert human rights into the foreign policy process; the rapid sequence of embrace and abandonment of this emphasis on human rights raised and then shattered expectations about a normative element in foreign policy. Fifthly, there was a widespread willingness, especially in Western Europe and Japan, to work towards various accommodations with the Third World so as to forge a compromise-new international economic order.

Without entering into any detailed discussion there has been disillusionment with each of these efforts. The world political system is moving back towards an embrace of statist selfishness as the dominating basis of foreign policy. Such a normative retreat can be exaggerated and interpreted as "a new reality" when, more accurately, it is only a temporary readjustment. Indeed, there always were pragmatic motives underlying the supposed benevolence of "the donor," whether "the gifts" were money, advice, or ideological guidance. Nevertheless, idealistic pretensions, and possibly accomplishments, at least created some impression of a nascent world community. This erosion of normative content in foreign policy tends to underscore the reality of a fragmented political order containing States grossly unequal in all respects. Such an image of conflictual hierarchy becomes the dominant, almost the uncontested, image of the character of international order. The debt dependency of the poorer countries, including virtually the entire Third World except for the major oil producers, now adds up to an amount in excess of $500 billion, fostering a situation that points to the fragility of the monetary foundations of international order and the new forms of post-colonial subordination that is the experience of most of the non-Western world.[30]

II—THE GEOPOLITICAL MAELSTROM

This interpretation of international order emphasises the retreat on the level of discourse and of policy from any serious expectations of normative growth. The evidence of this retreat is heavily influenced by the shift in orientation of the United States over the years. The power, wealth, and prominence of this single country is very important to the overall tone of international relations. Hence, the advent of the Reagan presidency is both the most recent and blatant confirmation of this basic assertion of normative decline, an explicit repudiation of idealistic initiatives.[31] The new American leadership places its emphasis on a conflictual view of international relations, a view in which the only outsiders that count are friends, that is, allies in the wider geopolitical struggle for dominance. The provisional decision by the Reagan leadership to hold up on the negotiation of a final version of a law-of-the-seas treaty because of the wealth-sharing provisions bearing on ocean mining, is indicative of a sceptical attitude towards co-operative approaches to international issues. Its vigorous, overt support for the counter-insurgency régime in El Salvador augurs a stepped-up emphasis on military approaches. Finally, the wonderfully symbolic claim that a campaign against terrorism will serve as a substitute in the Reagan Administration for the campaign on behalf of human rights in the Carter years (a campaign, incidentally, that even Carter virtually abandoned in the last two years of his presidency) is not only ideologically revealing, but suggestive of a new escalation of "double-think" discourse, considering that anti-terrorist tactics often involve reinforcing repressive régimes.

What also seems evident is the absence of any idealistic substitute for United States leadership. Western Europe and Japan, although perhaps comparatively more prudent at this stage on East-West issues, at least with respect to military power and intervention, are without any serious tradition of normative concern on an international level. Scandinavian

---

[30] See F. Janssen, "Third World's Debts, Totaling *500 Billion, May Pose Big Dangers," *Wall Street Journal*, January 28, 1981, pp. 1, 27.

[31] See, *e.g.*, Hobart, "A U-Turn Away from the Third World," *Washington Post*, March 5, 1981, p. 19.

countries, especially Sweden, are a partial exception to the preceding generalisation, but Sweden lacks the weight to exert much of an impact on the overall tone of international relations. The Soviet group adopts more an ideological rather than a normative approach, and although by virtue of its position and outlook, it seemed a progressive force especially in a Third-World context during the decolonialisation process. This favourable impression of a Soviet role has all but vanished in recent years. The massive Soviet military intervention in Afghanistan sealed this negative impression. Finally, the group comprising the Organisation of Petroleum Exporting Countries (OPEC), as a Third-World formation, could have used a fraction of its extraordinary wealth and dollar surplus to raise the hopes of the world as a whole. These oil-producers, although not acting more selfishly than most rich States, have not put forward any normative claims in a strong way aside from a vague and weak endorsement of the Third-World call for a new international economic order, and some routine contributions by way of development assistance. These oil-producers have been overwhelmingly preoccupied with their own security and development, and have not attempted to halt the process of normative decline.

As might be expected, the normative decline has been accompanied by an accentuation of militarist tendencies. World military spending is expected to top $600 billion in 1981, with pressure mounting at all levels to go still higher. A series of careful books warns about the growing danger of nuclear warfare.[32] The *Bulletin of Atomic Scientists* has moved the minute hand on its renowned clock closer to the midnight of nuclear war, going from seven minutes before midnight to four in its January 1981 issue.[33] What is worse, perhaps, is a revival of limited-nuclear war thinking, implying that nuclear wars are fightable, even winnable, without placing the heartland of the super-Power in jeopardy. These attitudes have been translated into new strategic doctrines and feverish weapons acquisition and deployment plans.[34] The prospects of limited nuclear wars in such vital theatres of geopolitical concern as Europe and the Persian Gulf are now widely discussed. Such a drift of super-Power thinking has led to the formation of a strong grass-roots anti-nuclear weapons movement in Europe over the last two years or so that is beginning to worry the NATO-oriented leadership.[35]

---

[32] *e.g.* L. R. Beres, *Apocalypse: Nuclear Catastrophe in World Politics* (1980); N. Calder, *Nuclear Nightmares* (1979); see also J. A. Leonard, "Danger: Nuclear War," 32 *Monthly Review* (1981), pp. 23–34.

[33] See lead editorial, B. T. Feld, "The hands move closer to midnight," 37 *Bulletin of Atomic Scientists*, Nr. 1 (1981).

[34] See interview with Daniel Ellsberg, "Nuclear Armaments," published as pamphlet (1980).

[35] For important statements see E. P. Thompson, "Notes on Exterminism; the Last Stage of Civilization," *The New Left Review*, Nr. 121, pp. 3–31 (1980); R. Williams, "The Politics of Nuclear Disarmament," *The New Left Review*, Nr. 124, pp. 25–42 (1980).

Another ominous sign in this anti-normative trend is the growth of grand strategy as a background for national foreign policy. Ray Cline, part of President Reagan's foreign policy entourage and a former high Central Intelligence Agency (CIA) official, is taken seriously when he writes a neo-Mahanian tract proposing a 22-nation all-oceans alliance to counter the combined weight of the Communist countries, including those currently antagonistic to one another.[36] More modest grand strategies call for an all-out effort to defend the Persian Gulf against any and all contingencies whether mounted from within or without.[37] Again, this world view is being embodied in a broadened conception of security requirements, in this instance, a justification for an all-oceans naval presence, reinforced by basing rights and widespread deployment of contingents of troops.

Finally, this new militarism, productive of anxiety and fiscal burden, requires justification to receive and retain public support. Such support in the West depends on whipping up fears of Soviet expansionism among the citizenry. A very fully orchestrated effort along these lines over the past few years has reshaped the neo-isolationalist post-Vietnam political climate in the United States.[38]

On the Soviet side, this impression is reinforced. Soviet military spending, its involvements direct and indirect in the internal politics of foreign societies, and its failure to produce new leadership all foster the impression of a fortress mentality, as well as a conception of security reliant on military intervention to suppress popular movements in countries along the Soviet periphery. This mentality feeds also on the United States militarist drift, thereby creating a feedback loop that accelerates the destructive spiral of the arms race. These militarist patterns may also be reinforced by the failure of either super-Power to solve domestic economic problems; there is an oft-noticed tendency in the political life of major States to exaggerate international dangers so as to discourage scrutiny of domestic failures. Such a destructive dynamic concentrating on military prowess has been impeded during the *détente* years (roughly 1972–78), at least symbolically, by other contrary undertakings including especially arms-control negotiations, but also trade and co-operative ventures such as cultural exchange and joint space activities. Removing these moderating aspects of the bipolar con-

[36] Spelled out in R. S. Cline, *World Power Trends and U.S. Foreign Policy for the 1980s* (1980); see also C. S. Gray, *The Geopolitics of the Nuclear Era* (1977).

[37] Most carefully argued in R. W. Tucker *op. cit.* in note 18, above; see also *Challenges for U.S. National Security*, a preliminary report, Carnegie Endowment for International Peace (1980); K. Kaiser and others, "Western Security: What has changed? What should be done?," report by directors of four foreign policy institutes (1981); "The Geopolitics of Oil," *Staff Report*, U.S. Senate Committee on Energy and Natural Resources (Dec. 1980).

[38] An excellent study of this mobilising dynamic in J. Sanders, *Peddlers of Crisis*, unpublished Ph.D. dissertation, University of California (Berkeley) (1980).

text leaves one with the strong sense that the Cold War has "heated" up again, quite possibly in a more dangerous way because of the political and military preparations for nuclear war, the overall precariousness of the world economy, and the sharpening global struggle for resources, markets, and capital.[39]

---

[39] Even the most judicious assessors are driven toward these conclusions. See, *e.g.* M. Howard, "Return to the Cold War?," and G. W. Ball, "Reflections on a Heavy Year," in 59 *Foreign Affairs* (1981), pp. 459–473 and 474–499.

DISARMAMENT NOW:

CATCHING UP WITH CRUCÉ

By

WAYLAND and ELIZABETH YOUNG

To see the history of attempts to reach disarmament in perspective, we must ask ourselves when they began. The earliest book we may regard as having begun our present search is *Le Nouveau Cynée* by the Parisian monk Eméric Crucé, which was published in 1623. Our own hopes and desires today resemble Crucé's utopia far more closely than other and more famous ones, than Grotius, than Kant, than Bentham; and it is strange that this calm, practical, and far-sighted visionary should be so little known and honoured. Crucé called for general and comprehensive disarmament down to the level required to maintain order within nation States, for national resettlement plans for the demobilised armies, for a "United Nations Assembly" covering the whole world as he knew it, and for a peacekeeping force to back up the decisions of the Assembly. All this was remarkable, but most remarkable of all was that he included Ottoman Turkey, Persia, China and the princes of India and Africa in his proposed "United Nations": he was the first European to count Islam and Buddhism and Hinduism worthy of inclusion in an ideal world order: it is only 10 years since we readmitted China into today's United Nations.

The history of the search for disarmament since 1945 falls, not neatly or satisfyingly, but roughly and confusedly, into six phases: first, from 1945 to 1947, that of Western unilateral conventional disarmament; secondly, from 1948 to 1952, that of Berlin, Korea, conventional re-armament and nuclear proliferation; thirdly, from 1953 to 1962, the ostensible multilateral search for general and comprehensive disarmament; fourthly, from 1963 until 1978, the bilateral phase of non-proliferation and cosmetic agreements. We are now in a fifth phase of Strategic Arms Limitation Talks, which began in 1969; and also, since 1978, in a sixth, in which some of the real questions and techniques have begun to emerge.

Although the West disarmed conventionally in the first phase, the Soviet Union did not; nor did the United States lay down her nuclear weapons. The Soviet Union refused America's Baruch Plan of 1946 for the control of nuclear weapons, to be followed by their destruction; and the United States refused the Soviet Union's proposal for their immediate and total destruction, to be followed by international control. Russia had already begun her nuclear weapons programme, and it was

25

in that year, 1945, that we in the United Kingdom and France began ours. The age of nuclear proliferation was on us. With the blockade of Berlin, the first *coup d'état* in Prague, and the Korean War, the West learned the effects of unilateral conventional disarmament, accompanied by the maintenance of nuclear weaponry. That was the second phase.

With the death of Stalin came the third phase. The level of armaments had piled up since 1949, and the first nuclear tests by the Soviet Union and the United Kingdom convinced American and European public opinion that both the economic burden and the danger of physical annihilation were intolerable. And the governments responded. The turning points of the third phase were the Anglo-French proposals of 1954 for general and comprehensive disarmament, and the Soviet-American Joint Statement of Principles of 1961, the McCloy-Zorin joint statement, which was endorsed by the United Nations.

The Anglo-French proposal was, after a year of real and useful negotiation, most dramatically torpedoed by Washington at the eleventh hour. There had been a change of mind; perhaps the convulsive resettlement of Western Europe brought about by the failure of the proposed European Defence Community, by the consequent creation of Western European Union, and by the rearmament of Germany, had contributed to a change of American priorities. At any rate, another moment was lost.

The McCloy-Zorin joint statement, seven years later, was swiftly followed by draft disarmament treaties from both the Soviet Union and the United States. But the matter ran into the sands again, the arms race continued, wars continued to break out, and the idea of disarmament, as opposed to arms control, was forgotten.

I—THE SEARCH FOR "GCD"

Let us examine this period more closely, 1953–1962, the period of the ostensible search for general and comprehensive disarmament. "General" meant that all nations should take part in the process, and "comprehensive" meant that the process should include all sorts of arms; not, "only nuclear," "only conventional," or "only offensive." "Comprehensive" differs from "complete" in that it means reduction of all types of weapons down to a level to be specified. "Complete" means the total elimination of a given type of weapon, as, for instance, in "complete nuclear disarmament." Thus disarmament may be comprehensive without being complete, and complete without being comprehensive. Complete and comprehensive disarmament made few and doubtful appearances even among the proclaimed or ostensible aims of governments, and none among their real aims. General and comprehensive disarmament, on the other hand, dominated the ostensible aims, and even fleetingly, from time to time, was accepted, with some trepidation, by some policy makers in the West and quite possibly in Moscow as well, as a real aim.

Many and diverse were the proposals made in those years, and much and excellent the analysis. Especially perhaps between 1958 and 1964, some of the best minds in the world were active on this problem. Why did they fail?

One reason was the absence of China from the negotiations. China had no nuclear weapons at that time, and only comparatively primitive conventional weapons, but the Soviet Union and the United States both knew well what China would be able to do in the future. This is not to say that China would have failed to go along with a comprehensive test ban and with super-Power reductions. Through no fault of her own, China was not given the opportunity and the most populous country in the world cannot be expected to stand outside the door and applaud the sounds which filter through.

Not, therefore, at the end of every vista, but quite a short way along it, was the Chinese obstacle, or, should we say, the non-Chinese obstacle. At first China's absence from the United Nations and thus from the negotiations was due solely to the United States. After the Sino-Soviet split Russia tacitly acquiesced in the American boycott. Disarmament was only one of many goals which American administrations at that time sacrificed to their non-recognition of China, in other words to the well-known moralistic strand in United States foreign policy. It took Secretary Kissinger to change this policy and, when history comes to judge him, it may well be more interested that he corrected the long-standing errors of a generation than that he committed his own, since they, though sometimes atrocious, were short and sharp.

II—Faith and Reason

An equally important reason for the failure to secure disarmament was the perennial conflict between Russian secrecy and American openness. Beneath the deadlock of the early 1960s lay the oil and water of faith and reason. The Russians are creatures of faith and fear. Truth is what has been declared to be true by a sound authority: first the Church and the Tsars, now the party leaders. Science must serve the Party, else it is not science, since the Party, as is well known, embodies the scientific truth of Marxism-Leninism. For centuries the Russians have spent more talent and money than any other European country on trying to keep their own secrets and find out each other's, and as they treat each other, so they treat the rest of us. Their stories turn inward, to the family hearth, and their wisdom inwards, to the soul.

Americans are creatures of reason and acquisition. Truth is what has been found not to be untrue in a process of hypothesis, test, replication, counter-hypothesis, comparison, and so on, and truth is rewarded with success and material wealth. American stories turn outward: to the forest, the frontier, the sea, and the mastery of matter.

Was there another side to it? Is it possible that it was not only their inheritance which made the Soviets paranoid in the early 1960s but that the United States might herself have contributed something? At that time the United States was immeasurably superior to the Soviet Union in the strategic field, and had been so ever since 1945. Even though the Western democracies had then dismantled their conventional war-fighting armies, yet American nuclear weapons, originally built with the help of British, Canadian, and some Free-French scientists, were alone in the world. Though nobody could stop Stalin blockading Berlin, infiltrating Iran, fomenting the Greek civil war, seizing Czechoslovakia and the rest, yet the United States could at any moment have wiped him and most of his people off the face of the earth with complete impunity.

The Russians had good reason to be terrified of American capability in the 1950s and into the 60s. They did not admit it (as the Chinese now admit they are terrified of the Soviet Union) because to do so would have been to weaken themselves. Furthermore, it would have been to hand over real perceptions which, in their book, is as important as handing over skills in ours.

But terrified they were by the ring of bomber bases from Libya to Greenland to Guam, by the ring of missile bases from Turkey to England; by the American missile-launching submarines, not only in the Atlantic and the Pacific, but in the Indian Ocean as well; and by the overwhelming superiority of the American means of nuclear delivery to the Soviet Union over the Russian means of nuclear delivery to America, in numbers, in payload and in accuracy. They used the Potemkin village technique to mislead the West and persuade it of their strength. Only in the summer of 1960 did the American Administration realise the small numbers of Soviet long-range bombers and missiles.

III—CUBA, VIETNAM, FIRST STRIKE

Only a few months after the McCloy-Zorin Joint Statement of Agreed Principles on the Basis of which Disarmament might be Negotiated, President Kennedy, having met Mr. Khrushchev (and having been brow-beaten and patronised in a most ill-judged manner) stepped up Minuteman production, and chose Vietnam as the place where he would show the Russians he was not going to be pushed around. His choice led to the most dreadful war in history; an eight-year war in which the greatest Power in the world expended on a very small country of rural Asia, which had already been at war for 25 years, a quantity of munitions ($15\frac{1}{2}$ million tons) which may have been more than all the munitions used by all mankind in all other wars together: and was beaten. Nuclear weapons were not, and could not be, used.

It was also about the same time, in 1962, that President Kennedy's Secretary of Defense, Mr. Robert McNamara, made a speech at Ann Arbor declaring that some of the Minuteman missile force, then becoming operational, would be targeted in a counter-force role. Mr. McNamara was talking about a second (or retaliatory) counter-force strike, not a first; but how were the Soviets, given the general human tendency to project one's own habits of thought on to others, to be sure that was what he was really saying? How could the United States think it knew which Soviet missiles would be used in a hypothetical first strike and which would be reserved for a second strike? It could not. It could not therefore intend to target its missiles on Soviet second-strike missiles alone, and must be intending to target them on all Soviet strategic missiles. And this would be a first, counter-force, strike capability and posture.

Though Zorin had just agreed with McCloy, the other arm of Soviet policy took the only action open to it. The Soviets could nowhere near match the United States in Intercontinental Ballistic Missiles (ICBMs) or bombers, and though they had short-range submarine-launched cruise missiles, their massive submarine-launched ballistic missile programme lay still in the future. It would be years before they could catch up. Still, we now know, they were at that time placing the orders which in the next decade made their strategic forces in many ways superior to those of the United States. Something had to be found to correct the threats discernible in Mr. McNamara's speech. What the Russians had in some number were Intermediate Range Ballistic Missiles (IRBMs) and, as no-one who was alive then will ever forget, they decided to put some of them into Cuba.

What was intended by Moscow as a rectification of an imbalance suddenly threatened with aggravation, was perceived in Washington as a new and direct threat to the continental United States. There followed the so-called Cuba Missile Crisis, and the Western World applauded the nerve and skill with which the Kennedy brothers got it out of the danger they themselves had led it into.

If there is hostility between two people, two nations, two camps of nations, and if one is much stronger than the other, but does not intend physically to crush the other, then the stronger has certain difficult duties. It is the stronger who must convince the weaker of his goodwill: it is the stronger who must take the first step, propose what should be done, be patient with the other's fears, be especially consistent. It cannot be said that United States foreign and defence policy was such, during the years of American military preponderance over the Soviet Union, as to give much chance of disarmament.

The Ann Arbor-Cuba Missile Crisis killed general and comprehensive disarmament as a true ambition. The giants had brushed, and did not like it. The Soviets placed orders for new generations of ICBMs, for an

Orbiting Bombardment System, for Anti-Ballistic Missiles (ABM), for Anti-Satellite Satellites, for aircraft carriers, and for their nuclear Submarine-launched Ballistic Missile force. The United States, mainly occupied with Vietnam, began to develop Multiple Independently-Targeted Re-entry Vehicles (MIRVs) and, later, Anti-Ballistic Missile systems as well.

Appearances had to be kept up and during their own build-up, the Soviets were content to co-operate with the Americans: the world entered the fourth phase, the phase of non-proliferation and cosmetics. In 1963 the Partial Test Ban was signed. It did not affect the progress of the central Soviet-American arms race: the rate of Soviet and American testing was higher after than before. China and France did not even sign. But it was a good Clean Air Act: the first victory for the environment lobby.

IV—Cosmetics

There followed a spate of agreements not to do things that no-one would want to do: not to plant nuclear weapons on the seabed, not to use nuclear weapons in an accidental or unauthorised way, not to militarise the moon or to put nuclear weapons into orbit around the earth, not to introduce nuclear weapons into Latin America. Despite the existence of near consensus at the Geneva Disarmament Committee on a wide-ranging disarmament package, the Russians and Americans were able to impose on the international community their version of a Non-Proliferation Treaty (NPT), one by which the non-nuclear weapons countries undertook not to seek to get nuclear weapons and the nuclear weapons countries undertook not to tempt them to break that oath, which meant: to help only each other to get nuclear weapons. Neither France nor China signed. A few non-nuclear weapons States, the ones most at risk in a naughty world and most capable of getting nuclear weapons, refused to undertake anything at all and continued with the nuclear programme which would allow them to acquire nuclear weapons later if they saw fit to do so. The Treaty's promises of assistance concerning the civil use of nuclear power did not carry enough conviction to bring this group in.

Implicit in American anti-proliferation policies during the 1960s was an assumption that the two super-Powers had common interests, not only in preventing other States from acquiring or further elaborating nuclear weapons, but also in regulating their mutual competition. The possibility of bilateral Strategic Arms Limitation Talks was raised, and the prospect of using them to curb United States ABMs was attractive enough to the Soviet Union to engage its interest. Strategic Arms Limitation negotiations began in 1969 behind almost totally closed doors, and in 1971 produced a first clutch of agreements. The limits agreed were well above existing deployments; Soviet *numerical* superiority in strategic weapons was accepted (and United States *qualitative* superiority assumed by the Americans). Throughout the 1970s the talks went on, against the background of a continuing Soviet build-up of nuclear, chemical and other weapons, and of an increasingly wide-ranging navy. "Parity," sought by the Soviet Union since 1962, had arrived. News that emerged showed a continued determination to avoid reductions and to leave the general thrust of the arms race untrammelled. In 1977, President Carter, new to the scene, and taking at face value the Soviet Union's regularly expressed desire for disarmament, proposed "deep cuts" in strategic weapons, "even to 50 per cent.," instead of the faint trimming of the arms race that President Ford and Mr. Brezhnev had unveiled the previous year. The suggestion was rejected by the Soviet Union with contumely and forgotten by the West with facile equanimity. In 1979, a second SALT agreement was signed by Mr. Carter and Mr. Brezhnev. At the time of writing it has not been ratified by the United States: if it is not ratified during the first part of 1981, it will, in part at least, have to be renegotiated.

Meanwhile, the possibility that some arms levels might nevertheless be reduced did not entirely escape attention, and virtually unrelated cockpits, permanent or recurrent, existed for its discussion. These include the Committee of the Conference on Disarmament (CCD), comprising 31 countries meeting in Geneva; the Mutual and Balanced Force Reduction Talks (MBFR), made up of 11 countries having troops stationed in Central Europe and meeting in Vienna; the Review Conferences, including those of the Non-Proliferation Treaty, the first of which was held in 1975 and the second in 1980, the latter breaking up without a final text; and of the Final Act of the Conference on Security and Co-operation in Europe (CSCE), which included some microscopic "confidence building measures," mainly about advance notice of manoeuvres, and was followed by two review conferences, the first in Belgrade in 1977 and the second in Madrid in 1980–1. At President Carter's suggestion, a whole row of bilateral Soviet/United States discussions started up, on subjects such as the Indian Ocean, Anti-Satellites, and trade in conventional arms. Most lasted for a few meetings and then collapsed. Trilateral talks—including the United Kingdom—on a Test Ban go on. Lastly, there was the Special Session of the United Nations General Assembly in 1978 devoted solely to disarmament, to which we shall return. For the moment it is enough to recognise that the pursuit of a common world interest, whether by accident or design, began to be hampered by this proliferation of unrelated talking-places.

Since 1962, the date we arbitrarily chose for the end of the ostensible pursuit of disarmament and the beginning of super-Power parallelism in the NPT, the world has come to realise more and more clearly that it is for a while going to have to rely increasingly on plutonium for energy.

The generally uninhibited arming by the super-Powers of the two sides in the Arab-Israeli and in the Iran-Iraq wars, the use of the oil price by the Organisation of Petroleum Exporting Countries (OPEC) as a political lever, the Soviet invasion of Afghanistan—all are hastening our rush towards plutonium. Nothing can stop it, and nothing can alter the fact that the more plutonium there is in the world's energy cycle, the easier it will be both for nations and for bandit and terrorist forces to get some and make bombs with it. The answer is not to cancel the fast breeders (though perhaps we could delay them a little), nor is it to mount armed guards at every street crossing and railway bridge in the world. Nor even does it lie in such super-exclusive devices as the so-called London Club (that is, the advanced white world and Japan) which was persuaded by the United States to block various loopholes in the NPT by introducing further *de facto* controls of its own (which amounted to an admission by those who promoted the NPT that their brainchild had failed). The International Nuclear Fuel Cycle Evaluation (INFCE) confirmed that there were no technical fixes to control proliferation.

The only answer is still, as it always was, to seek to remove the reasons for which nations and groups want nuclear weapons. Breeders are a new technology, outside the arms race, which merely makes disarmament more urgent again.

V—The Neglected IRBMS

Within the arms race there has been for 20 years a situation which was not fully understood in the United States, and which makes disarmament more urgent for Western Europe, for China, and for the Middle Eastern countries. In SALT I and SALT II, the United States was talking to the Soviet Union about limiting strategic weapons. But what is strategic? As far as we in Europe knew, the United States and Soviet Union were discussing only the systems with which they can hit each other, and not those with which they cannot. The shorter range Soviet systems which, by their exclusion from SALT were deemed tactical, were nevertheless capable of reaching London, Paris, Peking, etc., from the Soviet Union. If one is living in, for instance, Bonn, the possibility of its immolation strikes one as entirely "strategic" whatever the range of the missile which immolates it; Helmut Schmidt it was who in 1977 finally succeeded in opening American eyes to this simple fact.

The Soviet Union has for 20 years had some 700 IRBMs targeted on Western Europe. It eventually became possible to dismiss them as old and soft, but a new, hard generation, the SS-20s, is now being added to them. We in Europe saw the reaction of the United States when some IRBMs were taken to Cuba in 1962. We in Europe have had 700 of them, against which we have no defence, facing us for 17 years, and neither the United States Government nor any other Western government had ever requested, or even suggested, their removal. At last, in 1979, NATO decided to counter them with Cruise Missiles and Pershing IIs, to be installed in Western Europe. This decision, justified though it may be, still further complicates prospects for Europeans and world-wide arms-control negotiations. In particular, the prospect of Pershing IIs being deployed in West Germany, four minutes away from their pre-sumed targets in Russia, has lit a fuse of alarm in Moscow. It is now proposed to discuss Soviet IRBMs and various American systems bilaterally between the two countries.

Soviet IRBMs can hit Western Europe. So, since West European governments, not so much cannot trust, but have no right to require, the United States to immolate American cities for their sake, the IRBMs make it unthinkable that the United Kingdom or France should give up their independent strategic forces as a result of negotiations between the Soviet Union and the United States.

The IRBMs can hit Israel. This over the years has led Israel to use the Zionist vote in the United States to exact the maximum of American weaponry for Israel. In case the United States should ever abandon Israel, or even reduce arms deliveries, Israel has acquired a stash of untested nuclear weapons, and no United States pressure has induced the Israeli Government to sign the NPT: all of which has led other States in the region to seek strength from the Soviet Union, and Iraq to pursue a nuclear programme that the Israelis claim is weapons oriented; and all of which has led to the destruction of the Lebanon, and perhaps now of Iran, and to a shifting chain reaction down through Libya, the Sudan, Ethiopia, into the morass of racialist Southern Africa. Israel and South Africa co-operate in nuclear matters and South Africa is certainly well on the way to being a nuclear-weapons Power as well as a supplier of uranium.

They can hit Pakistan and India, and China; indeed the Soviet Union has uttered nuclear threats to China, which has forced that country into a *de facto* alliance with the United States and Western Europe.

They can hit South Korea, where a proposal to withdraw United States support was met by first steps towards the acquisition of nuclear weapons. The proposal to withdraw was itself withdrawn.

And they can hit Japan.

Except in Latin America, there is little indeed in the lesser arms races of the world which cannot be traced back to the central arms race, and at the same time, little in them that can be dealt with in super-Power negotiations. Many thoughtful men have recognised this since the two super-Powers imposed their kind of Nuclear Non-Proliferation Treaty on the rest. Governments recognised it, but found it hard to identify any initiative to seize, in the face of joint Soviet-American determination.

President Carter's 1977 proposal for "deep cuts" would have been germane, but it proved the merest flash in the pan: not only rejected by the Soviets, but supported neither by his startled allies nor even by his own, unprepared, government machine. The essential idea was sound, but it lacked both the intellectual structure and the diplomatic underpinning that are necessary if a major shift in world affairs is to be achieved.

We suggested earlier that the militarily superior government is best placed to take a first step to reduce tensions and restore equilibrium. This is not the view of the Sóviet Government, the strength of whose ideological commitment is often under-estimated in Western Europe and the United States. Even if the Soviet leadership are disillusioned with it, it is on the assumed truth of Marxism-Leninism that the legitimacy of the Soviet system depends. The Soviet Union is the only one remaining of the nine European empires which existed in 1900—British, Russian, French, Dutch, Portuguese, German, Italian, Spanish and Belgian—and there is nothing in Marxism which makes an empire more likely to endure. Tell a Muslim or a polytheist to adopt the liberalism of Macaulay and Mill, the positivism of Comte or the idealism of Croce, and you do him no inner violence. But tell him to adopt the pre-destinarian materialism of Marx, and you require him to deny his identity and invent himself anew. The ideology of Marxism-Leninism may be a lid to hold the Soviet Union down, but one must doubt it can be a cement to hold it together. It seems to be a foregone conclusion that the Russian Empire will break up, like the others. The time it does, we must expect to be a time of great danger for the world: a moment which may last for years.

Marxist-Leninist dogma, on the other hand, holds as a basic tenet that the Soviet system is bound to triumph and that in the meanwhile, the role of the Soviet Government is to secure such a "correlation of forces" in the world—including military forces—that "capitalism" and "imperialism" collapse without initiating war, either aggressively, or in self-defence. Soviet disarmament proposals and support for "peace" and unilateral disarmament movements in Europe and elsewhere are part of this ideologically mandatory "peace" policy.

The likelihood of an explosion within the Soviet Empire, considered in the light of the new (but, if President Reagan has his way, temporary) "correlation of forces," does not mean we should not seek disarmament. Only that, when we seek it, we should remember that the Russians have a trauma left to live through which the rest of us have survived. For a number of reasons we must certainly continue to pursue disarmament. For many years now the military spending of the rich nations has equalled or exceeded the entire turnover of the poor nations. The poor nations are themselves spending an increasing proportion of the resources available to them on arms. New generations of weapons and new kinds of deployment make "mutual deterrence" look a less reliable way of preventing war. The militarisation of space has now started in earnest; the consequences are incalculable, given the importance of satellites for command, control and communication, for navigation, for early warning, and their vulnerability to attack, whether from earth or from space. All this will put the reliability of most long-range weapon systems in question. The political and military effects of this on the North Atlantic alliance, are imponderable.

VI—AN AGREED GOAL-STRUCTURE

It is likely we shall never hit on or achieve measures of arms reduction until we learn how to fit them into some agreed structure of goals. The point is not that the goals should be attained, or even attainable: if the nations can agree that a teleology or goal structure makes sense in itself, and that nothing shall be done which goes against it, that nothing shall be done that is beside it, and that everything that is done must be fitted into its rightful place in the structure, then certain consequences may be expected to flow.

First, each measure or redisposition or treaty will be more likely to endure and to serve its purpose, since to destroy or distort it would destroy something greater than it, namely, the goal structure itself. Secondly, the endurance of each measure would smooth, not hinder, the achievement of the next, since their relation to each other would already be established. And thirdly—perhaps most important—would be that those States which were outside would be able to see what was happening and would co-operate.

VII—INSTITUTIONAL REFORMS

The 1978 Special Session may in time turn out to have marked the beginning of a real change. Certain reforms were agreed which have already triggered others: the Russians and Americans were deprived of their previously permanent co-chairmanship of the Geneva Committee and with it was dismissed the tacit claim that their major responsibility for the arms race endowed them with commensurate privilege in disarmament and arms control negotiations. The Geneva Committee has now been reorganised; France and China have joined it; and it has already started to examine a chemical warfare ban, which had long been bogged down in bilateral negotiations between the United States and the Soviet Union.

The other great reform was that the United Nations General Assembly was once again recognised as the proper body to devise, coordinate, and oversee the machinery for negotiating and securing disarmament. It would do this through its own *First Committee* (which includes the whole membership of the United Nations) now to be exclusively concerned with disarmament affairs; through the deliberations of the revived *Disarmament Commission* (also of the whole membership) which is now charged to "consider the elements of a comprehensive programme for disarmament"; through negotiations in the reformed (Geneva) *Disarmament Committee*; through improved facilities for research and inquiry in the United Nations Secretariat; and through the mandatory reporting-back from the various review conferences and bilateral and regional negotiations. A second Special Session on Disarmament is to be held in 1982: can we now say we are catching up with Crucé?

Implicit throughout this complex organisational structure is a purpose, a theoretical structure, which cannot be much different from the GCD which was devised in the 1950s and 1960s. That is to say that it must indeed be general and comprehensive as we defined them earlier and it must rest first on the old McCloy-Zorin principle that imbalances may not be generated by the process of disarmament itself. Any imbalances which now exist must be reduced or done away with during the process, and the parties must know not only what arms are destroyed but what exist (whether by remainder or by new manufacture) at all times during the destruction. At some point, though later than it would have been in the early 1960s because of today's increased inventories, the idea of the minimum balanced deterrent will probably have a role. To ensure that it can, limits on anti-satellite weapons and on all kinds of anti-missile weapons will need to be slotted into the programme at an early stage. Our argument is that the idea of GCD, which around 1955 was elaborated as a practical and not too long-term goal, and as such was ostensibly adopted by governments, should now be turned to the only purpose it could ever really have served: a structure of theory into which must be fitted the practical goals which can in fact be achieved.

To speak of creating a theoretical structure may appear less farfetched and alarming now we are beginning to have the elements of a practical structure for disarmament negotiations. That we have is thanks, in large part, to French initiatives at the Special Session on Disarmament. The French Government saw itself as untarnished by the failures of the previous 20 years in which it had played no part. President Giscard himself went to the Special Session and made a number of specific proposals which showed at once a coherent philosophy, and an awareness of the need to tackle central problems openly and head on, rather than peripheral, easily-negotiated, dead ends as in the old CCD (the Seabed Non-nuclearisation Treaty, the treaty banning some forms of environmental modification, etc.). One of his most valuable suggestions was for something the present writers have long advocated: the devising and setting up of an international agency for the monitoring by satellite of disarmament measures—and indeed of military dispositions in general. It is not sufficient for the rest of us if our governments are told by their senior allies what the latter think fit we should know about the military postures and the arms control record of the other side. It is

our world as well, and our lives are at risk as well. Both neutral and alig-
ned countries have a right to their own information, coming from their
own observation satellites, and this could most conveniently be done
through a United Nations agency. Opinion in certain countries with the
technical know-how is favourable, and great experience has been gained
over the years in the art of interpreting intelligence data by, among other
public bodies, the Swedish International Peace Research Institute in
Stockholm and the International Institute for Strategic Studies in
London. The experience could be drawn on for the build-up of a United
Nations monitoring agency.

One other beneficial technique which is yet to be officially advocated
is the Single Informal Negotiating Text (SINT). The largest ever international conference, the Third United Nations Conference on the Law of
the Sea, has been in session since 1973. Between 1975 and his recent
death its Chairman, Dr. Hamilton Amerasinghe of Sri Lanka, had
something called a Single Informal Negotiating Text drawn up,
circulated to delegations, and published. It is revised in the light of what
passes at each session of the Conference. This has had three good
results. First, although some countries, and especially the super-Powers,
refused to be immediately impressed by it, yet in time they found that
everyone else was in fact negotiating on it, and they fell into line.
Secondly, the existence of this series of well-judged texts, and their
widening acceptance, made disguised imperialist claims, particularly by
the Soviet Union, harder and harder to maintain. The Soviets have
perhaps fallen into line with what one might call normal world opinion
quicker at this conference than at any other. Thirdly, and most
important, the fully agreed portions of SINT, even though it has not
been formally adopted, have already begun to be treated as "customary"
international law. Two-hundred-mile fishery zones are fully accepted.

Now, the introduction by its Chairman of a corresponding SINT into
the Special General Assembly on disarmament could, it seems to us,
have all the good results in that field which it is already having in the
other. It would pre-empt the otherwise-to-be-expected super-Power bids
to have everything remitted to them or made dependent on their
approval. It could pre-empt many Russian stonewall positions. And
above all it would be a way of getting into the bloodstream of the world's
body politic the first drafts of that structure of theory without which we
are destined to stumble hopelessly from cosmetic expedient to cosmetic
expedient while the risks and the bill mount ever more hideously high.

THE POLITICS OF FORCE:

ANALYSIS AND PROGNOSIS

By

EUGENE V. ROSTOW

THE editors and I agreed that this paper should "conjecture" about the law on the international use of force in the year 2000.* How simple! The words of our agreement determine my answer. They presuppose the survival of a political system consisting of more or less independent States: otherwise how could we talk of the "international" use of force? The question therefore also presupposes the survival of a system of international law distilled from the nature of the political order—*i.e.* a system articulating the norms necessary to the coexistence and co-operation of States which claim to be equal in dignity and even in "sovereignty," all formally committed to respect each other's territorial integrity and political independence. Given the stubborn loyalty of people in the modern world to the idea of nation and State, our assumption seems not too outrageous.

If, then, the State system we perceive in our mind's eye has not become a Soviet Imperium 20 years hence, it follows that the law on the international use of force will continue to evolve in the pattern which began to take tangible shape at the Congress of Vienna, and has developed coherently, though hardly in a straight line, ever since.

Of necessity, this hypothesis implies that the North Atlantic Treaty Organisation (NATO) allies, Japan, and China will soon adopt rational and effective foreign policies to master the present crisis in international politics. If it is plausible to indulge in such Panglossian optimism at all, I should conclude that by the year 2000 the actual law of State practice will be much closer to the rules of the United Nations Charter than is the case today—not because men will by then have become angels, but because a sustained Western policy of containment will have convinced the Soviet Union that the imperatives of survival in the nuclear age permit no other solution.

If the United States should fail in that effort, the task of forecasting the condition of international law in the year 2000 would be sad beyond bearing, and hardly an appropriate theme for an American professor.

---

* Inevitably, this paper draws on my earlier writing on the subject, particularly Chap. 9 of *The Ideal in Law* (1978): "Is the Charter Going the Way of the Covenant?"

38

I—THE MODERN STATE SYSTEM
IN THE PERSPECTIVE OF LAW

How should the contemporary State system—the system we perceive in our mind's eye—be described? How did it develop? Where is it going? And what are its customs, mores, or "rules" with regard to the international use of force by States and from States? Are these propositions "rules of law" in any meaningful sense, or no more than admonitions, expectations, hopes, or aspirations? Are they rules of convenience, rules of thumb, rules of the game, or pretence—cynical statements not intended to govern behaviour but to give an aroma of sanctity to the funerals of statesmen?

To anticipate, my view is that the propositions put forward in this way as normative should be considered rules of law only if they define the pattern of behaviour deemed right by the society of nations, and that society seeks effectively to enforce compliance with them.[1]

When we think of international relations, the modern mind confronts two quite different perceptions or hypotheses, each rooted in experience, each consistent in part with what actually happens. The first is the echo of earlier history, Hobbes' vision of the state of nature—the notion that the external realm is a jungle; that foreign policy requires us to go about fully armed, prepared for Pearl Harbours at any moment; and that clubs are trumps. The modern view, equally tenacious, is that the society of nations exists; that it normally exists in a state of peace; and that peace is a system, a legal system based on the balance of power, and maintained by laws of magnetic attraction and repulsion and (sometimes) by the active co-operation of the most powerful States.[2] These two models—Hobbes' and Kant's—clash in our minds. They clash also in the forum, where the Kantian superego tries endlessly to tame the aggressive instincts of Hobbesian man. The diplomatic history of the last 200 years could be written as a counterpoint of these two themes.

The idea that peace is a condition to be achieved by the deliberate efforts of diplomacy is one of the major achievements of modern civilisation. In earlier centuries, at least since the fall of Rome, peace had been viewed as a rare blessing, brought about for brief periods by the lucky conjuncture of wise princes and the balance of power. Professor F. H. Hinsley contends that the modern State system began in Europe towards the middle of the eighteenth century as part of the deep and pervasive

---

[1] I have defended this view in *The Ideal In Law* (1978), Chapters 1 and 9, and in Chapter 9 of *Peace in the Balance* (1972). My definition of "law" in this context is not far from Professor Hedley Bull's notion of "order" (which he contrasts with "law") in *The Anarchical Society* (1977).

[2] A. Vagts and D. F. Vagts, "The Balance of Power in International Law: The History of an Idea," 73 AM. J. INT. L. 555 (1979).

change in consciousness we call the Enlightenment.[3] Here, as in so many
other aspects of our thought about society, Montesquieu led with abid-
ing influence.

Montesquieu put aside the older yearning for Europe's lost unity,
which has exerted (and still exerts) such a powerful influence on the
European imagination. While the idea of Europe was strong, and the
cultural identity of Europe was real, Montesquieu stressed, the fact was
that the States of Europe had become autonomous, and could not be
joined together through marriage, conquest, or federation in a new version of Charlemagne's Empire. He directed attention to the autonomy of
the European States, and their relations in peace and war. As Hinsley
comments, Montesquieu and his contemporaries saw that "Europe was
a diversity as well as a unity—a unity because of its diversity."[4]

"For Montesquieu," Hinsley writes, "Europe was a single whole. 'The
state of things in Europe is that all the states depend on each other . . .
Europe is a single state composed of several provinces.' But it was
because of the multiplicity of its several states that, to him as to
Machiavelli, it represented progress as opposed to the stagnation of
Asia; and he showed in De L'Esprit des Lois (1748) an acute sense of
the fundamental nature of the rivalry between its states. Although they
belonged to the same collectivity, it was impossible to subject them to a
single law like that which governed the individuals in a single state. In
some cases offensive war was justified as a form of defence; there was a
right of war and of conquest; the most that could be hoped for was that
the different provinces would do each other as much good as possible in
peace and as little harm as possible in war."[5]

Many other powerful eighteenth century minds addressed the
problems of war and peace in the new political order of the period—not
only the legal writers, but Voltaire and Rousseau, Hume, Gibbon, and
Kant as well. In their view, self-defence was the only justification for one
State to make war on another—defence against actual attack or the
perceived risk of attack. At least that was the rule they thought should
be deemed to apply among the States of Europe. The world beyond
Christendom, in the language of the day, was another matter.

These were hardly the only ideas on the international use of force
current towards the end of the eigteenth century. The statesmen of the
time were by no means willing disciples of contemporary intellectuals.
The rulers of Europe, liberated from the "just war" doctrines of the
Church, assumed they had an absolute right to make war on each other,
and some of them acted accordingly. The competition for empire overseas had its repercussions on the peace of Europe itself. And the French

---

[3] *Power and the Pursuit of Peace* (1963). See also his 1980 New Zealand lectures, *The
Decline and Fall of the Modern International System* (unpublished).
[4] *Power and the Pursuit of Peace* (1963), p. 162.
[5] *Ibid.*

Revolution and its demonic aftermath reminded the world that the dream of universal empire after the style of Alexander and the Caesars could still become an evil force menacing the life of all States and all peoples.

The Congress of Vienna, convened to restore the European State system, reflected both the trauma of the war and the altered climate of European opinion. Thus it became something quite different from what its convenors had in mind—the catalyst for a process which created a new State system, based on ideas and procedures unknown to the diplomats of the Old Régime. The world political system was not "restored." It was transformed.

With the benefit of hindsight, it is now clear that the men of the Congress of Vienna—Castlereagh, Talleyrand, Metternich, and Czar Alexander—belong in the Pantheon among the heroes of our civilisation. They were derided and abused by many of their contemporaries. Some of the finest and most generous spirits of the nineteenth and twentieth centuries have scorned them as hopeless reactionaries— defenders of the "status quo" against "progress"; believers in "legitimacy" rather than "self-determination" as the rightful basis for the authority of States; and above all unsympathetic to the romanticism of the age about to dawn. They have been in eclipse for more than 100 years; many books and articles still echo the violent diatribes of Shelley, Byron, and other luminous enemies of the perennial Establishment.

But the failure of the settlements of Versailles and of San Francisco—after 12 years in one case, and about 25 in the other—highlights the extraordinary character of what the architects of the Vienna settlement accomplished. They built a structure of peace which served the world well for a century; it proved to be an environment which fostered and nurtured a great flowering both of culture and of social progress. Contemplating what has happened since 1919, we should recite the names of the diplomats of Vienna with respect, if not with awe. They set in motion both a new code of values about the use of force in international relations—occasionally stated, but even more influential when unstated—and a new pattern of diplomatic practice through which those values became admonitions and precepts, then habits, then *mores*, and then obligatory rules of law in the most practical sense, governing the minds and therefore the behaviour of men. Despite the setbacks of the period since 1914, the self-evident truths of the Congress of Vienna remain the essence of the policies the nations profess on the subject today.

Between 1815 and 1914, the nations of Europe accepted the principle of collective responsibility—or at least of a measure of collective responsibility. Since all had an equal interest in the viability and character of the State system as a system, decisions affecting its structure or functioning were considered and discussed together—often decided by consensus. And, acknowledging that duties arise from circumstances, both the large and the small Powers recognised that the Great Powers had special responsibilities because of their military strength and potential—responsibility to limit their ambitions and concert their influence in the interest of sustaining the system of peace. So far as war was concerned, the goal of policy was not to abolish war but to confine it. Still influenced by the spectre of the Napoleonic experience, the statesmen of the early and middle nineteenth century found compromises which restricted their rivalry. Moderation and toleration remained the order of the day until the rise of Kaiser Wilhelm's Germany after Bismarck. It was taken for granted that States should seek political solutions for their disputes, and that force should be used only as a final resort. Strongly urged by the United States as early as 1794, international arbitration became a familiar feature of the diplomatic landscape. In 1872, the *Alabama* arbitration dealt with the responsibility of a State for the international use of force from its territory as a question of international law. Great Britain was held liable to pay substantial damages for its negligent failure to prevent the Confederate cruiser *Alabama* from slipping out of a British port to start its career of raiding the commerce of the United States.[6] It is hard to exaggerate the significance of that episode in the process through which the admonitions of philosophers about limiting the right to use force internationally became binding rules of law.

During most of the nineteenth century, the Concert of Europe and its occasional diplomatic Congresses functioned often and sometimes well to find diplomatic solutions for problems which might otherwise have led to war. In this sense, the nineteenth century diplomatic apparatus of Europe provided the model for the institutions of the League of Nations and then of the United Nations, including the Security Council and its veto. When wars came in the nineteenth century, they were confined, and their goals were limited. During the 100 years before 1914, war was a phenomenon of the political order, and within it, not a means of destroying it. The European wars of the nineteenth century never involved the destruction of States or of societies. In the end, they were smothered in diplomacy. The Crimean War, the Franco-Prussian War, and the war over Schleswig-Holstein did not greatly alter the political system of Europe or of the world.

Of course, the system functioned imperfectly, and of course in retrospect one can note episodes which weakened the confidence of each member State in the unity of the group: the Crimean and the Franco-Prussian wars, particularly. With the benefit of hindsight, it is clear that

---

[6] A. Cook, *The Alabama Claims, American Politics and Anglo-American Relations, 1865–1872* (1975).

these events sapped the foundation of a system built on mutual trust. But the Concert of Europe did function for a century, and its destruction in 1914 was not inevitable. It was destroyed not by flaws and contradictions in the ideas of its constitution, but by the shortcomings of the statesmen who betrayed them.

The effort to curb war through the methods which had developed in the wake of the Congress of Vienna suffered a tragic wound in 1914. Germany had violated the most fundamental rules of the Vienna system by seeking a position of dominance incompatible with its harmonies. Sensitive to the fragility of the Austro-Hungarian and the Russian Empires, the Powers reacted with panic to the Austrian attack on Serbia. And the First World War released reservoirs of violence and barbarity which most people thought had been permanently tamed by the advance of civilisation during the Victorian age.

After the First World War, the quest for peace initiated at Vienna was consciously resumed. As Professor Hinsley has pointed out, one of the most important features of the modern political system, marking it off from its predecessors, is that "after every war since the end of the eighteenth century—1815; after the wars of 1854 and 1871; in 1918; and again in 1945—the States have made a conscious and concerted effort, each one more radical than the one they had made before, to reform the international system in ways that were calculated to enable them to avoid another conflict."[7] At Versailles, that attempt to achieve radical reform had two major purposes—to bring the United States into world affairs as a Great Power, and to establish the League of Nations as the central forum of diplomacy.

Lord Devlin has written a revealing book on how Woodrow Wilson accomplished a mutation in world politics, both by leading the United States into the war, and by initiating the League of Nations as successor to the system started at the Congress of Vienna.[8] Before Wilson's time, the United States, born in the travail of European power politics, had lived apart as a neutral beneficiary of the Concert of Europe. Earlier than most of his contemporaries, President Wilson saw that history had made it impossible for the United States to protect their national interests in world politics by the methods of isolation and neutrality they had used for 100 years. Under the pressure of the German bid for hegemony, the European system had lost its capacity to maintain the balance of power which had helped to stabilise the long century before 1914. As a consequence, the United States was no longer protected by the British fleet.

The essence of President Wilson's vision was that the best course for

---

[7] "*The Decline and Fall of the Modern International System*", *op. cit.* in note 3, above, Lecture 1, *The Modern Pattern of Peace and War*, p. 6.

[8] P. Devlin, *Too Proud To Fight* (1974).

the United States in a changing world is to play a full part in processes of international co-operation intended to achieve and secure a new system of world politics ordered by law: a system more just than the imperial order of the past; more progressive and more enlightened; one which developed peaceful procedures to vindicate human rights and the self-determination of peoples. In such a world, Wilson believed, each State could live on terms of peace and friendship with every other, whatever its social philosophy, so long as it respected its basic obligations to the world community. And United States participation in the work of the League—and particularly in its peacekeeping efforts—would make it possible for the goals of the Covenant to be achieved.

The Covenant of the League institutionalised the chief practices of the Concert of Europe, and added an extremely important new factor to the realm of diplomacy—the Secretariat. The international civil service of the League, led by a Secretary-General of rank and prestige, became an autonomous influence, capable of mediation and conciliation, and, at its best, of leadership. After 1919, multilateral diplomacy was not an occasional dimension of world politics, invoked when necessary, but a continuous process, conducted at many levels and on more and more subjects. So far as the use of force was concerned, the Covenant did not quite outlaw war as an instrument of national policy—that step did not occur formally until the Kellogg-Briand Treaty was ratified in 1928—but it did accept the idea of compulsory conciliation, in its provision for a three-month moratorium in order to give diplomacy a chance to preserve the peace.

Manifestly, the quest for an organised peace under the League failed in the 1930s. The United Kingdom and France were overwhelmed and paralysed by events. It was beyond their power to stop Germany and Japan at the same time. Besides they could not bring themselves to believe that quarrels and aggressions in what is now called the Third World really mattered. The Soviet Union was foolishly kept in isolation, and the United States stood in the undignified pose of the ostrich, looking for an escape into the womb of the nineteenth century. As a consequence, the Powers made the same mistake they made before 1914—the mistake, be it said, they are repeating again: they allowed the momentum for war to build up in Asia and Africa and then to overwhelm the possibility of general peace.

II—THE RULES OF THE CHARTER
REGARDING THE INTERNATIONAL USE OF FORCE: THESIS

After the Second World War, the search for peace was resumed in the name of the Charter of the United Nations, and has been pursued with varying degrees of success ever since. For the men and women who had lived through the failure of the League, it was self-evident that the Second World War had come because the United States had not followed Wilson's advice, and because the Western Allies had not stopped aggression in Ethiopia, Manchuria, Spain, and Czechoslovakia, and prevented the rearmament of Germany and the occupation of the Rhineland, in violation of the Treaty of Versailles.

The Charter is not the whole of international law, any more than a written constitution or statute is the whole of the law on the subjects with which it deals. Like any document of positive law, the Charter must be read against a tenacious background of custom, practice, history, expectation, and hope. And, like any other document of positive law, its meaning evolves continuously in response to social and moral change, and to changes in its own code of aspiration as well. The Charter is thus an effort to reorient and in some areas to restate the pre-existing international law. It should be read in its matrix of purpose, with primary emphasis, always, not on the words alone but on the underlying theory of governance the words seek imperfectly to express and to fulfil.

What is that theory of governance, with regard to the responsibility of States for the international use of force?

The Charter articulates a number of axioms, postulates, and aspirations for the society of nations: to defend and advance fundamental human rights and the equality of men and women, and of nations large and small; economic welfare and social justice; respect for the integrity of treaties and other sources of international law; friendly relations among nations based on the principle of equal rights and self-determination of peoples; and, above all, international peace and security. These goals of the Charter system are to be sought through peaceful means, and never by the use of force—through political co-operation, compromise, mediation, arbitration, adjudication, and the good offices of friendly Powers and the organs of the United Nations.

If there is any one proposition about the Charter which history makes manifest, it is that its primary and overriding purpose is to minimise the use of force in international relations. All scholars on the subject do not agree about the extent of that restriction. But if the Charter does not revise international law in this regard, by making peace the first among its goals, it is hard to imagine what it can be supposed to intend.

The régime posited by the Charter with respect to the international use of force is reflected in two key passages of the document, Article 2(4) and Article 51. The modern law concerning the international use of force could easily be codified as an exegesis of these two Articles, and their application to the problems of contemporary international life. The proposition that each State is "sovereign" and entitled to territorial integrity and political independence is the major premise for every group of decisions which constitute the corpus of the doctrinal law on the international use of force.

Article 2(4) specifies that "all Members shall refrain in their international relations from the threat or use of force against the territorial integrity or political independence of any state," while Article 51 notes that nothing in the Charter "shall impair the inherent right of individual or collective self-defence if an armed attack occurs against a member of the United Nations, until the Security Council has taken measures necessary to maintain international peace and security."[9]

Article 2(4) is the critical change sought to be accomplished by the Charter in customary international law. Building on the Kellogg-Briand Pact and the jurisprudence of Nuremberg, it would deny States one of their historic "inherent rights" as sovereign States—that of making war on their neighbours at will. Under the Charter, States can use force internationally only in situations beyond the scope of Article 2(4); in instances of individual or collective self-defence; in circumstances which do not threaten or impair the territorial integrity or political independence of a State; or pursuant to an appropriate resolution of the Security Council.

The "inherent" right of States to use force internationally in ways which do not violate Article 2(4) is left unimpaired by the Charter. Some uses of force which fall into that category, *i.e.* assistance to a recognised State in suppressing a rebellion against its authority, will be discussed at a later point.

The expectation of the Charter was that the permanent members of the Security Council would agree on the peacekeeping policies to be applied by the Council in carrying out its responsibilities. When it became clear that no such agreement was possible, the enforcement of the Charter rules was remitted automatically to the "inherent" right of States to undertake policies of individual or collective self-defence in accordance with Article 51.

The background of Article 51 in customary international law is well developed. States have always been conceded the legal right to ask others for help in dealing with external and internal threats to their security, and, indeed, to co-operate freely with other States in the military area. They have also been conceded the right to use limited and proportional force in peacetime to defend themselves against armed attacks and other threatening and coercive breaches of international law for which there was no practicable diplomatic or judicial remedy. The classic paradigm of permissible self-help against the fact or the threat of external attack in peacetime is the situation of the famous *Caroline*

---

[9] In addition, Article 2(7) provides that nothing in the Charter confers jurisdiction on the United Nations to intervene in "matters which are essentially within the domestic jurisdiction of any state," except that this principle shall not prejudice the application of enforcement measures under Chapter VII.

episode in 1837, in which the British sent armed forces into New York to disperse a military group that had assembled along the Niagara River to assist an insurrection in Canada. The United States had failed to break up and arrest the armed band.[10] The United States did not contest the principle on which Great Britain acted, but argued that Britain should have given the United States more time to discharge its conceded legal obligation.

The principle of self-help recognised in the correspondence over the *Caroline* episode was applied widely and generally accepted as right in situations where the State claiming the right of self-defence had suffered a prior violation of its legal rights from the offending State, and the violation was of a certain quality involving coercion or violence, such as international raids, arms smuggling to rebels against the authority of the State, threats to the safety of citizens abroad, or breaches of neutrality. If a State was subjected to armed attack or other forms of coercion by or from another State, and no peaceful remedy was in fact available, it was universally accepted that it had a right to use a proportional amount of force against the State responsible for the breach—enough force under the circumstances to cure the breach.[11] Such limited uses of international force by way of self-defence are not acts of general war. And they are not deemed to threaten the territorial integrity or political independence of the State being attacked.

While each State is subject to the obligation to exhaust available peaceful alternatives before exercising its right of self-defence under Article 51, the Charter leaves to the State itself the right to decide in the first instance when to respond to what it regards as an armed attack, the imminent threat of armed attack, or a breach of international law which it regards as comparably coercive. A State need not obtain a ruling from the Security Council before using force in self-defence. The Security Council can support a State's decision, as it did when North Korea attacked South Korea in 1950, and as it did repeatedly in the course of the prolonged conflict over Israel's right to exist. The Security Council may disagree with the action of the State claiming a right of self-defence, and rule against the propriety of its decision: *i.e.* rule that its use of force

---

[10] Professor R. Y. Jennings has commented that in the *Caroline* case "self-defence was changed from a political excuse to a legal doctrine." *The Caroline and McLeod Cases*, 32 AM. INT. L. 82 (1938). See also *Digest of International Law* (1906), pp. 409–414, and *Digest of International Law*, (1969), pp. 211–236; D. W. Bowett, *Self-Defense in International Law* (1963); D. W. Bowett, "Reprisals Involving Recourse to Armed Force," 66 AM. J. INT. L. 1 (1972), and "Economic Coercion and Reprisals by States," 13 VA. J. INT. L. 1 (1972); I. Brownlie, *International Law and The Use of Force by States* (1963); M. S. McDougal and F. P. Feliciano, *Law and Minimum World Public Order* (1961); J. Stone, *Aggression and World Order* (1976).

[11] *e.g.* the Naulilaa affair, *Digest of International Law* (1943), p. 154, 2 U.N. Rep. Int'l. Arb. Awards 1011.

was a violation of Article 2(4), and therefore a breach of the peace or an act of aggression. This happened in effect during the Suez crisis of 1956, although the Security Council was paralysed by the British and French vetoes. Nonetheless, it was clear that an overwhelming majority of the world community had concluded that the United Kingdom and France, at least, had not been attacked, or threatened by attack, and therefore that their use of force against Egypt was not justified under Article 51.[12]

The much mooted case of Vietnam was the occasion for heated political passion and many charges of illegality. In fact, however, the legal issues in the Vietnam war were simpler and less equivocal than those of the Korean War some years earlier. Reviewing the literature with the advantage of distance reveals no basis for the claim that United States aid to the government of South Vietnam violated international law. Like East and West Germany and North and South Korea, North and South Vietnam were separate States for every purpose of international law, certainly after 1954 and for some years before that date as well. Whether one views the war as an attack by North Vietnam against South Vietnam, or as North Vietnamese aid to an insurrection within South Vietnam, the legal issue is the same. Under either hypothesis, the American position was legal, and that of North Vietnam and its supporters illegal.[13] This conclusion applies as well to the Allied invasion of Cambodia towards the end of the Vietnam war, since North Vietnamese troops were attacking South Vietnam from Cambodia, and the government of Cambodia was unable to stop them.

The Cuba Missile Crisis was the most extreme instance thus far of the exercise by a State of its inherent right of self-defence. The United States made no claim that a nuclear attack on it from Cuba was imminent. On the contrary, United States nuclear superiority at the time made it clear that a Soviet nuclear threat to the United States was not credible. The United States did take the position, which subsequent events demonstrated was correct, that the secret emplacement of missiles in Cuba, in violation of Soviet diplomatic assurances, was a substantial political-military threat, against the background of contemporary pressures in Berlin, in Laos and Cambodia, and elsewhere, though not an armed attack or even an imminent threat of armed attack. The United States elected to treat that threat as one justifying limited acts of self-help, including some use of military force. Article 51 is the only possible legal basis for the United States claim, although the United States Govern-

---

[12] See R. R. Bowie, *Suez 1956, International Crises and The Role of Law* (1974).

[13] For a review of the literature, see E. V. Rostow, Book Review, 82 YALE L. J. 829 (1973); R. A. Falk (ed.), *The Vietnam War and International Law* (4 Vols., 1968–1976); R. H. Hull and J. C. Novograd, *Law and Vietnam* (1968); and note 15, below.

ment of the day relied on another legal argument. Most of the non-communist world agreed with the American assessment.[14]

In this connection, a related use of force in international affairs should be noted: the placement of the forces of one State on the territory of another, at its request, to assure their common defence interests or, indeed, to assist the host State in dealing with domestic disorders, including riot, insurrection, or civil war. This practice is an aspect of customary international law accepted as the order of nature in the States system, and never seriously challenged under the Charter. Whether it should be treated as coming under Article 51 is not clear, and perhaps not important. The international use of force under these circumstances cannot be considered to violate Article 2(4), since it is intended to uphold and not to threaten the territorial integrity and political independence of the host State. For example, when civil war raged in Nigeria in the 1960s, it was considered altogether normal and legal for the United Kingdom, Egypt, and the Soviet Union to provide military assistance to Nigeria, although military assistance to the Biafran rebels would have been considered an armed attack against Nigeria and a breach of Article 2(4). The Organisation of African States and a number of interested nations made strenuous efforts to prevent any international assistance to Biafra. The minute assistance the Biafrans did receive from abroad was covert, and understood to be illicit. The Biafran case was discussed and treated by the international community as comparable to that of Greece in the late 1940s, although there were differences between the two episodes. In Greece, the internal rebellion was helped significantly from neighbouring communist States, a fact which was verified publicly by a United Nations Commission. The pattern of reaction by the international community in the Biafran case was the same as in the case of Greece: that is, the right of a State to assist another in suppressing a rebellion does not depend on whether the rebels attacking it are being helped from abroad. International assistance to the Greek rebels was condemned, while the action of the United Kingdom and the United States in helping the Greek Government was regarded as legal and proper.[15] Similarly, the United Kingdom and France have assisted a

---

[14] The best analysis of the Cuba Missile Crisis as a coercive threat is Albert and Roberta Wohlstetter, *Controlling the Risks in Cuba* (1965). See also H. S. Dinerstein, *The Making of a Missile Crisis, October 1962* (1976). Abram Chayes, at that time Legal Adviser of the State Department, has written an important memoir, *The Cuban Missile Crisis* (1974). I disagree, however, with its thesis that the United States position can be defended as an action by the Organisation of American States pursuant to Article 53 of the Charter, but not as an act of self-defence under Article 51. To me it is unthinkable that a regional organisation take such action without the prior approval of the Security Council, as required in Article 53.

[15] T. J. Farer, *The Regulation of Foreign Intervention in Civil Armed Conflict* (1974); J. N. Moore (ed.), *Law and Civil War in The Modern World* (1974); E. Luard (ed.), *The International Regulation of Civil Wars* (1972); R. A. Falk, *The International Law of Civil War* (1971); J. N. Moore, *Law and the Indo-China War* (1972); L. C. Buchheit, *Secession* (1978); J. J. Stremlau, *The International Politics of The Nigerian Civil War, 1967–1970* (1980).

number of African countries dealing with disorders or movements of revolution or secession, whether those revoluntionary movements were assisted from abroad or not.

Force is sometimes used internationally under customary international law and Article 51 to protect the citizens of a nation in a situation of distress or to remedy severe breakdowns in public order after earthquakes, riots, or other disasters. In the 1976 raid to rescue Israeli and other hostages being held at Entebbe in Uganda, for example, the government of Uganda owed a clear duty under international law to protect the plane and its passengers from the hijackers. Since Uganda was not fulfilling that duty, and the risk to the passengers was imminent, the prevailing view—a correct one, in my opinion—was that under Article 51 Israel was entitled to use the amount of force reasonably necessary to deal with the effects of Uganda's breach of international law.[16] Such actions do not violate the principle of Article 2(4), since they do not threaten either the territorial integrity or the political independence of the State where limited military operations occur. In the *Caroline* affair it was obvious that Great Britain was not waging general war against the United States, or planning to annex upper New York State.

Much of the modern law regarding the use of force in international Politics concerns the interpretation and enforcement of Article 51. In practice, the law of Article 51 has gone far beyond its text in adapting its principles to the realities of the political process during a period when the Security Council has often been paralysed by the rivalries of the Cold War and other political passions. Like every document in the history of law, Article 51 cannot be given a literal interpretation. In terms, it seems to apply only to members of the United Nations. But non-member States, like South Korea, have been given its protection. And the right to use force under Article 51 against "an armed attack" extends to the threat of armed attack, although Article 51 seems literally to apply only after an armed attack has begun. Such a construction would be absurd, as a practical matter, especially but not exclusively in a nuclear setting. As Elihu Root once wrote, under international law every State has "the right . . . to protect itself by preventing a condition of affairs in which it will be too late to protect itself."[17] There is no evidence that those who drafted the Charter or have since construed it contemplated any change

---

[16] J. A. Sheenan, "The Entebbe Raid," 1 *Fletcher Forum*, Nr. 135 (1977); T. E. Behuniak, "The Law of Unilateral Humanitarian Intervention by Armed Force: A Legal Survey," 79 MIL. L. REV. 157 (1978); Francis Boyle, *Entebbe Revisited* (1981); T. R. Krift, "Self-Defense and Self-Help: the Israeli Raid on Entebbe," 4 BROOKLYN J. INT. L. 43 (1977); M. Knishbacker, "The Entebbe Operation: A Legal Analysis," 12 J. INT. LAW AND ECON. 57 (1977); L. M. Salter, "Commando Coup at Entebbe: Humanitarian Intervention or Barbaric Aggression," 11 INT. LAW 331 (1977).

[17] Chayes, *op. cit.* in note 14, above, at p. 109.

in this basic rule of customary international law. On the contrary, long-standing usage in this regard has been relied upon as obviously sensible. In the celebrated *Caroline* episode the United States conceded that self-help might sometimes be justified to deal with the imminent threat of armed attack. And in the *Corfu Channel* case, the International Court of Justice held that Albania had committed a serious breach of its international legal obligations, justifying a limited use of force by the United Kingdom, in failing to issue public warnings about the presence of mines in the Corfu Channel, an international waterway. Albania was held liable for damages caused by the use of force from its territory—not by the Albanian Government but (presumably) by others—because the Albanian Government, the court inferred, must have known about the presence of the mines which caused serious damage to British ships found to be legally passing through the channel. Heavy damages were awarded against Albania for its "knowing" failure to act—hardly an "armed attack." In a demonstration of political balance, the court also ruled that the United Kingdom had used excessive force in responding to Albania's illegal act, although it did not award damages against the United Kingdom. Paradoxically, the principal evidence in the case concerned the mines which the Court ultimately ruled had been wrongfully swept by the Royal Navy.[18]

While States necessarily make provisional determinations that an attack has occurred when they exercise their rights of self-defence under Article 51, the Security Council has the final authority under the Charter to determine when a threat to the peace, a breach of the peace, or an act of aggression has taken place. It may then call on the parties to settle their dispute by peaceful means, recommend a settlement, provide a mediator or a diplomatic midwife, or recommend the submission of the dispute to the International Court of Justice. If these means fail, it may make legally binding decisions and, in extreme cases, apply economic or military sanctions in order to maintain or restore international peace and security. Under the Uniting for Peace Resolution passed during the Korean conflict, the General Assembly can make recommendations but not legally binding decisions on breaches of the peace and acts of aggression when the Security Council is unable to act.

Thus the third class of international uses of force contemplated as legal by the Charter consists of those undertaken pursuant to recommendations or binding decisions of the Security Council, either by the national forces of member States or by special United Nations forces. Not all such episodes, properly speaking, have been "enforcement actions" of the United Nations rather than procedures of self-defence encouraged, or not opposed, by the Security Council. Their legality under the Charter is the same in either case. In other instances, United

---

[18] (1949) I.C.J. 4.

Nations forces have been established more for diplomatic than for combat purposes—to keep combatants apart, and to reduce anxiety about possible breaches of cease-fire or armistice agreements, as was the case in the Middle East, Cyprus, and other troubled areas.[19]

Under the political circumstances of recent years, the power of the Security Council to make binding decisions on issues of international peace and security has not been used often. But on great occasions, when the major Powers can agree, the Security Council has acted, and acted with considerable effect. One such action occurred on October 22, 1973, when the Council voted a binding decision requiring the parties to the Middle Eastern conflict to negotiate a just and durable peace in accordance with the principles and provisions of an earlier resolution on peace in the Middle East, Resolution 242, which the Council had adopted in November, 1967.

Security Council resolutions are drafted in a political atmosphere, and avoid explicit language to which some of the nations might be sensitive. They must be interpreted, therefore, like the holdings of common law judges, in the light of the principles and propositions from which they necessarily derive. Read in this way, Resolution 338 of October 22, 1973, is of the utmost importance. By commanding the Arab States to make peace with Israel before Israel withdraws from any territories it has occupied since 1967, the Resolution authoritatively rejects the basic thesis of the Arab States that Israel has no right to exist. According to Arabs, the existence of Israel is in itself an "armed attack" on the Palestinian nation and people which in their view inherited the sovereignty of the whole territory of the Palestine Mandate from Turkey in 1922, or at the latest, when the United Kingdom gave up the Mandate in 1948. On the contrary, Resolutions 338 and 242 reaffirm the basic decisions of the League of Nations and a long line of decisions and other resolutions of the Security Council which uphold the legitimacy of the Palestine Mandate and the lawful emergence of Israel and Jordan as the successor states to Turkey in the territories of the Mandate, and declare the United Nations' special interest in the future of Jerusalem.[20]

The Security Council has not often authorised the use of force to carry out its "decisions." It has relied primarily on the slower processes of political persuasion to achieve compliance. This is the case today with respect to both Namibia[21] and the prolonged conflict over Israel's right to exist.

---

[19] Rosalyn Higgins, *United Nations Peacekeeping, 1946–1967* (1970); D. W. Bowett, *United Nations Forces* (1964).

[20] See E. V. Rostow, "The Illegality of the Arab Attack on Israel of October 6, 1973," 69 AM. J. INT. L. 272 (1975); and "Palestinian Self-Determination: Possible Futures for the Unallocated Territories of the Palestine Mandate," 5 *Yale Studies in World Public Order*, Nr. 147 (1979).

[21] [1971] I.C.J. 16, R. Higgins, "The Advisory Opinion on Namibia," 21 INT. & COMP. L. QU. 270 (1972).

The rules of the Charter with regard to the international use of force have been interpreted and restated with surprising consistency over the years since 1945 not only by the Security Council and by scholars, diplomats, judges, and ministers, but by a number of United Nations committees, commissions, and special bodies charged with codifying and expounding this branch of international law. Despite the intense political interest of many States in establishing exceptions which might legitimise categories of war they happen to favour—most notably, wars of national liberation, wars of communist revolution, and wars against the white régimes of Africa—it has proved intellectually and politically impossible to do so. The needs, interests, and anxieties of all States in this regard are the same. In the end, no State will vote for a doctrine which might be read to authorise guerrillas, mercenaries, or armed bands to operate against it from foreign bases, nor can it bring itself to abandon its inherent right under international law to obtain foreign help either against insurrection or invasion.

In 1950, the General Assembly, "condemning the intervention of a State in the internal affairs of another State for the purpose of changing its legally established government by the threat or use of force," solemnly reaffirmed "that, whatever the weapons used, any aggression, whether committed openly, or by fomenting civil strife in the interest of a foreign Power, or otherwise, is the gravest of all crimes against peace and security throughout the world."[22] And, in 1954, the International Law Commission defined as offences against the peace and security of mankind the tolerance by a State of the use of its territory by armed bands or terrorists planning to make incursions into another State, or by groups intending to foment civil strife in another State.[23]

A quite different General Assembly affirmed the same sentiments in 1970, and again in 1974. The General Assembly's 1970 Declaration on Principles of International Law Concerning Friendly Relations and Co-operation among States provides that "every state has the duty to refrain from organising or encouraging the organisation of irregular forces or armed bands, including mercenaries, for incursion into the territory of another state."[24] And the 1974 Definition of Aggression adopted by the Assembly defined as aggression "the sending by or on behalf of a state of armed bands, groups, irregulars or mercenaries, which carry out acts of armed force against another state . . . , or its substantial involvement therein."[25] The rule of law goes beyond these declarations, and imposes

---

[22] G. A. Res. 380, 5 U.N. GOAR Supp. 9, at 13–14, U.N. Doc. A/1775 (1950).

[23] Int'l. L. Comm. Report, 9 U.N. GOAR Supp. 9, at 11–12, U.N. Doc. A/2693 (1954).

[24] G. A. Res. 2625, 25 U.N. GOAR Supp. 28, at 122, U.N. Doc. A/8082 (1970). See Dean Rusk, "The 25th U.N. General Assembly and the Use of Force," 2 Georgia J. Int. And Comp. Law 19, 25 (Supp. l, 1972).

[25] U.N. Doc. A/RES 3314 (XXIX), Dec. 14, 1974, 69 Am. J. Int. L. 480 (1953). See J. Stone, *Conflict Through Consensus* (1977).

absolute liability on a State for the use of force by armed bands from its territory, so long as the host State knows or should know that such activities are taking place. Great Britain's liability to the United States in the *Alabama* case was based on its failure to prevent the cruiser from leaving the harbour, not on the British complicity in a Confederate plot. And the *Corfu Channel* judgment is even more categorical.

It is sometimes urged that these rules enshrine the *status quo*, and that an exception should be recognised on behalf of international assistance to revolutions which a majority of those voting in the General Assembly of the United Nations might consider to be just, especially for so-called "wars of national liberation." All authoritative doctrinal statements of international law and the conditioned reflexes of the State system deny the thesis. International law does not condemn revolutions which occur within States. It is opposed to international war, not to social or political movements seeking social change within the States which have been formed by history.

Confronting revolution or other civil strife within a State, the world community has a wide variety of choices. Outside States can sometimes influence the course of internal events through recourse to diplomacy or other peaceful means. They can help—or refuse to help—the government struggling to put down the rebellion. Or they can do nothing. What they cannot do is to assist the rebellion. This is an act no theorist has as yet been ingenious enough to reconcile with the principle of the sovereign equality of States. There are almost no States which do not contain groups which could be described as "peoples" claiming the right of self-determination. Spain, one of the oldest States of the international community, contains Catalonians and Basques who assert rights of self-determination. There are problems of this order in Belgium, in Canada, in the Soviet Union, in most of the States of Africa, and in many, many others. Each time an effort is made to formulate a rule which would allow force to be used internationally in behalf of "the self-determination of peoples" or other popular causes, the obstacle of statehood proves to be insuperable.

In Article 1(2), the Charter declares that it is one of the "purposes" of the United Nations to develop "friendly relations among nations based on respect for the principle of equal rights and self-determination of peoples, and to take other appropriate measures to strengthen universal peace." It is difficult to see how that statement of purpose expressly linked to the idea of universal peace can be interpreted as a licence for international war on a nearly universal scale. The self-determination of peoples is an aspiration to be pursued through political means, and not through the international use of force. Self-determination is not an absolute. Like any goal or prescription of international law, it must be accommodated to other equally authoritative goals or prescriptions applicable in the particular case. If elevated into a totem, the principle of self-determination would become a weapon with which to dissolve and destroy the State system. For international law and practice to acknowledge a right to use force internationally in behalf of such claims would be to repudiate the most basic principle on which the Charter is based: the principle of the equality of States, and their right to order their domestic affairs in accordance with their own ideas of social justice.

This is not to say that a State's internal affairs may never be a matter of international concern. The Charter does contemplate the use of peaceful means to promote the universal acceptance of human rights. And the precedent of international military interventions where minimal standards of decency are being violated has by no means vanished from our consciousness. Such humanitarian interventions—a limited and controversial category at best—are not considered to violate Article 2(4), because they do not threaten the territorial integrity or political independence of the State.[26] But the pattern of State practice, and the repeated formulations of international law by groups purporting to be authoritative, deny the claim of a legal right to use force in behalf of rebellions, secessions, or revolutions, whether labelled those of self-determination, national liberation, or one or another sect of communism. Under Article 2(7), only the Security Council can decide that events within a State constitute a threat to the peace.

International law prohibits the Brezhnev Doctrine as categorically as it forbids all other forms of aggression. The Soviet invasion of Hungary in 1956 and of Czechoslovakia in 1968 were instances in which the Soviet Union used force to depose governments which had changed their policies, and, in the Soviet view, had deviated from the true faith. The Brezhnev Doctrine thus rests on an idea which is the exact opposite of the principle of self-determination.

III—THE FALL OF THE CHARTER RULES: ANTITHESIS

The effective validity of these rules as law is an illusion despite the near unanimity with which they are pronounced.

As a government committed to crusade for revolution, the Soviet Union never accepted the Charter of the United Nations more than nominally and tactically, and always with grave reservations about interpretations derived from bourgeois conceptions of international law. The Soviet Union made its first expansionary moves before the Second World War—annexing the Baltic States and invading Finland. It has been pursuing the same policy at an accelerating rate ever since. In 1944

---

[26] M. S. McDougal, H. D. Lasswell and Lung Chu Chen, *Human Rights and World Public Order* (1980).

or 1945 its armies were accompanied by governments for both the East European States and for Germany.

Between 1947 and the early 1970s, in the name of the Charter, the United States and its allies conducted an active campaign to contain the process of Soviet expansion and maintain a balance of world power. In that period, the Charter norms against aggression were vindicated quite consistently and effectively in Iran, Greece, Turkey, Berlin, Korea, the Middle East, Africa, and Cuba. Since the collapse of United States policy in Indo-China some 10 years ago, however, world politics has been transformed by a series of large-scale and successful aggressions planned or supported by the Soviet Union. Under the impact of these events, the Charter norms are rapidly ceasing to correspond to the practice of States.

Even in the heyday of the Truman doctrine, exceptions to the apparent universality of the Charter were tacitly recognised. In the first instance, the United States and its European allies made no attempt to invoke the Charter against Soviet aggression in East Germany, Hungary, Poland, Czechoslovakia, and other countries of Eastern Europe. In fact if not in form, the area was treated as a Soviet sphere of influence, and the promise of free elections given at Yalta and Potsdam was ignored. The allies reacted effectively only when the Soviet Union attacked or threatened areas outside the Soviet protectorate—Greece in the late 1940s, Korea in 1950, and Yugoslavia in the early 1950s and again in 1968.

Secondly, the rules of the Charter have never been seriously invoked in connection with the process of African decolonisation. In the first stages of that process, groups seeking independence from France, the United Kingdom, and Belgium were rarely helped by forces from beyond the frontiers of their own colonies, and then only on a small scale. The spread of the practice of using force internationally in wars against white authority in Africa, and the increase in the scale of such interventions, is only some 15 years old. It began with attacks from neighbouring States against the Portuguese and then the Spanish provinces in Africa: attacks which no effective group in the world community was prepared to resist. Later, the technique was applied to Rhodesia. At the present time, the practice is epidemic and virulent throughout Africa. While the African States have often invoked the Charter in order to protect themselves—as in the Biafran case, the Katangese secession in the Congo, and a large number of other episodes involving the international use of force in Africa—neither the African States nor other members of the United Nations so much as comment on the illegality of most of the warfare now raging in Africa. State after State faces frontiers festooned with armed camps—the camps of troops actively engaged in aggression against neighbouring States. The troops may be exiled natives or mercenaries fighting for money or for ideology.

They may represent the cause of conquest, adventure, or racial warfare, or of one or another brand of revolution. Whatever their cause, the effect of what they do is the same.

The intensification of international conflict since the early 1970s rests on a basic challenge to the political and legal doctrines of the Charter. What is happening in Africa is no more than an extension of trends long manifest in the Middle East and the Far East. That challenge is encompassed in the theory of wars of national or indeed of ideological liberation. In legal terms, as was pointed out earlier, the argument is that international law should formally acknowledge the right of self-determination of peoples who happen to live within the States which constitute the atoms of the system of international politics. By treating "States" as fictions, and "peoples" as realities, the advocates of this theory claim that international law should recognise the right of States to use force internationally in order to assist movements of secession and other revolutionary movements against the authority of States, so long as they are labelled wars of self-determination or of national liberation. Furthermore, they claim that when revolutionary movements of this character gain sufficient momentum, no State should be allowed to provide assistance to the governments being attacked.

The first of these precedents would legitimise international assistance to peoples in revolt. Before the First World War, the Russian Government provided assistance to the Slavs of Eastern Europe—a process which contributed to the turmoil of the Balkans, and helped to bring on the war. The argument is made in behalf of the Palestinian Arabs today. It was the theory Hitler invoked to justify his seizure of the Sudeten province of Czechoslovakia in 1938.

The second theory much in vogue today is that of the non-intervention policy adopted by the United Kingdom, France, and the United States during the Spanish Civil War of the 1930s. That theory asserts that it is the duty of States to refrain from assisting either side in a civil war, at least when the conflict reaches the level of belligerency.

I should argue that international law cannot accept either the Sudetenland precedent, nor that of the non-intervention policy of the 1930s towards the Spanish Civil War. The Charter of the United Nations repudiates them. They do not correspond to what has until recently been the almost instinctive pattern of practice. And, most fundamentally, they are contrary to the necessities of peace in a political system which is and will remain a system of States.

The only workable norm of international law for situations of this kind is illustrated by the way in which the international community reacted to the Biafran case in the mid–1960s; to those of Tanzania, Chad, and Ceylon; and to that of Greece in the late 1940s. In all these instances, the international community regarded it as clear that governments could legally obtain international assistance in putting down insurrections, even when the conflict had in fact reached the point of "belligerency," while open or covert assistance to the rebels under such circumstances was treated as categorically illegal. In the Hungarian case of 1956, the Czech case of 1968, and the Afghan case today, the argument before the United Nations and elsewhere has not been that the Soviet Union could not legally assist a widely recognised government which asked for help in suppressing a rebellion, but that there was no such government, and therefore no such request for assistance. In all these instances, the Soviet Union invaded not to support but to destroy a government, although in each instance it carefully invoked the fiction that it was acting at the request of a recognised government to help it put down a revolution—or rather, a "counter-revolution." The United Nations intervention in the Congo which ended the secession of Katanga rested on exactly the same principle—that nations could assist the government of the Congo, at its request, but not the secessionists.[27] And in the Bangladesh war, the preponderant view of the international community, at least as expressed in votes in the Security Council and in the General Assembly, was that the Indian intervention in behalf of the secession of Bangladesh from Pakistan was contrary to international law. India did not claim its action was justified on humanitarian grounds. Only the Soviet veto saved India from explicit condemnation.[28]

The principle is particularly familiar to Americans. When France assisted the secessionist cause in America after 1776, everyone understood that French help for the American colonists was an act of war against Great Britain. It was treated as such, legally and politically. This is one of the categories of war the Charter now purports to forbid.

IV—Can There be a Synthesis?

What conclusions does this review justify, both about policy and about the role of law in the life of the society of nations?

Since the Charter of the United Nations was drafted and ratified in 1945, the nominal law on the international use of force has been clear—as law goes, remarkably clear. Its essential terms can be summarised more easily (and with less real controversy) than most branches of the law of tort or contract. Save for a few idiosyncratic universities, examinations on the subject would be written and ranked the same way in most Western and "non-aligned" countries—perhaps even in the Soviet Union.

---

[27] E. W. Lefever, *Crisis in the Congo* (1965), and *Uncertain Mandate* (1967). More generally, see the excellent articles of M. Krauss, "Internal Conflicts and Foreign States: In Search of the State of the Law," and R. Tyner, "Wars of National Liberation in Africa and Palestine: Self-Determination for People or Territories?," in 5 *Yale Studies in World Public Order* (1979), pp. 173, 234, and books listed in note 15, above.

[28] T. W. Oliver, *The United Nations in Bangladesh* (1978).

The actual law—the law-in-fact, the law of State practice—has been clear too, but in a quite different sense. For 25 years or so after 1945, the few spare propositions which are commonly regarded as the legal norms of the subject were obeyed about as much and enforced about as effectively as most law, except in Eastern Europe and some parts of Africa, where departures from the law were frequent, unchecked, and unpunished. Since the early 1970s, however, the situation has changed radically. The so-called legal "rules" have lost all normative influence on the behaviour of ever more numerous and important sectors of the State system. If present trends continue, the outcome is easy to foresee: the *soi-disant* "rules" will disappear altogether as a factor of immediate significance in world politics. The accelerating Soviet drive for empire, based on aggression as an instrument of national policy, has placed the West in a situation of growing peril. It would be suicidal for the United States and its allies to continue much longer to obey rules against aggression which are being systematically violated by the Soviet Union, its allies, and satellites. Unless United States diplomacy promptly rallies a coalition of nations to insist on restoring the authority of the Charter regarding the international use of force, the State system will disintegrate into complete anarchy. General war will surely result, unless the West should accept a *pax Sovietica*.

This is now the over-arching question of world politics. It was well formulated in a recent article by Sinnathamby Rajaratnam, Deputy Prime Minister of Singapore, in these terms: "Unless the Soviet challenge is made the core of United States foreign policy and met with the same resolve and sense of realism that the Soviets bring to their cause, then a Pax Sovietica is a high probability in the 80's. This is not what we in Asia want, but if that is the only item on the shelf that is what we will have to settle for."[29]

The choice—in my opinion, the only choice—before the West is whether the United States, its allies, and China accept responsibility for enforcing the Charter of the United Nations, or leave the task of world order by default to the Soviet Union, which would enforce rules of its own. The Soviet drive for hegemony has gone too far. It now threatens the world balance of power, and therefore the political independence of the industrial democracies, and of all the States which depend on them for security. They cannot further delay embarking on a programme to restore security through coalition diplomacy backed by deterrent military force. The Charter is the only possible basis for such a policy, since it is the only "code of détente" to which all the nations have formally agreed.

There are factors beyond faith in sweet reason which permit one to believe that the task of persuading the Soviet Union to accept this view is

[29] *New York Times*, November 16, 1980, Section 4, p. 21.

not altogether hopeless. The North Atlantic Treaty Organisation (NATO) allies, Japan, China, and like-minded smaller nations around the world, increasingly conscious of the threat of Soviet domination and the risks of anarchy, have ample power and potential power to insist that the Soviet Union finally accept the State system re-established at San Francisco in 1945 under the rules of the Charter regarding the international use of force. Since 1945, the Soviet Union has given lip service to the Charter, but has never considered itself bound by its rules.

Despite its formidable apparatus of power, the Soviet régime is weak and vulnerable, both in the Soviet Union and in other countries under its rule. And we may finally witness the victory of Nobel's old dream that the increase in the destructive power of technology would compel the nations to settle for peace. The argument has been put forward over and over again, and thus far has always been rejected by those who prefer war to peace. Will the bizarre arithmetic of nuclear weapons now carry the day?

One of the most thoughtful students of these problems, Professor Hinsley of Cambridge, has recently concluded that what he considers to be the world-wide acceptance of the Charter rules as legal norms, coupled with the paralysing implications of nuclear war, are changing the modern mind in fundamental ways, and therefore producing a new international system. He writes: "I derive some comfort from the belief that the conjunction of circumstances which proved fatal to the international system in 1914 and again in 1939 is unlikely to be repeated.

"The modern international system collapsed on those occasions because states continued to hold the view that they had the legal right to go to war. It also collapsed because states holding this view were confronted with massive shifts in their relative power which persuaded them in the last resort that war was a reasonable means of defending or advancing their interests. States hold this view no longer, and in the wake of the great acceleration of scientific and technological development that has taken place in the last forty years, and that still continues, they are unlikely ever again to make this judgment. Indeed, they are unlikely, such of them as have been caught up in this acceleration, to be confronted ever again with shifts in their relative power that will disturb the equilibrium between them. That shifts of power will continue to take place—this goes without saying, as does the fact that interests will continue to conflict. But these states have passed so far beyond a threshold of absolute power that changes in relative power can no longer erode their ability to uphold the equilibrium which resides in the ability of each to destroy all.

"With this I complete my grounds for suggesting that we are now witnessing the formation of an international system which will be even more different from the modern system than that system was from all its precursors, and which will be so because its leading states will abstain from war with each other. But since it will also be a system in which conflict and confrontation continue, between those states as between the others, let me conclude by reminding you that Immanuel Kant, he who first foresaw that precisely such a system would one day materialise, allowed that it would remain subject to constant danger from 'the law-evading bellicose propensities in man' but judged that, once constructed, it would survive for that very reason."[30]

It should be recalled in this connection that Professor Hans Morgenthau, for many years a leading advocate of *Realpolitik* in the study and practice of statecraft, reached the conclusion before he died that nothing short of "world government" could assure the survival of civilisation.[31] My own view of the matter is less radical, and perhaps therefore less capable of dealing with what must soberly be described as the crisis of world politics.

What Professor Morgenthau seems to have had in mind in his final cry of despair is a utopian world super-State altogether beyond the possibilities of history. World politics are now dominated by processes of interaction among many flows of pressure: national, international, and supra-natural; private and public; economic, religious, political, ideological and governmental. In my view, there is no way to escape the complexities and limits of world politics by invoking the simplicities of an imaginary and unattainable planet. The cultural and ideological differences among the nation States of the world are too profound to make anything like Morgenthau's notion of world government a conceivable alternative, save perhaps under Soviet hegemony. And if the Soviet Union has had so much difficulty in maintaining discipline in contiguous States ruled by parties which call themselves Communist, how would it fare in Africa, Islam, and South America? Would a *pax Sovietica* turn out to be very peaceful? In any event, it is not within my terms of reference to examine Professor Morgenthau's surprising legacy.

If I understand Professor Hinsley's insight, he sees an indefinite continuation of the present situation—no direct war between the United States and the Soviet Union—because of the destructiveness of nuclear weapons and what he assumes will remain the nuclear stalemate between them; but a steady agenda of active conflict at the conventional level in many parts of the world, including conflict initiated by the Soviet Union and conducted either by Soviet or proxy forces.

I see the process differently.

In the first place, I cannot agree with Professor Hinsley that the Soviet Union has as yet come to believe that war is not a reasonable means of

---

[30] *The Decline and Fall of the Modern International System, loc. cit.* in note 3, above, Lecture 2, "The Rejection of War," pp. 8–9.
[31] Francis A. Boyle, "The Irrelevance of International Law," 10 CALIF. W. INT'L L.J., 193, 218–219 (1980).

"advancing its interests." On the contrary, it has used war, and the threat of war, for these purposes on a steadily increasing scale since 1945, and it is now busy doing so every day in a number of carefully selected theatres around the world. Its campaign has been conducted thus far largely by proxy forces, except in Eastern Europe and Afghanistan. And it is being carried out at the conventional level or that of the KGB.

It is true that between 1945 and the present time the most basic rule of the Cold War has been that Soviet and United States forces not shoot at each other. That rule has not yet been violated; it is felt on both sides to set an ultimate limit to hostility in the relationship between the two countries. During the Berlin airlift, the Soviet Union buzzed Allied planes, but did not shoot them down, nor did the Soviet Union interfere with Allied shipping during the hostilities in Korea and in Indo-China. The Cuba Missile Crisis strained the taboo, but did not quite breach it.

But the rule cannot survive if the pressures of the Soviet drive for empire continue at anything close to their present level of intensity. The Soviet lunge for dominance in Asia, in the Persian Gulf, in Africa, and in the Caribbean cannot be contained by parrying Soviet thrusts and making counter-thrusts, in the style of the British naval strategy against Napoleon. That phase of the contest will almost surely develop when the West wakes from its somnambulism of the past decade. But I do not believe the contest can be confined for long in that way. The Soviet invasion of Afghanistan is an ominous straw in the wind. The use of Soviet forces in Afghanistan is a fundamental change in the habits of the Cold War. The Soviet leaders decided to move because they considered the United States under Carter too weak and indecisive to stop them. Western leaders were shocked, although they should have known better. They have been clinging to the illusion that the Cold War is over and that "détente" is a political reality rather than an aspiration. Unless Western policy promptly and decisively checks the Soviet rush for dominance, those leaders will be even more shocked when for the first time the Soviet armed forces sink an American or Allied warship, shoot down an American or an Allied plane or satellite, or attack an American or an Allied military installation.

In short, Professor Hinsley sees the future as an indefinite continuation of the present pattern. To me, that forecast seems most unlikely. The course of world politics is too unstable to permit such an outcome. Unless stability is restored, there will be an explosion. Too much is at stake. The conflicts now going on around the world are not for coaling stations in the Pacific and other peripheral targets. The serious men who govern the Soviet Union have not invested 35 years of collosal effort in a campaign to achieve "status," "equality," "recognition as a Great Power," and "a place in the sun." As they say over and over again, they believe that what they call "the correlation of forces" will dominate the future of world politics. That is what they mean. And that is what they are trying to do by building military superiority at a break-neck pace.

The relationship between the use of conventional and nuclear forces is too complex and uncertain for anything like the present pattern to survive. Surely, as Professor Hinsley assumes, the United States must maintain its second-strike capabilities (*i.e.* nuclear stalemate) in order to make certain that the Soviet Union and other States are unable to use or plausibly to brandish nuclear weapons in world politics. But United States nuclear second-strike capability is of no value if it is viewed as a licence for conventional aggression through proxies or otherwise. Yet that is precisely how the present situation should be described, and precisely what Professor Hinsley contemplates for the future as a state of "peace." To my way of thinking it would be more accurate to describe it as a state of anarchy or even of war—limited war for the time being, but war nonetheless.

Thus far in the Cold War, Soviet probes revealed that even when the West had a nuclear monopoly, and then overwhelming nuclear superiority, Western nuclear power would not be used to stop Soviet conventional force attacks on secondary targets, although the threat could be invoked to control escalation when frustration developed, as was the case in Korea and later in Cuba. By the time of the Vietnam campaign, however, United States hints of that kind were no longer credible, and did not work. The Soviet-American nuclear relation was close to stalemate: therefore, the United States no longer controlled the process of escalation. In 1982, or at least by 1985, the question is whether the Soviet Union can paralyse any Western *conventional* force reaction by plausibly threatening a *nuclear* strike to which the West could not rationally respond. For there are circumstances in which it would be nearly inconceivable that the President of the United States order a nuclear attack on Soviet cities in response even to a direct Soviet attack on United States forces or installations. If the Soviet nuclear arsenal were so large that it would be capable of destroying large parts of the American population after an American reprisal, would the American President, however enraged, press the button to initiate that reprisal? More important, would the Soviet leaders believe he would do so? Was Soviet policy in Afghanistan and the Persian Gulf region based on some such calculation as early as 1980–81?[32]

For this reason, I disagree with Professor Hinsley that nuclear stalemate is enough, although I fully agree with him that nuclear stalemate is indispensable to the West, and that nuclear weapons have

---

[32] See *The SALT II Treaty*, Hearings before the Committee on Foreign Relations, United States Senate, 96th Cong., 1st Sess. (1979); E. V. Rostow, "SALT Two—Catch 22," *Wingspread Briefing*, (1979); E. V. Rostow, "The Case Against SALT II," 67 *Commentary* (1979), pp. 23–32.

changed and are changing the magnetic field of world politics. The period since nuclear stalemate first became a perceptible factor in world politics in the mid-1960s has been the worst in the Cold War. The pattern of international aggression sponsored and assisted by the Soviet Union has spread far beyond Eastern Europe and the Asian borders of the Soviet Union. The Arab attack on Israel in 1973 and the final stages of the war in Indo-China—both strongly supported by the Soviet Union—were flagrant violations not only of the Charter but also of agreements the Soviet Union had made with the United States and other nations. The West did nothing to prevent or remedy these acts of aggression. Nor has the West checked the strategically critical Soviet campaign to gain control of the Persian Gulf. That prolonged and well-conceived effort has involved Soviet violations of the Charter in Angola, Ethiopia, Aden and Afghanistan. In 1980, the Soviet Union supported the Iraqi aggression against Iran—timed, like so many other Soviet moves, to take place during the final stages of an American electoral campaign. That aggression has initiated a process which the Soviet Union hopes will allow it to tighten its grip on Iraq, Iran, Syria, and many other States, and bring severe pressure on Egypt, Israel, and Saudi Arabia as well.

The Soviet bid for dominance in the Middle East is not to be compared with its earlier moves against South Korea, Vietnam, Angola, and other targets. Those places are useful tactical outposts. But the Persian Gulf and the Middle East are the strategic epicentre of world politics, the fulcrum on which the Soviet strategic planners expect to move the world.

Everyone in the West realises in an uneasy way that the process of Soviet expansion in the Middle East and elsewhere threatens the vital interests of the United States and its Allies. But there is no agreement on how and why these acts threaten vital interests, or what should be done about them.

The reason for confusion in answering this fundamental question is that the West has failed to work through the trauma of its experience in Vietnam.

In the aftermath of Vietnam, everyone who discusses Western foreign policy should clearly address this primordially important question: What *are* the vital national interests of the United States, the interests for which they may have to fight? Are the vital interests of the United States, Japan, Canada, and the West European nations the same? And where does China stand? A consensus on these matters could in itself prevent war by miscalculation.

It is often said that the ways of world politics are less bipolar than they used to be, and that power is now diffused. The overwhelming lead of the United States and the Soviet Union in nuclear arms makes this proposition untenable. The Soviet Union is pursuing a policy of indefinite expansion, and has now challenged the capacity of the United

States to provide a nuclear umbrella even for its most vital interests. The Soviet and United States lead in the field of nuclear arms is so great that no other nation could catch up effectively within a reasonable time. It follows that third nations cannot protect themselves against the risk of Soviet coercion or attack save through alliance with the United States. This is the meaning of China's *rapprochement* with the United States since 1971. And it is why the idea of a third-force Europe is without substance. Given the pressures of Soviet policy, and the impossibility of altering the nuclear equation significantly, the security interests of Western Europe and Japan (and many other States) are identical with those of the United States. The European and Chinese nuclear arsenals do not exist as independent nuclear deterrents, but as devices to force the hand of the United States during periods of crisis when the United States might happen to have a weak government, or at least a government which differed fundamentally with the views of China or the European States.

Soviet control over Western Europe and Japan would give it such preponderant power as to threaten the political independence and territorial integrity of the United States. Everyone understands that the United States must at a minimum prevent a Soviet take-over of these vital areas. However, Europe and Japan do not exist in geographic isolation. There are areas and countries vital to their defence: in the Far East, Japan could be invested from China, South Korea, Taiwan, or the Philippines, or from combinations of bases in the Southern and Western Pacific. And Europe, under siege on the Eastern Front, is being enveloped from the Middle East, and threatened from the North as well. If Europe should fall, China, Japan, and many other countries would conclude that the United States had been finally defeated and that further resistance to Soviet domination would be useless. The consequences would be bleak. Those nations would become neutral or align themselves with the Soviet Union in patterns that would recall the status of Poland, Finland, or Vichy France. And the peoples of the Soviet Empire, who hate the evil of its government, would give up all hope of liberty.

Can the United States and its Allies protect their interests in world politics by drawing a Maginot Line around certain areas, and ignoring the rest of the world? That approach was tried once. It resulted in the Korean War. Can the security interests of the United States and its Allies be defined in terms less comprehensive than those of the Charter? Thus far, all such attempts have failed for the same simple and fundamental reason: the world is round. The Soviet strategy of imperial expansion, world-wide in scope, is a dynamic process focusing now on one area, now on another, and is constantly nourished and strengthened by the Soviet perception of its emerging military superiority. No region of the world can be excluded in advance from the agenda of concern, for each may be used as an instrument of control as Soviet campaigns develop. It is hard to imagine areas of the world more remote from the United States than Afghanistan and the Yemeni States were 15 or 20 years ago. Yet the United States has rightly asserted an interest in their independence. In the context of Soviet policy they have turned out to be staging areas from which to attack Iran, Saudi Arabia, and the Persian Gulf region generally.

It follows that the twin forces on which Professor Hinsley concentrates—the formal acceptance of the norms of international law as obligatory and the hallucinatory threat of nuclear weapons—compel more than an avoidance of direct warfare between the Soviet Union and the United States, and a continuation of conflict between them at the conventional level through proxies and covert forces. Such a course could permit the Soviet Union to take the fruits of victory without having to make war. Or, what is far more likely, it could detonate general war, and, in all probability, nuclear war. At a given moment, it will become impossible to keep the demon in its cage. The "game of nations" is not in the least like chess; it is a psycho-social phenomenon of immense force. Nuclear and conventional forces do not exist in separate compartments; they are controlled by the same people, subject like all human beings to feelings of pride, shame, anger, humiliation, ambition, and above all fear. We cannot recall too often Thucydides' comment that the true cause of the Peloponnesian War was the rise in the power of Athens, and the fear this caused in Sparta.

Reviewing the condition of world politics at the moment, I conclude with Professor Hinsley that modern war is terrible to contemplate. I go further. I consider both World Wars catastrophes for civilisation, although I think the Allies, having failed to act prudently before 1914 and 1939, had no alternative in each case but to fight. It follows, I should contend, that the ultimate national interest of the NATO Allies, Japan, China, and many other nations is an interest in achieving a stable State system governed by the rules of the United Nations Charter about the international use of force. I therefore suggest that the only feasible major premise of policy for the United States, its allies, China, and other nations which prefer peace and reject Soviet domination is a concerted policy of deterrence which would require the Soviet Union and other errant nations to accept the Charter norms regarding the international use of force. Aspirations which would go beyond that limited goal, like Professor Morgenthau's, would collide with the undeniable pluralism of world cultures about which Professor Adda B. Bozeman has written.[33] But even a planet full of widely different cultures ought to be able to agree on minimum rules of world public order, codifying the terms of

---

[33] "On the Relevance of Hugo Grotius and De Jure Belli ac Pacis for our Times," 1 *Grotiana* 65 (1980).

their mutual interest in peaceful political and economic intercourse. The best evidence that such a task is feasible is the Charter itself, and the repeated efforts to alter its rules with regard to the international use of force, all of which have foundered on the rock of State sovereignty.

The role of law in human society is fundamental. Man can never stop striving to realise its promise. The quest for peace in the society of nations is like every other aspect of man's struggle for justice, and against evil. It goes through periods of progress and periods of reaction. The norms of a legal system can remain norms even if they are not uniformly and universally obeyed. But if they are broken with impunity, and if there is no effective pressure to restore them as genuine standards of conduct, we must conclude that they have ceased to be norms, and have become no more than pious dreams. That is what is happening today to the rules of international law about peace. When law fails as a system of peace, mankind is left with the dismal choice between anarchy and tyranny. Even that choice is more apparent than real. In human experience, states of anarchy have been brought to an end more often by tyranny than by a return to law.

The heart of what I urge here is that the United States, its allies, and China prepare themselves to insist that the Soviet Union and its satellites finally embrace the rules of the Charter of the United Nations regarding the international use of force. Those rules cannot survive unless they are strictly and reciprocally observed. The United States and its allies desire nothing better than a system of world peace governed by the Charter. But they cannot achieve that goal singlehanded. Unless the Soviet Union is persuaded—persuaded by a determined collective effort—to give up its imperial ambitions, and adopt the rules of peaceful coexistence as the United Nations Charter defines them, the United States, its allies and friends will have no choice but to defend their interests as best they can. War is far more likely to come if the industrialised democracies are weak than if they are strong, united, and above all committed to a clear programme to save and safeguard the peace before it is too late.

CRISES AND SURVIVAL

By

CORAL BELL

THE final 20 years of the twentieth century will almost certainly prove a time of exceptional danger for the survival of mankind, or at least of his present civilisations. And within that 20 years of danger, the most dangerous hours will be those when the decision-makers of the nuclear Powers are choosing their lines of action in the context of some international crisis. Thus the techniques of what is optimistically called "crisis management," or less optimistically "crisis diplomacy" or "crisis bargaining," will substantially affect the chances of whether human societies as we know them will live or die or suffer some strange mutation. That is not a particularly reassuring thought when one reflects on some past instances of crisis diplomacy, especially some in the very recent past during the Carter presidency.

I—ORIGINS OF CONCEPT

The term "crisis management" has tended to replace the older "crisis diplomacy" since the time of the Cuba Missile Crisis in 1962. Mr. Robert McNamara, then President Kennedy's Defense Secretary, was reported to have remarked in the aftermath of the crisis that there was no longer any such thing as strategy, only crisis management, and the academic study of the subject took off from then. But actually the new term has always been rather a misleading or mistaken one, in that the word "management" conveys an overtone-image of calm, prudent allocation of resources with a view to judicious maximising of future benefits. It would be agreeable if real diplomatic crises allowed such luxuries, but they do not. Decisions are much more likely to be improvised in a spirit of controlled desperation and within a fog of uncertainty. So the older terms, "crisis diplomacy" and "crisis bargaining," are essentially more realistic. But it is difficult to avoid altogether the phrase "crisis-managers," since the policy-makers concerned are hardly ever professional diplomats, usually politicians and strategists.

II—NATURE AND PROVENANCE OF CRISES

Before we look at crisis diplomacy, however, we must look at the nature of international crises and the most likely provenance of those which must be expected to trouble the society of States during the next two decades. Literally the word crisis means no more than "decision-point" or "turning-point." Its use in political and economic affairs seems to

68

have derived from an earlier usage in medicine. The crisis of a fever was the point at which the patient's condition moved upward towards restored health, or downward towards death. When we reflect on the potentialities of the nuclear age, the medical analogy acquires a certain macabre appropriateness.

Crises are normally episodes in persistent long-term conflicts, and the conflict will not necessarily be ended because the crisis is successfully negotiated. The Cuba Missile Crisis of 1962, for instance, was an episode of a few weeks' duration in the long-term conflict between the United States and the Soviet Union. The management at the time seemed relatively satisfactory to the United States and its allies, by the two primary criteria normally applied, the interests of peace and the interests of Western power. But it did not end the conflict between the United States and the Soviet Union. On the contrary, the outcome stimulated Soviet decision-makers to adopt certain policies which, 20 years later, are visibly part of the reason why that conflict is now more acute and evenly-balanced than it was in 1962.

Obviously, the most desirable state of affairs would be one in which the underlying conflicts were resolved, and therefore future crises were avoided, and thus did not return to be managed. But the policy-makers of the society of States are somewhat in the position of locomotive-drivers at the controls of great ungovernable steam-engines, with rather primitive brakes, or no brakes at all, making their ways in the assumed interests of their respective passengers over a faulty network of rails to uncertain destinations. The possibility of disastrous collisions is inherent in the nature of the system. Nevertheless, it is the system history has endowed us with, and it can only be changed gradually if at all. The policy-makers must do what they can within the limits it imposes. So they have needed to evolve rules and signalling devices to reduce the probability of collision, and mitigate the risk of a general "pile-up," if there is a derailment. Those rules and devices are what I would call the conventions of crisis.

Given that crises normally arise from existing conflicts, the logical way to predict the probable crises of the next 20 years is to look at current and prospective conflicts, and assess which ones involve large enough interests to be likely to generate serious crises. Unfortunately there is no shortage of prospective "scenarios," to use the jargon of the crisis-analyst's trade. The conflict between the Soviet interest in maintaining Eastern Europe as a strategic buffer-zone under its own political control, as against the nationalist resentments of the peoples of that area, is certain to continue to produce tensions that will periodically rise to crisis-point, as in Poland in 1980. The central balance of power is bound to shift back and forth as it has done over the past two decades, as the United States and the Soviet Union wax and wane *vis-à-vis* each other in military and economic strength, and as they expand and contract their respective spheres of influence. The Russian invasion of Afghanistan was the most recent crisis of that sort. Many régimes, in the Third World and elsewhere, will go through "crises of legitimacy" as their grasp on their respective peoples weakens. The fall of such régimes (as for instance the fall of the Shah in 1979) will produce shock effects through the whole society of States, often with a sequence of "after-shocks," as the Iran-Iraq war was one of the "after-shocks" of the fall of the Shah. The conflicts within regional balances (or imbalances) as for instance between Israel and the Arab States, or between India and the other countries of the Indian sub-continent, or between rival candidates for the leading role in the Arab world, will go on producing intermittent crises. So will the new system of sovereign States in Africa, and the older system of sovereign States in Latin America: probably the crises between South Africa and its black nationalist neighbours will be the most dangerous of these. In Asia the societies neighbouring on both China and the potentially quite substantial People's Democracy of Greater Vietnam (incorporating Laos and Cambodia) will certainly experience periodic crises, as those formidable entities come to terms with each other and their other neighbours. The long-running conflict between China and the Soviet Union shows no sign of resolution and is probably not likely to do so while China is (as it will be during the next decade) working to modernise its arms-structure. That process must inevitably increase the Russian sense of future danger, so one might expect the relationship to be particularly fruitful of crises. And as these crises involve direct confrontation between two nuclear Powers they must be regarded as potentially perilous for the rest of the world as well as the adversaries themselves. With a little luck the "security community" of the North Atlantic (Western Europe and North America) will manage to avoid hostilities within its own membership (except perhaps between Greece and Turkey) and may retrieve and maintain a wary *détente* with the Warsaw Pact Powers, as far as the potential European theatre of operations is concerned. But it will certainly be in endemic conflict with the Soviet Union and its allies over the resource-producing areas of the Third World, such as the Persian Gulf, and that particular conflict would evoke the most dangerous of all prospective crises, since both camps will be nuclear-armed, and might be fighting for what seemed to each their industrial life-blood.

III—CLASSIFICATIONS

There are various ways of classifying international crises, but the most useful, if one is contemplating so crisis-ridden a future as the next two decades may be, are those that relate to modes by which crisis may be controlled. The primary distinction I would suggest is between intramural and adversary crisis. An intramural crisis is one within the walls of a domestic society, or an alliance system, or a sphere of power.

An adversary crisis is one between Powers defining themselves and each other as adversaries. An illustration of the difference may be provided by considering the case of the conflict between the Soviet Union and China. Initially the crises to which that conflict gave rise were intramural crises: that is, they were within the walls of the Sino-Soviet Alliance of 1950, and might perhaps have been successfully managed had Russian diplomacy within that alliance been less heavy-handed. But, in fact, by 1969 these crises had been so ill-managed that they had clearly been transformed into adversary crises: China was defining the Soviet Union as the most dangerous of its enemies, and heavy border-hostilities had taken place. The essential characteristic of both adversary and intramural crises is that tension within the relationship concerned rises to a degree that threatens to transform the nature of the relationship. In the intramural case, the transformation is usually only from alliance to rupture, but in the adversary case it may be from peace to war. Two of the crises of the time of writing, Afghanistan and Poland, began essentially as intramural crises within the sphere of Soviet power. Both had the potential of transforming themselves into adversary crises, precipitating major hostilities. But this had been avoided up to the time of writing.

It would be reassuring if one could say that there exist regularised institutions or modes of procedure for resolving crises, and that these institutions are likely to develop further, and prove more effective, in the next two decades. Unfortunately that is not the case. In theory the United Nations does have procedures which are supposed to come into force when there is a threat to the peace, which is usually the case in adversary crises. But, looking over the long series of crises in the post-war period, there are few which can be said to have been resolved, or even managed, primarily by the Secretary-General or his officials. The United Nations is useful in crises, but mostly at what one may call the "tidying-up" stage, after the true confrontation has been resolved in one way or the other. The reason for this limited effectiveness on the part of the United Nations is that only the decision-makers of nation States have at their disposal the instrumentalities (such as armed forces) that are brought into play in such confrontations.

The actual crisis-managers are normally the chief decision-makers of the local Powers involved (each with his phalanx of advisers) and, if the crisis is serious, a committee round the chief decision-maker in each of the major capitals which may feel its interests potentially affected. Thus, for instance, in the case of the Iran-Iraq war of 1980–1981, the crisis-managers were on the one hand the President of Iran and the circle he had to consult, including the Ayatollah Khomeini, and on the other the President of Iraq and his closest advisers. But there would have been also a "crisis-group" charged with watching the evolution of events not only in Washington but in most other world capitals.

Crises since the Second World War
(Asterisk indicates substantial or fairly substantial hostilities)
Year

1946	Azerbaijan, Indo-China* I
47	Greece,* Turkey, Kashmir*
48	Berlin I, Czechoslovakia, Middle East I,* Indonesia*
49	Malaya* (insurgency)
50	Korea,* Chinese intervention in Korea*
51	Abadan
52	Kenya*
53	East Germany (riots), Morocco, Tunisia
54	Indo-China II,* Algeria,* Guatemala*
55	Cyprus I*
56	Hungary,* Poland,* Middle East II*
57	Syria-Turkey
58	Lebanon-Jordan-Iraq, Quemoy-Matsu, Berlin II
59	Indo-China III* (Laos)
60	Congo,* U-2
61	Laos, Berlin III, Cuba I* (Bay of Pigs), Goa
62	Cuba II (missiles), China-India,* Yemen*
63	Malaysia-Indonesia* ("Confrontation")
64	Cyprus II, Tongking Gulf, Panama, Mozambique*
65	India-Pakistan,* Dominican Republic*
66	Rhodesia*
67	Middle-East III,* Cyprus III
68	Czechoslovakia, *Pueblo*
69	Biafra,* Sino-Soviet, Ulster*
70	Jordan,* Cuba III (Soviet base)
71	Bangladesh*
72	Cyprus IV
73	Middle East IV,* Chile*
74	Cyprus V*
75	Portugal, Indo-China IV,* *Mayaguez*
76	Angola,* Spanish Sahara*
77	Ethiopia,* Somalia,* Zaire,* Cambodia-Vietnam-Thailand
78	Uganda-Tanzania,* Vietnam-Cambodia,* Zaire
79	Iran,* China-Vietnam,* North & South Yemen, Cuba, Nicaragua*
80	Afghanistan,* Teheran hostages rescue mission, Iran-Iraq,* Poland

The academic study of crisis management has unfortunately but inevitably, had to rely a great deal for its "models" on information derived from the Washington practice on these occasions. Only American sources have provided in adequate quantity the memoirs and "leaks" that (with luck) enable the analyst to reconstruct what actually happened, and why. In the case of the Cuba Missile Crisis of 1962, for instance, about 95 per cent. of the available information comes from American reporting of various sorts. If Moscow were as given to "leaks" as Washington, it would obviously be possible to construct a more balanced picture. But since that situation is not likely to develop, the best one can do is to correct the Washington-based model by historical retrospect of the European Great Powers, and with whatever information emerges from other capitals. Such evidence as is available seems to imply that the process in Moscow is reasonably parallel to that in Washington, though with perhaps more "inputs" from the Chiefs of Staff.

The crisis-managers group in Washington has had various names through the years. At the time of the Cuba Missile Crisis it was called "Excom" (Executive Committee). More recently it has been called "Washag" (Washington Special Action Group). Its numbers have varied around 12 (not including the president of the day) but its dominant figures seem normally to have reduced themselves to about two – or even one, in Dr. Kissinger's time. (He seems to have managed the 1973 crisis of the Middle Eastern war almost single-handedly). Personal qualities and closeness to the final decision-maker, rather than formal position, seem to determine roles. For instance neither the then Secretary of State, nor the then National Security Adviser seems to have been at all dominant in the Cuban crisis-group. The influential voices were those of the Attorney-General (Robert Kennedy), the Defense Secretary (Robert McNamara) and perhaps the British Ambassador of the time, Lord Harlech. Closeness to the President (John Kennedy) may seem to have been the important criterion, but it was not entirely that: ability to come up with useful ideas was more decisive, on the evidence.

I have suggested the term "conventions" for the procedures which may be seen in action in various episodes of crisis diplomacy.[1] That word is deliberately chosen to make it clear that what is normally involved cannot be accorded the status of law or moral norm, or be described as an institution (though legal and moral and institutional influences undoubtedly bear on these procedures). The word convention means two things: a mode of behaviour expected and recognised and understood in a particular society, and (as in the case of "the conventions of bridge") a set of agreed "signals" familiar to both partners and opponents. Both these meanings must be borne in mind when considering the conventions of crises, since "signals" are the primary instrumentality by which the possible pattern of events is bargained between decision-makers. A signal may of course be an actual verbal message, but as Dr. Kissinger once said, in some ways words are the least effective of signals. The most dramatic and usually the most effective are the alerting and movement of armed forces.

It might be objected that what I have called conventions ought merely to be regarded as rules of prudence, and I would agree that the distinction between the two is not very sharp. No doubt it is a rule of prudence not to eat peas from a knife but is it not also a convention, at least in Western societies? In many Muslim societies women are sequestered,

---

[1] See this writer, *The Conventions of Crisis* (1971).

and muffled in garments when they venture out. This is certainly a convention of those societies: but it is presented as originating in a rule of prudence, to safeguard their persons in rougher times. One might indeed argue that it is often only the lapse of time which is needed to turn a rule of prudence into a convention and then into a law. But whether they be regarded as conventions or merely as rules of prudence the following apparent maxims may be observed in the behaviour of decision-makers.

IV—THE CONVENTIONS OF CRISIS

(1) That one should not seek to win too much, since the other side cannot afford to lose too much. The most difficult and dangerous calculation in crisis diplomacy is that of estimating the degree to which the adversary's decision-makers are willing to accept defeat on an issue, which means estimating the level at which they value a position. In the Cuba Missile Crisis, one might argue, the danger of nuclear war arose because Khrushchev had originally miscalculated on this point, failing to realise that Soviet missiles installed in Cuba would be seen as an unacceptably large psychological defeat in Washington. What he perhaps omitted to take into account was the non-rational element in the Washington reaction, the American historical and emotional stake in the Monroe Doctrine, weighing far more heavily than the rather marginal change in the immediate strategic balance. (If one reads the full text of Khrushchev's first letter to Kennedy, the degree of his personal regret, alarm and consternation at this error emerges very strikingly, and undoubtedly it was that which enabled the Washington crisis-managers, "Excom," to treat his letter as the true signal from the adversary, rather than the formal Politburo letter which was received later and theoretically ought to have had the greater validity.) In the 1973 Middle East crisis, on the other hand, in which the Soviet Union actually did sustain, at least for a few years, very sweeping losses in diplomatic influence, amounting to the whole of its previous ascendancy in the Arab world except Libya, the defeat was so inexplicit and *sub rosa* that there was only a brief episode (about 24 hours) of crisis confrontation. Comparing the two cases, one might say that the "insiders" calculation of loss will probably always contain emotional elements not perceived or not estimated at their true weight by most "outsiders."

It is logical to assume that the side which feels itself to have the most at stake will be prepared to make the higher "bid" in terms of cost and risk. The Soviet sphere of influence in the Arab world was about 18 years old in 1973, dating it from the first Egyptian arms deal of 1955. But it was a fairly troublesome, unsatisfactory and unstable one, as the expulsion of Soviet officers from Egypt in 1972 had demonstrated to the Soviet leadership: it would thus probably have been difficult for any Soviet "hawk" at the time to make a case that it was of sufficient advantage to the Soviet Union to warrant the risks of confrontation with the United States. The American sphere of influence in Latin America has no doubt also been quite troublesome, unsatisfactory and unstable, but it had a kind of historical sacredness in American eyes, being almost a century and a half old in 1962.

The demonstrated effect that the higher the estimate (always subjective rather than objective) of the national stake involved, the higher the willingness to take risks and pay costs also applied in Vietnam. It was an "unlimited" war for the Vietnamese, in the sense that their future national identity, as far as the effective decision-makers in both Hanoi and Saigon were concerned, was staked on it. It was, however, a "limited" war for the United States: what was at stake was not survival, nor identity, nor substantial national assets, nor even a stable and valued sphere of influence: only a fragment of diplomatic prestige and credibility. The level of costs the United States was willing to bear to avoid that loss was large but limited, and was exhausted by 1973. The conscious or unconscious "signalling" of this fact was quite correctly read by the decision-makers in Hanoi as meaning that their final offensive originally intended for 1976, could be advanced to 1975 without serious risk.

The conscious or unconscious signalling of refusal to bear costs or risks in an issue was the decisive factor in the Angola crisis at the end of 1975. In this case the source of the crucial signal was the American Congress, which insisted on voting at the end of the year entirely to cut off funds to the operation in Angola. The Secretary of State had struggled hard to throw at least a protective shadow of ambiguity over the American reaction by a CIA operation, and by some channelling of funds to the Western-oriented factions, the Union for the Total National Independence of Angola (UNITA) and the Front for the National Liberation of Angola (FNLA). For a time his signals seem to induce a certain hesitancy in Soviet decision-making. The flow of Cubans and *matériel* to the Angolan People's Liberation Movement (MPLA) faltered for a few weeks in November 1975. But the post-Vietnam revulsion in Congress was too vociferous to be drowned out by conflicting signals from the Administration. The Congressional votes of December 1975 and January 1976, unmistakably conveyed "no contest" to Moscow: the Cuban operation went ahead at full steam again, and the MPLA were installed in government within three months. The Soviet reading of the Congressional signals that Western influence in Angola was not a matter for which the United States would take risks (or let the Secretary of State try a bluff) was quite accurate. One might make the generalisation that accurate reading of the other side's signals, and a flexible set of low-risk options to enable one to take advantage of the opportunities they indicate is a key to at least short-term success in crisis diplomacy. The option of using "proxies," demonstrated by the Soviet Union with the

Cubans in this encounter, and láter in Africa and elsewhere, is one for which the Western alliance has found neither equivalent nor answer.

(2) That communications with the adversary must and will be maintained, and should rather grow closer and more intensive as the confrontation sharpens than be diminished or broken off. The final "crystallisation" of this convention came during or just after the Cuba Missile Crisis, with the decision to establish the "hot line," direct teletype communication between the chief American and the chief Soviet decision-makers. This development tended to make intermediaries of the traditional sort unnecessary to the main diplomatic process, and also tended towards the exclusion of allies, though some of them (including the Chinese) also now have "hot lines" to Washington. The first serious use of the Washington-Moscow direct link was during the 1967 Middle Eastern crisis, by Kosygin to President Johnson. By the time of the 1973 crisis, the level of communication between Moscow and Washington was so full that it may be said to have amounted to consultation, and the modes used included Kissinger's journey to Moscow, and his day-by-day conversations with the Soviet Ambassador in Washington. This intensity of communication did not, however, obviate the need for the very loud signal constituted by the United States strategic alert of October 24, 1973. This was a signal that certainly reached, and was calculated to reach, many ears other than those of the Soviets: for instance the Israelis and the Egyptians (to reinforce their consciousness of the potential dangers of the situation) and the West Europeans (to dispel the suspicions of a Soviet-American "condominium" which had been generated there). How far there was any serious Soviet intention of moving troops to the area is still a moot point: President Nixon in a television interview in May 1977 implied that the Egyptian proposal had been for two divisions each of American and Soviet troops and pre-sumably the Brezhnev letter indicated the Soviet intention of moving its forces unilaterally if the Americans refused the bid, as they did.

(3) That one must "build golden bridges behind the adversary to facilitate his retreat." No situation could be more dangerous in the nuclear age than to box one of the nuclear Powers into a corner from which its decision-makers can see no way out, save general war or unacceptable humiliation. This is the point at which the meaningless conference, the bogus *quid pro quo*, and the anodyne United Nations resolution all find real usefulness, as face-saving devices to be pressed on the adversary with all diplomatic skills available. The removal of the United States Thor missiles from Turkey (they being obsolete and due for removal anyway) in the aftermath of the 1962 crisis was one such expedient. The institution of the Geneva conference at which the Soviet Union could be co-chairman, in the aftermath of the sweeping American gains in the Middle East during the 1973 crisis, might be deemed another. This was a clear contrast to the crisis-management of 1914,

when either Serbia or Austria would have had to accept an unacceptable humiliation. There will always be voices within the circle of decision-makers of the "victorious" Power, and among articulate opinion in that country which will denounce such expedient gestures as "appeasement" or as unnecessary concessions to the *amour propre* of the other side, or of its decision-makers, but devices of this sort are useful in the preservation not only of the system as a whole but of the domestic political position of individual decision-makers who have shown a willingness to accept setback philosophically. There is a sense in which Mr. Khrushchev's experience in the 1962 crisis was encapsulated into Mr. Brezhnev's reactions in the 1973 crisis, and if the system of conventions is to be strengthened and grow, these successive experiences must as far as possible constitute a *learning-curve for the decision-making élite as a whole*, not just for one individual decision-maker. That is the only manner in which the system could become stabilised, established and perhaps as long-lasting as the nineteenth-century one.

(4) That contingency plans, which inevitably will exist, and the strategic priorities which are assumed to be inherent in them must not be allowed to dictate the manner in which the crisis is managed. *Political ends must maintain ascendancy, not military means.* Everyone concerned with the Cuba crisis, especially the President,[2] was familiar with the baneful influence which the Schlieffen Plan (first devised by the German General Staff about the turn of the century) is said to have exercised over the German crisis-managers of 1914. Whether this baneful influence was a historical fact or not, its "memory" was an important check on any tendency to allow an undue weight of decision to rest on the shoulders of the military in 1962. Indeed, political considerations took precedence over military ones even at the tactical level. For instance, there was a "preferred line," as far as the United States Navy was concerned, for the American warships which were to stop the vessels making for Cuba during the operation of the "quarantine": the line which would keep them out of the range of the Mig aircraft based in Cuba. But this line would have allowed little time for the decision-makers in Moscow to change their minds before the moment when the ships must be stopped. It was therefore decided (on the suggestion of the then British Ambassador in Washington) to take the military risk of a different line, closer to Cuba, in order to allow more time fo reflection in Moscow. The assumed possible danger from the Migs never came to anything, and the extra time so bought may have been important.

The advice tendered by Chiefs of Staff must obviously be a major influence on the chief decision-maker in any serious crisis. If he is a former military man himself, that may help him to resist (or know how far to discount) alleged military necessities. President Eisenhower, for

---

[2] He had just been reading Barbara Tuchman's *The Guns of August*.

instance, was in a good position professionally to resist advice pressed on him by Admiral Radford and General Curtis Le May at the time of the 1954 Vietnam crisis. President Johnson, on the other hand, was less well equipped to judge, and seems indeed to have misconceived, the nature of the military prospects in Vietnam during the 1968 crisis of the war. The military as an element in the group of crisis-managers must perhaps have a professional tendency to base their advice on a "worst-case" analysis. On the other hand, it should not be assumed that they will always opt for military solutions: they may be more conscious than the civilians of what the strategic vulnerability of their own forces will be once the tanks begin to roll. During the first Berlin crisis, several of the policy-advisers in Washington and elsewhere were of the opinion that the Russian "bluff" should be called with an American tank column. It was the Joint Chiefs of Staff, and General Marshall as Secretary of State, who were adamant against such a move, undoubtedly on the basis of professional understanding of the real strategic disadvantages faced by the West if the Soviets proved *not* to be bluffing. Many Western contingency plans existed against various possible Berlin moves by the Soviets in 1961, but it was perhaps fortunate that none of them envisaged the actual event, the wall built across the city. The lack of a plan for that particular contingency caused a hesitancy in Western reactions, which no doubt helped allow the wall to become a fixture. Twenty years later, the wall may reasonably be seen as having been less a problem than a solution: a Soviet solution to the intramural crisis in the affairs of their East European satellites which had been occasioned by the tendency of so large a part of the population to "vote with their feet" for life in the West. Whatever one's sympathy for East Germans constrained to live in the Soviet sphere, the probability that a Berlin crisis would be the flashpoint for a Third World War has been much less in the years since the wall was built than it was before that time.

(5) That local crises will be met in local terms, and that even true crises of the central balance will be met at least initially in *conventional* terms. This is really the direct opposite of the ostensible doctrine enunciated by Mr. Dulles in 1954, of "massive and instant retaliation at places and by means of our own choosing," which appeared to imply that a Soviet bid in Angola or Afghanistan might be requited by reprisals against Kiev or Vladivostok. In that form the doctrine was totally incredible from the first, and it is somewhat of an injustice to Mr. Dulles's understanding of international politics to assume he was not aware of this. There are several passages in the same speech which indicate that he did not expect the doctrine to obviate all future Western losses. What he apparently hoped was to increase the level of uncertainties facing Russian decision-makers, so as to deter any propensity to undue risk-taking on their part. One can hardly say that he was successful even in this more modest endeavour: in fact Khrushchev,

who was to dominate Soviet policy-making for the next 10 years, undoubtedly pursued more risk-taking policies (Congo, Berlin Wall, U-2, Cuba) than either Stalin and the collegiate leadership before him or Brezhnev after him. The importance for crisis diplomacy of the local conventional balance and also the balance of local political forces, has been almost continuously illustrated ever since 1945. It is only in very special cases, with a symbolic value recognised on both sides (for example Berlin), that the strategic nuclear balance can be said apparently to "over-ride" the local conventional balance. Even for the central front NATO forces (often represented as being hopelessly and irretrievably weaker than the Warsaw Pact forces they face, though over most of the post-war period they have only been marginally so) the desirability has always been understood of building a reasonably viable theatre-balance. A "massive and instant retaliation" doctrine might conceivably be usable in crisis diplomacy, *either* by a Power which was so strong that the threat could inhibit any challenge, *or* paradoxically, by one so weak that it visibly had no other means of resistance. In the latter case, however, the Power concerned's decision-makers would probably have also cultivated an image of being prepared to die as a community rather than yield: what might be called a "Masada" strategem.

In more normal cases, for the middle Powers especially, enough local military capacity to hold ground until the processes of international crisis-management could take effect may prove the crucial factor. The business of reversing a military *fait accompli* (as in Cyprus after the Turkish invasion) offers almost insuperable difficulties. The capacity rapidly to reinforce a threatened line, or a potential "co-belligerent" (for instance Yugoslavia) with either *matériel*, or conceivably forces, would thus appear vital to maintaining the credibility of this convention, as far as the dominant Powers are concerned.

The deployment of tactical nuclear weapons in the European theatre does not reduce the importance of the conventional-forces balance there for ruling-out "pre-emptive options" which might otherwise be thought worth chancing in crisis situations. Tactical nuclear warheads provide a sort of reinforcement of the conventional forces' role in rendering unattractive any such opportunist moves. Their existence means that the adversary forces need to be kept dispersed in order to avoid presenting "high-yield" targets, and that in turn means that operations in the nature of massing for attack would be clearly signalled (some strategic analysts say by as much as a month), thus providing extra warning time for diplomacy to get under way. So they may be considered to have a peace-time function as part of the mechanism of surveillance, as well as the battlefield function usually ascribed to them. How long the interval for negotiation would be between the first conventional clash and the military demand to use tactical nuclear weapons would obviously depend on the forces-balance in the area concerned, and the general political relationship between the Powers: that is, on whether détente or cold war prevailed.

(6) That the other side's sphere of influence requires a special wariness and restraint when beset by intramural crisis through political dissent. The first exemplification of this convention was in the 1953 East Germany riots, in which the then American Secretary of State, Mr. Dulles, was extremely cautious, though he had just campaigned for the Republicans on a platform of "liberation" in Eastern Europe. He adhered to that convention again in 1956, despite the urging of some of the bolder spirits in the CIA for a "spontaneous" general uprising. And President Johnson maintained a similar caution during the Czechoslovak events of 1968.

(7) That the Powers will not allow their signals to each other to become infected with excess or misleading ambiguities through consultation with allies. This is really a convention necessary for the Western side rather than the Soviet Union to observe. No one in Washington seems likely to calculate that the decision-makers in Moscow will modify their choices in the light of representations from Bulgaria or Poland. But the nature of the Western political and logistic situation is so different that it is quite possible to imagine Soviet decision-makers counting on French or German or Italian complications to obstruct United States action in some future crisis. This would be considerably more likely if the French or Italian governments were coalitions including the Communist Party, a situation conceivable in the next two decades. There was a foretaste of that kind of difficulty in the 1973 crisis, in the obstacles placed by the West German and other governments in the way of the United States resupply operation to Israel.

The speed of events in many crises operates usefully to prevent the problem becoming acute: and in fact to exempt allied heads of government from the burden of choice. President de Gaulle said, after a briefing by Kennedy's envoy during the Cuba Missile Crisis, "I was glad to be informed: I would not wish to be consulted." The known necessity for speed operated not only to preclude the sharing of responsibility for decision, but also to rule out any possible Soviet calculations that the misgivings of allies would prevent decisive United States reaction. There are potential crisis-areas, however, especially Berlin and Eastern Europe, where the only effective action would be allied action, and where therefore this useful simplifying of the adversary's choices would not take place. Possibly the known existence, ahead of time, of a unified diplomatic "command structure," parallel to the unified military "command structure" would be a useful hedge against such calculations.

V—PAST AND PROSPECT

The four years of the Carter presidency were not a good period for Western crisis-management. In fact the set of events surrounding the fall of the Shah and the Soviet invasion of Afghanistan might well be cited as a case-study in how not to do it. It will not be possible to make an adequate analysis of what went wrong until the memoirs have been written and some of the documents are available, but in an initial retrospect one would say the difficulties arose from confused signalling, indecisive command and unrealistic assumptions about the basic nature of international conflict. As to the new set of policy-makers in this field in the White House and the National Security Council, all that it is possible to say at the time of writing is that they need all the skills that they can muster. If Western fortunes fare as badly in the eighties and nineties as they did in the late seventies, the prospects for the year 2000 will not be reassuring.

ENERGY AND A NEW WORLD ECONOMIC ORDER

By

C. A. SHAW

ACCURATE forecasting of events is a difficult business, thanks partly to the complexity of human behaviour, and also because taking due account of every factor becomes a monumental analytical task. There remains too the element of the totally unpredictable, the disaster of nature or the Act of God. Sometimes, however, future events lend to themselves an inevitability which results from the absence of viable alternatives. The difficulty then is in predicting the timing of events, especially as extraneous, unconnected occurrences can have a sudden, overwhelming influence. The First World War, for example, was predictable because of the increasing rivalry and rearmament of the eventual combatants, but who could have forecast that an assassination in a provincial Balkan city in the summer of 1914 would have been the trigger?

It requires no special foresight to predict that the current reliance of the world on oil, as the principal sustainer of its energy requirements, will lead to serious economic and social crisis in the future. It is much more difficult to predict the timing and number of crises the world will have to experience before diversification away from oil is taken seriously. Quite possibly an incident as improbable as that in Sarajevo may precipitate a chain of events leading to a constriction of supplies. The last decade saw two such occasions—the Yom Kippur War of October 1973 and the destabilisation of Iran in 1979. The Iran-Iraq conflict, which began in September 1980, is still in progress and conceivably may escalate further.

The critical influence which energy availability, security of supply and price has over economic events, can be expected to continue into the foreseeable future. How could it be otherwise unless important new sources of energy unexpectedly and rapidly appeared from nowhere? The energy scene is now the subject of such grave world-wide concern because there is virtually no prospect, short of a wholly unlikely discovery of vast new oil reserves which can readily be tapped, or the miraculous taming of the nuclear fusion reaction, of an abundant supply of energy at prices which even the wealthier, let alone the poorer, nations can afford. This conclusion arises from the assumption, which now has widespread geological foundation, that proven and probably Non-Communist World oil reserves will support existing rates of consumption for only a few decades. Even in the unlikely event that reserves double, the significance of this on the overall economic outcome would be minimal, by putting back in time the inevitable diversification away from oil by some years. In any case, it is not so much the modest size of the reserves as their concentration into limited and politically unstable areas, which arguably presents the greater threat to secure supplies. The real cost of tapping them, too, is certain to rise as the big, shallow and accessible reservoirs are exhausted first.

Perhaps there will be spectacular technical innovations of which we cannot currently conceive, which will revolutionise the energy scene. Personally I have my doubts, and I think it unwise to rely on them. The question in any case is not so much whether such innovations will occur, as whether there will be practical application of them on a sufficiently large scale by the year 2000 to make any significant impact on the world energy scene. I shall be arguing that innovation, although not necessarily spectacular, must be brought about urgently in the field of energy generation if serious world-wide economic and social disruption is to be avoided. Unfortunately, the optimum conditions for the encouragement of such innovation do not currently exist, nor is there sufficient impetus to create them.

I—The Decay of the Old Order

Until the last few years, new technology has enabled man to make ever greater use of natural resources such as metals and oil, to increase his material standard of living. As I explained in "Dilemmas of Supergrowth,"[1] that era is coming to an end due to the growing scarcity, and therefore the actual and inevitable trend towards rising real prices, of some critical natural resources, notably oil. The growing strength of the Organisation of Petroleum Exporting Countries (OPEC), and its willingness to cut back oil production in order to obtain greater price increases, was not difficult to forecast, given a rudimentary appreciation of the extent of world oil reserves. Indeed it presents a rough parallel to the power exercised by John D. Rockefeller and his Standard Oil Company in the United States at the turn of the century. Self-interest dictated that OPEC would function most of the time in this manner. Disagreements occur, but the inexorable trend towards rising real oil prices nevertheless continues. Falling oil production, long before depletion of reserves forces this to occur, remains the inevitable consequence of OPEC's actions. A further logical consequence, world-wide inflation coupled with deepening economic recession, is no longer a forecast but reality. We now therefore witness the onset of decline in the large industrial economies dedicated to mass production and conspicuous

---

[1] See this *Year Book*, Vol. 30 (1976), pp. 273–297.

consumption, based on depleting non-renewable energy. The trends have been visible for a decade and the evidence conclusive for more than half a decade. Yet only one major organisation in the world—OPEC—has stood resolutely for a new order, in which man would have to curtail his use of exhaustible materials. Articles are still written, and statements still made, by eminent economists, politicians and industrialists, castigating OPEC for stoking the fires of inflation and creating unemployment world-wide. OPEC is a convenient scapegoat on whom the industrialised countries, believing in a fool's paradise of cheap and plentiful energy, can blame their ills and vent their righteous indignation. The eminent critics are perhaps trying to avoid responsibility for their own bankrupt policies which are failing. Increasing material living standards are unquestioningly accepted in the West as both a political and an economic goal, because it is believed, rightly I judge, that most people in the world, both rich and poor, desire to enjoy the results. This desire therefore becomes an end which justifies the means of achieving it, even though the means are patently not available on a sustainable basis. The depth of the world economic recession in the opening years of this decade and, more importantly, its duration, will largely be dictated by the speed at which acceptance of the need for changed economic targets occurs, and investment decisions to meet the new targets are taken. Although oil will not run out by the year 2000, and both consumption and production of it may already have plateaued, leaving reserves available for several more decades, the prospect of stable supply at prices which industry and wage-earners can afford is too remote for reliance on oil to be a sensible policy.

The vital first element, the catalyst and precursor of a new economic order, is to develop new forms of energy from sustainable, renewable sources.

II—A False Start

Economic recession is caused by many interrelated factors over which economists dispute amongst themselves. The 1980 world-wide recession has, in my judgment, two factors of special significance contributing to it which economists and politicians of developed countries have been painfully slow in recognising, if indeed recognition has yet taken place. These are: (1) Continued over-reliance on oil; (2) The slow development of alternative energies. Both factors are interrelated and stem from failure to learn at the time the lessons of the Yom Kippur War of October 1973.

(1) *Over-reliance on oil*

The lessons of 1973 were, the conclusions still remain, and the consequences for the future will continue to be, the same. They are:

(a) Oil is a depleting, irreplaceable natural resource whose production, cost, and therefore price in real terms, will rise as the more accessible reserves are exhausted.

(b) The major reserves are concentrated in a relatively small number of countries, many of which are politically and socially unstable. Some two-thirds of known reserves are in the Middle East, which has had, since 1945, on average a war about every six years. The prospects for the future in the Middle East appear, currently, to be deteriorating in two respects—internal social unrest (*e.g.* Iran and Saudi Arabia), and international friction (Iran and Iraq). The occupation of Afghanistan by the Soviet Union represents a further dimension.

It was unnecessary and ill-advised of the developed world to await the appearance of social and military disturbances in the Middle East before taking seriously the threat which was so obvious. The political climate for the developed world to institute tough internal economic changes existed from the end of 1973 up to perhaps 1975. Public opinion awaited the decisive change of direction and its accompanying costs, with an air of resignation. The opportunity was not taken. In reality, the United States Congress and President debated endlessly the creation of a mammoth new energy policy, and eventually in 1978 they spawned a midget. General Motors thought about building a small car, and kept right on producing "gas-guzzlers." The United Kingdom Government introduced incentives for home insulation and then withdrew them. Japan continued its gargantuan programme of industrial expansion, prepared to outbid rival nations if necessary by paying the highest prices for available oil. Some steps were taken to diversify energy sources—a greater emphasis on coal, for example—but these lacked conviction.

(2) *The slow development of alternative energies*

As the sense of crisis ebbed away after October 1973, the urgency evaporated from programmes for developing new sources of energy. The first flush of funds into energy research dwindled, and emphasis returned once again to the satisfaction of the short-term whims of electorates. The Departments and Ministries of Energy of the developed nations have, meanwhile, managed to convey the impression of a welter of sponsored research activity, which protects them and their political masters from too much criticism. Meanwhile, the consumers of the world have gone back to many of their energy-squandering habits, whilst complaining ever more stridently, in tune with the economists and politicians, about OPEC's alleged greediness.

III—LOSS OF PURPOSE

After October 1973, OPEC made a realistic and lonely stand for common sense, and pushed up real oil prices with the air of a stern headmaster administering corporal punishment to an errant pupil, adding the words "it hurts me more than it hurts you." The industrialised world, observing enviously how OPEC's newly won wealth was giving birth to conspicuous consumption on vast prestige projects, believed otherwise as it suffered economic pain in the form of inflation and unemployment. However, after the initial price rises following the Yom Kippur War, OPEC's resolve began to weaken as "moderation" took root in the wake of the political and diplomatic offensive waged by the developed nations, led by the United States. Perhaps the offensive managed to create a feeling of guilt amongst some OPEC members. This "moderation" contributed in large measure to the loss of purpose amongst the developed nations to press ahead with their escape from reliance on oil. Subsequently, the destabilisation of Iran in 1979 strengthened once again the hand of the OPEC hawks, and led to a doubling of the price in less than 12 months. Ironically, Ayatollah Khomeini can surely claim without fear of contradiction to have achieved more than any other single person in history towards the conservation of oil, although this was hardly his prime objective. That the industrialised countries should allow their economic well-being to be so overwhelmingly at the mercy of one cleric, is evidence on its own of the short-sighted and Micawberist policies they have been pursuing. Only the shock effect on oil consumption of the sharp increase in price has saved the world from a much deeper recession even than that now being experienced.

The over-production of oil in 1980 resulted more from economic recession and its consequential effects on oil demand, coupled with the effects of oil price increases on demand, than from any increase in production. Indeed oil production fell in 1980, yet even so a surplus remained. OPEC members, however, have been at pains to replace the supplies disrupted by the Iran-Iraq conflict, in response to their misplaced concern for the short-term economic plight of the world. Once again, therefore, OPEC's resolve has weakened, thereby threatening the budget of many an energy research project in the industrialised world, and lulling the developed nations into a false sense of security.

To the rescue, in some measure, have come ironically the Soviet Union, and the Ayatollah's own *bête noir*, Mr. Saddam Hussein, the President of Iraq. Respectively, the Russian occupation of Afghanistan and, more immediately, the Iran-Iraq conflict have re-emphasised the risks of continuing to rely on oil, while simultaneously increasing the cost to the West of policing the Arabian Gulf area. Hopefully, but not certainly, the politicians and economists of the West can read the writing on the wall this time, and pursue an irrevocable shift away from oil.

Ironically OPEC is seeking, quite reasonably, to redress the economic balance between the industrialised North and the under-developed South. It is providing the latter with subsidised oil, and cheap loans with which to buy it. This is the equivalent of giving to a drug addict a supply of cheap heroin, and a loan to pay for it and to buy his own gravestone. The under-developed world, greatly though it may feel the high cost of oil, is thankfully only marginally dependent on it, and is therefore better placed than the developed world to adopt alternative energies when they are available. Once he has decided to give up drugs, the addict certainly needs support and encouragement while he is suffering from withdrawal symptoms, and as he starts out on a new life. Indeed withdrawal may be in stages, not overnight. Likewise OPEC should confine its help of under-developed countries to the minimum supply of cheap energy consistent with a policy of tiding them over until new energy sources are available. The provision then of financial support, coupled with technical input from developed countries, to help introduce the new alternative energies into the under-developed countries, should be of top priority, so as to get those countries on the road to sustainable economic development.

IV—Whither Economic Growth?

The pace of technological change, some people claim, has quickened in recent decades and is now at its fastest ever. If the yardstick is electronic gadgetry, then perhaps I agree, but it does seem to take longer now to develop and construct new projects than used to be the case. Planning permission, environmental constraints and even the process of corporate or governmental approval can take years. The complex web of computerised techniques and electronic controls which go hand in hand with modern projects can take much longer to design and construct than the more simple equipment of former years, and start-up problems too often take longer to iron out. In the time now taken from conception to commercial production of a modern airliner, the Second World War had begun and ended, with all its revolutionary military hardware conceived, developed, produced and rendered obsolete by yet further inventions. The pace of change in the field of energy developments has so far been painfully slow, and on current evidence it seems highly unlikely that anything short of economic catastrophe would alter this. If, therefore, an orderly progression to alternative energy is to be achieved by the year 2000, nothing short of a major shift of economic and political priorities stands any chance of succeeding. Alternatively we must wait until necessity dictates, which is hardly a strategy to be recommended.

Unless alternative energy is given immediate and top priority, it will not be possible to have significant capacity (say a 20 per cent. replacement of oil) in place by the year 2000. Yet probably a 50 per cent. replacement is the minimum needed if the world is to stand a reasonable chance of avoiding the serious economic and social upheavals which will result from interrupted oil supplies at some stage, perhaps repeatedly, over the next 20 years, and perhaps for prolonged or indefinite periods. How can this galvanisation of research and development be achieved?

V—Towards a New World Energy and Economic Order

A two-pronged programme along the following lines by the principal industrialised nations, represented by the International Energy Agency (IEA) and the Organisation for Economic Co-operation and Development (OECD), holds the best prospect of success: (1) Heavy investment in non-renewable energy projects, preferably using materials available within those countries, in order to buy time and obtain improved short-term security of energy supply; (2) Agreement and action on common policies aimed at reducing oil consumption, coupled with joint co-operation in alternative energy research and development.

(1) *Buying time*
Coal, nuclear and gas must figure prominently in the programme to buy time. They have longer-term futures in many, mostly advanced, countries. But for most under-developed countries, with little, if any, coal or gas, and without the expertise or capital to enter the nuclear age, these sources of energy have little or no role to play in their future. If the IEA/OECD countries were now turning quickly away from oil, the likelihood of supplies being unavailable or prohibitively expensive for everbody, including the under-developed countries, would be reduced. Over-production would become the rule rather than exception, and price increases would be less than would otherwise have occurred, and this in turn would threaten to undermine IEA/OECD resolve to continue with their diversification policy. This latter influence would need to be recognised at the outset, so that the joint policy was not allowed to falter. Firm control of oil import levels and uses would be a continuing requirement.

The mining and burning of coal are environmentally detrimental, although modern techniques are capable of reducing the ill-effects considerably. Nuclear power has its risks of radiation and of nuclear proliferation. The radiation risks have perhaps been exaggerated by some protest groups, but I certainly would not wish to live near to a nuclear power station and would feel happier if we could reduce our reliance on them. However, if public demand for rising material living standards is so insistent, the price of co-existence with the nuclear radiation risk and the environmental pollution of coal has to be paid. Remote location of nuclear power stations will reduce the consequences of an accident without removing it altogether.

Nuclear proliferation, however, is another matter. An energy crisis is more likely to bring this about by sparking off a stampede towards nuclear power. A coherent international policy designed to supply those countries who have not yet chosen the nuclear route, with energy from other sources, both short-term and long-term, is most likely to keep nuclear proliferation, and the risk of nuclear war, to a minimum. This factor adds additional support to the proposal for IEA/OECD energy diversification, because improved prospects for obtaining oil at reasonable prices would tend to dissuade non-nuclear countries from taking the plunge.

Gas suffers from the same strategic disadvantages as oil—60 per cent. of Non-Communist World proven and probable reserves lie in the Middle East. Insofar as IEA/OECD or under-developed countries possess gas reserves, exploitation will help to buy time to diversify into alternative sustainable energy sources. As there is probably as much gas remaining in the world as oil, but with gas usage only 40 per cent. of oil's, gas has an important role to play in helping to bridge the gap until renewable energy is available.

Reserves of coal, although capable in theory of replacing oil and fueling the world for perhaps centuries, seem to be confined in any quantity to a very limited number of countries, principally those like the United States and Soviet Union who already have a variety of fuels available, and the expertise to develop new ones. Although the price of coal, like that of gas and to an even greater extent, is generally well below that of oil, the difference is likely to shrink once international market penetration has increased. As internationally traded commodities, however, the significance of both coal and gas to all but a few developed countries will probably be small.

(2) *Common policies for oil conservation and alternative energy*

The principal weapon in the struggle towards improved energy conservation, as OPEC has somewhat fitfully proved, and as any first year economics student could quickly conclude, is price. Unfortunately the IEA/OECD countries in general have been so concerned about the combined inflationary and recessionary effects of rapidly rising oil prices that they have tended to keep domestic energy prices as low as possible in the circumstances. The United States, whose domestic oil and gas reserves are in serious decline, has lacked the political will and realism to take appropriate fiscal measures to curb energy consumption, partly because of the ineptitude of President Carter's handling of Congress, and partly because of the short-sightedness of Congress itself. Elsewhere, as fast as OPEC has pushed up the real price of oil, consumer countries have allowed their domestic taxes on it to fall behind the rate of inflation, thereby partly neutralising the price incentive for the man in the street to conserve energy. The tedium and frustration of the motorist in queuing for petrol when it was short, particularly in the United States, has arguably to date had a greater impact than the increasing price of gasoline on the consumer's willingness to conserve. Ironically the Ayatollah must again take most of the credit for the progress that has been made towards conservation and changed attitudes.

The United States, by far the greatest squanderer of energy and, partly as a result, now the largest importer of oil, has adopted an energy conservation policy of sorts, which uses price as the main incentive to conserve oil and gas consumption, and also to stimulate production. Price de-control of domestically produced oil was scheduled to be completed by October 1981 but President Reagan brought forward this step immediately on taking office. World market prices for oil now therefore apply. Partial de-control of gas will have taken place by the end of 1984, unless President Reagan speeds things up. Gas prices will then only equate with 1979 world oil prices, unless the policy changes, and domestic taxing of oil and gas consumption will remain derisory. One element of existing United States policy is to encourage a switch from oil to gas consumption as a means of cutting down oil imports. Yet proven conventional domestic gas reserves are only the equivalent of 10 years of existing production levels, and the probability of vast new gas fields being found is very small. Piped imports from Mexico and Canada, and Liquefied Natural Gas imports from Algeria and Nigeria are unlikely to provide more than a small proportion of United States requirements in future. It seems barely credible that the world's greatest economy can consciously adopt such a short-sighted and potentially disastrous policy.

At the opposite end of the spectrum, the United Kingdom, in spite of the prospect of self-sufficiency in oil and gas, for a decade or two anyway, has adopted a much tougher pricing policy. Gas prices to consumers, particularly to industry, have been pushed up relentlessly to narrow the gap between electricity and gas. Although gas is still cheaper than United Kingdom crude oil, which is priced at world levels whether for export or for refining in the United Kingdom, the gap there too has been narrowing. In terms of energy conservation the policy has succeeded, with energy demand falling 5.3 per cent. over the first half of 1980 even though industrial production fell only 2 per cent. The cries of public anguish bear witness to the policy's impact and to the realism and political courage required to have pressed ahead with it. Unfortunately there have been adverse side-effects. Other industrial countries, and particularly the United States, have not followed suit and therefore United Kingdom industry has had to absorb an element of additional energy cost which its competitors have been spared. In the case of petrochemicals, the very raw material of production itself is involved. Ironically we have witnessed the closure of United Kingdom factories using North Sea oil and gas as feedstock, whilst the United Kingdom Government draws billions of dollars of tax revenue from the sale of crude oil abroad to countries who use it to supplant United Kingdom industrial production.

Although the United Kingdom Government has pursued the most correct energy conservation policy of all the industrialised nations, arguably it has gone too far, too fast from a political and economic viewpoint. The Government now appears to be recognising this. This dilemma, however, highlights the need for IEA/OECD nations to co-ordinate their energy taxation and pricing policies so as to neutralise these distortions. The United Kingdom's experiences will probably have taught all IEA/OECD countries not to be one move ahead of the game.

Should all IEA/OECD countries then proceed only at the speed of the slowest? Certainly all would need to be persuaded to move swiftly towards common pricing and taxation of energy for an effective policy of oil conservation to be implemented. This step is a vital prerequisite also of a strategy for new alternative energies, of a sustainable and secure nature, for these may have to be tax free, or even to receive subsidies, if they are to emerge quickly enough.

VI—THE KEY ROLE OF SAUDI ARABIA

How then are IEA/OECD policies for the pricing and taxation of energy to be agreed and implemented quickly, in time to make their impact by, say, 1985 at the latest, so that alternative energy research and development programmes have time to bear tangible fruit before the end of the century? Probably the only feasible way, assuming that politicians and the energy departments of the IEA/OECD countries are unlikely to agree much before the millennium unless they are given some external encouragement, is for OPEC to take the initiative. If Saudi Arabia, with the largest single influence in OPEC and the champion to date of "moderation," can be persuaded to turn for its economic advice to opinion other than that channelled through the United States State Department, it may realise that "moderation" is not in the interests of the world at large, not even of the United States. Saudi Arabia has it within its power, through its 20 per cent. of world and almost 30 per cent. of OPEC oil production, to persuade the IEA/OECD countries speedily to adopt common conservation policies. It has the most power within OPEC to influence the oil price, through manipulation of its own oil production levels. It is known to be seriously concerned about how to handle its huge dollar revenues from oil, and how to contain the social, economic and religious pressures building up as a consequence of the vast construction projects of many kinds which are in progress within the country. Saudi Arabia's own internal interests would surely best be served by a deal with IEA/OECD which enabled it perhaps to halve its oil output gradually during the 1980s. Provided the IEA/OECD countries had adopted, and were implementing, common oil conservation policies, their requirements would in any case be falling. Other OPEC members, both hawks and doves, would probably give Saudi

Arabia their support because this would be in line with OPEC policy heretofore of curbing production in pursuit of real price increases. Indeed Saudi Arabia has been criticised by OPEC hawks for not yet significantly reducing production. Saudi Arabia, through OPEC, is therefore uniquely placed to persuade the IEA/OECD nations to agree amongst themselves. It should not give them too long to do so.

There are international political benefits which Saudi Arabia can expect from such an initiative. It would surely become the acknowledged leader of OPEC and of the Arab world, with an increased authority it has sought but not yet achieved. Its standing amongst under-developed nations would also be much enhanced, because its contribution towards the development of a new economic and energy order could hardly go unrecognised. Its support, and that of other OPEC countries, for the poorer countries of the world, by tiding them over with subsidised oil supplies and funds, would be gratefully appreciated.

The rising price of oil brought about by reducing production would protect Saudi Arabia from a too rapid reduction in its income. Internal criticism and religious unrest aroused by the influx of foreigners and the excesses of personal wealth, would be easier to hold in check. Internal security would consequently be easier to maintain. Its security from outside interference would also be greater because the significance of its oil production would lessen. It would be an enormously powerful and influential country, not so much any more due to the size of its oil production, but because of its ability to change the course of history.

From the viewpoint of the IEA/OECD nations, and indeed of the Non-Communist World, a more stable Saudi Arabia producing five million barrels per day of oil would be far preferable to the greater risk of upheaval, and disruption of supplies, at 10 million barrels per day.

VII—The Materialistic Void

The raging fires of materialism, which so consume the wealthier parts of the world, and which make such heavy demands on the dwindling world fossil fuel reserves, themselves need to be quelled. Alternative human aspirations need to be fostered to fill the void which materialism creates and will leave behind it as its embers die. This theme I developed in "Dilemmas of Supergrowth"[2] and, like the rest of the paper, it remains as valid today as when it was written. The stimulus of cultural and leisure pursuits, therefore, remains a central part of a viable economic, and energy-conservation, policy. This provides the vital social safety valve to relieve the frustrations of material aspirations unfulfilled.

---

[2] *Op. cit.* in note 1, above.

VIII—Renewable and Recoverable Energy

Technology to date has focused on large-scale conversion (refineries, power stations) of concentrations of easily transformed materials (oil, coal) into convenient forms of energy (petrol, electricity) for mass distribution and consumption. The sources of renewable energy of the future are already freely available through the continuing cycle of nature, are already distributed relatively thinly across the globe, and must therefore be produced and consumed in close proximity. Technologists have the job of harnessing this energy—emanating in one form or another principally from the sun—for use where it is needed, cutting capital and operating costs to a minimum consistent with long-term reliability and safety.

Tapping of renewable energy

It is too early to forecast accurately which specific processes for the tapping of renewable energy will succeed, and in any case there will be continuing improvements and modifications developed from the basic processes. Nevertheless there are clues and pointers which now indicate that the following routes are likely to be utilised widely in the future: (1) Direct conversion of sunlight into heat or electricity. This will clearly become of considerable importance in the equatorial countries, and elsewhere also, especially if attached to effective storage schemes. (2) Biomass—the development of new or improved strains of trees and plants with the object of achieving rapid growth, efficient harvesting and ready conversion into heat, by direct combustion, or into more sophisticated fuels by processing, for example, sugar cane into alcohol for transportation fuels. (3) Wind power—the generation of electricity, or the substitution of electricity usage through direct pumping. These routes emphasise the value of looking anew at traditional methods of harnessing the power of the elements, coupled with the advances of modern technology.

Storage

Practical methods of storing energy in large quantities so that it can be used at peak periods on demand, particularly on a seasonal basis, would satisfy an important need, especially in the colder climates. It would also have wider world-wide application in ironing out the peaks and troughs of demand which span a normal 24 hour period. Efficient, effective methods of storage will reduce the required capacity for energy generation, and therefore can make an important contribution to satisfying needs.

As with foodstuffs grown in summer and consumed throughout the whole year, storage of vegetable matter for conversion into energy is one approach which is certain to have widespread use. Another is the collection of surplus heat in summer, or from exothermic chemical reactions, or of waste heat generated whether from power stations or from other sources, for accumulation in heat storage reservoirs. The technical problems requiring solution would seem to lie principally with the storage medium and a containment system. Underground hot water storage, at sufficient depth for the temperature to be balanced by that of the surrounding rock, is another promising approach.

Conversion

Nature's own storage reservoirs—air and sea water—can be used within limits for converting the sun's energy through the use of heat pumps, which extract heat from one medium and transfer it to another. The sea is a natural heat reservoir, and methods of tapping it on a large scale will surely be developed, with particular application to coastal communities. Similarly heat pumps for extracting energy from the air and from effluents before discharge are also likely to increase dramatically in use.

Avoidance of energy use and waste

As the prices of, and the taxes on, energy increase there will be a greater propensity for consumers to avoid incurring expenditure on energy—this point has already been covered in the main text. Apart from this factor, there are a number of technical options for the avoidance of energy consumption: (1) Heat conservation—by greater and more efficient use of insulation; (2) Energy conservation—through more efficient machinery which consumes less energy while fulfilling the same purpose; (3) Agricultural developments involving crop selection and rotation so as to minimise the use of artificial fertilisers based on oil and gas; (4) Combined heat and power whereby electricity is generated in conventional power stations situated close to consumers of the hot water effluent. This is particularly appropriate to towns and cities, and will be more efficient still when used in conjunction with heat pumps and storage.

A healthy economic climate, within which research into, and development of, new energy can proceed apace is an essential prerequisite for the rapid emergence of successful processes for the tapping of renewable or recoverable energy. As already explained, much has yet to be done to create and maintain this healthy climate. Some of these new sources of energy will need to be suitable, not only for the industrial conurbations of Chicago and the Ruhr, but also for the villages of India and Brazil.

CONCLUSIONS

The developed nations of the world, particularly the IEA/OECD countries, will have available to them the full potential range of opportunities for developing new energy sources from the simple extension of existing methods (for example, the improved cultivation of trees) to the development and introduction of complex new technologies (for example, photovoltaic cells or the possibly unobtainable goal of nuclear fusion). The under-developed countries, on the other hand, may find more sophisticated technology beyond their scope and may be driven to exploiting relatively few simple routes. In both cases an enormous research, development and practical implementation effort will be required from the developed countries, not only to meet their own requirements but also in order to help along their poorer neighbours. Again I must emphasise how important it is that the right economic climate, including pricing régime for conventional energy, is created and maintained to bring about a sustained impetus towards these goals.

In this potential programme for the development of new sources of renewable energy lies the principal hope for recovery from prolonged and persistent world recession. Without stable and secure energy supplies, recovery and the maintenance of a healthy economic environment are unachievable. Even if spontaneous economic recovery begins, now or shortly, it is unlikely to be maintained without large injections of capital into new areas of development and technology. New energy is by far the most important potential recipient of capital investment. Indeed by investing heavily in this field as soon as economic methods become available, the nations of the world will ensure the most rapid recovery possible from recession, assisted by the multiplier effect. The inflationary effects of rising fuel prices cannot be brought under control, and therefore the deflationary impact of rising prices neutralised, until over-reliance on oil has been consigned to the history books.

While economic planners argue whether world oil consumption will rise or fall by the end of the century, the absence of an active, existing programme to slash it, preferably by at least 50 per cent., represents a threat to the welfare of hundreds of millions in the industrialised world and a deferment of the hopes of even more millions in the under-developed world. It is to be hoped that, in the absence of a will to act on the part of the West, OPEC, led by Saudi Arabia, will take the initiative in driving the IEA/OECD countries into adopting common oil conservation policies and a rapid development of alternative renewable sources of energy. No other course seems likely to avoid serious world-wide economic and social disruption, with potentially disastrous consequences to civilised living, democracy, and freedom. No other course offers any substantial prospect of recovery from world recession.

OPEC AND THE WORLD ECONOMY

By

MICHAEL BEENSTOCK

WHEN the Organisation of Petroleum Exporting Countries (OPEC) raised the price of oil in 1973–74 a series of economic forces was unleashed that has reverberated through the world economy. The object of the present exercise is to review these developments in a comprehensive if necessarily brief way, and although only seven years have transpired since the initial oil price hikes it is possible to discern some fairly clear response patterns in the world economy.

We begin by considering the reaction of OPEC itself especially in terms of its oil pricing behaviour. This is followed by a review of macroeconomic developments in the countries of the Organisation for Economic Co-operation and Development (OECD) in relation to inflation, unemployment and the Gross Domestic Product (GDP). We then go on to consider the international financial consequences of the vast OPEC current-balance surpluses, their effects on the euro-currency markets and the recycling problem. Finally we review the economic response in the energy sector itself with regard to the consumption and production of energy outside OPEC.

I—OPEC

(a) *Oil pricing*

Following the initial oil price hikes in 1973–74 two fairly polarised prognoses immediately emerged. Perhaps the majority viewpoint was represented by the pessimists who believed that OPEC could charge anything and get away with it. On these assumptions oil pricing was essentially political and depended on the goodwill of OPEC. At the other extreme were the optimists represented, *e.g.* by Professor Milton Friedman who argued that in the past cartels of all sorts have broken down under market pressure and OPEC would be no exception. The argument went that the high cost of oil would elicit alternative energy supplies and energy conservation thus squeezing OPEC's market to the point at which the cartel would not be able to agree on the proration of production cut-backs. Each OPEC member (especially Saudi Arabia) would then go it alone and in the scramble for a limited oil market oil prices would collapse.

In practice neither of these predictions has so far been fulfilled as may be seen from Chart 1 where the real price of OPEC oil is plotted. The

chart shows that oil prices fell in real terms in the period 1955–1970 and
that even before the oil price hikes in 1973–74 the oil market tended to
tighten. The chart also shows that following the initial hikes oil prices
softened significantly so that by 1978 they had fallen by about 20 per
cent. It began to look as if the optimists were right. However, the Iranian
Revolution boosted OPEC's market power as Iran cut back its oil
production from 5.7 milion barrels per day in 1977 to only 1.77 million
barrels per day in 1980. This enabled OPEC to raise oil prices once
more and Chart 1 shows that the real oil price has more or less
recovered to its level in 1974.

Chart 1
Real Oil Price 1950–1979

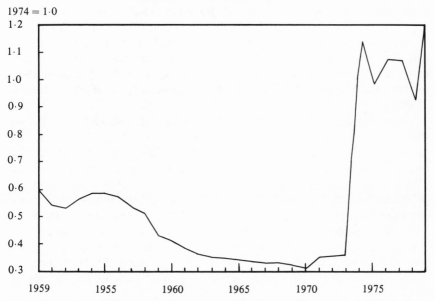

Source: *International Financial Statistics,* IMF (Price of Oil); *National Institute
Economic Review* (Price of world exports in manufactures).

Ayatollahs come and go and the oil market may be affected by
unexpected gluts as well as unexpected shortages. The basic question is
whether OPEC could stand united in face of an unexpected glut. In a
very real sense the cartel has already broken down since the meeting in
Venezuela in December 1979, when members could not agree on
uniform pricing. Instead each country has more or less been going it
alone and the Vienna meeting in September 1980 failed to repair the
damage. This does not matter when the oil market is tight but a
dangerous precedent has been set and should the oil market weaken a
downward price spiral could rapidly emerge. As it happens the conflict
between Iran and Iraq is likely to safeguard OPEC's market position for

the time being. Nevertheless, it is arguable that in the longer run the optimists may be right after all.

(b) *Development policy*

The question of where the OPEC money has gone is discussed later. Insofar as it has been invested in financial assets in the West it is arguable that some of the transfer of resources to OPEC over the current account has been recovered over the capital account. For example, in 1978 Aaa corporate bond rates in the United States were 8.7 per cent. at a time when world manufactured export prices in dollars were inflating at $14\frac{1}{2}$ per cent. per annum. On this basis OPEC was experiencing a negative real rate of return of minus 5.8 per cent. p.a. The comparable return for 1979 was minus 5 per cent. And as the OPEC surpluses accumulate over time the reverse resource transfer over the capital account becomes larger and larger. For example OPEC's cumulative surplus over the period 1973–1979 amounted to $231 billion. If the real rate of return remains at about minus 5 per cent. the reverse resource transfer over the capital account would run to about $12 billion in 1980 which compares with OPEC's current balance surplus of $67 billion in 1979.

Therefore elementary inflation accounting suggests that OPEC has been engaged in substantial reverse transfers to the West. However, this most probably pales into insignificance when compared with the historically unprecedented waste of resources that is generated by OPEC's desire to buy industrialisation. Perhaps nowhere is this more pronounced than in Saudi Arabia where countless billions are being "invested" in the country's future. However, the same kind of development policies were pursued by the late Shah, by Nigeria and other Gulf States. Future economic historians will surely be amazed by the monumental folly of these so-called development policies and their associated waste of resources which will serve as a landmark in the annals of history.

The fallacy of the Saudis is that industrialisation cannot be bought off the shelf and that the sophisticated western model is not appropriate for a desert community which in any event has oil resources that extend beyond any reasonable planning horizon. Plant and infrastructure are being developed which after a short term will serve as little more than industrial monuments and the social equilibrium will be adversely affected perhaps with the same kind of consequences as in Iran. Economic history teaches us that industrialisation comes from below not above, and a higher oil price is unlikely to alter this elementary lesson.

II—MACROECONOMICS

Since 1974 there has been continuous discussion about the impact of oil prices on inflation and unemployment in the OECD countries.

Unfortunately much of this discussion has confused a number of issues. In particular there has been a confusion between long-term and short-term effects, *i.e.* between the permanent and the temporary. We begin by considering the effects of oil prices on inflation in the OECD bloc.

(a) *Inflation*

Because the OECD is a net importer of oil import costs will rise when the price of oil increases. Since in 1979 oil imports were 4.2 per cent. of GDP the immediate effect of a 10 per cent. oil price increase is to raise the average OECD price level by 0.42 per cent. This at least is the first round effect and the story certainly does not end here. Domestic energy prices for coal, gas, etc. will eventually move in sympathy with oil prices although quite often governments have sought to prevent energy prices from fully adjusting to the higher price of oil.

In principle the story could end here with energy prices rising relative to other prices, and as we shall see this is what eventually happens. However, in practice workers may try to put in wage claims which compensate them for the higher prices and which will restore their real wages. If this happens wages will rise and as firms seek to compensate themselves for their higher labour costs prices will tend to rise. In this way a wage-price spiral may be triggered.

But such a spiral will not go on indefinitely unless governments print money to validate the higher price level. If, for argument's sake, they did not allow the money supply to change, the higher price level would cause a credit squeeze and a recession would develop. This in turn is likely to depress wages and prices. Indeed, it is perhaps plain to see that if the money supply remains unchanged the price level would eventually revert to its initial level. At this equilibrium the relative price of energy will be higher and real wages will be lower. If OPEC is to be paid more real wages and real incomes generally must fall in the oil consuming countries.

These considerations imply that higher oil prices initially generate inflation but this is eventually followed by deflation so that in the longer run oil prices on their own do not automatically generate inflation. Permanent inflation could only occur if monetary policy was allowed to expand in an accommodating fashion. Therefore the short-term inflationary effects largely depend on unrealistic attempts to protect real wages, attempts which must eventually be frustrated.

To illustrate this inflationary process on Chart 2 we report the results from a computer simulation derived from an econometric model of the world economy which has been developed at the London Business School.[1] In the simulation the price of OPEC oil is assumed to rise per-

---

[1] For a description of this model see G. Dicks and M. Beenstock, "An Aggregative Monetary Model of the World Economy," London Business School mimeo, October 1980.

Chart 2
Simulated Effect of 10 per cent. Increase in Oil Prices
on Prices and Output in OECD Countries

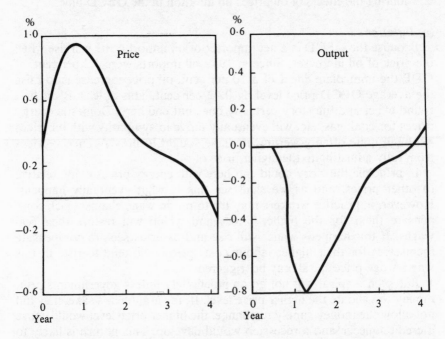

manently by 10 per cent. in the initial quarter. The simulation is carried out under the assumption that governments keep the money supply fixed. The chart shows that initially the higher oil price generates cost inflation such that after a year prices are raised by about one per cent. However, because monetary policy is assumed to resist these inflationary pressures, output becomes recessed. The bottom of the recession is reached during the second year when output is 0.8 per cent. below its initial level. The recession causes prices to fall which in turn has an expansionary effect on the economy. After four years output and prices return to their initial values and the process is complete.

These simulations suggest that an increase in oil prices has stagflationary effects which are essentially short-term and that these effects are distributed over a four to five year period. During 1979 oil prices more or less doubled, *i.e.* by an amount which was 10 times larger than the increase assumed in the simulations. This implies that world inflation was temporarily raised by about 10 percentage points and output fell by about 7 percentage points. Although these effects are temporary they are nevertheless highly disruptive and underline the importance of OPEC's pricing behaviour on the world economy's short term-prospects.

In the wake of the first round of oil-price hikes, OECD governments chose in 1974 to accommodate its inflationary effect by a temporary expansion in monetary and fiscal policy; consequently inflation was greater and the recession was less deep than if non-accommodatory policies had been adopted. In contrast the price hikes of 1979 have largely gone unaccommodated and so far this has been reflected in less inflation but a deeper world recession.

(b) *Gross Domestic Product*
From the previous discussion it follows that when oil prices rise and governments do not accommodate the inflationary pressures that ensue the economy becomes recessed. However, the recession will be temporary in a way that parallels the temporary nature of the inflationary pressures. Therefore, in the short run the economy will tend to be recessed but in the longer term GDP will revert to its "full employment" level.

It is probable that in response to higher real energy prices the "full employment" level of output will fall for two reasons. First of all, as we have already observed, real wage rates will fall and this will have the effect of reducing labour supply incentives so that employment is likely to fall voluntarily. Secondly, higher input costs will squeeze profits and this will adversely affect entrepreneurial initiative. Therefore on both these accounts it is probable that the long-run, or "full-employment," level of output in the OECD bloc will fall.

It is generally recognised that GDPs in the OECD countries have been adversely affected by higher energy prices. One estimate[2] of the adverse long-term effect implies that when the real price of oil rises by 10 per cent. "full-employment" GDP falls by about 0.2 per cent. This implies that the quadrupling of oil prices would eventually reduce the level of GDP by about 3 per cent. It should be noted that higher oil prices do not permanently impair economic growth. Instead, the growth rate will be more or less unaltered although the level of GDP will be permanently lower than it would otherwise have been.

So much for the long-term effects of higher oil prices on OECD GDP. On Chart 2 we illustrated the possible short-term effects which are measured by the percentage deviations of output from the "full-employment" level. This chart shows the output profiles that are implied by the inflation profiles shown in Chart 2, *i.e.* they are based on the same computer simulation of a 10 per cent. oil price increase. It has already been pointed out that the recessive effects are essentially short-term. However, the simulation assumes that governments do not accommodate the inflationary effects of higher oil prices by printing more money. If they did, the inflationary pressures would persist and the

[2] See M. Beenstock, *The World Economy in Transition* (1982).

recession would most probably be shallower. But this would simply put off the evil day unless governments were adept enough to contain these inflationary pressures.

(c) *Unemployment*

To a large extent the effect of oil prices on unemployment will occur via the recessive effects that have just been discussed. If governments do not accommodate the inflationary impact of higher oil prices there will be a deficiency of aggregate demand and Keynesian unemployment will be generated. However, we have already remarked that the higher cost of imported oil implies that real wages must fall. If on account of real wage resistance this does not happen firms will respond by reducing their demand for labour and classical unemployment will result. Whereas Keynesian unemployment reflects a deficiency in aggregate demand, classical unemployment occurs when real wages are above their "full-employment" level. Classical unemployment will only be removed when workers accept the appropriate real wage cuts that are necessitated by the higher oil prices.

The evidence suggests[3] that workers in OECD countries have tried to resist the real wage cuts implied by higher oil prices and have as a consequence priced themselves out of jobs. Indeed the average OECD unemployment rate rose from 3 per cent. over the period 1964–1973 to 4.9 per cent. over the period 1974–1979. The essence of the classical unemployment problem is that workers are trying to force their employers to recompense them for the higher price of oil. If they succeed it can only be at the expense of lost jobs.

III—INTERNATIONAL FINANCE

The oil price hikes radically transformed OPEC's international financial position and petrodollars have had an important bearing on international financial institutions. In 1973–74 it was widely feared that the international financial system might be unable to cope, but by now most of these fears have been largely allayed. We consider first the effect of OPEC on the structure of current balances.

(a) *Current balances*

The current balance is the balance on current transactions in the balance of payments and thus excludes capital flows. Higher oil prices increase the value of OPEC exports and unless OPEC can increase its imports by a commensurate amount the OPEC current balance will improve to the detriment of other countries. The so-called "high absorbers," *e.g.* Nigeria, are able to spend the extra revenue more readily on

---

[3] M. Bruno, "Import Prices and Stagflation in the Industrial Countries: A Cross Section Analysis," *The Economic Journal*, September 1980.

imports while the "low absorbers" such as Saudi Arabia have to accumulate financial surpluses because they simply cannot spend their extra revenues on imports.

Table 1 records recent current balance performance and shows that OPEC ran some very large surpluses. However, by 1978 this surplus had all but disappeared and many individual members were running substantial deficits. This decline was widely predicted since spending plans usually lag behind income and it seems likely that the recent recovery in OPEC's current balance following the 1979 price hike will be short-lived.

The table also underlines the precarious position of the non-oil developing countries who as a group have run substantial and persistent current-balance deficits. However, without OPEC aid the less developed countries (LDCs) would have been substantially worse off although the aid flow of about $5 billion hardly compensates for the higher oil import bills of about $24 billion per year (1980 prices) that the LDCs have to pay.

Table 1: Current Balances ($ billions)

	1973	1974	1975	1976	1977	1978	1979
OECD	10.5	−26	0.5	−19	−24.5	10.5	−37.5
OPEC	7.5	59.5	27	36.5	29	4.5	67
Non-oil LDCs	−7.5	−26	−31	−19	−12.5	−25.5	−34.5
Aid from OPEC	N/A	N/A	5.5	5.6	5.9	5.3	4.7

Source: OECD

The persistent current balance deficits of the non-oil LDCs make for an unstable element in the international financial system. As LDC debts accumulate the chances of a major default increase as vulnerable LDCs find that they cannot honour their debts or reschedule them on afford-able terms. A series of major defaults would severely test the stability of the euro-currency banks and there are many who believe that the world is very near such a precipice.

(b) *Recycling*

OPEC's current-balance surplus must be matched by an equal and opposite capital-account deficit with the non-OPEC world. In other words as long as OPEC runs surpluses it must spend them on financial assets outside OPEC. For example, the $59.5 billion surplus in 1974 (see Table 1) had to be matched by the accumulation of external financial assets worth $59.5 billions.

In 1973–74 there were numerous sceptics who were concerned that international financial institutions such as the euro-currency banks would not be able to cope with such a vast and sudden flow of funds. And even if they could absorb the flow it was felt that it would be invested precariously. It was therefore proposed to establish various recycling arrangements by which the OPEC surpluses would be on-lent to various deficit countries. Indeed a number of such recycling arrangements were set up under International Monetary Fund (IMF) auspices, but the vast majority of recycling was left to market forces. By and large the international financial markets have been coping fairly well although in certain cases loans have been poorly placed. But this has been the exception rather than the rule and it is not obvious that recycling through government agencies would have been any better. However, not all of the recycling has taken place through these euro-currency markets, as Table 2 indicates.

Table 2: Deployment of OPEC's Cash Surpluses ($ billions)

	1974	1975	1976	1977	1978	1979
Bank deposits	7.0	2.0	0.5	2.3	2.8	6.3
Euro-currency deposits	21.6	7.9	11.5	10.7	1.1	31.0
Government securities	9.1	2.0	2.2	3.4	−2.6	2.6
Direct & portfolio investment	7.1	12.8	13.2	9.8	5.8	9.0
To LDCs	4.9	6.5	6.4	7.0	6.2	6.9

Source: *Bank of England Quarterly Bulletin*, June 1980, p. 158.

The table shows that, when surpluses increase, OPEC initially goes short and bank and euro-currency deposits rise, *e.g.* as in 1974 and 1979. This is followed by a lengthening of portfolios through direct and portfolio investment. Nevertheless by the end of 1979 OPEC was still holding 50 per cent. of its overall portfolio in relatively short-term deposits. On this basis it must be concluded that OPEC has a marked preference for liquidity in which case banks are likely to bear the principal brunt of recycling.

It would also seem that OPEC has avoided government securities which are largely held as official reserves. This has benefited the United States Government, since the dollar remains the principal vehicle for reserves. It would further seem that the dollar has been the main beneficiary of OPEC's portfolio management so that perhaps as much as 50 per cent. of OPEC's assets are currently held in U.S. dollars.

In contrast sterling has scarcely benefited except in 1974 when there was a substantial influx into Treasury Bills. But this was not to be repeated in 1979 when OPEC's surplus surged once more although the data may eventually reveal that there was a considerable influx during 1980 when sterling appreciated by more than 30 per cent.

IV—THE ENERGY SECTOR

So far we have been concerned with the indirect effects of higher oil prices outside the energy sector. We now turn to the energy sector itself and explore the effects of higher oil prices on the supply and demand for energy.

(a) *Energy demand*

Chart 3
Ratio of Total Energy Consumption to GDP:
Developed Market Economies 1950–1978

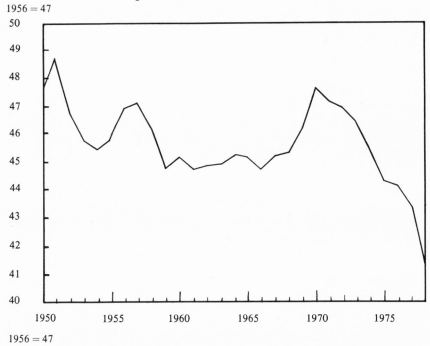

1956 = 47

1956 = 47

Source: *Statistical Yearbook*, United Nations (GDP for Developed Market Economies); *World Energy Supplies*, United Nations (Energy Consumption in Developed Market Economies).

Perhaps the best measure of energy conservation is the number of energy units required to produce a unit of GDP: the fewer the units the more energy efficient we are. Accordingly on Chart 3 we plot the ratio of total final energy consumption to GDP for Developed Market Economies over the period since 1950. The chart shows that energy efficiency has tended to rise over time. However, the gains in efficiency have been particularly marked since OPEC raised its price in 1973–74 and the latest observations suggest that these efficiency effects show no sign of abating. Therefore world-wide achievements in energy conservation have been quite pronounced and there is every indication that even more adjustments are in the pipe-line.

Chart 4
Real Energy Prices to Final Users*

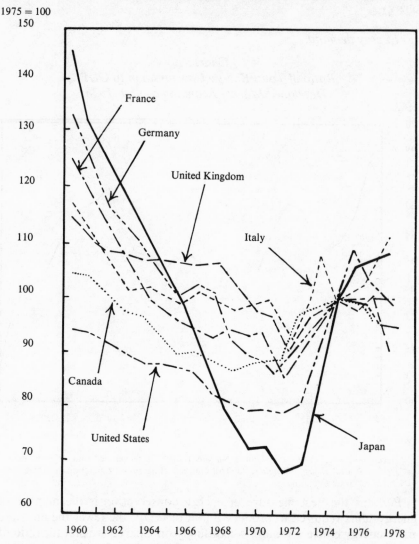

1975 = 100

* Index of combined energy prices to final users consisting of: energy component of consumer price index (excluding gasoline) divided by the total index of consumer prices; energy component of wholesale price index divided by a composite of prices of labour and capital; and gasoline prices divided by total index of consumer prices. Each component was weighted by its respective share in total final energy demand.

Source: *Economic Outlook*, OECD, Paris, July 1980, p. 118.

These conservation measures have reflected the changes in real energy prices in consumer countries brought about by the oil price hikes. The nature and scale of these price changes are indicated on Chart 4 for seven of the principal industrialised countries. The chart shows that prior to the price hikes real energy prices had been falling with the greatest rate of decline in Japan and the smallest rate in the United States. Without exception this decline was reversed in the aftermath of the oil price hikes with the strongest reversal in Japan and the weakest in the United Kingdom. On average, however, the quadrupling of oil prices had by 1979 only raised real energy prices to final users by about 15 per cent., or to where they were in the mid-1960s. This suggests that energy prices have not risen as far as they should since real oil prices are double their 1950 level (see Chart 1), yet energy prices have not even reverted to their 1960 relativity, let alone their real value in 1950.

The main reason for this discrepancy is the intervention of government in the pricing of energy. In many countries, such as the United States, government regulations determine energy prices, or the cost of energy reflects government taxes. If these taxes are not set in *ad valorem* terms an increase in the price of oil would cause domestic energy prices to rise less than proportionately. This is particularly true of petrol prices where prices at the pump largely reflect excise duties. For example, in 1970 these taxes amounted to 75 per cent. of petrol prices in the United Kingdom. By 1979, however, these taxes only amounted to 35 per cent. of pump prices. Because the energy price response has been so muted the achievements in the area of energy conservation are all the more remarkable. This implies that if and when governments allow the full energy price adjustments to take place further progress in energy conservation can be expected.

(b) *Energy supply*

Few subjects are as controversial as the cost of generating alternatives to OPEC oil. In 1974 there were numerous optimists that shale oil and syncrude could be developed at competitive prices and there were many who believed that the ultimate "back-stop" technology was the breeder reactor which could produce virtually limitless quantities of low cost energy. In the event none of these expectations has so far been fulfilled. Syncrude costs have not been competitive and there have been major environmental obstacles to cheap production. There has also been a waning of enthusiasm about the widespread use of nuclear energy and the episode at Three Mile Island in Pennsylvania has substantially boosted the anti-nuclear lobby. In any case nuclear costs have escalated too.

Government price intervention has also been an obstacle to energy development especially in the United States where as already mentioned energy prices have been held back. This has reduced the incentive to produce energy and the cheap energy lobby remains very strong.

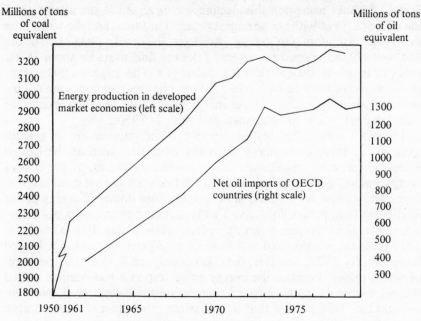

Chart 5
Energy Production and Oil Imports in Industrial Countries

Sources: *World Energy Supplies*, United Nations; *Energy Balances*, OECD, Paris.

The record on energy production in the Developed Market Economies is shown on Chart 5. After two decades of sustained growth energy production began to falter in 1971 reflecting the peaking of United States oil production at that time. Perhaps it is no coincidence that OPEC timed its price hikes at a time when non-OPEC energy production had levelled off and even declined. In 1976 and 1977 energy production recovered although a large proportion of this was due to oil production from the North Sea and Alaska.

(c) *The world oil market*

International trade in energy is predominantly concerned with trade in oil although there is a substantial trade in coal and liquefied natural gas. Therefore the balance between domestic energy consumption and production is largely met through oil imports, in which case the world market for oil reflects the state of this imbalance across the nations of the world.

By far the greatest source of net oil demand on the world market originates in the OECD countries. As OECD oil imports grow relative to the supply of oil on the world market the price of oil will tend to rise and vice-versa. Chart 5 shows the growth of OECD oil imports over the period 1962–1979. The chart has two distinct phases. Up to 1973 oil imports grew steadily and this growth was particularly marked in the early 1970's when energy production in the OECD countries grew more slowly. Since the oil price hikes of 1973–74 OECD oil imports have grown more slowly and have been much more erratic. This has proved to be so despite the deceleration in indigenous energy production and reflects the lower output growth and energy conservation in the OECD as a whole.

Chart 6
OPEC Oil Production

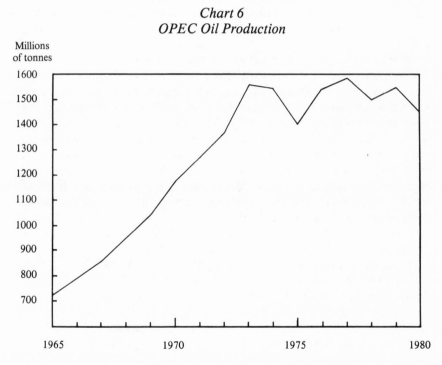

Source: *BP Statistical Review of the World Oil Industry* (1980)

The deceleration in OECD imports has inevitably been reflected in OPEC oil production which, having steadily expanded in the 1960s and early 1970s, ceased to grow after 1973. By raising the price of oil the demand for OPEC oil has fallen from what otherwise would have been the case and Chart 6 suggests that OPEC so far has managed to prevent its market from either expanding or contracting. Had its market contracted through over-pricing it would have been necessary to prorate cut-backs and this would have triggered political strains within the cartel that might have threatened its unity. But it should be remembered that the demand for OPEC oil is the residual between two very large numbers, *i.e.* between energy production and consumption outside OPEC, and if energy production rises relative to consumption the market for OPEC oil could dwindle rapidly. If the former rises by 10 per cent. and the latter falls by 10 per cent. OPEC's oil market would almost be entirely wiped out and oil prices would crash.

(d) *Economic welfare*

Have higher oil prices been good for the world as a whole? The majority view is perhaps that OPEC has done the world a social service by signalling to the market that energy is becoming scarce and the world economy has been forewarned about a prospective energy shortage. Indeed, there has been a spate of "doomwatch" projections which indicate that before the end of the millenium an energy "crunch" will occur which will severely constrain economic growth.

The minority view is that OPEC is no different from any other cartel that raises prices to boosts its profits at the expense of others. Moreover, it is not a zero-sum game because the world is forced to conserve energy when this is socially unnecessary. According to this view OPEC has raised its price above the long run scarcity value of oil. If indeed energy was expected to become scarce at some future time market forces would have raised prices gradually prior to 1973. Indeed oil prices in real terms began to firm up after 1969 under market forces. On this basis the OPEC price hikes have been artificial, abrupt and anti-social, and it is perhaps surprising how since 1973 numerous analysts have convinced themselves about a forthcoming energy crisis when they discounted this prospect prior to 1973.

History tends to repeat itself. More than a century ago, W. S. Jevons, the renowned Victorian economist, calculated that the Industrial Revolution in Britain would come to an end before the end of the nineteenth century on account of a shortage of coal. It is quite possible that present day pessimists are making the same mistake. If so, OPEC's oil pricing policy has adversely affected society as a whole.

ESCALATION IN SOUTH AFRICA

By

DONALD WOODS

WHEN historians come to survey the last quarter of the twentieth century they may well wonder how the developed democratic countries of the West could have remained so blind for so long to two areas of vital concern to them—Iran and South Africa. They will be able to see how for more than a decade the West believed its policies on Iran were in their best interests; then how this complacency was exploded by an uncontrolled revolution which not only displayed widespread hostility to Western policies, peoples and governments, but also jeopardised vital oil supplies in a manner neither foreseen nor anticipated by any Western foreign service. Whether they will find many parallels in the Western response to the South African crisis will depend largely on Western policy for this area during the years 1982–1987, because all the indications are that these will be the crucial years in determining South Africa's future political structures, and the Western response during this period could well define Western relationships with South Africa until well into the next century.

Certainly parallels exist already between Western attitudes to South Africa today and to Iran up to the fall of Shah Reza Pahlavi. Although Western governments had reservations about the Shah's autocratic rule, they believed that diplomatic and trade relations and military alliances with the Shah should continue for economic and geopolitical reasons, and in the interests of what was thought to be "stability" in a State regarded as a "bulwark against communism." Western governments have more than reservations against the present South African régime and officially condemn the apartheid policy, but maintain the same readiness to recognise the Pretoria government diplomatically, to retain and increase trade and investment links and, unofficially, to regard South Africa's military capacity as an asset in the global rivalry between East and West.

The world knew well by 1980 what an illusion the Shah's "stability" had been, and the world will see during the 1980s the shattering of a similar illusion of stability in South Africa, but the reasons for the successful projection of both illusions abroad for many years deserves special attention. Undoubtedly the link is information. Just as the Shah managed for a long time to get his version of Iranian reality projected abroad to the virtual exclusion of the version of those who eventually overthrew him, so the South African Government contrives, in spite of all the foreign journalism critical of apartheid, to project abroad the

111

essential elements of the South African picture it needs for the prolonga-
tion of economic support and diplomatic acknowledgment. It is basically
a picture of a hard-headed and embattled régime, admittedly representing a minority, but beginning slowly to come to terms with the need for
reform—a régime which is pragmatically permitting the erosion of the
edges of apartheid, with the implied intent of permitting, ultimately, the
erosion of the inner core itself: *given time*. Meanwhile, so Pretoria would
like the West to remember, it is a rich field for investment, a good trading partner and a reliable business dealer, paying its debts promptly and
arming to the teeth to prevent "communist-backed terrorists" from
delivering its gold and uranium-rich economy to the Soviet camp. Like
most convincing illusions, it is based on a shadow of truth—at least in
some respects. But before examining the illusion, let us first examine the
substance of apartheid.

I—APARTHEID ENTRENCHED

To most people outside South Africa "apartheid" means simply an
objectionable policy of racial discrimination applied against the
country's blacks. But apartheid is much more than that. It is a device
whereby 12,000 whites, with the direct support of 2,700,000 other
whites, retain for the country's total white population of 4,800,000 all
significant political and economic power in dominance over the
country's black majority of some 25 millions. The 12,000 are members
of the Afrikaner Broederbond, an élite organisation which screens and
selects all candidates for public office, including premiers and cabinet
members, and the 2,700,000 are supporters of the governing Afrikaner
Nationalist Party which is the public arm of the Afrikaner Broederbond.

The core of apartheid is the retention of the vote in white hands. All
the other manifestations of apartheid—including 317 apartheid laws
banning a full range of inter-racial activities such as sex, sport, dancing,
drinking, work and residence—are peripheral. Any of these peripheral
laws, including the Pass Laws (requiring all blacks to carry identity
booklets) could be abolished without affecting the core of
apartheid—the key question of the vote.

The Afrikaner Broederbond, founded in 1918, came fully into control
of South Africa in 1948 with a narrow electoral victory by the Afrikaner
Nationalist Party over Jan Smuts's conservative but less extreme United
Party. Since then it has consolidated its hold on the country through a
battery of statutes passed during the ensuing 32 years, so that today the
governing party could not be unseated by the electoral process. Even if
its parliamentary group of 135 members were to split in half, each half
would have a comfortable majority over the tiny Progressive Federal
Party opposition of 18 members. But in any case the South African
Parliament is a parliament in name only. The real power is at Broederbond headquarters in Pretoria, and the edicts coming from there are

drafted, also in Pretoria, by Broederbond-selected civil servants before being sent down to Members of Parliament in Cape Town for rubber-stamping into law.

The ruling body within the Broederbond (Brotherhood) is the Executive Council of 15 members, whose present chairman is Gerrit Viljoen, a university professor. Although South African cabinet ministers, including Prime Minister P. W. Botha, are members of the Broederbond, no member of the cabinet is a member of the Broederbond's executive council.

II—SOUTH AFRICA'S EXTERNAL IMAGE

The pertinence of the Broederbond to South Africa's image abroad is clear. It was the Broederbond which decided in the mid-1960s to cause massive funds to be allocated to external propaganda and lobbying. Initially these propaganda and lobbying attempts were crude and unsuccessful. Working with right-wing groups in the United Kingdom and the United States—in London with the Committee of Ten, which placed newspaper advertisements—the South African Department of Information tried to portray apartheid as a benevolent system of "separate development" in terms of which South Africa's blacks, while admittedly segregated from whites politically, socially and to some extent geographically, were not badly off economically.

The strategy did not work because nobody was really fooled. It could easily be shown, for example, that far from being better off in South Africa than anywhere else in Africa, South Africa's blacks were economically worse off than in 11 other countries in Africa, and that in spite of South Africa's enormous wealth compared with other African countries, South African blacks had among the worst infant mortality rates in all Africa through the poverty diseases of malnutrition and kwashiorkor.

Early in 1978 the Broederbond decided to take a new tack in external propaganda—to employ more subtlety and to switch emphasis from public advertising to private lobbying. In Washington, conservative or middle-of-the-road senators and congressmen were taken to discreet dinners in the best restaurants, and talk was less of apartheid than of South Africa's anti-communism, military strength, investment yields and readiness to "reform." There was a similar approach in London, Paris, Bonn and other Western capitals, and the strategy was broadened to include financiers, industrialists and bankers. But the Western media remained a problem, so funds from the propaganda budget were diverted to attempts to buy influence in selected publications. The two best publicised attempts were aimed at the *Washington Star* and the London-based magazine *West Africa*, but there were many other clandestine attempts, through share-dealings via middlemen, and at the same time Western journalists were invited to South Africa, feted extravagantly, and shown the most favourable aspects of the country.

It was only when such spending reached indiscreet levels and when substantial portions of the funds were diverted to the private pockets of some government officials that inter-departmental jealousy in Pretoria led to revelations triggering off the "Muldergate" scandal—Dr. C. P. Mulder then being head of what was euphemistically called the Department of Information. The scandal, which caused the Broederbond to decide that Premier Vorster and Dr. Mulder should pay the price for such indiscretions, led to a re-structuring of the entire propaganda operation. Vorster and Mulder and Dr. Eschel Rhoodie, Mulder's deputy, were removed from office and even more subtlety in propaganda was ordered.

Throughout 1980 the propaganda exercise abroad increasingly became low-key and low-profiled. Public statements by ambassadors were reduced to almost nil, newspaper advertisements ceased entirely and more emphasis than ever was placed on discreet dinner parties and receptions for bankers. As far as the external media were concerned, it was decided to use the "karate" method—making use of one's opponent's own momentum. Since television crews and newspaper correspondents showed no inclination to stop covering what they could in South Africa, a real effort would be made to make things inside the country seem a lot better. The most visible areas of South African life would therefore be improved, and to this end—at the instigation of two members of the cabinet, Premier P. W. Botha and Dr. P. G. Koornhof—some of the peripheral edges of apartheid would be eroded: and not only eroded, but seen to be eroded.

The peripheral edges chosen were sport, recreation and entertainment. Blacks were allowed to join sports clubs and to play in the same rugby and cricket teams as whites, to go onto previously "whites only" beaches and to the best hotels, restaurants and bars. That, consequently, is now the official policy.

III—THE INTERNAL PROBLEM
OF LEGITIMATION

Internally, such an exercise requires extreme delicacy of judgment by the Broederbond because the ever-present possibility of a right-wing backlash has to be considered as a major factor in all Afrikaner Nationalist politics. It is not that the Broederbond is essentially out of sympathy with the right-wingers, the Broederbond being essentially a right-wing conservative organisation dedicated to preserving white Afrikaner sypremacy, but its executive council has a broader vision than its grass-roots supporters of how to retain such supremacy.

The delicate balance the Broederbond has to strike is to make the international community believe that apartheid is being phased out while assuring the grass-roots followers that it is not. The task is complicated further by the fact that some influential Broederbonders such as Dr. A. P. Treurnicht believe such a balance is impossible to strike and that the only way to preserve the core of apartheid is to preserve the edges of it as well. The two viewpoints within the organisation are personified by two members of the present cabinet—Dr. Treurnicht on the relative right and Premier Botha on the relative left. Botha, heavily influenced by his Minister of Defence, General Magnus Malan—also a Broederbonder—believes in the edge-erosion process, and the executive council is, at least at first, going along experimentally with the Botha-Malan approach. However, it is probable that at the first sign of significant grass-roots objection to blacks on beaches or in sports teams or hotels the executive council would swing back to the Treurnicht approach and shore up the edges of apartheid again.

Malan has a slightly different reason for urging the relatively liberal approach, which is called, in Afrikaans *verlig* and its proponents *verligtes*. The relatively right-wing approach is called *verkramp* and its advocates *verkramptes*. (*Verlig* means open-minded and *verkramp* narrow-minded.) Malan, commander-in-chief of the army for years in the border war against the South-West Africa People's Organisation (SWAPO) in Namibia, believes in the long-established saying that in a war of insurrection victory will go to those who win allegiance of the "indigenous peasants" (for which read "blacks"). The main flaw in Malan's approach is his gross underestimation of the degree of policy-change necessary to win this allegiance. He, and the *verligtes* generally, appear to think that a black revolution can be averted by (a) opening certain doors to an aspirant black middle-class, and (b) negotiating away all but the core of apartheid. Treurnicht and the *verkramptes* somewhat more realistically, believe that the overwhelming majority of blacks will never be contented with anything less than black majority rule. In their view the erosion of the edges of apartheid, far from preserving the core of it, will hasten the inevitable onslaught on it.

It is typical of most whites in South Africa that these are the only two options they see—the *verligte* and the *verkrampte* options—when the truth is that neither option matters much. The enormous black majority, so airily discounted in this all-white, all-Afrikaner debate, is already on an inexorable march which its leaders will not consider halting until a black majority rules South Africa. When anyone suggests to people outside South Africa, or to whites inside the country, that an armed victory by black South Africans is not only conceivable but probable within the next five years, the response is invariably total scepticism.

Much of the reason for that scepticism has been bought for hundreds of millions of rands worth of partially-successful propaganda—a great deal of it unwittingly transmitted by perfectly impartial news media abroad. As in Iran under the Shah, the news coverage within a largely closed society has severely prescribed limits; what often looks like good coverage in such circumstances given that impression because such societies are not entirely closed, and appear with significant realism to be considerably open. It is possible, for example, to allow television crews and foreign correspondents to roam all over South Africa, filming and recording all that they can see and hear—without allowing anything like a true picture of the country to emerge. All the significant black leaders are inaccessible to such inquiry. The last vestige of such accessibility died with Steve Biko in September 1977, and even then Biko's was not a complete accessibility to interviewers in that, like other credible black leaders (Bishop Desmond Tutu is one such), there are limits of political discretion to what can be said for publication in such a situation, even for publication outside. Most of the significant leaders are operating underground; are in bush training camps outside; are in exile overseas; are banned; or are in jail on Robben Island political prison. In any case few blacks in South Africa would ever open up completely to such interviewers.

IV—REVOLUTIONARY PREPARATIONS

The two main liberation movements, both banned, are the African National Congress (ANC) and the Pan-Africanist Congress (PAC). Both are committed to war. The ANC is the senior of the two movements. It remains under the leadership of Nelson Mandela, who is in his eighteenth year of imprisonment on Robben Island, and his deputy, Oliver Tambo, who is the black leader-in-exile. Formed in 1912, the ANC relied on peaceful protest, negotiation and petitions until the early 1960s, when it turned to its commitment to violence in response to the refusal of whites to consider any kind of significant negotiation towards equal rights for blacks. Outlawed, it turned to the Western democracies for aid, and was rejected partly because of Western diplomatic and economic ties with Pretoria and partly because the socialist programme of the ANC was regarded as too radical in Western capitals (the ANC stated it would nationalise the gold mines). The ANC, feeling rebuffed by the West, turned to the East for aid and received it immediately, in money, weapons and training. It also received, as a matter of course, such limited aid as the newly-independent African States could provide.

Originally the youth wing of the ANC, the Pan-Africanist Congress was to have the same experience. The young leaders who formed the PAC, such as Robert Sobukwe, criticised the ANC for remaining too passive for too long, for getting too involved, as the PAC felt, with white communists and for laying too little emphasis on the Africanist character of the coming revolution. In the latter sense the PAC was foreshadowing the Black Consciousness movement of a decade later, although in the years to come it would broaden its ranks to include whites, Indians and Coloureds, defining as "Africanist" or "African" anyone owing fealty to Africa. Both movements have had from the 1960s considerable following. There is little doubt that if most black South Africans could express their real allegiances freely today, they would follow one or other of these mass movements. The PAC had a more spectacular start in the business of armed conflict—launching attacks on white towns and police stations—but was poorly equipped in weaponry, often pitting pangas, spears and axes against the automatic weapons of the white police. Inevitably these half-cock attacks failed and the PAC realised it would have to follow the ANC route of training guerrillas externally, raising funds in the international arena, and restricting attacks to isolated acts of sabotage until the externally-trained force was adequate to the task of serious invasion. The PAC's main external base was to be Dar-Es-Salaam, and most of its guerrilla training camps are in Tanzania. After the death of Robert Sobukwe in 1978 a leadership-struggle began externally with attempts to remove Potlako Leballo from the post of leader-in-exile, and that struggle is yet unresolved.

Both the ANC and PAC decided to take a longer-term view and to prepare their strike forces more assiduously than had the guerrilla forces of Robert Mugabe and Joshua Nkomo in their campaign against Rhodesia's whites. Some of Mugabe's guerrillas were thrown into combat after only weeks of training, and some after only months. The average ANC and PAC guerrilla has had several years of training and the weaponry of the ANC, in particular, is the best available.

The main question, for years, was when to strike in force—not by conventional invasion but by large-scale infiltration back across the South African border, and an inhibiting factor was the Rhodesian war. While this continued, the logical infiltration regions along the Limpopo River and from Mozambique into the Eastern Transvaal and Northern Natal were not easily accessible, nor would they be so until Mugabe's newly-independent Zimbabwe was stabilised and Machel's Mozambique consequently recovered from the side-effects of the conflict.

It seems that the collapse of the Smith régime in Rhodesia occurred a year or two before all the black nationalists concerned expected, Mugabe included, and that this collapse caused the ANC and PAC to reassess their own plans for large-scale infiltration. In the light of the rapid escalation of events in Zimbabwe and the peripheral effects of this on Mozambique, it seems probable that purposeful ANC and PAC infiltration of guerrillas into the Northern and Eastern Transvaal and into Northern Natal will begin to occur early in 1982, and that the South African government will have border wars other than the SWAPO conflict in Namibia to contend with. The border war in Ovamboland, Northern Namibia, now involves some 50,000 white South African troops at a cost of £4 million a day. The area of conflict covers only 400 miles of border, but South Africa has more than 2,000 miles of border to defend if the Limpopo and Natal fronts open up as expected, and in terms of money alone, apart from manpower, the cost will escalate to stupendous amounts.

V—CONFRONTATION WITH REALITY

(a) *Military realities*

Acts of sabotage within South Africa are on the increase. The most dramatic of these—the most sophisticated operation of its kind yet attempted—was the blowing up of Sasol (oil-from-coal) refineries by the ANC in 1980 with the complete escape of the saboteurs. Although television viewers outside South Africa saw the results of this attack, there are few glimpses of the large forces of the black movements training in their camps in several African countries—partly because the ANC and PAC do not want too much to be known of these camps, for obvious reasons, and partly because there is as yet no widespread interest in the West in the existence of the black guerrillas.

As in the Zimbabwe conflict, initial international interest tends to be focused on the white forces. Not only are they more accessible to television crews and correspondents, but it suits the Pretoria government's "information" strategy to be as open as is expedient about them. Any impression of white military power on the television screens of the West is helpful to Pretoria's private reassurances to bankers and industrialists that white control is invincibly permanent. Thus shots of aircraft, or warships, or disciplined infantrymen in camouflage uniforms are not only permitted by the Botha government but encouraged. The result is that people in the West have a mental impression, if often only a subconscious one, of immense white power in South Africa, opposed by minimal black forces, if any. Similar impressions were created, even in the last months of the Shah's rule in Iran, by footage of the superbly-trained and splendidly-equipped Tehran guards—the Shah's élite.

It is true that white South Africa is hugely wealthy, heavily-armed and formidably-prepared for modern warfare. What is questionable is how well-prepared white South Africa is for the kind of violent challenge that will face it in the future. Its strengths are similar, if on a larger scale, to the strengths of the white Rhodesians displayed for most of the Zimbabwe war. With a disclosed military budget of over one billion pounds (the amount actually spent is considerably higher), South Africa has a standing army of 20,000 white soldiers, 1,700 black soldiers, 35,000 white conscripts and 150,000 reservists. The air force has 9,000 servicemen and the navy 5,000. There are 20,000 white police and 13,000 white police reservists.

Pretoria claims that the average white South African soldier will prove a more formidable adversary than the average white Rhodesian soldier, on the grounds that the latter had a "settler mentality" and was not truly fighting for "his" country, whereas the white South African "has nowhere else to go" and will fight "to the end." This is a myth. The available evidence actually indicates the opposite—that the white Rhodesians were probably the best bush fighters in the world, man for man, with a remarkably low rate of psychological failure in combat. Young white Rhodesians generally had a lifelong knowledge of the bush and a romantic "macho" attachment to it, whereas the average young white South African today is a city-dweller whose entertainment is more likely found in a disco or nightclub than on a crocodile hunt. The South African military have been said to be disturbed by the high rate of drop-out from their bush camps by young recruits suffering mental strain and psychological inadaptability to combat conditions. While this does not suggest that white South Africans will not make tough fighters it does indicate the fragility of the comparative myth *vis-à-vis* the white Rhodesians.

The other myth, that white South Africans are solidly united in deter-mination to fight to the end, also deserves closer examination. During the past five years as many as 4,000 young white South Africans have avoided military service, and many of these, mostly English-speaking, have emigrated rather than "fight for apartheid." An unknown number have simply refused conscription and risked prosecution, although relatively few have been prosecuted because Pretoria does not want to lower white morale through the attendant publicity such prosecutions would entail. One reason why such details are not known is that the Defence Act bans publication of all military or paramilitary matters without the approval of military spokesmen, and these spokesmen would rather lose the conscripts than publicise defections or refusals.

A further myth, the significance attached to the claim that Afrikaners are more rooted in South Africa than English-speaking whites are, is based on the fact that the latter have six countries which are English-speaking, and predominantly "white," for purposes of immigra-tion—Canada, the United States, Ireland, the United Kingdom, Australia and New Zealand—whereas Afrikaans is spoken only in South Africa. This myth is also fragile, because: (a) immigration into all these countries is difficult and highly restricted; (b) Afrikaans-speakers would not be linguistically stranded in a number of areas of Holland, Belgium and western West Germany; (c) most Afrikaners can speak English well; and (d) numbers of Afrikaner Nationalists have already indicated an inclination to feel politically at home in Argentina, Bolivia, Chile and Paraguay.

As to commitment, if it is conceded, which it must be, that about three million Afrikaner Nationalist men, women and children would be highly motivated to fight for their supremacy in a homeland legitimately theirs by the long tenure of over 300 years, it is equally clear that more than 20

million black men, women and children would be at least as highly
motivated to fight for the same homeland which is even more
legitimately theirs by the longer tenure of several hundred more years.
The Afrikaner Nationalist claim that there were no indigenous tribesmen
in South Africa when white settlers landed at the Cape of Good Hope in
1652 has no basis in historical fact, although it is assiduously taught in
South African schools. It is part of the self-delusion necessary to preserve a degree of self-justification for apartheid.

(b) *Political realities*
  Self-delusion is fostered in a variety of ways within the white South
African community. This is possible because, in spite of some apparent
signs of an open society—Parliament, an Opposition, some newspapers
free to publish at least a measure of criticism of the State—white South
Africa is in fact a remarkably closed society.
  The State (with which I equate the Broederbond) controls all radio
and television programmes and transmissions, censors books, plays and
films, owns all the Afrikaans-language newspapers, and severely
restricts, by more than a hundred regulations under more than twenty
statutes, what may be published in the English-language press. To give
one example, when the film *South Pacific* was screened in South Africa,
certain scenes were cut, including Cable's song about race prejudice:
"You've got to be taught to hate and fear." News and commentaries, on
radio and television, aim broadly at one vision of South Africa and
another of the world outside. Wherever possible the world outside is
depicted as a place of violence, disaster, economic problems, unemployment, communist influence and decadent frivolity. Earthquakes in Italy,
muggings in New York, race riots in Boston, dole-queues in Britain,
political or economic problems in black-ruled Africa—these are the
most delectably presented items of world news. Conversely, problems in
South Africa are played down as much as possible and literally nothing
adverse to the Pretoria government or its policy is permitted. No critics
of apartheid ever appear on South African television screens to oppose
official policy or testify to the true measure of black anger and resentment.
  Propaganda, as such, is subtly transmitted. A radio programme called
"Survey of Current Affairs" is broadcast daily. Most of the broadcasts
are sober, factual accounts of demonstrably accurate statistics on irriga-
tion, hydro-electricity or industrial development, but interspersed with
these are broadcasts, in the same sober tone of voice, depicting anti-
apartheid students abroad as communists or anti-apartheid churchmen
as subversive. Figures from public life overseas projected as having high
standing include the likes of Ian Paisley, Enoch Powell, Franz-Josef
Strauss and any right-wing Senator or Congressman in the United States
or Member of Parliament in the United Kingdom.

Propaganda both internally and externally emphasises South Africa's "whiteness." Black faces are seldom seen on the television screen. One of the plans mentioned during the Muldergate scandal was to try to bribe the judges of the Miss World contest to choose Miss South Africa—to remind the world of that same whiteness—and sports stars abroad like Gary Player have received government funds to help project the white image. Player was one of the first prominent figures to hold shares in the State-run newspaper, *The Citizen*, an instrument of apartheid propaganda. If the main message to the world is: "There are many whites in South Africa, they are embattled but powerful and basically well-intentioned, they are good business partners and very anti-communist," the main message to whites internally is: "You are better off here than anywhere else in the world—be prepared to defend your privilege." Along with the euphoric picture of idealised life (which would be marred by realistic statistics showing the highest *per capita* incidence of tension-diseases in the world, the highest *per capita* prison-population in the world, the highest *per capita* execution-rate in the world and one of the highest *per capita* crime-rates in the world), goes the necessity to project a level of white unity that does not exist.

(c) *Social and cultural realities*

Few government politicians make a speech without failing to state that Afrikaners and English-speaking (white) South Africans have grown closer and are more united than ever before. In reality, the opposite is the truth. In private each category refers repeatedly to the other in tones of contempt or resentment. Publicly terms of opprobrium such as "hairyback" (Afrikaners) and "Rooinekke" (English-descended) are regarded as jokes, but privately they are often freely expressed with feeling when no member of the other group is present. Essentially the Nationalist Afrikaners regard the English-speaking as being less com-mitted to the fight for apartheid (which is broadly true), too productive of such relatively liberal institutions as the English-language Press, universities and churches, and generally too rich and too dominant in the economy. The English-speaking whites, outnumbered two-to-one by the Afrikaners, resent Afrikaner dominance in politics, the civil service, the military and the multi-national corporations, and tend to look down on most Afrikaners culturally. Generally, the strenuousness with which such feelings are denied publicly is matched only by the vehemence with which they are expressed privately, but by tacit common consent the myth of close unity is seldom openly questioned.

Another myth constantly fed not only to the white South Africans but abroad as often as possible is that South African blacks are deeply divided politically and culturally along tribal lines. But the truth is that tribalism is not the political factor in black South African politics that it is further north, in places like Zimbabwe. Membership and leadership of the ANC, the PAC, and the Black Consciousness Movement (BCM) has consistently been across tribal lines, and in fact tribalism as such is strongly condemned by all three movements. Culturally and linguistically most blacks have more in common than the Afrikaner and English-speaking whites do. The Nguni group of languages (Zulu, Xhosa, Swazi, Ndebele) are all similar and are spoken by some 15 million blacks. Besides, the traditional language of black politics at policy-making and leadership levels is English.

(d) Geographic realities

The question most people abroad must ask themselves about the white leaders of South Africa is: "What are they trying to do?" To that could be added the subsidiary question: "Do they think they will succeed?" The most simple answer to the first is that they (the Broeder-bond, and through them the leaders of the Afrikaner Nationalist Party, and through them the party followers) are trying to perpetuate their political and economic control of South Africa. But again, the answer is not exactly that simple, and an elaboration covers a reply to the second question. Their view of "South Africa" is not precisely the geographic view held by the rest of the world.

In attempting to divide and rule the blacks, the government has designated nine areas, mostly along the perimeter of the country, as "black homelands" which are to be regarded as independent or autonomous, or at least in varying stages of self-rule. Parts of what used to be Zululand were set aside for the Zulus, the Transkei and Ciskei areas for the Xhosas, Vendaland for the Vendas, and so on. This was in preparation for a law which decreed that no blacks could exercise any political rights except in their designated tribal area. This "Bantustan" policy, as it came to be called because for years the official government word for blacks was "Bantu," was and is consistently rejected by almost all blacks, for the following reasons: (i) the Bantustans together add up to no more than 14 per cent. of the land area of South Africa, and blacks do not see why they, 87 per cent. of the population, should be crowded into 14 per cent. of their own country; (ii) the Bantustans are desperately poor areas, with virtually none of the mineral, industrial or agricultural wealth of the country; (iii) blacks deny that their aspirations should be limited to anything less than full civil rights throughout South Africa, where their ancestors lived before the whites came, and they see through the attempt to divide them tribally as well as geographically. So although Broederbonders may claim to be sacrificing parts of South Africa to dilute the political claims of blacks, they are the only people on earth who see matters in that light. None of the countries of the world have yet recognised the independence of any of the Bantustans, nor is any such recognition in prospect.

Such a formula as that of the Bantustans represents Afrikaner

Nationalist gropings for some kind of rationale to justify their position. They want to seem, if only to themselves, to make at least some such gesture in the direction of fairness. Its inadequacy and its rejection focus attention again on the question of whether they think they will succeed in retaining political and economic control. Probably few of them ever confront this question squarely enough to think it through. Arithmetically theirs is such a forlorn hope that possibly the mass unconscious mind of Afrikaner Nationalism has split off from reality to live in a world of wishful thinking where the future need not be considered in any detail. As part of this syndrome, there is possibly a kind of fall-back to the thought that: "If we cannot ultimately prevent black majority rule, at least we can delay it for as long as possible."

(e) *Future realities*

It seems certain that South Africa has the nuclear bomb. What is far less certain is how such a weapon could possibly be used against a black majority most of whom live near to white towns, villages and farms because their labour is needed. Unlike most garrisons under siege, the whites do not confront an enemy across a moat or battlement—their enemy is within the garrison itself, and it numbers five out of every six persons.

How will the final challenge to apartheid come? If the challenge depended on the infiltration of guerrillas alone, it could perhaps be withstood for many years, aided by the possible ineptitude or general inadequacy of the guerrillas themselves. If it depended on urban rioting or urban terrorism alone, this could be contained for as long as its incidence was localised. If it depended on industrial action by black workers alone, such strikes could presumably be broken in key sectors through lavish pay-rises. If it depended solely on rural attacks on outlying farms, as in Zimbabwe, this could probably be endured for at least as long as the white Rhodesians endured it. If it depended on external pressures, such as an oil boycott, alternative sources of crude oil could be found—at exorbitant prices. But the final challenge to apartheid is not likely to be any of these things in isolation. Its force, and the speed of its success, will depend on how many of these events occur in combination. Clearly, if they all occurred simultaneously or came to be occurring simultaneously after becoming factors in the clash one by one, Pretoria could not long remain in control of the situation.

One final factor in the equation is the stance of the super-Powers. The Soviet Union already supports the black side, if only indirectly via arms and money. The United States, even under a conservative Administration, can hardly risk alienating all Africa and the Third World, with the implied threat to trade and investment and in view of Nigeria's oil resources, by appearing too supportive of a detested white minority.

The angry young leaders of South Africa's black townships say with more vehemence in 1981 than ever before: "Black man, you're on your own." While this is not entirely true, it has an ironical ring, because what is more true is what the same young people could well be saying to the executive council of the Broederbond and to the national cabinet of South Africa, when the final phase of the conflict begins: "White man, *you're* on *your* own."

SOUTH AFRICA'S SEARCH FOR A NEW POLITICAL SYSTEM:

THE GOD THAT FAILED AFRIKANERDOM

By

COLIN LEGUM

"Experience teaches us that, generally speaking, the most perilous moment for a bad government is one when it seeks to mend its ways. Only consummate statecraft can enable a king to save his throne, when, after a long spell of oppressive rule, he sets out to improve the lot of his subjects. Patiently endured so long as it seemed without redress, a grievance comes to appear intolerable once the possibility of removing it crosses men's minds."

de Tocqueville

THE world has lived for so long with the problem of apartheid in South Africa that it is now in danger of failing to notice that the apartheid era is approaching its end. This failure to grasp the momentous change occurring in the Republic and the dangerous new period upon which it has entered is explained by the fact that the apartheid *system* itself still exists although the *ideology* of apartheid has already been abandoned. Most political analysts and commentators fail to look beyond the ramparts of the apartheid State to its foundations, where the ideology on which the system rests are already undermined. Without its ideology, the apartheid system must itself inevitably crumble. The only questions are how long it will take—a decade or less? What course will the transition process follow: one of negotiation or violence? Would violence be limited or extensive?

The Afrikaner establishment which drew up the blueprint for the apartheid system, has lost its faith in it; however, while all but a dissident minority have been forced to the realisation that apartheid does not work, they are trapped by indecision about what practical alternative to put in its place.

It has taken the ruling power group within Afrikanerdom 33 embittering and frustrating years to learn that their ideology cannot be translated into effective practice. Their dream has faded of creating a multi-national State based on separate development, which would offer racial harmony, a secure future for the white minority under Afrikaner dominance, and justice for blacks. Instead of the promise of greater racial harmony, it is now widely acknowledged that racial bitterness is greater than before; that the threat to white survival has increased; and that Afrikaner survival itself is no longer assured. The Afrikaners' disillusionment with

125

apartheid has been traumatic, threatening to divide them anew, and setting old comrades-in-arms at each other's throats.

The apartheid experience has taught the country a number of expensive lessons. The most important of these is that economic integration has gone beyond the possibility of either separating the races physically into viable black States and a predominantly white State in any part of the country let alone in the 86 per cent. demarcated for exclusive white control; or of creating parallel white and black economies.

The 1948 elections, which brought the first apartheid régime to power, was fought on the slogan that "White South Africa would be made whiter." The Afrikaner nationalists' pledge was not only to stop the influx of blacks into the "white" urban areas, but to reverse the flow through an efflux of those already there, with a 30-year target date for its achievement. Instead, by 1978, there were almost twice as many blacks in the urban areas as in 1948; and no practical system of achieving influx control had yet been devised.

A central concept of the apartheid ideology was that all urban black workers would become only "temporary sojourners," with no entitlement to citizenship rights or to permanent residence in the "white" areas. That idea has now been officially abandoned. So have two other basic concepts of that ideology. (1) The solution proposed for the country's 750,000 Indians was that they would be offered the choice of repatriation to India, or to stay on as aliens with no political rights in their own segregated residential and business areas—a community living beyond the pale. None accepted repatriation and, instead, they are now being offered representation within the parliamentary system itself. (2) While the 2,500,000 Coloureds were not offered their own separate homeland, their political rights—entrenched in the Constitutions—were to be extinguished to remove even that small element of direct representation they enjoyed in Parliament. A major constitutional crisis was invited and successfully faced during the debate on removing the Coloured people's voting rights. Now a change is proposed to give Coloured voters an even bigger say in Parliament than before their right to vote for only white Members of Parliament was removed from them.

The only aspect of the apartheid ideology which has met with any success at all has been the policy of creating separate black homelands, of which three (Transkei, BophutaTswana and Venda) have already been made "independent," while a fourth (Ciskei) will soon join them. But even in this area of homelands' development there were major setbacks. Three of the homelands still resolutely refuse to accept the form of independence being offered to them. The most important of these is KwaZulu—the "ethnic homeland" of the Zulus, who outnumber the whole of the white population. Moreover, two of the central assumptions behind the creation of "independent" homelands have been falsified by events. The first was a premise that Africans ruling themselves in their own republics would co-operate harmoniously with the "white core State"; in fact, all these relations have been hostile in varying degrees. Even more important, the crisis over the future of urban blacks (always the Achilles heel of apartheid) has grown sharper over the years because they overwhelmingly reject the idea of becoming citizens of their "ethnic homelands" and so losing their claims to full citizenship rights in South Africa. A second premise was that the enlarged homelands could be made economically viable. A Government commission recently concluded that there is no way in which this aim can be achieved—a finding now also accepted by the Minister of Finance, Senator Owen Horwood, who told a monthly business publication, *International Letter* (Paris), that "South Africa is phasing out apartheid because it does not work . . . the plan to set up homelands for the various tribal groups has not proved economically viable."[1]

As the idea of independent homelands was the cornerstone of the separate development envisaged by the apartheid ideology, these failures have been critical in wrecking the plan.

I—The Transition Period

South Africa has already entered on a transition period—away from apartheid towards something quite different and, as yet, unknown. The central issues are no longer whether apartheid can work or not, or whether it is fair or not. Already, the debate in South Africa itself is about the kind of political system that will *replace* apartheid—a system which will require an entirely new constitution; one which will reflect the altered power relations between whites and blacks, which have already occurred; which will allow for the redistribution of the country's resources and the sharing of political and other rights among the four major ethnic communities; and which will offer acceptable safeguards to the white minority community.

While white power groups (especially within Afrikanerdom) have not yet decided on a practical alternative system, they are at the same time unable and/or unwilling to continue to implement all the original ideas of apartheid—except, possibly, in regard to the homelands, population removals, urban influx control and migratory labour.

Seven major features characterise this difficult transition period:

(1) *A time of change.* Concessions are being made to ease the tensions within the society and in response to growing pressures that would otherwise be too difficult to resist. Examples of such concessions are the granting of some political rights to Coloureds and Indians; acceptance of the inevitability of a permanent urban black population; allowing

---

[1] Quoted in *Financial Times* (London), February 4, 1981.

trade-union rights to black workers, albeit under administrative constraints; providing free primary and secondary education for all black
children; easing up considerably on the industrial colour bar. However,
none of these changes fundamentally alters the political status quo in
that it still excludes the black majority from exercising any political
rights in the central Parliament.

(2) *A time of governmental indecision.*   Instead of the formerly assertive
and confident régime, we now have one that is engaged in manipulating
the system in an effort to avoid or, at least, to delay for so long as
possible making fundamental changes. Critics of the régime are right to
point out that all the proposed reforms are intended to maintain white
power by different means, and that they should not be taken seriously as
steps towards changing the political system in any fundamental way.
But the critics make a serious mistake in failing to recognise that
whatever the motives behind the reforms, they are nevertheless fundamentally important in that they do alter the balance in the power relations between whites and blacks—a point that will be presently
elaborated.

Only if success is predicated for the régime's manipulative techniques
in seeking to prolong white minority rule indefinitely, is it in any sense
correct to dismiss all concessions and changes as being no more than
"window-dressing." A more correct interpretation would be to see the
attempts at manipulation during this difficult transition period as only a
necessary stage in a dynamic process of change. Seen in this light, the
régime's attempts at manipulation (*e.g.* by trying to forge a collaborative
partnership between an "inner core" of black élite groups and the white
élite, or to buy off pressures by raising urban wages) are only signs of the
dying paroxysms of apartheid.

(3) *Continuing repression at a time when the Government is seeking to
become less repressive.*   Just as in the pre-revolutionary period in
Russia when the use of the knout flourished alongside a growing
measure of liberalism in education and the political system, so also in
South Africa there is an intensification of repressive measures in some
areas (*e.g.* tighter censorship, further control over the Press and a further
erosion of the rule of law) at the same time as new areas of opportunity
for blacks are being opened up in the economy and in education. These
negative aspects are seen by many simply as evidence of the true face of
a repressive régime; yet it is also possible to see this tightening control
not as evidence of growing reaction but as a response to a situation
which is becoming increasingly harder to control. It could be argued (as
I would) that the régime would much prefer to be less repressive than in
the past if only it could advance safely along the road of reform without
encountering ever-growing opposition. This is the dilemma described by
de Tocqville in the passage quoted at the head of this paper. In terms of
the analysis offered here, a further growth of repression in this period

should be treated as evidence that the ruling power groups have begun to lose their ability to control the situation.

Why, it will be asked, should a régime which has made itself notorious by its harsh laws and tough security measures now wish to behave less repressively? Precisely because it now realises that the repression it used in trying to enforce apartheid has alienated blacks, as well as sections of the white electorate (including Afrikaners) and Western opinion. If the manipulative techniques now being attempted by the régime are to stand any possible chance of success, it becomes necessary (from their point of view) to win over the support of important elements in the black community, and to lessen the violent resentment felt especially by urban blacks.

(4) *Growing divisions within Afrikanerdom.* Despite all the myths about *volkseenheid* (unity of the Afrikaner nation), a careful reading of their history shows that there has been no time in the evolution of the *volk*—from the days of the earliest Cape settlement, through the period of expanding frontiers and the Great Trek, during the Anglo-Boer War and the formative period of the Afrikaner National Party (*circa* 1901–1912), and right up to the commencement of apartheid in 1948—when the Afrikaners were not, in fact, strongly divided notwithstanding their loyalty to common ideals of religion, culture, language and a separate identity from that of English-speaking South Africans.

The ideology of apartheid united the Afrikaners in a way they had never been united before; the apogée of their unity was reached with their first electoral victory in 1948. It remained strong (though not without some early schisms) until the closing period of Dr. Verwoerd's premiership in the early 1960s when more potentially dangerous schisms began to appear with the emergence of the *verkramptes* (inward-looking, rigid conservatives) who formed their own *laager*, albeit a small one, within the *Herstigte Nasionale Party* (HNP). The dividing issue then was over the first signs of retreat from a full-blooded apartheid programme; the HNP correctly foresaw that apartheid was being abandoned step by step. Neverthless, for the sake of the aspiration of *volkseenheid*, the majority of *verkramptes* chose to remain within the ranks of the ruling National Party (NP).

It was during the time of Verwoerd's successor, John Balthazzar Vorster, that the internal schism widened. A second group of Afrikaners, the *verligtes* (the enlightened, more liberal-minded elements) followed Verwoerd's earlier critics in openly advocating a softening of the application of the apartheid ideology by removing what they described as "petty apartheid," *i.e.* laws which they argued exacerbated race relations unnecessarily and which threatened the central strategy of apartheid. However, Afrikanerdom was not polarised between the *verligtes* and the *verkramptes*; both these political extremes within the Afrikaner establishment remained minority groups. The majority formed the Centre, the so-called *standhoudendes* (those who "remained faithful to the stand" of apartheid, but not to the full-blooded version of the ideology expounded by the *verkramptes*). Vorster, while himself some-what more sympathetic to the *verligtes* than to the *verkramptes* (whom he demolished in a power struggle within the Afrikaners' citadel, the Broederbond) remained a man of the Centre.

His successor, P. W. Botha, was a spokesman of the *verligtes*. With his election, the Afrikaner leadership, for the first time since 1948, passed into the hands of an enlightened reformer: in Mrs. Thatcher's language, "a wet." This development produced a much sharper conflict between the two extreme wings of the party, with the Centre still in the majority. It was always possible for Mr. Botha to take on and defeat the *verkramptes*, as Mr. Vorster had succeeded in doing within the Broeder-bond; but unlike his predecessor, Mr. Botha could not be sure of carry-ing the Centre with him. He therefore needed time to prepare the ground and select the issues most likely to win over the Centre; so, while he preached the urgent need for reform, he delayed implementing his own proposal for change. Mr. Botha's tactics made his policies appear ambiguous. On the one hand, they served to rally more support behind the *verkramptes* and, on the other, they spread confusion among supporters of the Centre. This is not the place to argue whether more determined leadership on Mr. Botha's part could not have carried the day; the fact remains that a skilful party tactician, as he has proved himself to be in the past, believed he could not safely move forward with-out more careful preparation.

Thus, at this crucial time of transition, the dominant white power group found itself paralysed by internal splits—with one group wishing to go back to the pure apartheid ideology of 1948; a second group want-ing to march forward to some different political system which was only hazily sketched out; and a third, but the largest, group favouring reform within an adapted apartheid system. The fury and bitterness aroused by these controversies recall the worst times of conflict in Afrikaner ranks, *e.g.* when General J. B. M. Hertzog joined hands with General J. C. Smuts and the English-speaking electorate to form the United Party in 1936.

It is seriously open to question whether, even if Mr. Botha were to succeed in the end in consolidating his hold over the ruling party, the reforms he appears to have in mind would go anywhere near to meeting the minimum demands of even the most moderate of representative black leaders. However, if Mr. Botha were to fail, the immediate out-come would be, at worst, to strengthen the *verkramptes* and, at best, that victory would go to the Centre; in either case, the white leaders during the critical transition period would be much less flexible than Mr. Botha; this would bring closer a violent confrontation between whites and blacks, and so further sharpen the division among the whites themselves.

(5) *Growing black confidence.* The apartheid experience had two results not foreseen by the architects of its ideology, although it was always predictable. The first was to politicise Africans, Coloureds and Indians on a larger scale than ever before, and to thrust them together into a loose black alliance. The second result was greatly to sharpen their militancy, especially of the youth. The rise of a militant Black Consciousness was assisted by the success of the armed struggle movements in the countries on South Africa's borders; the victories since 1974 in Angola, Mozambique and Zimbabwe contributed importantly to bolstering black morale at a time when their own movements, because of bannings and other legal harassments, were unable to offer much serious opposition to apartheid.

The black opposition continues to reflect the complex pluralist nature of South Africa's society, while the choice of political weapons reflects the character of the diverse constituencies as well as differing ideologies, *e.g.* the central importance of an armed struggle as against non-violent but radical political methods of struggle; revolutionary confrontation as opposed to a reformist and constitutional approach; total rejection of any idea of homelands as against the notion of using the homelands as potential centres of political power. Whatever these differences, the black opposition—whether moderate, radical or revolutionary—are agreed on a single objective: the creation of a non-racial society based on the principle of majority rule, *i.e.* total opposition to any idea of adapting the status quo in the direction of a power-sharing constitution which would still leave the white minority in a dominant position.

A close interaction exists between the internal and the external black opposition movements. While foreign opinion tends to give more importance to the exile movements and the still evolving armed struggle, there seems little doubt that, without minimising its potential impact, it is the internal opposition that is crucially important. The nature and development of the internal opposition requires a separate study, but a few general observations are relevant to this particular analysis.

A new generation of black leaders has grown up during the years of apartheid. It is pertinent to recall that every black person under 33 has grown up under apartheid. Despite bannings, imprisonment and the outlawing of successive organisations, black politics are much livelier today than at the beginning of the apartheid era: they have moved from the periphery of the political stage to the centre. Political groupings are now to be found in practically every area in the country: all the homelands have their own forms of government and rival political parties which are closer to the grassroots than before; *Inkhata*, the movement led by KwaZulu's Chief Minister, Gatsha Buthelezi, is now the largest legal black political party in the country's history. Each of the major urban areas has evolved its own pattern of political organisations, ranging from students' and parents' associations and social welfare groups to trade unions and commercial associations. The role of the black churches is particularly significant; so are the local community action groups. Young blacks are engaged in raising community consciousness: it is the youth rather than the older generation which provides urban leadership. Opposition appears to be growing in favour of boycotting any institution, group or individuals identified with the administration or the white establishment; all contacts with such bodies or groups are regarded as "collaborationist"; but this boycott idea does not extend to a refusal to work with individual whites or particular groups not identified with the régime or groups supportive of the system. This attitude represents a trend of thinking among urban black youths rather than the dominant element in the black opposition. Nevertheless, this militancy acts as a constraint on more moderately-minded elements. In the eyes of young militants all concessions and signs of change are contemptuously rejected as "window-dressing."

Thus, at a time when white attitudes are beginning to show signs of change, black attitudes (especially among the young) are changing in the direction of total confrontation with white power. Should this trend continue to grow, as seems likely, and should the white power groups continue to delay fundamental changes, it will become increasingly harder to achieve any negotiated constitutional settlement.

(6) *Change in the balance of internal power.*   Before 1948 and, indeed, up to the early 1970s, the black society was to a very large extent composed of a passive, patient and unorganised mass of people having little confidence in their ability to challenge the dominant white society and possessed of little economic or political leverage on the system. The situation today is quite different in a number of major respects. Black political organisations are no longer so weak and confined mainly to the modern élites, or lacking in institutional strength. Black consumer power has greatly increased and is already a major factor in the country's economy. Black workers now play a larger and more responsible role in industry and commerce, and are no longer present simply as unskilled workers or in lowly positions; they are now more centrally entrenched within the economy. Black trade unions, though still relatively weak, are already capable of organising support behind both industrial and political demands, and can be curbed only by the use of force disruptive of the political process and of industry. The urban black communities have already demonstrated their potential for resistance as, for example, in the uprisings of the Soweto youth on two occasions, and the extensive school boycotts in Capetown and Port Elizabeth. The opportunities provided by the homelands' institutions have created new centres for legal political opposition which were not available before. Finally, the external support now enjoyed by the black opposition—from African States, the communist world as well as the West—has added a new dimension to their capacity to organise themselves and, no less

importantly, has greatly strengthened their morale. Moreover, this element of international intervention has become a significant constraint on the South African Government's use of its power.

(7) *Growing uncertainty among whites about their future.* This loss of certainty is unquestionably the most profound change that has taken place during the years of apartheid. In 1948, white South Africans were totally confident, indeed arrogantly so, of their ability to maintain their supremacy. They felt they could count on the superiority of their political, economic and military power, and on their numbers, to withstand any onslaught against themselves. The feeling now is quite different. The extent to which gnawing doubts about white survival has seeped into their community is widely reflected in the speeches and writings of prominent men, particularly among Afrikaners themselves. Typical of this new attitude is the analysis presented by Willem de Klerk, a considerable figure in Afrikaner circles, writing in a pro-Government newspaper[2]: "If I choose uncertainty as the theme for the starting-point of the New Year, it is anything but the uncertainty of what 1981 holds for us about which I am writing. It is specifically about the uncertainty among whites (and Afrikaners) about our political future. It lies at the heart of virtually every political discussion; uncertainty about whether there are enough guarantees for white authority (*seggenskap*) and whether we are not possibly on a slippery slope ... The content of this uncertainty is that we, the whites, are increasingly worried about whether the black peoples will push us out of our environment (*leefwereld*); whether they will push us in the direction of power-sharing; and whether they will then overwhelm us with their numbers to establish a black majority government and thereafter destroy the kernel of our *volk*, its traditions, its rights and its opportunities for existence.

"This is somewhat sharply formulated, but I am convinced that the great majority of whites more or less regularly have passing thoughts about this, or that they sit and brood about it. Nor can we really hide it from the blacks. They know it; they mock it; and they even frighten us with their threats about what will happen on the day of reckoning."

De Klerk then goes on to say that the questions raised by this uncertainty cannot be safely tucked out of sight, and proceeds to describe the core of the problem as he sees it: "We cannot maintain ourselves through our numbers, whatever the arguments to the contrary. In terms of white/black ratio we are not significant; the ratio between the Afrikanervolk and other nations in South Africa makes us a minority, with no casting vote; the ratio between the skilled and the blacks' lack of training (and all that goes with this) will lessen. Whoever has the advantage in terms of labour power and growth in the numbers being trained can determine the pace. (By the end of this century there will be

---

[2] *Rapport* (Johannesburg), January 4 and 11, 1981. The translation is that of the author of this paper.

more black and brown graduates, with comparable qualifications, than all the Afrikaners put together). We cannot maintain ourselves through military power. Such power has never succeeded throughout history. Armed force is only a very short-term answer. It leads to terrible consequences and the overthrow of order; to war with international dimensions involving ourselves, because the big powers desire what we have. A black 'independence war,' with bullets, terror, strikes, crime, violence, all against the background of Communism in Southern Africa. Good, we will hold out and hold out and, perhaps, still hold out—until we break."

Similar statements to de Klerk's appear regularly in Afrikaans political and academic publications. The real significance of this loss of white certainty about their future is that the Afrikaners now feel themselves to be on the defensive—a complete reversal of the situation in 1948. They have come to understand that their political and economic power is not limitless, and that time is no longer on their side: two ideas with which white South Africans have always comforted themselves in the past.

What this means in cold political terms is that the white power groups have begun to understand that they can no longer expect to maintain control on their own terms. Manipulative techniques can, at best, be only a short-term expedient. In the words of Prime Minister Botha: "We must adapt or die. Revolution is not a remote possibility. It can only be averted if the Government looks at the interests of all population groups, not just of the Whites."

Can the process of catering for black interests be stopped once it gets properly under way? Those who oppose Mr. Botha—like General Hendrik van den Berg, the former head of South Africa's Bureau of State Security (BOSS)—argued that: "The systematic removal of discriminatory measures and other crash programmes for improving the quality of life must inevitably lead to the removal of the final form of discrimination—political discrimination."[3]

The General is no less realistic in some of his other statements, *e.g.* that "the urban black population is the Achilles heel of the ruling party"; that the battle for the support of the black élite has already been lost; that the greatest threat to the country is not a "total onslaught" by external forces, but comes from the country's internal political and social circumstances; that South Africa is in "a classic pre-revolutionary situation."

II—Is There a Way Out
of South Africa's Dilemma?

At the approaching end of the apartheid era, most South Africans, white and black, are in substantial agreement that the country now faces a straight choice between reform or revolution. Even a professional

---

[3] *The Star* (Johannesburg), February 4, 1981.

optimist like Mr. Harry Oppenheimer, chairman of the Anglo-American Corporation, has expressed the view that South Africa now has, perhaps, five years in which to put its own house in order or else face armed revolution. And, as already cited above, Prime Minister Botha has warned that the possibility of revolution cannot be ruled out. Only the Afrikaner *ultras* still cling to their obstinate view that it is still possible to maintain a status quo based on white supremacy; but while this minority group is capable of frustrating meaningful reform, any success they have in that direction would only contribute to opening the floodgates to revolution.

Two serious obstacles stand in the way of fulfilling the hopes of the great majority of South Africans who favour reform: the problem of reaching agreement on an acceptable new constitution; and how to persuade the white electorate about the imperative need to accept bold constitutional reforms—reforms which, if they are to be acceptable also to the black majority—would necessarily extinguish their present exclusive right to make the laws of the land.

Where in history has a powerful minority ever surrendered its power, except when under irresistible pressure? While the pressures on the present system are already heavy, and while they will predictably continue to grow, the point has not yet been reached where a substantial part of the white electorate believe they cannot hold out—if not indefinitely, then at least for the foreseeable future. If the time still left for reforms is indeed anything as short as that indicated by Mr. Oppenheimer—or even twice as long as the five years he mentioned—the prospects of getting the consent of the white electorate must be judged to be very slim indeed. This would suggest that South Africa is heading in a revolutionary direction rather than towards change through reforms.

Yet, is this necessarily so? Is it the only possible interpretation of how the conflict situation is likely to develop? A different way of evaluating the competing elements in the power struggle would require making different assumptions about the rigidity, or unbreakable unity, of the Afrikaners than is generally believed to be the case, as well as about the black challengers' willingness, or capacity, to engage in a full-blooded revolutionary struggle. This different approach would also require that we treat *violence* and the sense of *white insecurity* as positive rather than as negative factors in the process of change.

While it remains a possibility that the sense of white insecurity could result in a majority of Afrikaners swinging towards the *verkramptes* in making a last-ditch stand, it is no less likely that they might choose to follow the Afrikaner establishment, provided only that Mr. Botha can succeed in his aim of uniting the *verligtes* and the Centre of the ruling party, as well as of winning the support of the English-speaking electorate. Mr. Botha could then begin to introduce the economic, social and political changes he has so far only talked about. One of these reforms would be to begin transforming the character of parliament from being an exclusively white parliament into a multi-racial body by, at first, introducing an element of Coloured and Indian representation into it. This tardy reform, which would still exclude the black majority from the central political system, would assuredly serve only to deepen the country's internal contradictions. The majority of Coloureds and, perhaps also of Indians, would substantially boycott the elections for their representatives to a parliament that would exclude Africans. Nevertheless, even if Coloured and Indian representatives were to be elected on minority votes, their election would end the era of an all-white parliament, while their votes would further strengthen Botha's position in parliament. At the same time, the representation of the minority non-white communities in parliament would only serve to point up the glaring inequity of a parliament with no African representation. Since the apartheid régime has already decided that urban blacks must be treated as a permanent element in "white South Africa," and not simply as an extension of the homelands, the next obvious move would be to include them in the parliamentary system. Thus, step by step, the principle of a multi-racial parliament would be established. The methods whereby this was achieved should be seen as *techniques* for circumventing the present veto powers of the Nationalists' parliamentary caucas and of eroding the influence of the white electorate, as well as a means of getting whites to accommodate themselves to the inevitability of power-sharing.

However, the black majority could not possibly be expected to be satisfied with the minority share of the power that would initially be offered to them and would therefore, predictably, continue their struggle by a variety of methods, including boycotts, strikes and a greater element of violence, such as urban "terrorism." Such a rising level of violence, coming from both internal and external sources, would provide further positive evidence of the limits of white power and of the inadequacies of limited reforms. The interaction between greater *violence* and a greater sense of *white insecurity*—with its predictable impact on the economy—could fairly rapidly produce a situation in which the alternative of accepting the need to make fundamental constitutional reforms would become irresistible.

At some point during this process of increasing conflict, the army leadership might be expected to play a more decisive role—as is already happening. The present army hierarchy is fully on the side of the *verligtes*, and might reasonably be expected to remain so. The likeliest assumption is not that South Africa would come under army rule, let alone that it would become a military dictatorship, but that the civilian power would come to rest more firmly on army support rather than on the Afrikaner electorate. This would force a different choice on Afrikaners: loyalty to their army or to Afrikaner unity. In such a situation the army should be seen as a positive force for change.

The culmination of the political process suggested by this alternative analysis would be an agreement to hold a National Convention of representative white and black leaders to work out an acceptable new constitution. White and black South Africans are already broadly agreed about the need for a new constitutional dispensation; only the Afrikaner *ultras*—a tiny minority of the whole population—still dissents from the broad consensus on this issue. There is no shortage of constitutional models to satisfy the country's complex problems and needs. Alternative models have been exhaustively debated for a number of years in white political circles. They include differing versions of partition; a variety of federal proposals; confederalism along the lines of an adapted Swiss system; a "constellation" of independent States, functionally linked through economic institutions, as favoured by Mr. Botha.

The snag about these alternative constitutional proposals is that, so far, none of the representative black leaders has been ready to join in the debate. Leaders like Oliver Tambo of the African National Congress and Chief Gatsha Buthelezi are at one in their approach to a programme of constitutional reform which, in their view, must contain two basic principles: majority rule and a non-racial (as distinct from multi-racial) society. They are also in agreement that the precise details of any constitution incorporating these principles should be worked out at a conference of the effective representatives of all four racial communities. (It is important to note that the question of whether South Africa should be a unitary or a federal State is not a contentious issue among black leaders.)

This idea of a National Convention finds wide support in African, Coloured and Indian political circles. It is also endorsed by the official parliamentary opposition, the Progressive Reform Party; and it is finding increasing support among Afrikaner intellectuals. Only the ruling National Party remains strongly opposed to the idea. This obviously constitutes a formidable impediment; yet a National Convention could provide the ultimate way out of the impasse that would inevitably be reached once the present phase of limited reforms has been exhausted—a phase which, predictably, could not last for longer than 10 years at most and, more probably, for less than that time.

CONCLUSIONS

The apartheid era is approaching its end. In historical terms, apartheid will be seen to have been the watershed between a white-ruled South Africa and a majority-ruled South Africa. The Republic has now entered upon a dangerous period of transition from the old order to the new. The white minority has not yet lost its *will* to rule, but it has begun to lose *confidence* in its ability to retain exclusive political control. Afrikaners, who remain the dominant political element, have no clearly thought-out strategy for what should take the place of the god that failed them: apartheid. They are engaged in a strategy for maintaining control and for white survival, while trying to formulate their ideas about how to achieve the latter objective. The Afrikaner electorate remains the rock core of resistance to meaningful change, and no Afrikaner leader is powerful enough to push through a policy of bold reforms in the teeth of this opposition. Although the present government leadership is potentially capable of influencing white opinion, it remains under severe constraints when it comes to implementing even limited reforms involving the dismantling of the apartheid system.

While the white ruling groups have been pushed on to the defensive, the black majority now feels confident that the tide has already changed in its favour. Although black political organisations are far from being united, no disagreement exists over objectives as between moderates, radicals and revolutionaries; only their tactics are different.

The choices facing South Africa are reform or revolution, with the time-factor now crucially important in determining which of the alternative routes the Republic will take in the post-apartheid era.

An analysis of the present situation which rests on the principal assumption that Afrikaners cannot under any circumstances be moved away from their inflexible opposition to fundamental constitutional changes, leads to the conclusion that revolutionary change is unavoidable. A different analysis, taking a more dynamic view of the interaction between growing black pressures and the limits of white powers of control, as well as of the impact of sharpening internal contradictions, suggests that a constitutional settlement still remains a possibility—even if, as seems most likely, the transition period is marked by increasing repression and greater violence. The white society does not see repression as either desirable or as an effective way of safeguarding its future; nor do the black challengers regard violence from their side as desirable, but rather as a necessary, though minor, element in their struggle. These two trends should be interpreted as inevitable elements in the process of drastic change now occurring in South Africa.

THE AFRICAN CONDITION:

PROPHECIES AND POSSIBILITIES

By

TIMOTHY M. SHAW

> "Ex Africa semper aliquid novi"
> —Pliny the Elder, *Natural History,* Book Eight.

> "What comes out of Africa is neither new nor exciting, nor seeming likely to be such, but what is old, predictable and boring. The liberating nationalism of twenty and thirty years ago was nearly always a joyful lift to the spirit ... the formative experience of Africa's under-30s one of deepening crisis apparently beyond cure by any familiar remedy; whether ... in a painfully large and spreading gap between the few rich and many poor, or in political systems which falter or collapse, or in the broadening shadow of inter-state rivalry and conflict. More and more often, from all I hear, there is a new consciousness of choice: that Africa must revolutionise itself and soon; or go, and sooner, entirely to the devil."
> —Basil Davidson, "Beyond the flags and anthems,"
> *New Statesman,* March 24, 1978, pp. 391–392.

> "To know the future we must look into the past and the present"
> —A. M. Babu, "Postscript" to W. Rodney, *How Europe Underdeveloped Africa*
> (1972), p. 316.

> "(ECA projections) show abundantly clearly how poor Africa's performance has been in the last decade and a half, and how dim the prospects are for the rest of the century, assuming the persistence of the present mix of public policies in most African countries and assuming also the continuation of the present international economic system. Even if Third World countries succeed in bringing about a fundamental restructuring in the world economic order, unless there is a corresponding restructuring of the economic order at the national and regional levels in Africa, the region as a whole will benefit only marginally, if at all, from changes in the world order."
> —Adebayo Adedeji, "Africa: The Crisis of Development and the Challenge of a New Economic Order. Address to the Fourth Meeting of the Conference of Ministers and Thirteenth Session of the Economic Commission for Africa, Kinshasa, February-March 1977" (Addis Ababa: ECA, 1977), pp. 4–5.

> "Africa has no future"
> —V. S. Naipaul, *New York Times Book Review,* May 15, 1979, p. 36.

THE continent of Africa is poised half-way between the achievement or recapture of formal "independence" in the early 1960s and the year 2000. The first 20-year period has been characterised by a rediscovery of Africa's identity as well as by a realisation of the continent's unpromising inheritance; the second 20-year period is likely to be characterised by a reconsideration of established development strategies, as the opening quotation from Basil Davidson suggests, as well as by a recognition that divergent responses pose difficulties for the continent as

139

a whole.[1] In short, the rest of this century may be a period of insecurity and instability and of decay and disintegration at national, regional and continental levels.[2]

However, out of this process of reflection, re-evaluation and reorganisation—a second African revolution—may emerge a transformed continent, one no longer constrained by a pervasive inheritance of dependence and underdevelopment. But this transition will be protracted and painful, resisted by established interests both within and outside Africa. Without such a transformation, however, the future may be even less promising, as projections indicate a growing gap between demand and supply. Forecasts and foresight require, therefore, that Africa reconsiders its past inheritance and performance both to avoid difficulties expected in the mid-term future and to transcend the dilemmas anticipated in the second set of social transformations. In sum, Africa's next 20-year period may involve more contradictions, conflicts and changes than the first post-independence era, so adding support to Pliny's own observation about the continent.

A further vindication of Pliny's remark is found in the 1979 BBC *Reith Lectures* by Ali A. Mazrui, the first series to be given by an African scholar. In his catholic and controversial *tour d'horizon*, Mazrui highlights a number of paradoxes, including those of poverty amidst plenty and marginality despite centrality: "The continent itself seems to be well endowed with resources but a disproportionate number of people in the population of the continent is undernourished and underprivileged. Africa is the most centrally located of all the continents, but politically it is perhaps the most marginal. This anomaly has implications for *pax Africana*...."[3]

I—AFRICA'S INHERITANCE

Such paradoxes, or contradictions, cannot be explained without reference to Africa's past. And if the continent's contemporary constraints are a function of its past, then its future, as indicated in the quotation from A. M. Babu, is the result of both past and present. But, despite the caution of Adebayo Adedeji and the gloom of V. S. Naipaul, Africa may have a promising future if it can overcome its inadequate inheritance and transcend current contradictions (see Section V below).

Future studies are rather underdeveloped on the continent. But they have already had an impact, as seen in the April 1980 Lagos Declara-

[1] For an overview of these projections and policy responses see T. M. Shaw (ed.), *Alternative Futures for Africa* (1981).

[2] For several different forecasts and scenarios see C. Legum *et al.*, *Africa in the 1980s: a continent in crisis* (1977); Helen Kitchen (ed.), *Africa: from mystery to maze* (1976); and Jennifer Seymour Whitaker (ed.), *Africa and the United States: vital interests* (1978).

[3] A. A. Mazrui, *The African Condition: a political diagnosis* (1980), pp. 72 and 116.

tion on the creation of an African Economic Community for the year 2000. This first-ever African economic summit was a response by the continent's leadership to various warnings by the Economic Commission for Africa (ECA), both from its Executive-Secretary, Dr. Adedeji, and also from a joint Organisation of African Unity (OAU)/ECA symposium on the future (under-) development of Africa to the year 2000.[4] But alternative policies and plans take time to effect. Meanwhile, the prospects for satisfying Basic Human Needs (BHN) or for augmenting continental autonomy are receding as recession and inflation in the North intensify the developmental difficulties of the South.[5]

II—Africa's Future

As if Africa's past and present were not sufficiently cautionary, projections based on such trends point to major problems before the end of the present century. As Dr. Adedeji warns, "Africa, more than any other third world region, is faced with a development crisis of great portent."[6] Forecasts based on established data suggest that inequalities both within and between African States will continue to increase, with profound implications for national, regional and continental integration. However, given the pessimism of most projections, there is little incentive to retain current strategies and linkages. Instead, Africa might either adopt a greater degree of self-reliance (national and collective) or experience a series of more-or-less revolutionary changes. Hence the attempt to design the continent's future despite the apparent limitations of post-independence planning at the national level.[7] If OAU/ECA-sponsored restructuring is either insufficient or ineffective, then Africa may be further impoverished and marginalised into the twenty-first century.

The major features of Africa's rather depressing prospects are now reasonably clear and agreed, as suggested in Tables One and Two. According to the World Bank's *World Development Report for 1979*, the continent's economy is projected to grow less rapidly than that of

---

[4] See A. Adedeji, "Development and economic growth in Africa to the year 2000: alternative projections and policies," and "Africa towards the year 2000: final report on the joint OAU/ECA symposium on the future development of Africa," in Shaw (ed.), *op. cit.* in note 1, above, Chap. 11 and App. C.

[5] On the North-South confrontation see, *inter alia*, *North-South: a programme for survival* (1980), IBRD, *World Development Report, 1980* (1980), and T. M. Shaw, *Towards an International Political Economy for the 1980s: from dependence to (inter)dependence* (1980).

[6] A. Adedeji, "Africa: the crisis of development and the challenge of a new economic order. Address to the Fourth Meeting of the Conference of Ministers and the Thirteenth Session of the Economic Commission for Africa, Kinshasa, February-March 1977" (1977), p. 8.

[7] On the prospects for self-reliance and planning see T. M. Shaw, "From dependence to self-reliance: Africa's prospects for the next twenty years," 35 *International Journal* (1980), pp. 821–844; and "On projections, prescriptions and plans: towards an African future," 14 *Quarterly Journal of Administration* (1980).

any other region: at a rate of about 4 per cent. per annum between 1980 and 1990. But given the continued high level of population growth, the Gross Domestic Product (GDP) *per capita* may rise by just over 1 per cent. per annum over the decade. This "dismal outlook" is related to Africa's inheritance of dependence and underdevelopment: very open economies in which there are neither sufficient gross domestic savings (less than half of the Third-World average of 22 per cent. of GDP) or investments, but which exhibit an over-reliance on foreign assistance and capital, and inadequate agricultural and industrial production along with an overemphasis on "services" or bureaucracy. Hence an increase in

Table One: Alternative Growth Rates for Africa:
by Income Category and GDP

Countries by income categories at 1970 prices	Growth Rates (%)		Shares of Africa's total GDP (%)		
	1962–75	Forecast	1975	1980	1990
Major oil exporters	6.9	7.5	34.5	37.9	45.0
Non oil-exporting countries					
Between $300–400 per capita	5.8	6.0	8.6	8.8	9.0
Between $200–300 per capita	4.1	5.0	30.0	29.0	27.2
Between $100–200 per capita	4.1	4.0	13.6	12.6	10.6
Below $100 per capita	2.6	2.5	13.1	11.3	8.2
Total non oil-exporting countries	4.0	4.4	65.5	62.1	55.0
Total developing Africa	4.9	5.5	100.0	100.0	100.0

Source: ECA estimates cited in Adebayo Adedeji "The crisis of development and the challenge of a new economic order in Africa."

Table Two:
Alternative Growth Rates for Africa: by Subregion and GDP per Capita

Subregions	Growth Rates (%)			Income Per Capita (US $)		
	1962/64– 1972/74	Forecast 1975–85	1985–90	1975	1985	1990
Northern	4.2	5.9	5.6	559	990	1,300
Sahel	−0.5	3.1	3.3	157	212	249
Western	3.0	5.3	5.7	322	538	708
Central	2.3	3.0	3.3	322	431	506
Eastern and Southern	2.4	3.0	3.4	231	311	368
Total Africa	3.1	4.9	5.0	342	551	703

Source: FAO *Regional Food Plan for Africa*, (1978) 54.

external indebtedness to about 10 per cent. of exports is projected. By 1985, the World Bank expects Africa's debt-servicing burden to double to equal 20 per cent. of exports and to increase further to 28 per cent. by 1990.

The World Bank's latest projections may be more pessimistic than those of the ECA or the Food and Agriculture Organisation (FAO) as indicated in the tables. However, even if Africa's short-term growth rate is 5 per cent. rather than 1 per cent. per annum, the benefits of such growth will be unevenly distributed both between regions and between types of countries. The richer States in Table One and richer regions in Table Two are expected to grow faster than the poorer States and regions. So Algeria, Gabon, Libya and Nigeria on the one hand and Congo (Brazzaville), *Côte d'Ivoire*, Tunisia and Zambia on the other hand are predicted to grow faster than, say, Benin, Sudan or Tanzania. And the already more affluent Northern and Western regions are anticipated to become relatively richer in comparison to Central, Eastern and Southern, and Sahelian regions.

Moreover, inequalities are expected to intensify within, as well as between, States, further retarding the prospects of meeting BHN by the end of the century. And while African States remain vulnerable to external pressures and events, their national and collective power remains embryonic. Planning is essential if two prerequisites of national development and order are to be achieved; namely, the satisfaction of BHN and the realisation of effective national power. Until most peoples on the continent have sufficient food, water, housing, educational and health facilities and until African régimes have sufficient financial, industrial, educational and strategic resources and reserves, sovereignty will remain a chimera. But neither of these goals—BHN and power—can be achieved easily, involving as they do difficult choices for, and considerable resistance from, both internal and external forces.

III—AFRICA'S RESPONSE

The dominant reaction in Africa to the elusiveness of BHN and power—one that is reflected in the April 1980 Lagos Economic Declaration—is self-reliance. But this development-orientation is as problematic as it is popular. So whilst contained incorporation with the world system is recognised to be deleterious, alternative strategies remain ambiguous in results or idealistic in conception. Nevertheless, the meagre benefits of external association and the emerging problems of extroversion in the 1980s have generated a new scepticism and creativity amongst analysts and activists.

Continued incorporation within the world system has led to neither growth nor redistribution for the majority of States and peoples in

Africa.[8] Rather it has facilitated structural as well as politico-military intervention by extra-continental interests. The former, structural, incorporation has advanced furthest in the case of the select few "semi-industrial" countries on the continent. Unlike the majority of "peripheral" States, this minority in the "semi-periphery" has increased its rate of growth through association with the countries and corporations of the "centre": *i.e.* the OECD.[9] But the benefits of such interaction are not available to either the majority of States in Africa or to the majority of peoples living within the semi-periphery itself. It is not available either because of internal opposition (the national or comprador bourgeoisie is minimal) or external disinterest (national markets and resources are marginal). In particular, resistance from excluded workers, peasants and unemployed, as well as from alternative fractions of the ruling class, make a sustained semi-industrial strategy problematic.

To avoid such opposition and instability, resort may have to be made to populism and rhetoric. Philippe Lemaitre suggests that: "If any of the successful semi-industrialising states follow a 'China model' they may become very ideological; in all probability they will be 'Marxist-Leninist.' Those which follow a 'Brazil model' may eschew ideological language entirely; or they may invent various original ideologies, largely nationalist and a bit xenophobic in content. The doctrine of 'authenticity' now preached in Zaire may be a foretaste of such ideologies."[10] But semi-industrialisation is not an option for most African countries and peoples. And as the processes of dependency and underdevelopment intensify, the structural and temporal crises of the majority as well as the minority will be exacerbated. For them the choice is not sovereignty but survival. As Thomas Kanza argues, "There are only two choices for Africa: survival or suicide."[11]

Claude Ake, however, raises the prospect of a third way, neither semi-industrialisation with continued dependence nor self-reliance via disengagement. This third possibility—fascism—is, Ake argues, related to the particular form of political economy presently found in Africa in which neither revolution nor reform are readily realisable. Instead, given the unpromising projections and trends and given the elusiveness of both dependent capitalism on the one hand and self-reliance on the other hand, Ake suggests that a " . . . third historic possibility which lies before Africa is a march to fascism. This could come about in a situation where

---

[8] See T. M. Shaw and M. J. Grieve, "Dependence as an approach to understanding continuing inequalities in Africa," 13 *Journal of Developing Areas* (1979), pp. 229–246; and "The political economy of resources: Africa's future in the global environment," 16 *Journal of Modern African Studies* (1978), pp. 1–32.

[9] See T. M. Shaw, "The semi-periphery in Africa and Latin America: sub-imperialism and semi-industrialisation," 9 *Review of Black Political Economy* (1979), pp. 341–358.

[10] P. Lemaitre, "Who will rule Africa by the year 2000?," in Helen Kitchen (ed.), *op. cit.* in note 2, above, p. 274.

[11] T. Kanza, *Evolution and Revolution in Africa* (1978), p. 79.

there was protracted economic stagnation, but not yet revolution . . . one thing that would surely be needed in ever increasing quantities in this situation would be repression. . . . It would appear that the choice for Africa is not between capitalism and socialism after all, but between socialism and barbarism. Which will it be?"[12] One reason for the possibility of fascism arising in Africa is the disjunction between apparent political power and real economic poverty. In such a situation, ruling classes cannot maintain themselves through economic development or redistribution because they do not control such processes as these are externally-determined. Rather, they can only retain political hegemony through the exertion of authority over the means of control, the means of production being foreign-owned: "The effects of the global struggle on the relation between the ruling classes of African countries and those of the bourgeois countries are very important. Against the background of economic and technological dependence of African countries, we may call this relation a patron-client relation. These contradictions are connected and may be treated collectively as one major contradiction: the one between political power and economic power. The African ruling class is the political power while the ruling class of the bourgeois countries is the economic power. The reality of economic dependence limits the political power of the African ruling class, while the reality of the political power of the African ruling class may to some extent limit the economic power of the ruling class of the bourgeois countries to manipulate and exploit Africa. The limitations frustrate both sides, and the parties involved strive to overcome them. So, despite the fact that the interests of the African ruling classes coincide in some respects, the two classes are also in struggle."[13]

The emerging response to such contemporary and continuing contradictions and to (under-) development through (inter-) dependence is to advocate some form of disengagement and self-reliance. Adedeji and the ECA reflect this new perspective: the "imperative that African states should reformulate their policies and economic strategies and instruments with a view to promoting national and collective self-reliance."[14] Self-reliance means not more of the same—*i.e.* more foreign finance, technology, skills, and exchange—but rather a fundamental reassessment of all external linkages. Instead of the criteria for development being externally—or internationally—defined they would be based on internal needs (not wants). Such a break, or decoupling, would be designed to maximise internal exchange and national autonomy and to overcome externally oriented growth and local disarticulation. It would also

---

[12] C. Ake, *Revolutionary Pressures in Africa* (1978), p. 67.
[13] *Ibid.* pp. 27–28.
[14] A. Adedeji, *op. cit.* in note 6, above, p. 18.

improve the prospects of avoiding the potential problems posed by pro-jections for the continent based on present trends.

The general adoption of self-reliance would advance African develop-ment in at least three ways. First, it would improve the rate and quality of development at the *national* level. Secondly, it would enhance autonomy and unity at the *continental* level. And thirdly, by reviving African institutions and images it would advance the continent's interests at the *global* level. It would serve to reduce, therefore, the tendency of fragmentation in the national and continental political economies and to support Africa's collective demands for a New Inter-national Economic Order.

Collective self-reliance would tend to minimise the dangers of a few semi-peripheral countries emerging on the continent to replace indigenous continental institutions as the focus of linkages between global and national régimes. But given the demise of Pan-Africanism, the essential, intermediate, continental level of agreement is likely to prove the most problematic. As Adedeji himself remarks: "Regionally, there is an urgent need for concentrating on achieving an increasing measure of collective self-reliance among African states. . . . Indeed, economic cooperation among African states is a *sine qua non* for the achievement of national socio-economic goals, and not an 'extra' to be given thought to after the process of development is well advanced. African states have also to learn very soon how to insulate economic cooperation institutions and arrangements from the vagaries of political differences."[15]

It is the intensification of such inequalities and differences—based increasingly on sub-structural rather than on super-structural factors—that poses a challenge to African solidarity as well as to its self-reliance. The emergence of a group of more socialist régimes with the "second wave" of decolonisation (especially in Southern Africa) and revolution (especially in middle Africa) undermines the easy consensus that characterised continental politics in the mid- to late-1960s. There is now a strong and growing faction in the OAU that defines development and foreign policy in more materialist terms based on somewhat dialectical assumptions. It is no longer persuaded by the rhetoric of Pan-Africanism and good neighbourliness. And it conceives of self-reliance as an adjunct to socialism rather than as an aspect of embourgeoise-ment. Such alternative definitions and expectations of self-reliance at both national and regional levels may come to pose problems for Africa in planning and projecting, let alone seizing, the future. As Kanza notes: "The African states are still undecided as to which economic system they should adopt, although such a choice is fundamental to national development, planning and economic expansion. . . . [They] are increas-

---

[15] *Ibid.* p. 16.

ingly finding themselves faced with an absolute choice: should they adopt the traditional capitalist method, which means, in effect, dependence on foreign capital and subordination of their own development to the special interests of monopoly capitalism? Or should they, on the contrary, take the socialist road and plan their development rationally in the general interest of Africa and its people?"[16]

IV—AFRICA'S DILEMMAS

Despite threatening forecasts and hortatory pleas from the ECA and other institutions—and despite the 1980 Lagos Economic Declaration—Africa exhibits a considerable caution in adopting and advancing self-reliance. Notwithstanding, prevailing prophecies about exponential inequalities, if Africa does not seize the opportunity to begin adopting self-reliance soon, the opportunity will pass, with profound implications for regional cohesion and compatibility. According to Lemaitre, "the next 15 to 25 years present relatively positive opportunities for Africa's semi-industrialising countries, but a bleak picture for the largely agricultural ones. The minority able to exploit such an opportunity include Algeria, Nigeria, Zaire, the politically special case of South Africa, possibly Egypt, perhaps Zambia and Morocco, one day (but only later in time?) Angola."[17] This minority in the semi-periphery may become further integrated into the OECD nexus, so advancing its own strategy of semi-industrialisation. The majority in the periphery, however, will continue to stagnate and even regress, becoming further marginalised.

For the small, weak, open, agriculturally-based and highly-dependent States of Africa national self-reliance may not only be a preferred policy; it may be an inevitability as disengagement is "forced" upon the Fourth World by the integration of First, (Second?), and Third Worlds.[18] I. W. Zartman points to some possible problems related to such increasing inequalities on the continent, with their policy as well as political implications: "By the 1980s, the spread in the level of power sources is certain to increase, even dramatically. Within the decade, Algeria or Nigeria may be more developed economically than South Africa, and Zaire might also be included in the list . . . several effects are likely to ensue. First, the more developed members may become more attractive to outside influence, even if greater amounts of influence will now be required in order to have an effect. Second, at this stage of development, internal gaps between socio-economic levels are likely to be magnified, as are also gaps between the states which have surged

---

[16] T. Kanza, *op. cit.* in note 11, above, pp. 70–71.

[17] P. Lemaitre, *op. cit.* in note 10, above, p. 266.

[18] See T. M. Shaw, "Dependence to (inter)dependence: review of debate on the (New) International Economic Order," 4 *Alternatives* (1979), pp. 557–578.

forward and those many others which have been unable to do so . . . the chances for regional leadership are increased."[19] But this leadership on the continent is unlikely to be benign unless it is associated with a strategy of self-reliance and a quest for autonomy and equality at both national and regional levels. Until and unless (i) the norms of the OAU become more authoritative, and (ii) self-reliance is adopted by the clear majority of member countries (both rather unlikely prospects), then regional leadership by the semi-industrialised States is likely to involve a form of sub-imperialism, or regional dominance.[20] As Lemaitre recognises, the semi-periphery has a growing capacity (and need?) "to interfere in the internal affairs of the economically peripheral states."[21] The directions and decisions of these influential self-peripheral States' leadership are crucial, then, to the future of the continent in terms of internal stability, national equality, regional co-operation and continental cohesion. Hence the concentration of investigation and influence on them. The choice they make between fascism, semi-industrialisation and self-reliance will affect the whole of Africa as it enters the twenty-first century.

The future of Africa is intrinsically related, then, to the choice of development strategy made by the semi-industrial States, a "choice" that is already seriously constrained by their inheritance of close links with centre countries and corporations: " . . . the essential option of African states seems to be between governments controlled by internal middle-class groups openly allied to governments and corporations in the industrialised world, and the more 'socialist', more autonomous, and more self-consciously indigenous regimes."[22] If the richer States choose the former path of incorporation and the poorer countries have little choice but the latter path of self-reliance, then Africa's future will be characterised, as already indicated, by growing divergencies of policy and performance, ideology and interest. Such increasing and intensifying inequalities would retard the prospects of continental cohesion and co-operation and open it further to external influences and institutions.

However, the exacerbation of inequalities both within the between States may generate its own dialectic; namely, a series of increasingly revolutionary movements and events within the periphery, leading towards the establishment of new régimes characterised by greater degrees of socialism as well as self-reliance. In other words, if the basic human needs of most of the people are not met in either the semi-

---

[19] I. W. Zartman, "Africa," in J. N. Rosenau *et al.* (eds.), *World Politics: an introduction* (1976), p. 593. *Cf.* T. M. Shaw, "Africa," in W. Feld and G. Boyd (eds.), *Comparative Regional Systems* (1980), pp. 355–397.

[20] See T. M. Shaw, "Keyna and South Africa: 'sub-imperialist' states," 21 *Orbis* (1977), pp. 375–294.

[21] P. Lemaitre, *op. cit.* in note 10, above, p. 268.

[22] *Ibid.* p. 275.

periphery or the periphery then pressures will build for fundamental change throughout the continent: for "real" as opposed to "formal" decolonisation. This would necessitate a change in the assumptions of present projections of Africa's futures.[23]

V—AFRICA'S REVOLUTION

The prospect of more radical movements emerging throughout Africa by the year 2000 is enhanced by the distinctive patterns of decolonisation presently apparent in the remaining unfree territories concentrated in Southern Africa. The mode of transition to independence in Mozambique, Angola and Zimbabwe—and perhaps yet in Namibia and South Africa—stands in considerable contrast to that which occurred in most of the rest of Africa, and points to another way: that of a non-capitalist path.

These cases may become not only significant and suggestive models for the rest of Africa. The new régimes in Southern Africa also possess a range of resources—political and administrative as well as economic and infrastructural—that will enable them to contribute to increased intra-continental interaction and exchange as a way of facilitating and advancing self-reliance elsewhere on the continent. This group of countries may indeed emerge as a non-capitalist semi-periphery, able to satisfy basic human needs as well as possessing the power capability of influencing neighbouring States way from continued dependence. As Steven Langdon and Lynn Mytelka argue, change in Southern Africa is crucial to the theory and practice of socialism and self-reliance throughout the continent: "South-South trade in the African context could be especially useful on a continental basis. But the prospect of such development depends heavily on successful overthrow of the white-run regimes in Southern Africa. The possibility of that taking place is likely to be a central focus of much international concern in Africa, on many levels, throughout the 1980s. Self-reliant black regimes in Namibia, Zimbabwe and South Africa would make an immense contribution to alternative development strategy for all Africa, but considerable conflict would occur before such regimes finally emerge."[24]

Paradoxically, therefore, the region of the greatest degree of incorporation into the world system because of its mineral-rich, settler-dominated and strategically-important characteristics is likely to be the one that is crucial to the successful disengagement of Africa from the world system. The current conflict in Southern Africa has, then, a long-term structural as well as shorter-term symbolic significance. As

---

[23] See T. M. Shaw (ed.), *op. cit.* in note 1, above.

[24] S. Langdon and Lynn K. Mytelka, "Africa in the changing world economy," in C. Legum *et al., op. cit.* in note 2, above, p. 21.

Langdon and Mytelka conclude in their own preview of Africa in the global political economy, the orientation and outcome of this regional situation has both superstructural and substructural importance: "Armed conflict in southern Africa, though, is likely to be no more than the most dramatic African form of confrontation between dependence and self-reliance in the 1980s. We expect the contradictions of periphery capitalism in Africa to become more acute in most countries on the continent in the next decade, and we expect the struggles for change in such countries to become more bitter as a result. We are confident, however, that out of such conflict can come more equitable and self-reliant development strategies that benefit the great majority of Africans."[25]

The combination of change in Southern Africa, widespread domestic opposition and continuing global recession may come, then, to pose a serious challenge to the hitherto comfortable collaboration of many established African régimes with external capitalist institutions, particularly threatening the logic of the emerging semi-periphery. Together they could begin to upset many of the projections and scenarios now available and set the continent on a new path.

Without such basic, structural transformation, the majority of States and peoples in Africa would seem to be doomed to continued underdevelopment and impoverishment. But projections may generate their own "dialectical" response: from *Africa Undermined*[26] to a more self-reliant and self-confident continent as the next century approaches. By then, *The African Condition* may yet be transformed, as Mazrui himself imagines: "In the new dawn the poor and the meek of Africa may not inherit the earth but, hopefully, they will finally inherit their own continent."[27]

---

[25] *Ibid.* p. 211.
[26] See G. Lanning with M. Mueller, *Africa Undermined: mining companies and the underdevelopment of Africa* (1979).
[27] A. A. Mazrui, *op. cit.* in note 3, above, p. 89.

THE MAKING OF ZIMBABWE:

FROM ILLEGAL TO LEGAL INDEPENDENCE

By

MARGARET DOXEY

In view of Southern Rhodesia's virtual autonomy as a self-governing colony from 1923 and its political and economic dominance of the Federation created by the United Kingdom in 1953 to weld the two Rhodesias and Nyasaland into a single political unit, one would hardly have predicted that it would be the last of the three components of Federation to achieve full independence. That Southern Rhodesia—now known as Zimbabwe—would eventually be independent was never in doubt; having rejected union with South Africa in 1922 it was clearly destined for autonomy. Indeed it seemed to be in the vanguard of the march to decolonisation within the British Commonwealth. But the coalescing pressures for decolonisation from the colonies themselves, from the colonial Powers and from the wider international community which, with increasing acceleration, brought much of black Africa to independence in the 1960s, were complicated in the case of Southern Rhodesia by the determination of its tiny white minority (210,000 out of a total population of 4.5 million in 1965) not to concede majority rule. This paper examines the internal and external forces which contributed to the emergence of Zimbabwe as a fully independent State in March 1980, giving particular attention to the role of international organisations—the United Nations, the Organisation of African Unity (OAU) and especially the Commonwealth—in shaping the course of events.[1]

I—Background and Legacy

At the dissolution of the Central African Federation, conceded by the United Kingdom in 1963 at the wish of the people of Northern Rhodesia and Nyasaland who resented Southern Rhodesian—and white—dominance, these two territories became independent as Zambia and Malawi, joining the United Nations and associated agencies, the Commonwealth and the OAU. In the distribution of Federal assets and particularly in respect of military equipment, Southern Rhodesia came off well and its connections with Zambia remained close. Transport

---

[1] For detailed history see C. Palley, *The Constitutional History and Law of Southern Rhodesia 1888–1965* (1966); R. C. Good, *UDI: the International Politics of the Rhodesian Rebellion* (1973); Elaine Windrich, *Britain and the Politics of Rhodesian Independence* (1978).

routes linked the two countries, both landlocked and dependent on ports in Mozambique and South Africa, and they shared hydro-electricity from the Kariba dam which was situated on the Rhodesian side of the Zambezi. Much to the dismay of its white population, however, Southern Rhodesia was denied independence by Britain until African participation in government was further advanced; the 1961 constitution which gave limited and qualified franchise to Africans remained in force. The resentment of white Rhodesians at this denial of independent status to which they felt fully entitled undoubtedly swelled support for the Rhodesian Front party which won the 1962 election and (under Ian Smith's leadership) swept the board at a subsequent election in January 1965, winning all 50 "white" seats.[2] The party, which held power until the so-called "internal settlement" produced a multi-racial government in 1979, was dedicated to independence *without* majority rule and a referendum held in 1964 produced an 80 per cent. vote in favour of independence, although it was confined to registered voters and only 60 per cent. of the electorate went to the polls.

Stern warnings were issued by the British Government about the serious consequences of any unconstitutional seizure of independence and, as indications of the imminence of such a move became unmistakable, Prime Minister Harold Wilson warned the Smith régime of severe sanctions. There had already been resolutions at the United Nations General Assembly calling for the end of white privilege in Southern Rhodesia, majority rule before independence and the use of force by Britain to deal with any rebellion. The Afro-Asian bloc at the United Nations also demanded sanctions against South Africa, but here it was clear that the United Kingdom was only one of several Powers who might have influence on the South African Government. South Africa had left the Commonwealth and become a republic in 1961; it was a fully sovereign State. Southern Rhodesia, on the other hand, was still technically a colony, even if self-governing, and Britain was the constitutional sovereign Power.

On November 11, 1965, having taken some advance measures to limit and cushion the likely impact of economic sanctions, the government of Ian Smith issued a unilateral declaration of independence (UDI). This act put (Southern) Rhodesia outside the protection of the United Kingdom's suzerainty; it also reflected miscalculation of the long-term trend to majority rule in Africa. Perhaps there was over-confidence in the sympathy of members of the British Conservative Party which might soon have been restored to power. The Labour Party had won the 1964 General Election in Britain with a very slim Parliamentary majority. There was also the "kith and kin" argument; Mr. Wilson had already

---

[2] Ian Smith took the leadership of the Rhodesian Front Party from Winston Field in April 1964 and became Prime Minister.

stated that Britain would not use force against Rhodesia in any circumstances. Justifiably, there was reliance on support from South Africa and Portugal, although full recognition of Rhodesian independence was not forthcoming, even from the former. There was certainly defiance of world opinion; criticism was attributed to an international communist conspiracy master-minded from Moscow. Ian Smith's Government also misjudged, in the long run, its ability to handle internal dissent, although it took nearly a decade for this to develop into a threat of alarming dimensions. However, the ability to survive economic sanctions, by circumventing or overcoming their harmful effects may not have been seriously misjudged from the Rhodesian side. Certainly the British Government's hopes of ending the rebellion "in a matter of weeks" through economic sanctions were soon shown to have been greatly misplaced. But Rhodesia's capacity to survive indefinitely, in isolation from the international community, without a restructuring of the political system to give major concessions to the black majority, was doubted by many informed observers from the outset. The kind of settlement which could be achieved, and *its* survival prospects were less clear, and here the role of international political organisations—the United Nations, the Commonwealth and to a lesser extent the OAU—proved very significant in the ensuing 15 years.

As long as a government was functioning in Rhodesia, which was the situation throughout this period, it was necessarily one of the prime actors in the negotiation of a settlement; the other was the British Government. From the outset, however, it was accepted British policy that the wishes of the majority African population were of direct relevance. This was the basis for the denial of independence in 1964 and was set out clearly as one of the six principles which the British Government insisted must form the basis of any settlement after UDI.[3] Given the unrepresentative nature of the Salisbury régime, to satisfy this requirement meant seeking popular approval for constitutional proposals (as in the work of the Pearce Commission described below), or bringing accredited representatives of the mass of the population to the bargaining table (as eventually happened at the Lancaster House Conference in 1979). But there were also other "actors" exerting influence on the situation. Britain was under continuous pressure from fellow members of the Commonwealth, particularly African members, to take firm measures, including the use of force, to increase the international isolation of the Smith régime and bring about its downfall, and these States were ready to veto any settlement of the constitutional crisis caused by UDI which did not also provide for an acceptable degree of African political advancement in Rhodesia. By discussing the Rhodesian

---

[3] See *Rhodesia: Documents Relating to Proposals for a Settlement*, Cmnd. 3171 (1966) (London, 1966), p. 3.

question with other Commonwealth Heads of Government, and then by taking it to the United Nations Security Council and supporting the imposition of mandatory sanctions, the United Kingdom itself accepted a direct role for international organisation and did not uphold the position that Rhodesia fell within British domestic jurisdiction.[4] Not only were the costs of settling with the Smith régime on terms unacceptable to the rest of the Commonwealth an ever-present, and growing factor in British calculations; it also became impossible for Britain to end international sanctions unilaterally. Independent African States who, on the one hand, sought to influence British policy directly and through co-membership of international organisations, also gave rhetorical and practical support and encouragement to the black population of Rhodesia in international fora, helped exiled nationalist leaders and, later, assisted guerilla operations. The rest of the Third World gave firm support, and the Soviet Union and its East European allies, as well as the People's Republic of China, lost no opportunity of denouncing colonialism and racism in Rhodesia (and elsewhere) and in furnishing arms, training and money for African nationalist movements.

The Rhodesian régime, for its part, enjoyed solid white support within the country and externally could look for assistance to its powerful neighbour, the Republic of South Africa and also, for nearly a decade, to Portugal which still exercised sovereignty over its African provinces. These friends provided Rhodesia with a buffer region of white supremacy, reducing its sense of isolation and making it easier to defy the rest of the world. But in the years following UDI, one can clearly discern a changing balance between all these actors, with the advantage shifting strongly away from Rhodesia and South Africa from the early 1970s onwards. For purposes of analysis the period between UDI and legal independence can be conveniently divided into four phases: (1) the first five years after UDI, 1965–70; (2) the early 1970s, to 1974; (3) the middle to later 1970s, 1975–78; (4) the period immediately preceding independence, 1979–80.

II—From UDI to Independence

(1) *1965–70*

This period, ushered in by UDI, made Rhodesia a prime target of pressure from African countries and produced its official designation by the Security Council as a threat to the peace. Initially, there was great political uncertainty as the United Kingdom tried on the one hand to discipline the rebel régime and on the other to negotiate terms of settle-

---

[4] It was ironical that Portugal should have made this claim, on Britain's behalf, to justify its non-participation in United Nations sanctions.

ment with it. Talks between Prime Ministers Harold Wilson and Ian Smith on HMS *Tiger* in 1966 and HMS *Fearless* in 1968 revealed the unwillingness of the Rhodesian régime to make concessions, judging that they could hold on and, presumably, win out in the longer run. Immediately following UDI, the United Kingdom formally assumed responsibility for the government of Rhodesia, although this remained nominal and had no practical effect in Rhodesia itself, where the government of Ian Smith remained in full control. But the British Government also imposed economic measures, including a complete ban on imports into Britain of Rhodesian tobacco (which had formerly found its main market there and accounted for one-third of all foreign exchange earnings in 1965) and sugar. Exports to Rhodesia of petroleum and petroleum products were also banned in December 1965, and by the end of February 1966 a total ban on imports and exports was in place. In addition, Rhodesia was removed from the Sterling Area, the Commonwealth Preference Area and the Commonwealth Sugar Agreement. British aid was suspended, capital flows to Rhodesia prohibited and the assets of the Rhodesian Reserve Bank (amounting to about £10 million) frozen in London. The United States, France, and other countries, particularly other members of the Commonwealth, took similar measures on a "voluntary" basis. Members of the OAU went further in imposing not only an economic boycott but also a ban on communications and overflying—measures they also applied to South Africa. A blockade of Beira, to prevent the off-loading of oil for Rhodesia, was authorised by the Security Council in April 1966, and maintained by British naval units until 1975. A year after UDI Ian Smith was still in power and Rhodesia had weathered the initial storm, but there was no international recognition of its independence and two highly acrimonious Commonwealth Prime Ministers' meetings, in Lagos in January and London in September 1966, had revealed the strength of Commonwealth feeling that more must be done to end the rebellion and force African political advancement. Failing this, the Commonwealth was likely to break up.

In response to these pressures, Britain asked the Security Council to declare the situation a threat to the peace in terms of Article 39 of the Charter and impose mandatory sanctions. The ensuing resolution (Nr. 232 of December 16, 1966) was the Council's first resort to such measures. The sanctions covered the export to Rhodesia of petroleum, arms, ammunition, military equipment, vehicles and aircraft, and the import from Rhodesia of tobacco, sugar, meat and meat products, asbestos, copper, chrome, iron ore, hides and skins—key commodities in her export trade. There was a further tightening of United Nations sanctions in resolution 253 of May 29, 1968, which brought a total ban on trade with Rhodesia and the severance of many communications links. It also established a Committee of the Security Council to monitor the implementation of sanctions.[5] But in spite of this intensified political and economic pressure, the Rhodesian régime stood firm, well buttressed by South Africa which ignored the United Nations resolutions and provided obvious routes for exporting (at a discount) and importing (at a premium). Oil, a vital commodity, was immediately made available from South Africa.

Inside Rhodesia, solidarity and defiance among the white population were quite marked and a new constitution—which strengthened the role of the chiefs but generally worsened the political position of the African population—ushered in a republic in 1970. This brought further demands at the United Nations for sterner measures, including the severance of postal and telecommunications links and sanctions against South Africa, and the use of the veto by the United Kingdom and the United States (the latter for the first time) to block them. It also seemed by 1970 that African nationalist movements had been firmly suppressed. Both the Zimbabwe African People's Union (ZAPU) led by Joshua Nkomo and the Zimbabwe African National Union (ZANU) led by Ndabaningi Sithole, had been banned since 1964 and their leaders detained in prison. Exiles were forced to give leadership from outside the country.

(2) *1970–74*

Rhodesia entered the 1970s in rather better shape than might have been expected given its obvious vulnerabilities. No doubt the self-confidence of the whites under the strong leadership of Ian Smith and the Rhodesian Front party had been strengthened by the degree to which the economic effects of international sanctions were being circumvented, with the help of South Africa and Portugal, and overcome by efforts of government and the private sector. Stockpiling and conservation of scarce commodities; utilisation of surplus capacity for industrial development and import substitution; government subsidies for white tobacco farmers and encouragement for agricultural diversification were helpful in the defence of the economy and for keeping up morale. Faced with a serious shortage of foreign exchange, which could only become worse, and in response to British financial sanctions, the Rhodesian régime had blocked the servicing of external debts, including a World Bank loan, and instituted rigid exchange control. A complicated system of "no currency involved" deals was instituted.

---

[5] The Security Council Sanctions Committee issued annual reports beginning in 1968: the twelfth and final report, covering the period from December 16, 1978 to December 15, 1979, appears in *Security Council Official Records*, 35th yr., Special Supplement Nr. 2, Vol. 1, 1980. Chapter VIII records that on December 21, 1979 the Committee ceased to exist. On that date sanctions were officially removed by Resolution 460.

Overall, security and secrecy prevailed.[6] It also proved possible to shift some of the burden of sanctions on to the shoulders of the less-privileged African population. Subsistence farming provided some cushioning of unemployment, although the growing African population meant a very large annual inflow of job seekers to the labour market for whom no jobs were available. This was to be one of the most serious long-term strains on the economy and no doubt also encouraged enrolment in the guerrilla forces at a later stage.

In this period, Britain tried once more to achieve a settlement. The Conservative Party returned to power in 1970, with Mr. Edward Heath as Prime Minister and his Foreign Secretary, Sir Alec Douglas Home (Lord Home), worked out a set of proposals with Ian Smith which were acceptable to the two governments. Britain's own commitment, spelled out in the six principles, and reinforced by pressure from the Commonwealth and the United Nations, meant that these proposals also had to be approved by the people of Rhodesia as a whole. It could not conceivably be claimed that the Rhodesian Government spoke for them all and Mr. Heath had already had a taste of Commonwealth opposition to any soft line on Southern Africa at the 1971 Heads of Government Conference in Singapore where his plans to sell arms to South Africa for "external defence" were vigorously challenged—and dropped. Now in January 1972, the Home-Smith proposals for a settlement in Rhodesia, which did not offer majority rule in the foreseeable future and maintained an income qualification for Africans on the higher voters' roll, were carried to the African inhabitants by a Commission of Inquiry headed by Lord Pearce, charged with testing their acceptability. And it was clear, as reported by Lord Pearce, that they overwhelmingly rejected them.[7] In fact the acceptability issue injected new life into Rhodesian African politics. The African National Council (ANC) was founded on December 16, 1971, to oppose the settlement. It was chaired by Bishop Abel Muzorewa, the head of the United Methodist Church in Rhodesia, and was not banned as other African political groups had been because of the need to test African opinion.[8] The rejection of the Home-Smith proposals by Africans indicated not only the politicisation of the rural population of Rhodesia but their commitment to majority rule, distrust of the Smith régime and willingness to follow the advice of

---

[6] See H. R. Strack, *Sanctions: the Case of Rhodesia* (1978), for a good account of the Rhodesian sanctions experience. See too M. P. Doxey, *Economic Sanctions and International Enforcement* (1980), chapters 5–7.

[7] *Report of the Commission on Rhodesian opinion under the Chairmanship of the Rt. Hon. the Lord Pearce*, Cmnd. 4964 (1972) (HMSO, London). The Commission was in Rhodesia from January 11 to March 11, 1972.

[8] A useful compendium of documents on African nationalist movements in Rhodesia is C. Nyangoni and G. Nyandoro (eds.), *Zimbabwe Independence Movements: Select Documents*, London, Rex Collings, 1979.

leaders who preferred to wait for a better deal.[9] Considering that many of the nationalist leaders were in prison, the verdict of the African people was even more impressive.

This was a serious setback to the British and Rhodesian Governments' hopes for a settlement, but in other respects the early 1970s seemed reasonably promising for the continuation of UDI. The Rhodesian economy was coping with sanctions—there had even been some growth in Gross National Product (GNP)—and in 1971 the United States Government lifted the chrome boycott under the Byrd amendment.[10] This was seen in Rhodesia as a "swallow" which might make a "summer" in due course. Moreover, South Africa under the leadership of Mr. Vorster was trying to develop better relations with African countries—the so-called "outward" policy—and seemed to have had some success. South Africa was also willing to assist the Rhodesian forces in countering terrorist acts of violence which began in earnest although on a very small scale at the very end of 1972. Guerrilla warfare was one small cloud on the horizon which was to grow steadily bigger; but there were others more immediately threatening as the period progressed. In the first place these were years of increasing difficulty for Portugal, faced with the growing scale and success of guerrilla warfare in its African territories. The cost of remaining a colonial Power was becoming intolerable and elements of the army were increasingly disaffected. The *coup* which in 1974 ended over 40 years of rule by Dr. Salazar in Portugal was to bring major changes in Southern Africa as well. It meant a new balance of forces, new problems for South Africa, and a transformation of the Rhodesian situation and the outlook for white supremacy.

Secondly, there were signs of a new unity in the hitherto bitterly opposed African nationalist groupings. On December 7, 1974, the leaders of ZANU and ZAPU were released from jail in Salisbury as part of a new effort by Ian Smith to achieve a settlement and at a meeting in Lusaka, also attended by Bishop Muzorewa, they pledged to unite with the ANC.

Although this unity was paper-thin, and was subsequently to tear apart in different directions, it did presage a long-run danger to white supremacy particularly in the possibility of a ZANU/ZAPU alliance.

(3) *1975–78*
During these crucial years, particularly once Angola and Mozambique had become independent in 1975, the position of the Rhodesian

---

[9] The Pearce report noted that "mistrust of the intentions and motives of the [Rhodesian] government transcended all other considerations," in the African rejection of the Home-Smith proposals, Cmnd. 4964, p. 80.

[10] Strack makes a special study of the Byrd Amendment which was in effect until 1977, *op. cit.* in note 6, above, pp. 146–164.

régime markedly deteriorated, both internally and externally.[11] Instead of Portugal providing a bulwark of white supremacy and support in the international community, the new Portuguese Government was unfriendly and there were two new hostile African States on the Rhodesian border, both applying sanctions and, at the same time, strengthening political opposition in the United Nations and the OAU. Moreover, guerrilla forces could now make incursions into Rhodesia from Mozambique with support from the government of Dr. Machel which had itself come to power after waging successful guerrilla warfare against the Portuguese. ZANU, now led by Robert Mugabe and its military wing ZANLA,[12] and ZAPU led by Mr. Nkomo with its military wing ZIPRA, had joint and separate backers in all parts of the world: from the neighbouring States of Botswana, Mozambique, Tanzania and Zambia (designated the Front Line States); from other Third-World countries; from Communist countries; and from considerable bodies of opinion in Western countries. In April-May, 1975, Bishop Muzorewa attended and addressed the Commonwealth Heads of Government meeting in Kingston, Jamaica; a clear sign of growing recognition of his status. And in 1976 ZANU and ZAPU, which were no longer part of the ANC, formed a loose alliance known as the Patriotic Front. Although there were continuing rivalries and differences, their unity was encouraged by the Front Line States who urgently wanted a legitimised settlement in Rhodesia. It was obvious that race war, further Cuban adventurism as seen in Angola, South African reprisals, and even the continuation of the existing situation could mean disaster for the whole area, killing all hopes of economic development and a better standard of living for the inhabitants.

The increasing scope of terrorism and guerrilla activity became very costly for the Rhodesian régime, which was hard-pressed to keep its defence forces fully equipped under sanctions, and it also had a serious effect on white confidence and morale. Tourism dropped off sharply, particularly after violent incidents at the Victoria Falls, and this meant a loss of much needed foreign exchange, and whites also began to emigrate from Rhodesia in significant numbers.[13] Worse still, South African support showed signs of waning. Under continuing attack from

---

[11] A 1975 commentary put the position thus: "It is not easy to foresee the future direction of Rhodesian politics. Both the African opposition and the white ruling group face an impasse. The nationalists have so far failed to establish a serious guerrilla movement. The Rhodesian Front has stayed in power and survived sanctions but presides over a government which is denied international recognition and over an economy which is stagnant." See M. Loney, *Rhodesia: White Racism and Imperial Response* (1975), p. 183.

[12] Mr. Mugabe who became the first Prime Minister of Zimbabwe in 1980 was Secretary-General of ZANU in the 1960s when it was led by Mr. Sithole. He was in jail or detention in Rhodesia until December 1974 and then went into exile. He successfully challenged Sithole for the leadership of ZANU and by 1976 was the commander of ZANLA.

[13] Between 1976 and 1978, the white population suffered a net loss of 37,000.

the rest of the world for its apartheid policy and for its involvement in Namibia, the South African Government felt that Rhodesia was becoming a burden and a danger and it wanted a settlement which would make its own problems more manageable. South African paramilitary forces were withdrawn from Rhodesia in 1975 and Ian Smith was encouraged to respond favourably to a new set of Anglo-American initiatives.

The United Kingdom, the United States and other Western countries were now extremely anxious to find a solution to the Rhodesian problem. The Middle East war of October 1973 and the associated Arab oil embargoes had focused attention on problems of national economic security; growing Soviet influence in Angola and the Horn of Africa, with Cuban military involvement, was also alarming. A peaceful settlement of the Rhodesian question would safeguard important raw materials, preserve Western influence and—it was hoped—the safety of Rhodesian whites, and remove a possible catalyst for the general spread of violence in Southern Africa. It would also bring to an end the continual criticism of the West by African countries, among whom Nigeria had assumed a new importance as a major oil exporter and with all of whom trade was steadily growing. Moreover, investigations of sanctions-busting by journalists, church groups and other private agencies, which after 1973 could be reported to the United Nations Sanctions Committee and be referred by it to governments for investigation, showed up the huge gaps which existed in the sanctions "net."[14] These allegations and reports confirmed the inefficiency of United Nations measures, and were also embarrassing for the United Kingdom which had taken the lead in reporting instances of suspected sanctions-breaking to the United Nations Committee and from 1966 to 1975 maintained a naval blockade of Beira, but was now found to be tolerating arrangements which made it possible for Rhodesia to receive ample supplies of oil.[15]

In 1976 it was not surprising to find a new flurry of diplomatic activity, with United States Secretary of State Kissinger and the British Foreign Secretary David Owen taking leading roles. In April, Dr. Kissinger's proposals for a settlement were published in Lusaka: they included majority rule in two years; the repeal of the Byrd amendment; the pledge of economic, technical and educational assistance from the United States and other Western countries for an independent Zimbabwe; an assured future in the country for whites as well as blacks. Dr. Kissinger subsequently met the South African Prime Minister on two occasions in West Germany and Ian Smith met them both for discussions in Pretoria. The Rhodesian leader agreed to accept majority rule in

[14] See particularly Commonwealth Secretariat, *Oil Sanctions against Rhodesia* (1978) and the annual reports of the Security Council Sanctions Committee.

[15] See T. H. Bingham and S. M. Gray, *Report on the Supply of Petroleum and Petroleum Products to Rhodesia* (1978).

two years, but subsequent conferences in Geneva and Malta proved unsuccessful. The Patriotic Front rejected the Anglo-American proposals and guerrilla war continued.

By 1978 the death toll in the guerrilla campaign was at least 12,000 and this third period ended with an official and dramatic change in policy on the part of the Smith régime. It conceded majority rule—which a decade before had been ruled out in Mr. Smith's lifetime—and negotiated an "internal settlement" with the African groups led by Bishop Muzorewa and Messrs. Sithole and Chirau. An executive council composed of these three African leaders and Mr. Smith took on the responsibility of government until constitutional change could be effected. Political and strategic issues were clearly decisive in bringing this turnabout. The economy had definitely suffered under sanctions, but it was not at collapsing point.[16] It was, however, in recession and the problems of sanctions which meant growing unemployment and a serious lack of new investment were compounded by rising military expenditure and inflation.

The question was now whether the United Kingdom and the United States would accept this internal settlement and lift sanctions? Ten years earlier they might have done so, but by 1978 the legitimacy of principles of non-discrimination and majority rule was unquestioned in the international community. They had been reiterated and supported by consensus at the United Nations; they were embedded in the Commonwealth Declaration of Principles and subsequent official pronouncements of Commonwealth Heads of Government; they made it impossible for anything less than one man one vote in Rhodesia to be accepted. This undoubtedly was the major contribution of the United Nations and the Commonwealth to the outcome of the long-drawn-out Rhodesian crisis. Through these organisations a boundary was set around permissible terms of settlement, defining what was acceptable and delegitimising any other schemes.[17] International sanctions, even if not decisive in economic impact, had symbolic and perhaps some practical effect in underpinning this international condemnation, and the claims and interests of black Rhodesians were sustained and reinforced by these means.

(4) *1979–80*

This final stage which culminated in the Commonwealth Heads of Government meeting in Lusaka in August 1979 and the ensuing

---

[16] See D. G. Clarke, "Zimbabwe's International Economic Position and Aspects of Sanctions Removal," 18 *Journal of Commonwealth and Comparative Politics*, Nr.1, March 1980, pp. 28–54.

[17] The role of the Commonwealth is examined further in M. Doxey, "Strategies in Multilateral Diplomacy: the Commonwealth, Southern Africa and the NIEO," 35 *International Journal*, Nr.2, Spring 1980, pp. 329–356.

Lancaster House Conference on the constitutional future of Rhodesia led to full independence and the end of white political supremacy. The Labour Party had held office in Britain from 1974, but in May 1979 the Conservatives were returned to power, with Mrs. Thatcher as Prime Minister. Although right-wing elements in the Tory party were, and had always been, in sympathy with Ian Smith and the whites in Rhodesia, and were anxious now for the United Kingdom to accept the internal settlement,[18] and lift sanctions—unilaterally if necessary—the message received by Mrs. Thatcher and her Foreign Secretary Lord Carrington before, and during, the Commonwealth Heads of Government meeting in Lusaka was that any acceptance by Britain of the internal settlement which was not acceptable to the leaders of the Patriotic Front was unacceptable to the rest of the Commonwealth and would be a prescription for further trouble. And clearly the rest of the Commonwealth was much more important to Britain at this stage than were white Rhodesians, although one of the British Government's responsibilities was obviously to try and safeguard the position of whites in any new constitutional framework.

In January 1979 the white—but not the black—population of Rhodesia had an opportunity to approve the "internal settlement" in a referendum, and a general election was held in March under the new constitution.[19] Sixty-four per cent. of the electorate voted and Bishop Muzorewa became the first black Prime Minister of what was now termed officially, "Zimbabwe-Rhodesia." But ZANU and ZAPU were banned and the election was marked by censorship of Press and radio, and much violence and intimidation. The new government was not acceptable internationally, or to the Patriotic Front, and it was now quite clear that a decisive outcome would come sooner rather than later, whether it was brought about by further negotiation or by force of arms. Zambia was suffering terribly as a result of spillover effects of sanctions and the loss of transport routes[20]; the war inside Rhodesia was "hotting up" and both Zambia and Mozambique were experiencing counter-incursions from Rhodesian forces; there was also the fear that the Patriotic Front would collapse and lead to further strife between ZANLA and ZIPRA. Nevertheless, the success of the Lancaster House Conference, convened after the Commonwealth Heads of Government meeting by the British Government with the Government of Bishop

---

[18] There was also a demand from the United States Congress that President Carter should terminate sanctions unless he determined it to be in the national interest not to do so. The President did so determine and delayed the termination of sanctions until after the successful conclusion of the Lancaster House Conference.

[19] A critical analysis of this constitution was made by Professor Palley. See C. Palley, *The Rhodesian Election* (1979).

[20] See *The Front Line States: The Burden of the Liberation Struggle* (London, Commonwealth Secretariat, 1978.)

Muzorewa and the leaders of the Patriotic Front as full participants, was by no means a foregone conclusion. Many thought it was bound to fail. It was a considerable achievement for all parties, and owed much to the skilful diplomacy of Lord Carrington who chaired it, and of others in the wings, particularly the Commonwealth Secretary-General Shridath Ramphal. Britain and the Front Line States were in agreement that it was a last chance for a peaceful settlement, and this was reflected in joint and separate pressure on the Patriotic Front leaders as well as on the Rhodesian Government. Many problems remained when the Conference concluded in December 1979, but it did produce an agreed constitutional settlement, arrangements for the pre-independence period and a cease-fire agreement.[21]

The constitution sets out provisions for citizenship, civil rights and a Parliamentary system with universal suffrage. The Head of State and Commander-in-Chief of the Armed Forces in the new Republic of Zimbabwe is elected by Parliament for five years and the Parliament itself is bicameral, with a Senate and House of Assembly. Taking the more important body first, the House of Assembly has 100 seats of which 80 are filled by members elected by voters on the Common Voters Roll and 20 by voters on the White Voters Roll. To be eligible for election, a person must have the vote, be at least 21 years of age and satisfy a residence qualification. The Prime Minister, who heads the government, is that person "best able to command the support of a majority of the members of the House of Assembly." The Senate has 40 members: 10 elected by members of the House of Assembly elected by white voters, 14 by members elected by those on the Common Voters Roll, 10 by the Council of Chiefs, and six nominated by the President on the advice of the Prime Minister. Senators must be at least 40 years of age.

All Zimbabwe citizens of 18 and over are eligible to be enrolled as voters, but whites (including Coloured and Asian citizens) are on a White Voters Roll "for so long as there is provision for separate minority representation in Parliament."

Legislation is passed by the House of Assembly and Senate (which has delaying powers) but there are special guarantees of the provisions relating to the representation of the white minority in Parliament. For seven years, these provisions can be amended only by a unanimous vote of the House of Assembly and two-thirds of the Senate; after 1987, they can be amended like other constitutional provisions by 70 per cent. of the Assembly and two-thirds of the Senate. In both cases, the Senate's power is to delay and not to veto.

---

[21] Southern Rhodesia: Report of the Constitutional Conference, Lancaster House, London, Sept.-Dec. 1979, Cmnd. 7802, (1980) (HMSO, London). See also, Lord Soames, "From Rhodesia to Zimbabwe," 56 *International Affairs*, Nr.3, Summer 1980, pp. 405–419, for an account of the strategy pursued by the United Kingdom Government throughout the Conference.

Immediately after the signing of the agreement, Rhodesia temporarily reverted to the status of a colony, with Lord Soames as Governor, and in the ensuing months the cease-fire was put into effect under a slender force of approximately 2,000 British and Commonwealth personnel. The guerrilla forces were invited to assemble in designated areas and campaigning for the General Election was permitted to all political parties.

All parties to the Lancaster House agreement had agreed to accept the authority of the Governor and comply with the pre-independence arrangements; to abide by the cease-fire agreement and the independence constitution; to renounce the use of force for political ends; and to accept the outcome of the elections and instruct any forces under their authority to do the same.[22]

The General Election took place on February 14, 1980, for the "white" seats, and on February 27, 28 and 29, for the "black" seats. It was monitored by a Commonwealth Observer group drawn from 11 countries, which ruled before the results were published that it was both free and fair[23] and it resulted in a clear victory for Robert Mugabe whose ZANU party won 57 out of the 80 African seats in the Assembly. This majority made his installation as Prime Minister inevitable; Joshua Nkomo became Minister of Home Affairs in a new government of national unity. On April 18, 1980, Zimbabwe became fully independent. It joined the Commonwealth and applied for membership to the United Nations. Sanctions had already been lifted by the Security Council in resolution 460 of December 21, 1979, a move anticipated by Britain on December 12, and by the United States on December 16. It was clearly in the best interests of the new State and of its neighbours that the economy should start moving again as quickly as possible.

CONCLUSIONS

It is too soon to say how things will work out in Zimbabwe. The whole area of Central and Southern Africa is beset with problems of an economic and political nature and South Africa, in 1980, is beginning to show signs of increasing and perhaps uncontrollable internal turmoil. Within Zimbabwe, the reallocation of land from whites to Africans, and the integration of the regular forces with guerrilla armies and "auxiliary groups" are daunting tasks, particularly if good race relations between the black majority and white minority are to be cultivated. That the Commonwealth and the United Nations played a considerable role in the unmaking of the UDI and the making of an independent Zimbabwe

---

[22] Cmnd. 7802, p. v.

[23] Members of the Observer Group, none of them British, served in their individual capacities and reported to Commonwealth Heads of Government through the Commonwealth Secretary-General.

under majority rule is undeniable, but one cannot conclude that either or both of these organisations would be equally influential in other situations. Southern Rhodesia was unique in that its status as a British colony preserved a constitutional role for Britain until independence was granted, and there was a rare international consensus on the need for reform of the political structure. Moreover, the majority of the population of Zimbabwe were, from the outset, seeking the same outcome as their external supporters, and this gave great moral strength to the sanctions which were fully legitimised by being imposed by the Security Council itself. The economic effects of sanctions were not decisive in bringing internal change, and in many ways they were successfully resisted or overcome, but the solidarity under pressure which has been characteristic of other cases of international pressure, notably Italy under League sanctions, and Cuba under Organisation of American States (OAS) sanctions, was restricted in Zimbabwe to the dominant white élite, and the symbolic effect of sanctions was correspondingly enhanced.

White Rhodesia was from the outset vulnerable to regional pressure, from South Africa—its ally—and from black African States. Its hope that the United Kingdom could tolerate, or even accept its illegal seizure of independence did not take sufficient account of the anachronistic and inequitable foundations of its privileged position, nor of British responsibility to African Rhodesians (and there was always a significant body of opinion in Britain prepared to support their cause) and responsiveness to Commonwealth pressure. In the long run, the Rhodesian whites had to find allies at home which entailed making significant concessions to their fellow blacks. This in turn encouraged the forces working for full enfranchisement of Africans and majority rule.

If the new State of Zimbabwe can retain the confidence and support of a substantial number of its white citizens and also satisfy legitimate African aspirations, it has a chance of becoming a model of political and economic development in Southern Africa. It is to be devoutly hoped that this will be its destiny.

"DISAPPEARANCES" AND THE INTERNATIONAL PROTECTION OF HUMAN RIGHTS

By

RICHARD REOCH

"The disappeared prisoners" is the name we give to members of our families who have been taken from our homes, in front of our eyes, or in their work places, colleges and universities, with eye-witnesses or strong proof of their detention. The people who detained them were members of the military intelligence services. They are being held in secret and all our efforts, such as writs of *habeas corpus*, affidavits of kidnapping, and letters and interviews with government officials, have been flung back in our faces with the following answer: "This person has never been detained."[1]

THIS statement, part of an appeal published from Santiago, Chile, in 1975, provides one of the earliest definitions of a phenomenon that, in the course of the last five years, has increasingly occupied the attention of the international community. "Disappearances" have been reported not only from Chile, but from countries throughout Latin America, Africa, Asia and the Middle East. Countries from which such reports came included, for example, Afghanistan, Argentina, Democratic Kampuchea, East Timor, El Salvador, Ethiopia, Equatorial Guinea, Guatemala, Haiti, Mexico, Nicaragua, the People's Democratic Republic of Yemen, the Philippines and Uganda.

In the years 1975 to 1980, in the context of the need for international protection of human rights, Amnesty International and other non-governmental organisations drew this phenomenon to the attention of the United Nations Sub-Commission on the Prevention of Discrimination and the Protection of Minorities, arguing that the disappearance of political opponents resulting from acts practised or tolerated by governments had become "one of the most serious human rights violations of our times."[2]

It has been suggested that the phenomenon of "disappearances," as it has developed in a systematic fashion, may be traced to Guatemala in the early 1960s, when "death squads" that included off-duty security personnel began operations against anti-government guerrillas. After the guerrillas were crushed in the late 1960s, the "death squads" continued to operate, abducting and assassinating opposition leaders and their

---

[1] *Agrupación de Familiares de los Detenidos Desaparecidos*, "Statement" (June 1975), Santiago, Chile.

[2] Amnesty International, Oral statement under item 8 of the 32nd session of the United Nations Sub-Commission on the Prevention of Discrimination and Protection of Minorities, Geneva, August 29, 1979.

sympathisers. However, it was only in the early 1970s that similar patterns began to emerge elsewhere in Latin America and in Africa, Asia and the Middle East. Although there is no evidence yet that would enable anyone to point convincingly to a pattern of deliberate international transfer of the phenomenon, it has nevertheless become a feature of gross violation of human rights on a large scale, crossing cultural, political and geographical boundaries.

Efforts are now underway to attempt a definition of the term "disappearance," to collect information about individual cases, assign responsibility for the practice as it has developed in each country, and to establish an international mechanism to monitor and react to reports of "disappearances." As indicated in Part IV of this paper, there has been a significant response from the intergovernmental community, through the establishment of a Working Group on Disappearances under the mandate of the United Nations Commission on Human Rights. Much of the information concerning "disappearances" and most of the initial international concern that contributed to the raising of the issue at the intergovernmental level, however, came from relatives of those who had "disappeared," lawyers acting for them and several non-governmental organisations, including Amnesty International.

In the instances of "disappearances" cited in Parts II and III of this paper, which help to outline the dimensions of the problem as currently in evidence, the research work of Amnesty International is used. It may be useful to sketch the basis on which that research has been done. Since it was founded in 1961, as the result of an appeal by British lawyer Peter Benenson in *The Observer*,[3] Amnesty International has concentrated its research and membership activities within a mandate defined by its international Statute. This mandate restricts the organisation to working for the release of prisoners of conscience (individuals imprisoned anywhere by reason of their political, religious or other conscientiously held beliefs, or by reason of their ethnic origin, sex, colour or language, provided that they have not used or advocated violence), for fair and prompt trials for all political prisoners, and for the abolition of the death penalty and torture or other cruel, inhuman or degrading treatment or punishment in all cases. The basis of the organisation's initiatives is research into individual allegations, conducted by a research department comprising some 70 staff at the International Secretariat in London. The underlying principle of that research is a belief that just as human rights defined in international law transcend the boundaries of nation, race and belief, so too does the responsibility for the protection of those rights. This principle implies a strict application of impartiality in the assessment of violations of those rights and a commitment to act in response irrespective of political considerations. Although Amnesty International itself, a

---

[3] P. Benenson, "The Forgotten Prisoners," *Observer*, London, May 28, 1961.

membership organisation relying on public support for its funding and campaigns, stresses the importance of individuals taking responsibility for human rights work, it also recognises and attempts to facilitate the development of regional and international human rights mechanisms of an intergovernmental nature. It has pursued both avenues in attempting to publicise and generate an effective international response to "disappearances."

I—THE TERM

The term "disappearance" as it is currently used to refer to particular forms of human rights violations found its way into the English language through the Spanish word "*desaparecido.*" Literally translated, *desaparecido* means "to be disappeared." The Spanish term *desaparecido*, used to describe these particular human rights violations, is believed to have been used first in recent years in Chile and Argentina. The English translation of the word—"disappearance"—is now, however, used to refer to situations that include a variety of elements, not necessarily limited to those found in the context of its origin.

The term may now be found to describe various situations where the relatives, friends and lawyers of an individual have reason to believe that he or she has been apprehended by government agents or kidnapped by people acting in collusion with the government; they are unable to find him or her or establish contact with him or her. The authorities refuse to acknowledge either the apprehension or the fact that the individual is in official custody; or, in the case of a kidnapping by a non-governmental group, the authorities refuse to investigate the kidnapping and the whereabouts of the individual, or refuse to make known the results of their investigation. In some circumstances, the authorities may have first acknowledged the apprehension, but subsequently claim that the individual is no longer in their custody. On the other hand, the relatives, friends and lawyers may have reason to believe that the individual is still in the authorities' custody or that the latter have killed him or her, although they have no way of establishing the whereabouts of or contacting the missing person.

In a case containing these elements, a number of human rights may be violated. These rights include, among others: the right to life, guaranteed in Article 3 of the United Nations Universal Declaration of Human Rights (1948) and Article 6 of the International Covenant on Civil and Political Rights (1966); the right to recognition everywhere as a person before the law, guaranteed by Article 6 of the Universal Declaration and Article 16 of the Covenant; the right to be free from torture, and from other cruel, inhuman or degrading treatment or punishment, guaranteed by Article 5 of the Universal Declaration and Article 7 of the Covenant; and the right to be free from arbitrary arrest and detention, guaranteed by Article 9 of both the Universal Declaration and the Covenant. The single human rights violation that is common to all cases of "disappearance" as described above is violation of the right to recognition everywhere as a person before the law.

In a submission to the 36th session of the United Nations Commission on Human Rights on February 22, 1980, Amnesty International drew attention to the problem of trying to define a "disappearance" in legal terms. In the experience of Amnesty International there are two essential elements in a "disappearance." The first element is that the arrest or kidnapping is not carried out by terrorists or common criminals but by government agents or by other groups directly or indirectly supported by the government. The second element is that the government subsequently refuses to acknowledge the arrest and the following detention. It denies that the person is being held under its jurisdiction and it also denies the need to carry out an investigation. As such, a "disappearance" represents a violation of human rights which is different from classic violations such as arbitrary arrest or incommunicado detention, because in those cases at least the authorities accept responsibility for the fact that the person is in their custody.

Because the government refuses to accept this responsibility, all legal provisions such as declarations, conventions and covenants negotiated by international or regional bodies have no application. All such instruments presume that the person who claims that his or her rights are being violated will have remedies, that his or her representatives can take legal action against the perpetrators. A disappeared person has no remedies because the authorities simply deny knowing his or her whereabouts.

Government denial may take various forms. It can be explicit, in the form of a statement. It can be implicit, involving a deliberate failure to acknowledge the apprehension. However, there may be cases in which the failure to acknowledge is not deliberate and cannot necessarily be construed as a denial. This could happen in instances where legal safeguards and administrative procedures are weak for all prisoners and where procedures that would guarantee due process are absent. Another form of denial arises from a situation in which the apprehension has been conducted by seemingly non-official agents or "unknown agents," but the authorities refuse to investigate the case or to make known in full the results of the investigation. Such refusal could in certain instances be construed as constituting grounds for belief that the government is involved in the apprehension or condones it. Such refusal could also be tantamount to an implicit denial of its own role in the case. Finally, there have been instances, involving a denial, where, following an initial admission of the apprehension, the government has later announced either that no such apprehension took place or that the individual has been released, even if he or she has not reappeared.

A further element which is present in some "disappearances," but not all, is the risk that the individual who has been apprehended may be subjected to torture and/or killed. Unacknowledged detention creates the conditions for the perpetration of torture or secret execution. Unacknowledged detention may itself be considered a form of cruel, inhuman or degrading treatment. However, it is necessary in a given situation to distinguish between the probability and the possibility of torture or murder. Assessing the risk varies from country to country and must take into account past and current practices. The risk itself, however, is not likely to be an element in a strict definition of the term "disappearance." Nevertheless, as the case studies in Parts II and III clearly indicate, torture and murder have frequently been the systematic concomitant of abduction.

II—DISAPPEARANCES IN LATIN AMERICA

It would be possible to cite brief evidence from numerous Latin American nations. It may be more useful to present a more detailed portrait of the problem in two countries: Chile and Argentina. Information about "disappearances" in both countries varies (in itself an indication of the problems that surround an understanding of the situation); the elements, insofar as they are known, also vary. Amnesty International estimates that since September 11, 1973 more than 1,500 people have "disappeared" following their arrest by Chilean security forces.

Direct evidence about individual victims of "disappearances" is difficult to obtain because many victims are simply killed and very few are actually released so that they can give an account of their experiences. Nevertheless, the Expert on the Question of the Fate of Missing and Disappeared Persons in Chile has already produced some extremely useful reports on "disappearances" in that country. His conclusions are also relevant for other countries where similar practices take place. In his most recent report the Expert concluded that in at least 600 cases there is no doubt that the persons were arrested by State authorities and that their fate has not been clarified. The report also concluded that the failure to identify and punish those responsible for "disappearances" might well encourage some to see "disappearances" as an acceptable method of operation in the administration of national security in the future.

All legal remedies taken between 1973 and 1978 had failed to persuade the government to acknowledge its responsibility for the abductions, regardless of the testimony of many witnesses. By September 1978, despite hunger strikes by relatives of "disappeared" prisoners, international pressure and evidence provided by the Catholic Church, the government still had not changed its basic position of denying any responsibility for the "disappearances."

On November 30, 1978, the situation changed when 15 bodies were found in a disused lime quarry in Lonquén, about 32 miles south of Santiago. All the bodies found were those of people who had been detained or abducted in October 1973 and whose names were included in the lists which had been made public by the *Vicaría de la Solidaridad*. A *Ministro en Visita* was appointed by the Supreme Court, Adolfo Bañados, together with the magistrate for the area of Lonquén to take charge of the investigations.

On April 8, 1979, Judge Bañados handed over the investigation of the Lonquén killings to military justice. He reported to the Santiago Appeals Court that the bodies buried in the lime kiln corresponded to those people who were detained or abducted on October 7, 1973 in the region of Isla de Maipo and that he was handing over his findings of "simultaneous multiple crimes" to a Military Tribunal. At the beginning of July 1979, a Military Court ordered the trial of eight police officers accused of murdering 11 of 15 people whose remains were identified at Lonquén. It subsequently found the accused guilty of "ill-treatment resulting in death" of the eleven.

On July 12, the accused appealed for release under the provisions of Decree Law 2191, which declared an amnesty for certain types of crimes (including murder) committed during the state of siege from September 11, 1973 until March 10, 1978. On July 31, the accused were released on bail despite the opposition of one judge, Sergio Dunlop, who declared that the police were "responsible for an event of extreme gravity" and did not deserve to be released on bail. The eight accused were granted unconditional liberty under the amnesty on August 16, 1979.

The ruling of the Military Court was challenged by the relatives of the 11 victims, who claimed that if the Supreme Court upheld this decision, Chile would be in breach of international obligations under the Geneva Convention ratified in 1950. The decision would also be in violation of the International Covenant on Civil and Political Rights which was ratified by Chile in 1972. They also challenged the court's verdict that the eight police officers were guilty of "ill-treatment resulting in death," claiming that the police were guilty of multiple homicide.

Cardinal Raúl Silva Henriques responded to the court ruling by issuing a plea to the authorities to return the remains of the victims to their families. Members of the committee of relatives of the missing prisoners, with the backing of the church, began a hunger strike in support of the demand for the return of the bodies. On September 11, 1979—the sixth anniversary of the military coup—the Martial Courts announced that they would return the bodies of the Lonquén victims to their families. On September 14, the relatives received the news that their dead ones had been buried secretly.

The relatives of the victims pursued the case through the courts. Their lawyers submitted a complaint to the Supreme Court against the Military Prosecutor who had ordered the secret burial and against the Director of the *Instituto Médico Legal*. They also appealed for the appointment of a special judge to investigate the reasons for this secret ceremony and demanded that appropriate charges be brought against those responsible for failure to obey the original instruction of the Military Courts.

Various official explanations were offered to the relatives through the Press and in other ways. It was stated that only one body had been positively identified; that it had not been possible to identify with certainty the remains of the other 14 and that the Military Prosecutor was perfectly within his rights to order the burial of the other remains in a common grave.

The Supreme Court reached its verdict on January 4, 1980. It cancelled a written reprimand previously served on the Military Prosecutor and declared that his action had been perfectly legal. In so doing, the court rejected the complaint submitted to it on behalf of the Lonquén relatives. No special investigation would be made. The final ruling of the Supreme Court on this matter set a disturbing precedent. It implied that a State, by manipulation of its national legal institutions and system and by strategic use of special decree laws, could evade internationally agreed norms for the treatment and protection of prisoners, leaving those individuals (either dead or in secret custody) or their relatives with no domestic means of redress.

The problem of "disappearances" in Argentina involves an estimated 15,000 individuals who have "disappeared" since the military coup of 1976 that brought General Jorge Videla to power. In June 1979, Amnesty International published a list of more than 2,500 known cases of "disappearances." In February 1980, it released the text of testimony by two Argentine refugees, Oscar Alfredo González and Horacio Cid de la Paz, who between them spent 15 months in five secret detention camps. The two men are among the very few "disappeared" people who have ever managed to escape. Their testimony represents an astonishing account of the scope and systematic character of an official operation. Amnesty International spent months cross-checking their testimony against its own records and information obtained from reliable sources in Argentina; it was able to corroborate many of the details in the two men's testimony.

They testified to a consistent pattern supervised in meticulous detail by military and police officers. Torture and interrogation were followed by a period of what they called "concentration camp" life with regular punishments and beatings, and finally, for most prisoners, "transfer"—the euphemism for death. Most of the victims had been taken from their homes or places of work without any semblance of legality by armed agents of the security forces. The two men estimated that 800 people passed through the camps they were in during their 15 months in captivity, and they provided details on more than 300 of them.

Both men were taken first to *Club Atlético*, a building in Buenos Aires which served as an initial depot for prisoners where they saw their first "operating theatres," as the torture rooms were called. It had three, each furnished with a *picana* (electric cattle prod) and metal table, to which prisoners were bound naked. They said the treatment was essentially the same for all prisoners. According to the two men, torture could go on for hours, day after day: "Between sessions of the *picana*, they would use the *submarino* (holding our heads under water), hang us up by our feet, hit us on the sexual organs, beat us with chains, put salt on our wounds and use any other method that occurred to them. . . . They would also apply 200-volt direct current to us. . . . Everything was done under the supervision of a doctor, who checked our blood pressure and reflexes: 'We've got all the time in the world, and this will go on indefinitely.' "

The army, navy, air force and federal police all had men in the "task forces" which did the kidnapping and operated in the camps. Generals, colonels and other high-ranking officers were among those whom González and de la Paz said they saw at the camps. When a kidnapping was approved, police and other security services would reportedly "surrender" an area of several city blocks to let the abduction squad operate.

Some of the victims described by González and de la Paz had been politically active, others were only related to political suspects, and there was no apparent reason for the abduction of some. Others were taken for the purposes of extortion.

The ultimate fate for most prisoners was the "transfer," according to the testimony. They were usually "transferred" in groups of 30 to 50. Guards were overheard telling such a group that they would be given injections of a tranquiliser because they faced a long and difficult journey. Shackled and blindfolded, they were loaded into lorries and never seen again. A prisoner who had served as a doctor in the camps told González and de la Paz that he had discovered that some "transferred" prisoners were given injections of a powerful sedative, then taken by lorry and loaded onto an aircraft, "from which they were thrown into the sea, alive but unconscious." Particularly at seasons when Atlantic currents changed, corpses bearing the marks of torture have been washed ashore on the Argentine coast.

The striking feature of the testimony is the detail with which the two men were able to reconstruct the elements indicating systematic State involvement in the kidnap, detention, torture and elimination of victims. They cited, for example, six "task forces." Task Force One was controlled by the Federal Police. Task Force Two was controlled by the Argentine Army and closely connected to Intelligence Batallion 601, based in the Federal Capital. Task Force Three was controlled by the Navy, with one of its subdivisions, 32, operating out of the Navy Engineering Institute. Task Force Four was under Air Force control. The Federal Police and Ministry of the Interior had joint control over a Federal Co-ordination, Intelligence and Counter-Intelligence task force. A Special Task Force was controlled by the First Army Corps and brought together personnel from army headquarters, the federal police, national gendarmerie and the prison service.

This allegation of widespread official involvement was corroborated independently by a mission of inquiry of the Organisation of American States in 1979 which confirmed the accuracy of reports that "disappeared" prisoners had been summarily executed by members of the armed forces: "due to the actions or the failure to act on the part of the governmental authorities and their agents, numerous serious violations of fundamental human rights were committed in the Republic of Argentina between the period covered by this report 1975–1979 ... persons belonging to or connected with government security agencies have killed numerous men and women subsequent to their being placed in detention."[4]

On September 12, 1979 the Argentine Government gave its final reply to the inquiries of the relatives of missing persons by issuing law 22.068. Under this law either the State or a relative may declare a person who disappeared during the previous five years dead. The date of death will be taken as the date on which the "disappearance" was first registered. In view of the facts presented in this testimony, law 22.068 may be seen as no more than an attempt to confer retroactive legality on grossly illegal actions.

III—Disappearances in Africa and Asia

In the five years from 1975 to 1980, countless people "disappeared" altogether or were known to be the victims of abductions and political killings in Afghanistan, Democratic Kampuchea, Equatorial Guinea, Ethiopia and Uganda. The list of countries is not exhaustive; it serves merely to highlight the extent to which the right to life, liberty and security of person was effectively suspended for whole populations. The different situations in these countries, in which there have been changes of government or changes of policy within the same period, are also reflected in different techniques and structures for the liquidation of real or suspected political opponents. From these countries and from others on the two continents, it is possible to cite a range of instances in which "disappearances" have occurred and which have come to the attention of Amnesty International and other bodies.

---

[4] Inter-American Commission on Human Rights, *Report*, Washington, 1979.

In September 1979, Amnesty International published evidence that "a consistent pattern of gross violations of human rights" existed in Afghanistan and in February 1980 an Amnesty International delegation visited the country two months after the new Government of President Babrak Karmal had come to power. The visit enabled Amnesty International to confirm on the spot the human rights violations it had previously reported. Amnesty International subsequently presented a memorandum to the government and since then has expressed concern that its recommendations should be implemented to include those alleged supporters of the previous government already in detention at the time of the mission, and the many hundreds of political prisoners subsequently arrested after anti-government demonstrations.

In its 1979 report, Amnesty International estimated that thousands of political prisoners were being held without trial—some 12,000 in Kabul's Pul-e-Charchi prison alone; these included instances where whole families, women and children included, had been arrested together with those suspected of political offences. It described a government policy of imprisoning any individual or member of a political group the government considered was in actual or potential opposition to its policies. In most cases political prisoners were denied all contact with their families and with the outside world.

Prisoners had been summarily executed without trial and many others simply "disappeared" after arrest. An Amnesty International list of "disappeared" individuals believed to have been executed or killed while in detention included two ministers of the Government former President Daud and the well-known scholar and statesman Mohammed Moosa Shafiq, who had been Prime Minister of Afghanistan in 1973.

The pattern of gross violations at that time was confirmed by the administration itself; on November 16, 1979, the Ministry of the Interior had reportedly begun publication of a list of as many as 12,000 names, mainly of political prisoners, who according to the government had died in Kabul jails in the period after April 1978. It also evidently intended to publish at a later date the names of other prisoners who had died in the provinces. In a letter of November 23, to President Amin, Amnesty International said it was shocked to read reports of publication of such lists, and also drew attention to reports that 800 children were named among those "disappeared" and requested that these lists, with full details pertaining to the 12,000 names, be furnished immediately. No response was received to this or to any other inquiry addressed to either President Taraki or later to President Amin.

On January 5, 1980, Foreign Minister Shah Mohammed Dost, representing the Government of Babrak Karmal, in a statement to the Security Council of the United Nations invited Amnesty International to visit Afghanistan. The same delegation which had visited Kabul in October 1978 was sent to Afghanistan to meet the new government. On

March 26, 1980, Amnesty International sent the President a memorandum based on the findings of the mission. It noted that thousands of Afghan citizens had "disappeared" after arrest during the period prior to December 27, 1979. It had been informed by those released that prisoners had been taken from Pul-e-Charchi prison at night and not seen again. Others had simply "disappeared" after arrest, and were believed to have been killed while in the custody of the security forces. The Ministry of the Interior revealed that it possessed a list of 4,854 people killed whose names it had not published; the list was far from complete. Many inquiries had been received about the fate of 9,000 individuals who had "disappeared" after arrest in the Kabul area. The government stated that those political prisoners who had not been released under the general amnesty of December 28, 1979, were presumed to have been killed before that date. The memorandum recommended that the government should undertake a full investigation of the cases of all individuals who had "disappeared" after arrest prior to December 27, 1979, and that it should publish the outcome of its investigations. The memorandum recommended that the government should avail itself of help from independent international organisations when tracing these people and that the government should make financial assistance available to the families who had lost their principal means of financial support as a result of the execution, "disappearance" or disablement through torture of the breadwinner.

The mission was informed that 15,084 prisoners had been released in the general amnesty of December 28, 1979. However, independent sources in Kabul estimated that between 3,000 and 4,000 prisoners had been released from Kabul's Pul-e-Charchi prison. Official statistics published in the January 1980 issue of the *Kabul Times* put the total number of prisoners released under the general amnesty from Pul-e-Charchi prison at 6,146. When questioned on the discrepancy in these figures, the Ministry of the Interior attributed the difference to the release of prisoners outside Kabul; a list of their names was in preparation. Amnesty International requested that it be sent a copy of the list. None has been received.

Another instance, reflecting the difficulty of obtaining official information about individuals who have "disappeared" after being taken into custody, is to be seen in the case of Ethiopia. The Government's "Red Terror" campaign, involving large-scale political arrests, mass killings and systematic torture, reached its peak in the capital, Addis Ababa, between December 1977 and February 1978. By May 1978, it had ended. But practices similar to those of the "Red Terror" continued in other parts of the country, especially in Asmara, Tigre, the Ogaden and the south.

A feature new to human rights violations in Ethiopia was the "disappearance" in July 1979 of some long-term political detainees and the abduction of a prominent church leader. On July 26, Amnesty International publicly expressed fears for the safety of a number of prominent political prisoners whose food, which was brought in daily, had been turned away by the prison authorities. This has usually meant that the prisoner has been summarily executed. Amnesty International cabled the Head of State, Lieutenant Colonel Mengistu Haile Mariam, urgently requesting assurance of the prisoners' safety and information concerning their whereabouts. No reply was received. No reliable information concerning their fate or whereabouts was subsequently received, and there was no corroboration of statements by government representatives that they had been transferred to other undisclosed prisons. At the end of July 1979, about 20 other long-term political detainees were released. On April 22, 1980, Amnesty International published the names of those who had "disappeared" in the hope that the international publicity might protect them if they were still alive. It had previously avoided naming Ethiopian prisoners for fear of reprisals against them or their relatives.

The United Nations Staff Council also appealed to the government on Human Rights Day, December 10, 1979, on behalf of two Ethiopian staff members, employees of the United Nations Economic Commission for Africa, who had been detained and not seen since 1978. They are Belay Melaku, a research assistant, and Azeb Abaye, a secretary.

"Disappearances" may occur during armed conflict or in the period after hostilities are reported to have ceased. A case in point is the fate of supporters of *Frente Revolucionaria do Timor Leste Independente* (Fretilin), the Revolutionary Front for an Independent East Timor.

During 1979 there were a number of reports of people "disappearing" after surrender or capture by Indonesian forces. Their present whereabouts remain unknown and there are fears they may have been executed. In February 1980, Amnesty International compiled a list of 22 such individuals. Some were reportedly killed immediately after surrender, but most simply "disappeared," either while in detention or, as in some cases, after release. These people were taken from their places of detention or picked up from their homes and have not been seen since. For example, in early 1978 Leopoldo Joaquim, a member of the Fretilin Central Committee, surrendered, was detained for several months and upon release was required to report daily to the local military command. In April 1979 he was escorted to the house of his niece, Maria Gorete Joaquim. Both were taken away, purportedly to Baucau. Neither has been seen or traced since. In March 1979, Dulce Maria da Cruz, also a member of the Fretilin Central Committee, was captured with her three-year-old child. She was taken to Dili and detained. Nothing has been heard of her since.

Amnesty International has urged a full investigation into the present whereabouts of these as well as of others said to have "disappeared" after surrender or capture. To its knowledge this has not been done.

Amnesty International continues to receive reports of new cases. It is not, however, in a position to estimate the total number of "disappearances" in East Timor in view of the obstacles to gaining access to the true situation.

Reports received by Amnesty International in 1979 and in 1980, allege large-scale summary executions of persons who surrendered under the terms of the amnesty or were among those captured. Furthermore, there are allegations that people who surrendered four years ago are now being executed for having assisted Fretilin. Reports also indicate that the East Timorese in general have been victims of reprisals, interrogation and arbitrary imprisonment. Amnesty International has also received reports of beatings of prisoners and persistent allegations of torture.

In April 1980 Amnesty International wrote to President Suharto to draw his attention to these concerns. It urged the Indonesian Government to carry out its own investigation into the present whereabouts of persons who had "disappeared" after surrender or capture; appealed to the Indonesian Government to co-operate in ensuring the International Committee of the Red Cross be permitted to expand its activities in East Timor beyond the provision of relief so as to include its other internationally-recognised functions of tracing missing persons and visiting prisons; and requested President Suharto to instruct Indonesian forces in the territory of East Timor to ensure the physical safety of former Fretilin supporters in compliance with the terms of the amnesty originally offered by the President.

In the light of the information Amnesty International had received, it considered such steps to be the minimum required. The minimum standards for the treatment of prisoners as set forth in the Geneva Conventions of 1949 governing areas of armed conflict prohibit torture and murder. According to internationally-recognised principles of law, all those alleged to have committed crimes are to be treated, judged and punished within a framework of legality which is consistent with respect for and protection of human rights.

No reply to this letter has been received to date by Amnesty International, nor has there been any evidence that the steps urged on the Indonesian Government have been implemented.

IV—INTERNATIONAL RESPONSE

As noted earlier, most of the initial international concern about "disappearances" in various countries came from the relatives of those who had "disappeared," lawyers acting for them, organisations to which they may have belonged or from non-governmental organisations working in the field of human rights. Inevitably, such concern was limited, in the first instance, to particular cases in individual countries. The issue was first placed on the international agenda by a 1978 resolution of the United Nations General Assembly which urged the Secretary-General "to continue to use his good offices in cases of enforced or involuntary disappearances of persons, drawing, as appropriate, upon the relevant experience of the Red Cross and of other humanitarian organizations."[5]

The Problem of Disappeared Persons was subsequently considered by the United Nations Sub-Commission on the Prevention of Discrimination and the Protection of Minorities at its 32nd session in Geneva on August 29, 1979, and the question forwarded to the 36th session of the United Nations Commission on Human Rights held in Geneva in February 1980. At that session, on February 29, 1980, the Commission adopted, without a vote, a resolution on the Question of Missing and Disappeared Persons.[6] The Commission decided to establish for a period of one year a Working Group consisting of five of its members, to serve as experts in their individual capacities, to examine questions relevant to enforced or involuntary "disappearances" of persons. It requested the Chairman of the Commission to appoint the members of the group. It decided that the Working Group, in carrying out its mandate, should seek and receive information from governments, intergovernmental organisations, humanitarian organisations and other reliable sources and requested the Secretary-General to appeal to all governments to co-operate with and assist the Working Group in the performance of its tasks and to furnish all information required. The Commission also requested the Secretary-General to provide the Working Group with all necessary assistance, in particular staff and resources they would require in order to perform their functions in an effective and expeditious manner. The resolution invited the Working Group, in establishing its working methods, to bear in mind the need to be able to respond effectively to information that came before it, to carry out its work with discretion and to submit to the Commission at its 37th session a report on its activities, together with its conclusions and recommendations.

As a result of the decision, the United Nations introduced for the first time in its history a procedure for possible immediate action in human rights cases. The United Nations human rights director Theodoor Van Boven told the Commission that the "burning and shocking" problem of "disappearances" could sometimes be eased by prompt intervention on behalf of the victims. He said that if the human rights division were to tackle the problem of "disappearances," it would require an additional £150,000, an extra nine full-time staff and a computer to deal with the

---

[5] United Nations, *Resolution 33/173*, December 20, 1978.
[6] United Nations Commission on Human Rights, *Resolution 20 (XXXVI)*, February 29, 1980.

mass of information on "disappearance" cases. His estimate of the resources required to put the decision into effect was not challenged by any of the 43 delegations comprising the Commission.

The Commission's chairman, Mr. Waleed Sadi (Jordan), announced the appointment of the Working Group: Mr. Mohamed Redha Al-Jabiri (Iraq), Viscount Colville of Culross (United Kingdom), Mr. Kwadwo Faka Nyamekye (Ghana), Mr. Ivan Tosevski (Yugoslavia) and Sr. Luis A. Varela (Costa Rica), all of whom were to act as experts in their individual capacities. At its first session from June 9 to 13, 1980, the Working Group elected Mr. Nyamekye as its chairman/rapporteur. It reported that it had before it reports of "disappearances" relating to some 15 countries from various parts of the world which had been transmitted by such sources as governments, the International Labour Office, the European Commission of Human Rights and non-governmental organisations in consultative status with the Economic and Social Council. After reviewing these reports the Working Group concluded that "the information before it warranted the deepest concern in particular for the danger to the life, liberty and physical security of persons subjected to enforced or involuntary disappearance and for the anguish and sorrow caused to relatives of those persons."[7] The second session of the Working Group was held in Geneva from September 15 to 19, 1980.

In a communiqué, the group said it was particularly alarmed by the reports it had received that "disappearances" continued to take place in several countries. The group also reviewed the action which had been taken between its first and second sessions in response to cases where immediate action was warranted to save lives.

According to the communiqué, "The reaction of governments to the group's initial approach has varied. Apart from the official invitation, one government has presented detailed information and another has offered cooperation in examining individual cases. The remainder have not fulfilled the group's expectations and consequently it decided to renew its appeal to those governments to cooperate with the group. The group also expressed its thanks to the Secretary-General for having appealed to governments pursuant to paragraph 4 of resolution 20 (XXXVI), to cooperate with and assist the working group in the performance of its task and to furnish all information required."[8]

During its second session the group met with government representatives and with representatives of organisations or associations directly concerned by reports of "disappearances" and met with the

---

[7] United Nations, *Working Group on Enforced or Involuntary Disappearances Concludes First Session*, HR/907, June 13, 1980.

[8] United Nations, *Working Group on Enforced or Involuntary Disappearances Concludes Second Session*, HR/2004, September 19, 1980.

Special Rapporteur on the situation of human rights in Chile, Abdoulaye Dieye.

The Working Group's first report to the United Nations Commission on Human Rights was issued on January 26, 1981, after its third session in December 1980. One question which arose was whether its report was to be confidential or not. At least one government was understood to have wished to communicate with the Working Group under existing procedures to guarantee confidentiality, but the group was believed not to favour such an approach to its work. The group could be hamstrung by continuing refusal on the part of governments to respond to its communication or by an insistence that it must function with discretion to the extent of imposing confidentiality procedures on all cases with which the group is concerned. The group itself is composed of experts and has the support of a small professional staff established within the Human Rights Division. It faced its first major diplomatic test when it reported to the Commission on Human Rights. Already, the group had faced first-hand the uncertainty that surrounded the problem it was set up to tackle. Mohamed Al-Jabiri, the Iraqi member, failed to appear for the first session of the Working Group, without explanation. By the time of its second session, the Working Group reported that he had resigned. Since receipt of his letter of resignation, there has been no independent contact with him and doubts remain as to his whereabouts and fate. The first report of the Working Group indicated that the United Nations had received specific information on between 11,000 and 13,000 "disappearances" in 15 countries. In March 1981 the United Nations Commission on Human Rights decided without a vote to extend the Working Group's mandate for another year.

CONFLICT IN NORTHERN IRELAND

By

HUGH SHEARMAN

THE writer of this paper contributed one on the same subject to the 1970 volume of this *Year Book*. Violence on a scale that attracted widespread attention began in Northern Ireland in 1968, a year of unrest in several other countries. Reaching serious proportions in August 1969, it has continued ever since, though with a somewhat declining death rate.

In retrospect it can be seen that 1970 was not a propitious time for attempting to elucidate a situation which has since revealed itself much more fully. The following decade has seen the publication of a variety of facts, figures and research material, all tending to put events in a perspective very different from that in which they were generally seen in 1970 and to bring into question some of the basic assumptions on which government policy, public comment and media reporting have depended.

I—THE IRISH BACKGROUND

The Government of Ireland Act 1920, set up two legislatures, one for Northern Ireland and one for Southern Ireland, linked by a common Council of Ireland. They had power over internal affairs and functioned within the constitution of the United Kingdom. At the second reading of the Bill in the House of Commons it was stated on behalf of the government that the purpose of the Act was to provide for "self-determination." Lloyd George at the same stage of the Bill referred to the idea of "two nations" in Ireland.

In 1921 Southern Ireland seceded from the United Kingdom, becoming a self-governing member of the British Commonwealth as the Irish Free State. Northern Ireland remained within the United Kingdom by its own choice. After some controversy about frontier demarcation and finances, an agreement was reached in 1925 in which the three Governments of the United Kingdom, the Irish Free State and Northern Ireland, each negotiating and signing independently, approved the existing frontier, abandoned the Council of Ireland, arranged for mutual recognition and consultation and recorded their resolve "mutually to aid one another in a spirit of neighbourly comradeship."

The secession of the Free State, the future Irish Republic, from the United Kingdom proved in many respects untimely. It occurred at a period when severe economic recession was imminent and not long before a considerable expansion of United Kingdom social services. By choosing to "go it alone," the Free State abandoned a claim to

182

participate in British social services and regional economic support.[1] Poverty, a high birthrate and an inert economy encouraged both large-scale emigration to Great Britain and at the same time a mood of rising nationalist aggression, the traditional psychological balm for internal national problems. This found expression mainly in irredentist claims to Northern Ireland. In 1937 the Dublin Government adopted a constitution, still in operation, in which was embodied a claim to sovereignty over Northern Ireland and referred in another of its articles to a prospective "reintegration of the national territory." The two countries, however, had never been united in a modern political sense except under British rule, and in the north there was a distinct sense of a separate Ulster national identity.

The British Government was conciliatory. Some constitutional and financial concessions were made. The wartime neutrality of what is now the Irish Republic was achieved under substantial British protection. When the Republic renounced membership of the Commonwealth, the British Government legislated to give Irish citizens virtually the same rights and privileges as British citizens, even to the extent of allowing them to vote in United Kingdom elections. Over a million Irish immigrants settled in Great Britain and were credited in the 1970s with having a controlling vote in about 50 marginal British constituencies.

Government in the Republic was strongly sectarian, as expressed in Eamonn De Valera's frequently quoted saying, "We are a Catholic nation." Protestants have nevertheless had a strong position in professional and administrative employments, like Phanariot Greeks in the Turkish Empire. Several individual Protestants, who have conformed to the pattern of Irish society, have reached high political office, including the presidency. On the other hand, Protestants have been unable to sustain their numbers in other employments, and their total numbers in the country have been halved in half a century by the social pressures exerted by an unsympathetic régime. Although aggregate Protestant emigration was lower than average, it was higher than average in the lower age groups.[2] The 1971 census showed a fall in the number of Protestants in 19 out of 25 employment categories. The theological severity expressed in the Cardinal Archbishop's declaration of 1931 that the Protestant church in Ireland "is not even a part of the Church of Christ"[3] has yielded to considerable surface affability; but an Irish-

---

[1] An Irish economist made the case in 1972 that if the Free State had remained in the United Kingdom its national income would then have been between 25 and 40 per cent. higher: R. Crotty in *The Times*, July 3, 1972.

[2] For a valuable study of these trends, see B. M. Walsh, *Religion and Demographic Behaviour in Ireland* (1970).

[3] *Irish News*, December 18, 1931.

American journalist noted in 1974 "pervasive but carefully hidden prejudice against Protestants."[4]

The irredentist claim to Northern Ireland has encouraged several campaigns of terrorist outrages against Northern Ireland. These ·were waged by the Irish Republican Army (IRA), a body banned by the Dublin Government but able to maintain surreptitiously its headquarters in the Republic. In the most recent period of violence it has been largely superseded by a more militant body, the Provisional IRA, the "Provos," while the older IRA has adopted a more political and social role. Another leftist paramilitary body in recent years has been the Irish National Liberation Army (INLA). An opinion survey under the auspices of the Economic and Social Research Institute, Dublin, found that in 1979 20.7 per cent. of respondents in the Republic supported IRA activities and 41.8 per cent. sympathised with IRA motives.[5]

II—THE GOVERNMENT OF NORTHERN IRELAND

Such a background presented the Government of Northern Ireland as set up under the Act of 1920 with immense problems. Apart from the difficulties of administering an outlying and economically depressed area, it had to face the political and security problems of having a land frontier with a rather unfriendly adjacent country while external relations and defence were wholly in the hands of the United Kingdom Government which was anxious to conciliate, or at least not to ruffle, the Dublin Government.

In security the Ulster Government had to try to do without calling in military aid by making what use it could of a police force, the Royal Ulster Constabulary (RUC), limited by statute to 3,000 men, backed by an auxiliary police force, the Ulster Special Constabulary. With these forces and making use of occasional internment of known activists, the Northern Ireland Government maintained peaceful conditions during nearly half a century. But in external relations the United Kingdom Government did little to counter the eloquent and often highly mendacious propaganda directed internationally against Northern Ireland from the Irish Republic.

Politically the Northern Ireland Government was dominated by the Ulster Unionist Party. This was not a party originally formed for government. It had been established round an Ulster Unionist Council founded in 1905 to unite all interests seeking to maintain the union with Great Britain. It was, thus, basically a coalition. Those who upheld the union could differ widely on other issues. Although Gladstone's decision in 1886 to take up the cause of Irish Home Rule had thrown Ulster

---

[4] T. J. O'Hanlon, *The Irish* (1975), p. 165.
[5] *Irish Times*, October 16, 1979.

Unionists into the arms of the Conservatives, their own traditions contained a large ingredient that was liberal and indeed radical.

This emerged in much of the legislation which came from the Northern Ireland parliament. Not professing to be ideologically either right or left, the Ulster Government was prepared to go ahead of Westminster in schemes of government involvement in industrial investment, control of agricultural production and marketing, the virtual nationalisation of transport and other progressive experiments in which other governments later paid it the compliment of detailed imitation. The Welfare State was adopted with little modification in detail for Northern Ireland, though Unionists at Westminster had sided with Conservative criticism of the form in which the scheme was unveiled there. The Ulster Government refrained from reproducing the restrictive industrial and trade-union legislation of the Heath Government.

Financially the Government of Northern Ireland had little freedom. The country was taxed at the same level as the rest of the United Kingdom and received back an allocation based on the principle that Northern Ireland services should have parity with those in the rest of the United Kingdom. The devolved government was financially efficient, and expenditure per head was often close to that in England. Thus in 1964–65, while public expenditure in Northern Ireland per head was 2 per cent. higher than that in England, in Scotland and Wales it was respectively 16 and 17 per cent. higher.[6]

Constant awareness of outside pressures caused the Unionist coalition to hold together, creating a background to parliament wholly different from that at Westminster. Many issues which at Westminster would have been debated between Government and Opposition were debated in Northern Ireland between wings of the Unionist Party, and often outside parliament.

Once the coalition was widely felt to be failing in its main purpose, particularly in the early 1970s and under the late Lord Faulkner, it began to break up into a number of smaller parties and splinter groups, all of which represented traditions which can be seen to have been components of the older and united party, which continued to hold a broad central position in the Unionist spectrum.

III—THE ELECTORAL SYSTEM

It has often been claimed that the preponderance of the Unionist Party was achieved by "gerrymandering" constituencies. Examination of what happened shows that this was not the case.

There were three levels of voting in Northern Ireland. Twelve members were elected to Westminster (not counting the university seat which

---

[6] *Royal Commission on the Constitution 1969–73*, Cmnd. 5460, Vol. I, Report, p. 178.

was abolished), constituency boundaries and franchise for this being wholly controlled by Westminster. Members were also elected to the 52 seats of the Northern Ireland House of Commons and to local councils.

New constituency boundaries for the Northern Ireland parliament were set up in 1929, when single-member constituencies replaced multi-member divisions. Omitting the university constituency, later abolished, Unionists, in all general elections during the 40 years from 1929 to 1969 inclusive, averaged 62.2 per cent. of the votes and 69.1 per cent. of the contested seats, while Nationalist and Republican candidates averaged only 14.6 per cent. of the votes but held 18.7 per cent. of the contested seats. In ratio of seats to votes, the Nationalist and Republican candidates were 15 per cent. ahead of the Unionists, and they still had an advantage when uncontested seats were taken into account.[7]

Successive Unionist Governments left the 1929 boundaries unchanged year after year, while substantial changes took place in population. By 1968 Unionists had come to hold the 14 most populous constituencies, mostly by large majorities. This implied large bodies of what would have been, from a gerrymandering point of view, "wasted" votes.

Local government boundaries had been fixed in 1923. They also were left unchanged, with only five individual alterations in half a century. Since they had been established on a system, prevailing at the time throughout the United Kingdom, which took account of valuation as well as of population, they became even more dissociated from actual population distribution than the parliamentary boundaries. An extreme but untypical case was the county borough of Londonderry where, in 1967, 35.5 per cent. of the votes gave Unionists 60 per cent. of the seats and 27.4 per cent. of the votes gave Nationalists the remaining 40 per cent. of the seats. For comparison, however, it may be recollected that, in 1974, 60 per cent. of the votes cast in two United Kingdom general elections were given against the party which nevertheless won both elections and formed the Government.

Local government election results showed little change in overall effect when compared before and after a drastic reform of the franchise, the voting system and the boundaries. In 1967, before the reform, candidates committed to maintaining the Union won 78.5 per cent. of the seats in the county borough of Belfast; and in 1973, after reform, they won 78.4 per cent. of the seats. In Northern Ireland as a whole, Unionists in 1973 got control of a slightly higher proportion of the 26 new councils than they had had of the 68 old councils elected in 1967.

Comparison of results shows that, although the system needed updating, both parliamentary and council elections in Northern Ireland had a much higher standard of proportionality than elections in Great Britain

---

[7] This and other illuminating background material is gathered in *The Northern Ireland General Elections of 1973*, Cmnd. 5851 (1975).

and that Republican candidates had on average a fair deal. Single-member constituencies, however, proved nearly as unfair to Labour in Ulster as they have been to Liberals in Great Britain. The whole issue of electoral integrity is important, since unfair elections were a major allegation of the Civil Rights movement from whose rallies and demonstrations violence began in 1968.

The emotive Civil Rights slogan "One man, one vote," which was much used in 1968, referred simply to the fact that, while in Great Britain the local government franchise had become the same as the parliamentary franchise, it was still confined in Northern Ireland to occupiers of rateable property and their spouses. In 1968, 941,785 persons had votes for the Northern Ireland parliament but only 694,483, or 73.74 per cent., had local government votes. There is no evidence that this favoured any particular political, social or religious group, and the assimilation of the two franchises in 1971 was not followed by changes in party-political results that can be attributed to there having previously been any general distortion.

IV—How People Have Voted

Voting in Northern Ireland has shown two significant trends—a steadily maintained and apparently increasing support for the Union with Great Britain, and an increasing dissociation of politics from religion.

In the first general election for a Northern Ireland legislature in 1921, 66.9 per cent. of the first preferences went to candidates committed to the Union. In the last general election for a Northern Ireland legislative in 1973, 74.7 per cent. of first preferences went to such candidates. Taking the first figure as an index, there is here a swing of 11.66 per cent. towards support for the Union.

Parallel with this there was a change in the religious composition of the population. In the 1926 census, Roman Catholics were 33.5 per cent. of the population. The 1971 census is less clear because so many did not answer the discretionary question on religious affiliation; but projections from the past, checked by distinctive family patterns, have produced general agreement in accepting a percentage of about 36.8 for 1971.[8] Again taking the earlier figure as 100, we have a swing of 9.85 per cent. in increased proportion of Roman Catholics. At once it will be seen that there is a correlation here that is quite at odds with the widely held assumption that Unionists are all Protestants and that Roman Catholics are all Republican in sympathy or that party-political and religious denominational names may be treated as interchangeable.

Voting trends shown in Northern Ireland internal elections are

---

[8] On this and on population trends in general, see P. Compton, "Religious Affiliation and Demographic Variability in Northern Ireland," in 1 *Transactions (New Series) of the Institute of British Geographers* (1976), Nr. 4, pp. 443 *et seq.*

reflected in Westminster elections. From the middle 1950s contests in all constituencies became the rule. In 1964, Unionists and Republicans contested all 12 Westminster seats and Labour contested 10 of them. Unionists received 63 per cent. of the votes, Labour 16.1 per cent. and Republicans 15.9 per cent. By this time the Northern Ireland Labour Party had committed itself to the Union.

What we seem to be seeing in post-War Northern Ireland elections is a hard core of political interests, oriented towards the Irish Republic, attempting to retain and increase its support from a Roman Catholic floating vote and failing to do so. It may well be that a major factor encouraging violence at the close of the 1960s was that the Republican cause was becoming desperate as votes steadily drifted away from it, producing a mood, if not a specific resolve, predisposing Republican sympathisers to seek to destabilise the whole social and political situation, hoping to gain from the resultant confusion what they had failed to gain by ordinary processes of democratic politics.

The extent of trends away from older Republican and "united Ireland" sympathies is not entirely revealed by party-political voting. Party programmes include many other issues; and many vote for a party for traditional, social or other reasons. But when the choice between the United Kingdom and the Irish Republic has been presented as a single issue, segregated from all other issues, support for the Union is more marked. In 1973 a plebiscite, popularly called the Border Poll, was held in Northern Ireland by the United Kingdom Government. Voters were asked whether they wanted Northern Ireland to remain part of the United Kingdom or be joined with the Irish Republic outside the United Kingdom. Republican parties boycotted the poll. The boycott was enforced on voting day by many acts of violence. There was a turn-out of 58.7 per cent. of the electorate, and 98.92 per cent. of the votes cast supported the Union with Great Britain, while 1.08 per cent. favoured the Republic. The highest overall voting turn-out in Northern Ireland under the existing franchise had been 72 per cent., so, even if all the voters between 58.7 per cent. and 72 per cent. had been in favour of the Republic, which is extremely improbable, it would have meant that only a fifth of the votes would have been against the Union.

In 1978 an "Attitude Survey," organised from Queen's University, Belfast, offered a range of political choices to respondents, two of them involving uniting Northern Ireland with the Irish Republic, under one government or federally. These two attracted the preference of only 39.1 per cent. of Roman Catholic respondents and only 16.9 per cent. of all respondents.[9]

---

[9] E. Moxon-Browne, *The Northern Ireland Attitude Survey*, an initial report, May, 1979, p. 25.

V—RELIGION AND POLITICS

The proportionate distribution of the population between Protestants and Roman Catholics in Northern Ireland is similar to that in the Netherlands. It is two-thirds and one-third in a population of $1\frac{1}{2}$ million, slowly gravitating towards three-fifths and two-fifths. On the issue of Ulster's orientation towards Britain or towards the Irish Republic, it can be seen from the foregoing that political opinion and religious affiliation coincide only to a limited extent. The much used expression "two communities" is misleading and has created much misunderstanding when applied to the political situation. There is a sense in which members of one religious body form a community, but this does not make all non-members of it into an antithetical community. In colloquial usage, Protestants in Northern Ireland are simply non-Roman Catholics, a very disparate population.

Historically an identification of Irish nationalism with Roman Catholicism has been close and strong, and it is in the Roman Catholic part of the Ulster population that the Irish Republican cause there has its base. In the earlier years of this century even the traditionally significant constituency of Londonderry could be represented at Westminster by a Roman Catholic Unionist. But from the early 1920s it became dangerous for a Roman Catholic who preferred the Union to "stand up and be counted." Lately this has changed again. All Unionist parties claim Roman Catholic support. The Alliance Party in particular has been able to combine a strong commitment to the Union with a claimed one-third Roman Catholic voting support and is led by a Roman Catholic.

The Roman Church, many of whose clergy come from the Republic, is widely regarded in Ulster as a political church which prefers not to "render unto Caesar." It has its own separate sectarian education system, financed from public funds but strictly separate from the non-sectarian State education system. Increasing numbers of laity, however, want their children to go to mixed schools. It is probably natural for Protestants to assume that, since conditions have been established in the Republic tending towards the obliteration of Protestantism there, the Church's hierarchy, in its zeal to end heresy, is eager to see the rule of the Dublin Government extended over Northern Ireland.

On the Protestant side there is a minority of very fanatical people; but on a Sunday the majority of Protestants will not be found attending a church. The broad centre of popular Protestantism is represented by the Orange Institution whose declared objective is to uphold civil and religious liberty. It requires a specific commitment from its members to respect the rights and liberties of their Roman Catholic fellow citizens. Its Ulster membership is wide, contains a large middle-class ingredient, and is guided by an ethos which seems much superior to that sometimes manifested in the movement's offshoots in Glasgow or Liverpool.

The fact that there is this tension between the Roman Catholic communion and nearly all other religious affiliations has caused too many commentators to imagine that violence in Ulster can be simplistically attributed to the irrational religious fanaticism of its inhabitants. The expectations which such· an interpretation arouses are constantly disappointed by the actual attitudes and behaviour of people.

The survey conducted under Professor Rose in 1968 found that 81 per cent. of Protestant respondents and 83 per cent. of Roman Catholic respondents said that relations between people of their respective religious affiliations in the areas where they had grown up were "very good" or "fairly good." The great majority of both groups thought that Ulster people of different religion from themselves were "about the same" as themselves. And 66 per cent. of the Protestants thought that their own co-religionists in England were "much different" from themselves, while the same proportion of Roman Catholics had the same feeling about their co-religionists in the Irish Republic.

There was thus a strong shared sense of Ulster identity and of the alienness of outsiders, whether British or Irish, regardless of religious affiliation. "This sense of alienness from Englishmen and Irishmen of the 26 counties (the Irish Republic) is about equally strong," Professor Rose noted, "among Protestants and Catholics, the difference index approaching nil. The most surprising of all findings is that more than two-thirds of Protestants and Catholics think that Ulstermen of the opposite religion are about the same as themselves." He would not have been at all astonished at this had he been born in Ulster and lived there.[10] Shared experience of recent adversities has probably strengthened rather than weakened this sense of shared identity.

VI—Roots of Social Difference

It was an easy choice for Republicans to consolidate Roman Catholic support by representing that denomination as having been discriminated against by Unionists and Protestants. It was also a peculiar weakness of the Unionist Government that it did not monitor its own performance, did not know the social effects of its own policies, and so had no factual answers for its critics.

In 1969 the Cameron Commission of three persons was set up by the Northern Ireland Government of Captain Terence O'Neill to report on the causes of civil disturbances. It was required to work with great rapidity and had no power to compel attendance of witnesses or examine on oath. In its list of causes of civil disturbances it gave first place to inadequate and unfair allocation of public authority housing to Roman Catholics.[11] This conclusion was based on allegations made to it about

---

[10] R. Rose, *Governing Without Consensus*, 1971, p. 214.
[11] *Disturbances in Northern Ireland*, Cmnd. 532 (1969) (N.I.).

seven out of 68 local authorities then functioning. As a result the housing powers and duties of these authorities were given to a single centralised Housing Executive which built fewer houses and has been in more or less serious difficulties ever since. Professor Rose in 1971, however, showed that his 1968 survey had not found evidence of discrimination against Roman Catholics in the housing patterns of any of the six counties and two county boroughs.[12]

In 1975 the volume of the 1971 census dealing with religion was published.[13] This made possible the collating of religious affiliation with extensive information simultaneously collected on housing conditions. Roman Catholic households and Protestant households (here consisting only of Presbyterians, Church of Ireland and Methodists) had been housed respectively as follows:

	Roman Catholics per cent.	Protestants per cent.
Own home	42.3	46.3
Public authority tenancy	40.9	32.6
Private tenancy	16.1	20.6
Others	0.7	0.5
All	100.0	100.0

This shows that, in proportion to their numbers, Roman Catholic households had been 25 per cent. more generously provided with public authority housing than their Protestant neighbours. Answers to other questions on housing showed that this advantageous position had not been offset by any marked inferiority in their accommodation in other respects.

Another area in which discrimination was alleged was employment. The 1971 census showed 5.6 per cent. of Protestant workers unemployed but 13.9 per cent. of Roman Catholics. In other words, 94.4 per cent. of the Protestants were then employed and 86.1 per cent. of Roman Catholics, so that it had apparently been about one-twelfth more difficult for a Roman Catholic to obtain employment, a significant but not very large difference.[14]

---

[12] Rose, *op. cit.* in note 10, above, p. 293.

[13] *Census of Population, 1971*, Religion Tables, Northern Ireland.

[14] The form in which census questions were worded resulted in census figures for unemployment being over 30 per cent. higher than the number of persons registered as unemployed in April 1971, when the census was taken; but the census figures have to be used, since they alone enable religion and unemployment to be collated. There seems no reason not to accept as fairly correct the proportions indicated by the census figures.

In a paper already cited,[15] Compton in 1976 pointed to the validity of the view that Roman Catholics were disadvantaged "not so much as a result of discrimination but because of their larger family size." The following table, based on the 1971 census, shows the close correlation between unemployment and birthrate, as birthrate manifests its effects in the excess of young persons over old.

	Great Britain ('000)	Northern Ireland ('000)	N.I. Roman Catholics ('000)
Persons in age group 15–25	7,826	241	80
Persons in age group 55–65	6,413	150	38
Excess of young over old	1,413 (22%)	91 (61%)	42(111%)
Total unemployed	759	51	24
Unemployed as decimal fraction of excess of young over old	0.54	0.56	0.57

There is not space in this paper to explain the social mechanisms which cause this correlation of unemployment with excess of young persons; but one cause lies in the fact that unemployment hits younger age groups much more severely than older[16] and so is more prevalent in social groups which have a higher birthrate. Size of family—small or large—also affects readiness to pursue higher education or to take up "dead-end" jobs when young. These, and other traceable social habits of Ulster Roman Catholics, are mathematically sufficient to account for Roman Catholic disadvantage in employment without any need to suppose a significant factor of discrimination.[17] Furthermore, actual direct evidence of discrimination has not been forthcoming. A Fair Employment Agency, established in 1976, discovered only eight proven cases of religious discrimination in employment up to March 31, 1979.[18]

Great social changes, however, are taking place in Ulster. B. M. Walsh in a paper already cited[19] had found a Roman Catholic birthrate in Northern Ireland 40 per cent. higher in the early 1960s than that of other denominations and "higher than any recorded in Europe in recent years with the exception of Albania." But Compton in 1976 showed that

---

[15] See note 8, above.

[16] An article, "The Youth Mountain," in The Economist, May 27, 1978, noted unemployment for under-20s in the EEC and America as being then three times higher than the general rate. For Northern Ireland the heavier incidence of increased unemployment among the young is illustrated in Economic and Industrial Strategy for Northern Ireland (HMSO, 1976), pp. 85 and 86.

[17] I am indebted to much illuminating unpublished research material from Dr. Colin Baskett, based on analysis of census reports.

[18] Fair Employment Agency for Northern Ireland, annual reports.

[19] See note 2, above.

there was a 9 per cent. drop in this birthrate between 1961 and 1971 and that the difference between marriage patterns inside and outside the Roman Catholic part of the community "had narrowed considerably" as Roman Catholics in Ulster began to catch up on their Protestant neighbours in family planning. Though they had lagged behind all Western Europe in this, the speed of change, now that it had set in, "has been much greater than occurred in the rest of western Europe."[20] It would appear that equality in birthrates is a necessary prerequisite for a just, peaceful and stable society, and that a movement towards that equalisation has set in strongly.

VII—VIOLENCE

It is possible to exaggerate the extent of violence in Northern Ireland. During its prevalence more people have been killed in traffic accidents than in political violence, and most people have been able at most times to live peaceful and normal lives, largely untouched by events which have often been given highly dramatic treatment by the world's Press and by television. At the same time the statistics of 10 years will show how deeply the lives and feelings of the whole population must have been affected.

Violent deaths from August 1969 to August 1979, numbered 1,956, made up of 319 from the regular army, 93 from the Ulster Defence Regiment, a locally recruited and mainly part-time force within the army, 90 from the Royal Ulster Constabulary, 39 from the auxiliary police, and 1,415 civilians, an expression which includes members of political paramilitary bodies. Over 20,000 people were injured, some very gravely, and 6,550 explosions were reported.[21]

To put the impact of these figures into perspective—if events comparable with the scale of population had occurred in Great Britain—there would have been 66,500 dead, including 14,000 members of the armed forces, about 700,000 injured, and over 200,000 explosions. Keeping the peace has at most times kept 30,000 men and women under arms, the equivalent of a million people in Great Britain.

The United Kingdom Government's interpretation of this conflict, and hence the strategy used in dealing with it, appears to have arisen largely from considerations not directly connected with Northern Ireland. The British Labour Party has been strongly influenced by its dependence on the Southern Irish vote in its constituencies. The Conservative Government of Edward Heath, anxious to enter the European Economic Community (EEC), and to do so in company with the Irish Republic, had to win the favour of governments which, through past default, had been

---

[20] See note 8, above.
[21] Figures from Royal Ulster Constabulary.

given virtually nothing but the Dublin Government's account of conditions in Northern Ireland. United Kingdom Governments accordingly took an attitude of critical severity towards the Northern Ireland Government, and the latter showed a singular incapacity to gather and present facts which might have amply vindicated its performance in many fields.[22]

Among other changes which the British Government forced on the Northern Ireland Government was the dismantling of the internal security system by largely disarming the police and disbanding the auxiliary police. Republican activists increasingly took advantage of the opportunities thus offered to them. When the United Kingdom Government increased the military presence in Northern Ireland in 1969 and accepted overall responsibility for security, this was represented not as an intervention to protect United Kingdom citizens but as an exercise to stop a purely internal conflict of two supposed "communities." Although the conflict developed quite clearly as being basically an attack on British people by avowedly anti-British paramilitary forces, the criterion of allegiance was not overtly allowed to be used in security vetting.

Violence continued with increasing momentum. Less than a week after Britain had signed the Accession Treaty preceding entry into the EEC, 13 people were killed by army bullets in an incident in Londonderry, in January 1972. Coming at that awkward time, the event seemed to stimulate the British Government to a further effort to put the blame for the growing chaos on those who were the victims rather than the creators of that chaos. In a dramatic gesture the parliament and Government of Northern Ireland were suspended and then abolished. A bureaucratic dictatorship was established under a Secretary of State, William Whitelaw.[23]

In 1973 a general election was held for an Assembly. Brian Faulkner, later Lord Faulkner, as leader of the Unionist Party, contested it with a manifesto which said, "Unionists are not prepared to participate in government with those whose primary objective is to break the Union with Great Britain." Having secured substantial electoral support by this

---

[22] For example, in spite of the grave doubt which Rose in 1971 threw on the Cameron Commission's sweeping allegations about religious discrimination in public authority housing, Lord O'Neill in 1972 was still commending the Cameron Report as a "textbook" for reform, in *The Autobiography of Terence O'Neill*, p. 114. Had his Government been effectively monitoring the results of its own social policies and legislation, he would have had an inkling of what the 1971 census was going to show and could have forestalled those unjust charges about housing discrimination which, in the event, the Ulster Government dumbly accepted and needlessly suffered for.

[23] Although the Government of Ireland Act 1920 reserved full power to the Westminster parliament, it may be held that the circumstances of the tripartite agreement of 1925 had recognised a degree of sovereignty in the Northern Ireland Government and given it an implied federal status. British constitutional custom has usually been understood to imply a principle of *quamdiu se bene gesserit* when subordinate legislatures have been established. No charge of misbehaviour was made against the parliament and Government of Northern Ireland.

undertaking, he and some of his colleagues accepted appointments to an Executive, handpicked by the Secretary of State. Six out of 14 members of the administration were members of the Social Democratic and Labour Party (SDLP) which had been recently formed and had the declared aim of taking Northern Ireland out of the United Kingdom and into the Irish Republic. The SDLP had secured less than a quarter of the Assembly seats and votes. Before confirmation of their appointments, members of the Executive were required to negotiate a compromising agreement with the Government of the Irish Republic in a form also inconsistent with Unionist manifesto undertakings. This was too much for the Ulster public, and a general strike brought the Executive to an end. All the Unionist participants in it had committed political suicide.

The "direct rule" régime which has since governed Northern Ireland has legislated largely by Orders in Council. It has removed most local government decisions from elected persons and given them to bodies not effectively answerable to the public. This has had the effect of placing a crippling burden of what would normally be local government business on Northern Ireland members of the Westminster parliament. Top posts in the "direct rule" régime have in practice been reserved for Englishmen.

A constitutional convention was elected in 1975, charged with the task of considering future constitutional arrangements for the government of Northern Ireland. The convention gave much consideration to "power-sharing" between parties. The conclusion come to by a substantial majority was that statutory power-sharing at executive or cabinet level would not work. It would produce deadlocks between executive and legislature, or it would place individuals forming a minority in such an executive in a false position in relation to their own party in the event of a majority of the executive, supported by a majority of the legislature, pursuing a policy unacceptable to that minority party.

It was proposed, therefore, that much executive business should be devolved to parliamentary committees, with chairmanships made generously available to opposition members. This approach owed much to the example of Congressional committees in the United States and to the increasing influence of committees at Westminster. It was supported by about two-thirds of the members of the convention and was presented in open-ended terms which left scope for much further negotiation of detail. The Wilson Government, however, at once turned it down and made no use of any of the work of the convention.

Meanwhile atrocities and outrages continued. The feeling of inadequate protection, and the suppression of normal open political life, had encouraged the underground development of large loyalist paramilitary bodies which occasionally engaged in recklessly irrelevant reprisal killings, sometimes feuded with one another, but mostly remained rather inactive. They were a product of conflict and not its cause.

A large proportion of the Republican outrages involved use of the territory of the Irish Republic, either as a base from which an action could be initiated, a refuge for those who had committed a killing or bombing, a place from which explosive devices inside United Kingdom territory could be set off by distant control, a route by which arms and explosives could be introduced into Northern Ireland, or a location for a command headquarters for terrorist activities. At all times the British Government has refused to quantify the incidents which have thus involved the Republic. In October 1972, Mr. John Laird, a member of the suspended parliament, lodged details of 529 fully documented cases of attack on Northern Ireland from the Republic's territory up to June 1972, with a senior official of the United Nations Secretariat. By the time of writing, it is probable that full and comprehensive research could show that the number of such cases has reached five figures.

When this is taken in conjunction with the Republic's continued claim to United Kingdom territory,[24] its unwillingness to extradite persons sought for murders in Northern Ireland, the burning down of the British embassy in Dublin, the murder of a British ambassador in Dublin and the murder of a naïvely exposed member of the British royal family, there can be seen to have been a situation between States which is perhaps unthinkable anywhere else in the world. Within Northern Ireland it has created almost total disbelief in British Government integrity and profound distrust of any contacts that take place between the London and Dublin Governments.

It is hardly the business of this paper to project the future. That future will be shaped to some extent by the "direct rule" régime's policy of de-industrialisation, leading to a level of unemployment in Northern Ireland often twice that in Britain. It would appear that the Irish Republican enemies of the United Kingdom are so fiercely and resolutely dedicated that no "political solution" is going to deter them from their chosen course, only military defeat. As for a political settlement for Northern Ireland, none is likely to be generally acceptable that does not provide a freely democratic devolved parliament in which the electorate is trusted and there are no contrived advantages or handicaps for any party or candidate. The fact that there are now at least four main parties in Northern Ireland, every one of which is electorally in a minority, could make for open and lively government if genuine democratic institutions were restored.

---

[24] The claim seems inconsistent with the Republic's commitment to one of the principles of the Helsinki agreements of 1975.

COMPARATIVE
INTERNATIONAL POLITICS

By
N. G. ONUF

THE era of systems-thinking in Political Science dates from the mid-1950s. David Easton gave currency to the term "political system" in 1953, and major statements on how to study such systems appeared a short while thereafter.[1] Input-output analysis, general systems theory, equilibrium models all competed for attention. Even though students of foreign governments and relations among States were especially stimulated to abandon exclusively institutional and historical studies for brave new ways to comprehend political reality, there were signs even before the end of the decade that emergent fields of Comparative and International Politics were to part company in their preferred systemic formulations.

In Comparative Politics the structural-functional orientation popularised by Gabriel Almond prevailed as the convenient tool for investigating not just governments but anything political. In principle all political systems were subject to comparison because they all, regardless of form, share certain distinctively political functions. In practice this meant comparison of diverse systems nonetheless sharing important features qualifying them to be called States. The result was an ample but bounded universe of items for comparison.

Structural-functionalism inspired what has come to be called the comparative movement, penetrating most areas of political inquiry except, peculiarly enough, international relations.[2] The stated object of comparing systems is theory-building. While failing to create theories of any consequence, the effort was marked by a surge of conceptual clarification, taxonomic ordering and empirical enrichment. Substantial though these gains are over previous scholarship, they succeeded mostly in fueling rising epistemological expectations structural-functional comparison could never fulfil.

Opinion leaders in Political Science turned increasingly to neopositivist epistemology prevailing in philosophy of science, which provided damning critiques of anything functional and legitimated the

---

[1] D. Easton, *The Political System* (1953); G. A. Almond, "Comparative Political Systems," *Journal of Politics* (1956), pp. 391–409; D. Easton, "An Approach to the Analysis of Political Systems," *World Politics* (1957), pp. 383–400. The term "system" has of course been used unsystematically for centuries.
[2] G. A. Almond, *Political Development* (1970), p. 25.

quest for properly hypothetico-deductive theory.[3] Whether the rise of neopositivism and the quest for formally stated theory as the basis of "real" science are benighted misadventure or passage to enlightenment cannot as yet be told. It can only be said that theory development in any form, or by any name, must be preceded by a period of conceptual and taxonomic growth. This would indeed seem to have been the pattern with all major advances in human understanding.

As much as its sister field of Comparative Politics, International Politics initially celebrated the pursuit of theory in systemic terms. Yet there resemblance ends. Few of the gains associated with the comparative movement characterise current studies of international relations. Particularised research strategies by whatever epistemological warrant yield collective incoherence, while conceptual and taxonomic under-nourishment make the pursuit of theory an unimpressive and frequently maligned endeavour. The field dissolves from within, its makers increasingly unsure even that it exists.

There are doubtless a number of factors contributing to such a remarkable parting of ways, with such untoward consequences for International Politics as a field. Principal among them must be the appearance in 1957 of Morton A. Kaplan's exceptionally well-developed, apparently hypothetico-deductive models of six possible international systems.[4] Kaplan's formulations dwarfed all other claimants to favour. Their specificity and formality created the impression, its seems unduly, that Kaplan had avoided functionalist fallacies and complied with neopositivist strictures on the nature of the theory enterprise.

One burden of this paper is to show how and why Kaplan's success stifled systems thinking applied to international relations. A second burden is to sketch what might have been, had the comparative movement a proper chance. In the absence of anything to compare, what came to be was an all too natural, almost narcissistic preoccupation with the international system, meaning of course the Western State system.

George Modelski and Fred W. Riggs, in particular, early developed complementary structural-functional formulations to permit comparison of international systems.[5] Had these important but ignored initiatives been built upon, International Politics might not have fallen so far

---

[3] One of the more energetic attacks on structural-functional comparison from a neopositivist vantage point is R. T. Holt and J. E. Turner, "Crises and Sequences in Collective Theory Development," 69 *American Political Science Review* (1975), pp. 979–994. Almond, *op. cit.* in note 2, above, retrospectively conceded the change in fashion by referring to his work, rather apologetically, as "heuristic theory."

[4] M. A. Kaplan, *System and Process in International Politics* (1957), Part I. "Hypothetico-deductive" is not Kaplan's description. It is typical of commentaries on Kaplan's work and was used specifically by O. R. Young, *A Systemic Approach to International Politics* (1968), p. 10.

[5] G. Modelski, "Agraria and Industria: Two Models of the International System," and F. W. Riggs, "International Relations as a Prismatic System," 14 *World Politics* (1961), pp. 118–181.

behind its sister field. Comparative Politics might also have benefited, because the relatively unbounded nature of international political phenomena encourages recourse to the comparative literature of Anthropology and Sociology, where structural-functionalism arose and long flourished.[6] Multicultural international history, systemic in cast but conceptually indifferent, might even have lent its extraordinary descriptive range and contextual richness to the integration of two now entirely separate fields of Political Science in an openly interdisciplinary manner.[7]

I—The International System

To understand current partiality for one system and correlative disinterest in the comparative study of International Politics, we must examine Kaplan's claims and contributions on behalf of systems thinking, thereby to establish the sources of his appeal. Kaplan presented his six models, which he now calls "theory sketches,"[8] as particularly suitable for theory-building because they contain a small number of elements abstracted "from a far richer historical context."[9] Called variables, these elements are arranged in several classes, the principal ones being "essential rules" and "transformation rules."[10] Collectively these rules provide for the identity and regulatory activity of hypothetical systems in equilibrium. Transformation rules are merely statements of failed essential rules. If any one essential rule fails, they all fail, and the system transforms.

Kaplan strengthened the impression that the rules represented a logical arrangement by insisting that fewer rules were impossible. While a larger number were possible, they would make his model less suitable as the basis of an eventual theory whose deductions would have generalised import. We surmise that no other rules would present themselves no matter who read the historical record. Furthermore, rules

---

[6] See M. Harris, *The Rise of Anthropological Theory* (1968), and A. W. Gouldner, *The Coming Crisis of Western Sociology* (1970), for major critical assessments.

[7] The more so as multicultural international history gains in conceptual awareness and comparative intent. Contrast A. B. Bozeman, *Politics and Culture in International History* (1960), with M. Wight, *Systems of States* (1977), and R. G. Wesson, *State Systems* (1978).

[8] "The six international systems ... are partial theory sketches that permit research programs of both comparative historical and analytical types." See M. A. Kaplan, *Towards Professionalism in International Theory* (1979), pp. 96–97.

[9] Kaplan, *op. cit.* in note 4, above, at p. 8.

[10] Kaplan's terminology is confusing. While two classes of variables are called rules, the remaining classes are called variables—actor classificatory variables, capability variables and information variables. Yet the variables he specifically called variables he tended to treat as parameters of stipulated, constant value for a given system state. Furthermore, the rules are not merely variables, but statements of variable relationships, containing or implying independent and dependent variables in each instance. Thus, in Kaplan's peculiar formulations, rules are pairs of variables, while variables are constants. At least he has used these labels consistently and exclusively.

as a logical arrangement of postulates and deductions in hypothetical models would appear to function as hypotheses testable in terms of real systems.

In articulating his models Kaplan actually never talked about their deductive and hypothetical properties. He did enumerate a series of hypotheses about regulatory processes which on inspection turn out to be actor centred and not at all system related.[11] He also claimed that if a host of unspecified conditions were met, his models would be predictive. This is a trivial claim, however, because it is true of any model.

The language of variables, rules and system states allows Kaplan to observe what certain systems look like at a dizzying level of abstraction. What he observed he stated as if it were being explained. John J. Weltman and Kenneth N. Waltz have each characterised Kaplan as a bad logician.[12] If the rules were not logically intended, however, then Kaplan can be no more than a bad historian. He made errors in culling the record, perhaps, and in reconstructing it so sparely. He may, as Waltz claimed, have lost the system as a distinctive reality in the process.[13] Certainly he befuddled his audience by not sounding like a historian.

Actually Kaplan's elaborate formulations are excess baggage. Four of the models were only imagined as possible systems in some future time, and their rules are whatever Kaplan chose them to be. The remaining models are the consequential ones for Kaplan, and for us, because they have historical referents. Stripped of jargon, they are readily seen as distilled wisdom about balance-of-power and loosely bipolar systems.[14] We need only turn to a book Kaplan co-authored on international law to find the Western State system historically treated, with little ado about essential rules and the rest. Balance-of-power and loose-bipolar systems are temporal manifestations of a continuous historical experience and not the disembodied abstractions we find elsewhere.[15]

---

[11] Only in his separate discussion of regulatory processes, *op. cit.* in note 4, above, Part II, did Kaplan allude to "systems hypotheses," and then only in passing, p. 87.

[12] J. J. Weltman, *Systems Theory in International Relations* (1973), pp. 57–60; K. N. Waltz, *Theory of International Politics* (1979), pp. 52–58.

[13] But see Kaplan, *op. cit.* in note 8, above, at pp. 12–13, 47–48; and S. Hoffmann, *Primacy or World Order* (1978), pp. 146–147.

[14] Note that one of Kaplan's imagined systems was called "tight bipolar." In common parlance the loose bipolar system is simply called bipolar. The degree of "looseness" is understood as being subject to considerable change and requiring empirical assessment at any point.

[15] M. A. Kaplan and N. de B. Katzenbach, *The Political Foundations of International Law* (1961), Chap. 2. Kaplan himself has held on to the view that his was a comparative analysis of different historical systems. *Op. cit.* in note 8, above, at p. 131. Nevertheless, specific studies undertaken by his students on the Renaissance Italian system and the twentieth century Chinese warlord system he characterises as "local international systems embedded in the general international system but apparently sufficiently insulated for long periods to permit independent treatment." *Ibid.* p. 162.

Both in its stated propositions and in its latent assumptions Kaplan's historical characterisation follows in the liberal tradition of assuming the constancy of an economic order and the consequent primacy of interest defined politically—the pursuit of power—in the operation of the system in any of its possible states. Liberal theory depends on the autonomy of the principal actors and on their rationality, understood to mean their acceptance of interest as the governor of behaviour. Economic liberalism defines interests differently only substantively. Kaplan clearly stands in the liberal tradition as applied to politics and in that tradition tends to reflect the views particularly associated with Hans J. Morgenthau, whose Machiavellian posture supposes that political values, like power and prestige, definitionally constitute a fixed fund.[16] If one actor increases his share from the fund, others' is diminished. Not to try to increase one's share is to run the risk of losing what one already has, making conflict inevitable. The attributes of conflict are decisively affected by such features of the system as the distribution of power, and this is the reason for engaging in systemic analysis.

Such is a liberal-evolutionary view of "*the* international system." In content it is as much Kaplan's as it is Morgenthau's. The differences between them are less epistemological than stylistic, and not at all substantive. It is also the substance of Stanley Hoffmann's view of the international system, which he nonetheless held up as antipodal to Kaplan's.[17] Here again differences being procedural and stylistic are less than meet the eye. Hoffmann simply sounded more like a historian.

Hoffmann perhaps even more than Kaplan insisted on partitioning the Western experience into discrete systems. As Waltz has shown, the result is a proliferation of systems with no clear criteria for distinguishing among them.[18] Enough change within a system, however much that is, means a change of system. The same tendency is more strikingly present in Richard N. Rosecrance's effort, published in 1963, to characterise no fewer than nine systems, one following on the other in Western international history after 1740.[19] Rosecrance combined Hoffmann's openly inductive method with Kaplan's substantive concern for systemic identity understood in terms of regulatory activity. Every

---

[16] As exemplars of the "Realist" position, both Morgenthau and E. H. Carr excoriated liberals as believing in the likelihood of a "harmony of interest." This too limited construction of liberalism wrongly excludes the laissez-faire doctrine, which realism strongly resembles, from the liberal tradition which, after all, has a "dismal," or conservative as well as a progressive branch. See H. J. Morgenthau, *Scientific Man vs. Power Politics* (1946), Chaps. 3, 4; E. H. Carr, *The Twenty Years' Crisis* 1919–1939 (2nd ed., 1946), Chap. 4.

[17] See S. Hoffmann, "International Relations: The Long Road to Theory," 11 *World Politics* (1959), pp. 315–362. Hoffmann's most useful statements on the nature of the system are in "International Systems and International Law," 14 *World Politics* (1961), pp. 205–237, and *op. cit.* in note 13, above, Chap. 3.

[18] *Op. cit.* in note 12, above, at p. 45.

[19] R. N. Rosecrance, *Action and Reaction in World Politics* (1963).

major war, as an instance of regulatory failure, must spell the death of one system and the cessation of war therefore the birth of another.

Writing in 1965 Charles A. McClelland redefined the problem of repeated system transformations by reserving the term "transformation" for changes such that no international system would then exist.[20] The criterion for determining that transformation had indeed taken place is quite clear in such a case. The decentralised character of a system constituted of autonomous, "sovereign" entities must give way to a centralised order. Inasmuch as there has been no such change over the last several centuries of the Western experience, we may freely speak of "the international system" as one continuous, evolving experience. McClelland and virtually everyone else writing on the subject ever since have seen fit to view the system in just these terms.[21]

For all their talk of systems numberless in principle, Kaplan and Hoffmann came to the same conclusion. They identified two system types—Kaplan, balance-of-power and loose-bipolar; for Hoffmann, stable and revolutionary—which together describe the history of the Western State system. The appearance of these two types in succession, in oscillation, really, contributed to the now prevailing image of one system, two phases, frequent transitions, indefinite duration, and apparently infinite capacity to rebound from major disruptions like world wars and absorb the impact of civilisational changes, like industrialisation, often described as revolutionary.

Recent monumental changes in the world are seen no differently. Unprecedented threats of destruction become a property of the system, namely, its stability. If there are but two states of the system, multipolar and bipolar, to use the now conventional labels for Kaplan's and Hoffmann's two system types, then one or the other may be the more stable and thus comport better with the structural reality of the balance of terror.[22] Note that answering the question of stability does nothing whatever to insure the system's survival. On the contrary, it clearly supposes that changes in the distribution of State power, themselves autonomous and inevitable, change the system's polarity and with it our survival prospects.

The passivity of liberal-evolutionary systems-thinking eventually

---

[20] C. A. McClelland, *Theory and the International System* (1965), Chap. 2.

[21] The major exception would appear to be Michael Haas, "International Subsystems: Stability and Polarity," 64 *American Political Science Review* (1970), pp. 98–123. Reference to "subsystems" sheds no light on the conceptual dilemma of one or many systems. It should also be noted that the study of analytical (sub-) systems—crisis systems, alliance systems, for example—is a vogue McClelland initiated. It takes for granted "the international system" as a frame of reference. C. A. McClelland, "The Acute International Crisis," 14 *World Politics* (1961), pp. 182–204.

[22] This is debated in a series of essays by Waltz, K. W. Deutsch and J. D. Singer and Rosecrance, conveniently reprinted by J. N. Rosenau (ed.), *International Politics and Foreign Policy* (2nd ed., 1969), pp. 304–355.

provoked an equally evolutionary but actively illiberal view of the Western State system, or "the modern world-system," as imperially created and dependency creating.[23] An adaptive capitalist economy supplants political relations of dominant Powers as the system's explanatory nexus. Rejected is the liberal assumption that the system of competitive politics operates in the manner of a marketplace economy. In its place is the illiberal argument that the global economy is rigged to operate as a marketplace for the few, not just to the exclusion of the many, but at their expense. The point of what passes for international politics is to maintain and service this rigged economy. To the extent that contests among dominant Powers are not merely illusory, they are an indulgence afforded the favoured few, again more at the many's expense than their own.

As competing constructions of Western international history, "the international system" and "the world-system" both fix on a single, continuous experience. To the extent that either construction is supported, as claimed, by theory, it must be a theory derived from and applicable to an empirical universe with exactly one item in it. However grandly sketched and richly elaborated, theories of the case are the weakest kind of theory, if theory at all.

II—Types of International Systems

The alternative to making theory for just one case is to delimit a universe of plausible cases, defined by an attribute common to those cases and only to them. The obvious candidate is decentralisation. All social systems without centralised political institutions are therefore "international systems."[24] But this is not enough. The universe of such systems is potentially huge and inevitably heterogeneous. Such circumstances call for comparative analysis as a precondition of theory-making, and this in turn depends on the classification of cases within the relevant universe. The choice of attributes to organise cases by is essentially a matter of the analyst's judgment. What seems to work out best for comparative purposes? Differences of judgment may give way to settled opinion, in the manner of normal science, or they may persist at even higher levels of refinement. In any event, exhaustive classificatory schemes enable comparative analysis, and the theory

---

[23] I. Wallerstein, *The Modern World-System* (1974); I. Wallerstein, "The Rise and Future Demise of the World Capitalist System: Concepts for Comparative Analysis," 16 *Comparative Studies in Society and History* (1974), pp. 387–415.

[24] To call them states-systems would be misleading inasmuch as they need not be composed exclusively of states. Wight, *op. cit.* in note 7, above, used this term narrowly to include systems only of states and determined that history has known only three: Western, Greco-Roman and Chinese between 771 B.C. and 221 A.D. Wight also noted the existence of systems including empires and systems of states as components. All such systems would come under the vaguer and more permissive term, "international systems."

enterprise as a whole, by pointing to the recurring relationships which demand a general form of explanation. Only by proceeding in this fashion can any writer speak of international systems as an object of inquiry.

Kaplan had a list of conceivable international systems. He and others were able to add to this list merely by applying their minds to it.[25] Never was it suggested that the list should be regarded as exhaustive. Nor were systematically comparative or general statements of any kind forthcoming. Modelski, by contrast, identified system types by the possible combination of two attributes ("system properties") characterising decentralised social systems, which is what all conceivable international systems are, whatever else they may be. The two attributes are size and degree of homogeneity.[26] The former refers to population and the latter to the proportion of the population participating in public affairs. Modelski provided descriptive labels for three of the four possible combinations: a small and homogeneous system is primitive, one that is small and heterogeneous he called agrarian, and one that is large and homogeneous an industrial system. Modelski launched an important departure from the literature on international politics and even more on international law by not calling the Western State system essentially primitive, as the model case of a decentralised system. Instead he argued that the Western State system has features of both agrarian and industrial orders, as would any international system. Agraria and industria are thus ideal types which occupy the end points of a continuum. Modelski also argues that this particular system was in transition from its largely agrarian origins to the industrial complexion of its dominant members.

Modelski accepted Kaplan's premise that the Western system is "subsystem dominant," meaning that the system's characteristics are established by characteristics of its most prominent members.[27] One could argue that attributes like size and degree of homogeneity inhere in the system itself, as well as in its members, and that a small system of big members, or a heterogeneous system of homogeneous members, is easily imagined. In fact, the Western State system would seem to be small, but rapidly growing and increasingly heterogeneous, thus moving from primitive toward agrarian and possibly on to the fourth type which Modelski neither named nor discussed. Such a system, being both large and heterogeneous, might be called feudal, to use the term in its informal sense. It is altogether plausible to present the Western State system as increasingly feudal, yet having pockets (regional subsystems) of a more

---

[25] See, for example, material by B. M. Russett, Kaplan and Young, also reprinted in Rosenau, *op. cit.* in note 22, above, at pp. 119–130, 291–303 and 336–345 respectively.

[26] Modelski, *op. cit.* in note 5, above, at pp. 126–130.

[27] Pp. 130–132. For Kaplan's argument on subsystem dominance, see *op. cit.* in note 4, above, at pp. 16–18, and note 8, above, throughout Chap. 1.

primitive, agrarian or industrial character. If the system is generally feudal, meaning large, stratified and decentralised, it would hardly be likely to function in the manner of the large, homogeneous industrial polities which appear to dominate it.

Modelski's typology, applied directly at the system level, rather than inferred from the character of its major members, can be supported by reference to an intellectual tradition quite alien to structural-functionalism. The clue is feudalism. This is Marx's most prominent category of pre-capitalist socio-economic orders. There are others, namely, primitive and ancient orders.[28] For Marx, primitive orders were indeed small and homogeneous, while ancient ones were small and heterogeneous, typically being urban slave economies. And an order that is both large and homogeneous would in Marxian terms be capitalist, while an order that is large and heterogeneous would be feudal.

If Marx and Modelski used what is effectively the same typology, their concrete descriptions of system types diverge in one instance. What Modelski called agrarian, suggesting land-based, dispersed economic activity, was for Marx ancient, meaning city-dominated (Athens, Rome). Modelski assigned several characteristics to an agrarian order which must be taken to represent the pervasiveness of tradition, kinship ties and ascription. These in considerable degree characterise both urban and rural life when the system is *small*. The term "agrarian" is clearly too inclusive and consequently imprecise.[29] Modelski's labels for his system types are less helpful than the typology itself, even though the latter is not fully articulated.

Riggs, from whom Modelski borrowed these labels in the first instance, characterised international system types in quite similar terms, but he avoided concrete descriptive labels altogether. Instead, he used ungainly conceptual labels, "refracted" and "fused," to represent agraria and industria as ideal types and "prismatic" for the intermediate model approximated by the Western State system. Even if Riggs managed to avoid projecting the wrong concrete associations with his choice of labels, their lack of sensible references consigned the scheme to near oblivion.[30]

Scholars in the field of International Politics have been loathe to further Modelski's and Riggs' important efforts to organise comparative inquiry in a theoretically fruitful way. This has come in part, as we have

---

[28] See especially K. Marx, *Pre-Capitalist Economic Formations*, with an Introduction by E. J. Hobsbawm (1965); K. P. Moseley and I. Wallerstein, "Precapitalist Social Structures," 4 *Annual Review of Sociology* (1978), pp. 261–268.

[29] This is a general failing among those using the term "agrarian." For an interesting attempt to establish all that the term includes, see G. E. Lenski, *Power and Privilege* (1966), pp. 190–210. See also below.

[30] Apparently the only work inspired by Riggs' essay is J. M. Rochester, *International Institutions and World Order: The International System as a Prismatic Polity* (1974).

seen, from the growing preoccupation with specific features of "the inter-national system." It has come in part from a smug but unwarranted belief that their scholarship has escaped the epistemological weaknesses of structural-functionalism, not to mention its much advertised con-servative bias.[31] It has also stemmed from a tendency among political scientists to invoke a narrow definition of politics and to relegate social orders lacking definite authoritative institutions to anthropology and sociology. Forgotten is the fact that a goodly proportion of all social orders, whether political by any given definition or not, happen to be decentralised in character and are therefore comparable as international systems.[32] A classificatory scheme for the comparison of international systems must therefore be appropriate for a universe of social arrange-ments which truly dominate human history. Appropriate in this instance means sufficiently refined to make sense of the varieties of human experience definitionally encompassed while simple enough to be of value in later stages of the theoretical enterprise.

We could begin by expanding and amplifying Modelski's typology, which uses a combination of physical and political attributes (size and homogeneity) to identify socio-economic types. There is a problem, how-ever, with the implicit causality of this arrangement. Specifically it suggests, though it does not necessitate, that political organisation (degree of participation in making crucial decisions for the order) deter-mines the type of socio-economic order. While this may or may not be the case, it would seem to be a premature and avoidable judgment.[33] It would be less problematic to use a pair of ecological attributes, one physical and one human, which then take the position of being provisionally antecedent to socio-economic and political organisation. Modelski's size attribute is not clearly human or physical and is rather crude as a result. An obvious attribute of physical ecology germane to the human experience is climate. The three immediately distinguishable climatic zones of the earth subject to intensive human occupancy are temperate, semi-tropical and tropical. Distinctive socio-economic and political experiences seem to be associated with each, as we shall see

---

[31] Conservative bias better characterises scholars choosing to work within the structural-functional tradition than structural-functionalism itself. A. L. Stinchcombe, *Constructing Social Theories* (1968), pp. 91–93; O. R. Young, *Systems of Political Science* (1968), pp. 36–37. Deliberately comparative structural-functional analysis should lend itself to control of any such bias.

[32] In this regard Young is a striking exception: "Over the bulk of recorded history man has organized himself for political purposes on bases other than those now subsumed under the con-cepts 'state' and 'nation-state.' " O. R. Young, "The Actors in World Politics," in J. N. Rosenau, V. Davis, M. A. East (eds.), *The Analysis of International Politics* (1972), p. 127.

[33] A thorough treatment of this question in genetic terms, with an affirmative answer, is E. R. Service, *Origins of the State and Civilization* (1975). For the negative answer, see M. Harris, *Cultural Materialism* (1979), Part I.

below.[34] The most salient attributes of human ecology would seem to be density of population. Again we commonly note three gradations—sparse, moderate and dense populations for a particular area—and impute distinguishable socio-economic and political consequences.[35]

Arranging the two sets of attributes in a matrix yields nine possible combinations, each of which represents a type of socio-economic and political system. Presumably all major instances of historical orders more or less fit into one or another of these typical systems. Labelling each type is bound to be influenced by what appear to be the appropriate historical examples and lends itself inevitably to counter-judgments by those with different readings of the historical record. Nevertheless a brief rationale for each label is attempted.

SYSTEM TYPES

Climate	Population Sparse	Moderate	Dense
Temperate	Feudal	Commercial-Imperial	Industrial
Semi-Tropical	Ancient	Bureaucratic-Imperial	Corporatist
Tropical	Chieftainly	Agricultural-Imperial	Involuted

To begin, I should observe that the term "primitive" is reserved for those simple, egalitarian societies dependent on hunting, gathering and possibly rudimentary horticulture. Wherever found, they support extremely modest populations. The term "agrarian" refers to any land-based economy and probably fits as a general label for most orders that are sparsely or moderately populated. Primitive orders are not agrarian because their use of land is not sufficiently systematic. Chieftaincies

---

[34] Speculation on the relation of politics and society to climate goes back to Montesquieu and, after a long period of disrepute, is being revived in the context of apparent global climatic change. The nomenclature of North and South, now in high fashion, actively if not always explicitly refers to climatic zones, as economists especially seem to understand. See, for example, W. A. Lewis, *The Evolution of the International Economic Order* (1978). If North equals temperate and South tropical, current nomenclature fails to characterise semi-tropical for political purposes. Wallerstein's category, "semi-periphery," though juxtaposed between the temperate core and mostly tropical periphery, is economically and politically but not geographically determined. It tends to include semi-tropical regions but is not restricted to them. Wallerstein, "The Rise . . . ," *cit.* in note 23, above, at pp. 403–404, 415.

[35] For a survey of anthropological speculation on the relation of population density to socio-economic and political organisation, see M. H. Fried, *The Evolution of Political Society* (1967), pp. 196–204, and for a strongly stated argument of causal relation, see M. Harris, *Cannibals and Kings* (1977).

would appear to be close to the lower threshold of agraria, while ancient orders, being urban and slave dependent, approach the upper threshold. Because of their reliance on hinterland agrarian activity, systems of the latter type nonetheless appear to be agrarian. Maritime societies, so typical of temperate zone, moderately populated systems, are classed as agrarian on the basis of technological and social attributes.[36] In the tropics even the densest populations hew to the agrarian pattern.

Turning now to specific labels, chieftainly systems involve simply organised hierarchies engaged in sporadic warfare and trading relations. Chieftaincies occur in all climates, but they persist in a stable form in the tropics because impenetrable vegetation deters the far-flung but loose organisation of feudalism and the concentration of economic activity typical of urban, slave-based societies. While temperate zones do not lend themselves to economic concentration either, unless of course the population increases markedly, relative openness permits confederations of chieftaincies, all the variations of which may be loosely described as feudalism. Ancient systems are also generally capable of maintaining the order beyond the urban core, but doing so frequently involves an increase in population density sufficiently to result in bureaucratic empires, which have been a well-known phenomenon throughout the semi-tropical world.

The relatively less hospitable physical circumstances of the temperate world, especially seasonal extremes, slow population growth and make the emergence of commercial empires less likely than their semi-tropical cousins, bureaucratic empires. By contrast the severely constraining features of tropical life suggest that the imperial phase is likely to be externally fostered, prompting population growth suitable for more systematic exploitation of the tropical environment. Plantation economies seem rarely to evolve spontaneously. The pattern of over-intensive land use in the absence of colonial supervision, identified by Clifford Geertz as agricultural involution, would also seem to require external fostering.[37]

The emergence of industria from commercial empires requires little comment. The emergence of corporatism from semi-tropical empires is another matter. It should be noted that such empires frequently collapse or are destroyed. Should they survive, they fall into the situation of having outstripped their ability to utilise new resources and provide sufficient growth to keep up with the needs of an expanding population. The result is a tendency for major interests to organise themselves to assure a continuing share of the steady or declining welfare available in that order. The same phenomenon of major sectors in a society squaring

---

[36] On the general resemblance of maritime and agrarian orders, and on specific differences, see Lenski, *op. cit.* in note 29, above, at pp. 191–192.
[37] C. Geertz, *Agricultural Involution* (1966).

off and settling in also seems to characterise industrial systems which have reached the limit of their capacity to grow. In this light the emergence of increasingly influential functional managers in States and in the industrial world as a whole may be understood as merely an emerging post-industrial form of corporatist order.[38]

The labels themselves connote socio-economic and in some instances political qualities. Ancient and industrial systems are not politically designated because no one form of political life is typically associated with them. In both instances the socio-economic type may be accompanied by highly centralised to less centralised, pluralistic polities. More generally the prime political variable of the degree of centralisation in decision-making must be regarded as analytically separable from socio-economic organisation. All socio-economic types admit to substantial variation in the degree of centralisation, even if some system types, for example, imperial systems, would generally display more centralisation than would other system types, feudal systems being an example.

Although the tendency towards centralisation within a system may be useful to know, it is not the same thing as centralisation of the system. All of the system types identified here are decentralised. Rarely is there one empire, ancient city State, modern nation-State or whatever in the system. The rule is plural centralisation: at least a couple, usually several, sometimes many more or less centralised entities coexisting in the system. The instance of singular or systemic centralisation is so rare that the ideal, or prediction, of a World State-like order deserves the jaundiced reception it usually gets. In short, our system types are all multi-unit systems which, as a bonus, may do double duty in classifying variously centralised units, or subsystems, within international systems. Misplaced emphasis on the latter function follows from our myopic, unit-level view of social reality rather than what we might call a civilisational view.

It might be possible to provide a political label for each system type by noting the degree to which political roles are present at the system level.[39] This is another way of asking if a system, or type of system, is system or subsystem dominant. As such it is an empirical matter. While the degree of unit-level centralisation obviously affects the way the system works, we need not stipulate, as Kaplan does, that a system of

---

[38] The best general statement on the nature of corporatist orders, their semi-tropical fluorescence and their increasing post-industrial incidence is P. C. Schmitter, "Still the Century of Corporatism?" 36 *Review of Politics* (1974), pp. 84–128. On post-industrial corporatism as a phenomenon transcending states individually, see D. Bell, "The Future World Disorder: The Structural Context of Crises," *Foreign Policy*, Nr. 27 (1977), pp. 388–392.

[39] This procedure was suggested by D. Easton for identifying the political in primitive systems. "Political Anthropology," in B. J. Siegel (ed.), *Biennial Review of Anthropology, 1959* (1959), pp. 238–247. Easton expected a continuum of system types to emerge.

highly centralised units for that reason alone is subsystem dominant. Centralised units in an industrial order may choose to promote system level political roles to manage their relations more efficiently or they may insist on their autonomy at any cost. We need not assume that either choice is a norm for that system type, so that departures from the norm have to be explained away individually. Dominance is even harder to typify in feudal systems, for example, with their complicated and confining relationships between greater and lesser subsystemic centres. Systems of the corporatist type also defy conventional thinking about the dominance of territory-centred units because the functional division of labour at the system level is likely to be decisive. This is an important point made by scholars who contrast the state-centric paradigm, as they call it, with the emergence of large-scale transnational activity and attendant fragmentation of States' activity.[40]

Comparison using the nine-cell matrix of international systems presented above also permits a more refined, or less arbitrary, view of systems transformation than currently found in the literature.[41] The transformation problem may be constructively understood as a change in type of system. Obviously transformation need not be progressive or linear, since movement from any particular cell may be in two, three or four directions (depending on its location in the matrix) to adjacent cells and could conceivably even jump to distant ones. The identification of transformations presupposes general, material causes, which, after all, define the conditions for the existence of a given system type, and encourages investigation of the specific, process-oriented features of each such transformation. Comparison of historical systems, not as transforming but as a sequence of types between transformations, may thus enable general statements about contextual pressures and systemic responses resulting in transformation.

Short of such overt theorising, a comparison of types between transformations in a given historical system can help us read that system's history without taking for granted the liberal-evolutionary view fostered by those living inside the system's unfolding reality. Consider the several hundred year history of the Western State system, which reveals several transformations in system type.[42] If we look back to the system's origins in fifteenth century Italy, the system was apparently

---

[40] The starting place in the burgeoning literature on this point is R. O. Keohane and J. S. Nye (eds.), *Transnational Relations and World Politics* (1972).

[41] Recent treatments of the transformation problem include Rochester, *op. cit.* in note 30, above; E. L. Morse, *Modernization and the Transformation of International Relations* (1976); D. A. Zinnes, "Prerequisites to the Study of System Transformation," in O. R. Holsti, R. M. Siverson, A. L. George (eds.), *Change in the International System* (1980), pp. 3–21.

[42] For another, more recent view of international history as a succession of system types, but without any consideration of the transformation problem, and with a different construction of the temporal boundaries of the successive systems of Western international history than presented here, see E. Luard, *Types of International Society* (1976).

well urbanised and on the threshold between temperate and semi-tropical. It would thus seem to fit the corporatist model with princes, merchants and prelates all consequential to the system's working. The Italian system also bore characteristics of a commercial-imperial system, in the instance of Venice's role. And the system was quite plausibly flavoured by remembrance of the ancient systems of Greece and Rome.

Rapid northerly migration brought on an altogether feudal system. Illiberally interpreted, the classical balance of power is recognisable as a typical feudal institution in which the ascendant Power (Spain and then France) is held in check by shifting alliances of somewhat lesser Powers. After two centuries or more, population growth in the temperate core of the system transformed it slowly into an imperial order of the nineteenth century, with commercial rather than bureaucratic or agricultural tendencies except where colonisation was involved. Bipolarity in our own time would appear to consummate the tendency towards empire—competing empires, really—with all three imperial types manifest in different zones of the globe.

Where is our international system going now? If multinationals functionally supplant the territorially fixed (feudal-imperial) actors, as some suggest will happen, we would see an increasingly corporatist system, both in the temperate and semi-tropical zones. A largely corporatist system, populated with overly mature (post-industrial) and never maturing (Mediterranean) members, would have gotten there without going through an industrial phase, although the presumably interdependent industrial Powers may well represent a transitional subordinate system at the present time. Meanwhile, the post-colonial tendency toward tropical involution would undoubtedly continue, pushing the system closer to the corporatist-involutional threshold of system types.

If alternatively the rise of the multinationals is overrated and the contemporary State system proves durable enough to contain political tensions and continues to support a healthy global capitalism, including rapid economic growth in the tropics, then we might see the gradual transformation of the global system from its imperial incarnation into something legitimately qualifying as industrial. Even then features of its feudal-imperial past would linger on.[43] Previous transformations were, after all, rarely quick and clean-cut enough to present us with anything resembling pure types.

Neither this generalisation nor any other we might devise with respect to the evolution of the Western State system necessarily fits the case of

---

[43] This assumes that at least in the short run a healthy capitalist order does not outgrow its need for the State system as a protective umbrella. In the longer run a healthy capitalist-industrial order, just as must as a stagnant corporatist, post-industrial order, could result in the transcendence of multinational functional actors. See also Wallerstein, "The Rise ... ," *cit.* in note 23, above.

any other international system. Only comparative inquiry will tell. And only then are we prepared to venture into the realm of theory, not just theory of the case, but theory applicable to the universe of international systems.

THE HOSTAGES INCIDENT:

THE UNITED STATES AND IRAN

By

ALFRED P. RUBIN

On Sunday, November 4, 1979, several hundred young supporters of a theologically-based political faction in Iran took control of the American Embassy compound in Teheran and the 63 Americans inside, most of them properly accredited diplomats. In addition, three American diplomats who happened to be in the Iranian Foreign Ministry building at the time were placed under restraint there. By November 20, 13 of the Americans, all either black or female, were released. One other was released later when he fell ill. The remaining 52 were held in Iran until January 20, 1981, when they were released as part of a complex transaction by which some Iranian Government money in the control of United States banks was transferred back to the control of Iran. Some of the money was transferred to a third party under arrangements that would permit the money to be used to settle commercial debts of Iran. As part of the transaction the United States agreed not to present any claims for injury to itself or its diplomats.

To tell the full story of all the events leading to the Iranian seizure of the American Embassy in Teheran, all that went on during the 444 days the hostages were held, and all the ramifications of the release transaction is far beyond the powers of the author. The world has still not learned all there is to know about the analogous but less successful Boxer Rebellion in China in 1900–1901 and the siege of the foreign Embassy quarter at Peking. To attempt a complete recounting of all the dramatic events in Teheran and every failed attempt at negotiating a settlement at this short remove in time is patently impossible. But it is possible, with the help of some personal reminiscences and tactful omissions, to outline how the United States decided to use the tools of the international legal order to help resolve the situation, how it abandoned those tools without any apparent consideration of the consequences or with any better prospect of success using any other tools, how the extraneous claims issues came to dominate the situation, and how the resulting arrangement led to the release of the hostages only, and unnecessarily, at the expense of the stability and security that might have been preserved by more adroit leadership.

I—TAKING THE CASE TO THE UNITED NATIONS

(a) *The preliminary attempts to open bilateral negotiations*

Immediately on seizing the hostages, the Iranian faction in apparent control of them demanded political concessions by the United States as the price of their release. Those concessions included the removal to Iran of the ailing Shah, who had been admitted to a New York hospital on October 22, 1979, and American confession to complicity in various human rights violations by the Shah's Government as well as apologies for involvement in Iranian internal politics over the previous 30 years.

The immediate United States reaction was to refuse to deport the Shah, to indicate that military force would not be attempted to release the hostages, and to leave open the possibility of investigating the history of United States involvement in internal Iranian politics. Apparently to gauge the scope for diplomatic manoeuvring with Iran, President Carter authorised Ramsey Clark, a former Attorney-General under the Johnson Administration reputed to be well respected in many newly independent countries, to meet with Iranian authorities. Before Clark could reach Iran, the nominal government in Iran resigned. The government that emerged refused to receive the mission. Other attempts to open communications with whoever could be identified with the government of Iran also failed.

(b) *The U.N. Security Council and Secretary-General*

On November 9, 1979, the United States began to seek help through the United Nations. A letter signed by the Permanent Representative of the United States was presented to the President of the Security Council requesting that the Council "urgently consider what might be done to secure the release of the diplomatic personnel being held and to restore the sanctity of diplomatic personnel and establishments."[1]

The President of the Security Council, Mr. Palacios de Vizzio of Bolivia, issued a statement almost immediately indicating that after consultations among the members of the Security Council he was authorised to express the Council's "profound concern" and to "urge in

---

[1] U.N. Doc. S/13615 of November 9, 1979, in International Court of Justice, *Case Concerning United States Diplomatic and Consular Staff in Tehran (United States of America v. Iran), Memorial of the Government of the United States of America* (hereafter cited as *US Memorial*) Annex 42 at p. 133 (January 1980). Not all the American hostages were diplomatic personnel under the definitions contained in the 1961 Vienna Convention on Diplomatic Relations, 500 U.N.T.S. 95. In addition to Consular personnel within the sense of the 1963 Vienna Convention on Consular Relations, 596 U.N.T.S. 261, there were also some Americans with no special status. The right of the United States to protect them diplomatically rested on general international law and the terms of the Treaty of Amity, Economic Relations and Consular Rights between the United States and Iran signed on August 15, 1955, 284 U.N.T.S. 93.

the strongest terms that the diplomatic personnel being held in Iran be released without delay."[2] At about the same time the President of the General Assembly, Mr. Salim A. Salim of the United Republic of Tanzania, expressed his public concern with "the safety and security of American personnel now held as hostages" in Iran and appealed in a personal message to the leading Iranian political power at the time, the Ayatollah Khomeini, for the release of the hostages.[3]

The responses of the Ayatollah and various Iranian spokesmen were not encouraging. A statement dated November 10, 1979, by the Ayatollah to the Personal Representative of Pope John Paul II alleged plots and conspiracies by the deposed Shah and President Carter and his predecessors as apparent justification for the seizure of the American Embassy in Teheran and the people within it, and ended by announcing "that we are neither afraid of military interference nor are we afraid of economic siege ... [but] we expect you to give paternal warning to the super-Powers and to demand of them the reasons for their wrong doings."[4] A letter to the Security Council restated Iran's grievances against the United States on November 13, 1979.[5] After considerable diplomatic activity, on November 25, 1979, the Secretary-General formally brought the attention of the Security Council to the hostages crisis which, he asserted, was a matter which in his opinion posed a serious threat to international peace and security.[6]

After a delay from November 27 to December 1, 1979, which it had been led to believe would enable an Iranian representative to attend the Security Council deliberations,[7] the Security Council convened. On December 4, 1979, it unanimously called on the Government of Iran "to release immediately the personnel of the Embassy of the United States of

---

[2] U.N. Doc. S/13616 dated November 9, 1979, in US Memorial Annex 43 at p. 134.

[3] U.N. Doc. GA/6076 of November 9, 1979, in *ibid.* Annex 44 at p. 135.

[4] *New York Times*, Sunday, November 18, 1979, p. 63. The statement appears as a full page advertisement inserted by the Embassy of the Islamic Republic of Iran in Washington.

[5] U.N. Doc. S/13626.

[6] U.N. Doc. 13646. Apparently the Secretary-General was acting under Art. 99 of the U.N. Charter, which authorises him to "bring to the attention of the Security Council any matter which in his opinion may threaten the maintenance of international peace and security." It is not known why the Secretary-General felt it desirable to state matters in a way significantly more urgently than was required to meet the threshold of Art. 99. Nor is it known why the United States did not itself call for an emergency meeting of the Security Council under Art. 35(1) of the Charter, which authorises "Any Member of the United Nations" to bring to the attention of the Security Council or the General Assembly "any dispute, or any situation" which might lead to international friction or give rise to a dispute.

[7] The Iranian letter requesting a few days' delay cited two Iranian holy days and the prospect that Iran's Foreign Minister, then Abolhassan Bani-Sadr, would attend. U.N. Doc. S/13650 of November 27, 1979. In fact, Foreign Minister Bani-Sadr was relieved of his portfolio on November 28 and no Iranian attended the Security Council meetings. A concise summary of the correspondence and surrounding procedures in the U.N. is in 17(1) *U.N. Chronicle* 5–13 (January 1980).

America being held in Teheran, and to provide them protection and to allow them to leave the country."[8]

Parallel to this activity, the United States on November 29, 1979, instituted proceedings against Iran before the International Court of Justice,[9] which unanimously made an Order on December 15, 1979, indicating provisional measures pending the Court's final decision.[10] That Order provided that "The Government of the Islamic Republic of Iran should ensure the immediate release, without any exception, of all persons of United States nationality who are or have been held in the Embassy of the United States of America or in the Ministry of Foreign Affairs in Teheran, or have been held as hostages elsewhere. . . ."

When the hostages were not in fact released, and in light of a report by the Secretary-General on December 22, 1979,[11] indicating his conclusion that "the expectation which had previously arisen for early progress towards a settlement of the crisis could, for the time being, not be fulfilled," the United States on December 22, 1979, requested that the Council meet at an early date to consider measures that should be taken to induce Iran to comply with its international obligations.[12] The Security Council met on December 29–31, 1979, and issued a new Resolution, 461 (1979), repeating its call of December 4 and "Decide[d] to meet on January 7, 1980, in order to review the situation and, in the event of non-compliance with this resolution, to adopt effective measures under Articles 39 and 41 of the Charter of the United Nations."[13] On January 6, 1980, the Secretary-General formally reported that the authorities in Iran "At present . . . are not prepared to respond to the call of the international community for the immediate release of the hostages."[14] A United States draft resolution under which the Security Council would "Decide" that all member States of the United Nations should forthwith impose a sweeping embargo on Iran was supported by 10 Security Council members, but failed of adoption on January 13, 1980, due to the negative vote of the Soviet Union.[15] In a bitter attack on

---

[8] Resolution 457 (1979) of December 4, 1979. It was adopted unanimously. The text is reproduced in 17(1) *U.N. Chronicle* 13 (January 1980) and 18(6) I.L.M., 1644–1645 (1979).

[9] See section (c) below.

[10] *I.C.J. Yearbook 1979–1980* 118–119 (1980); reproduced also in 17(1) *U.N. Chronicle* 7 (January 1980).

[11] S/13704, reproduced in 19(1) I.L.M. 248 (1980).

[12] S/13705, letter addressed to the President of the Security Council.

[13] Security Council Resolution 461 (1979) of December 31, 1979, operative paragraph 6. This Resolution was adopted by a vote of 11–0 with abstentions by Bangladesh, Czechoslovakia, Kuwait and the Soviet Union.

[14] S/13730. This document is reproduced in 19(1) I.L.M. 251 (1980).

[15] U.S. Department of State, *Current Policy*, Nr. 126 (January 13, 1980). This document is reproduced in 19(1) I.L.M. 254 (1980). A negative vote was also cast by the German Democratic Republic, which had replaced Czechoslovakia on the Security Council. Bangladesh and Mexico abstained. China did not participate. Tunisia, which had replaced Kuwait on the Security Council, voted in favour of the draft resolution. The debate of January 11 and 13 is well summarised in 17(2) *U.N. Chronicle* 22–26 (1980).

the Soviet veto immediately after the vote had taken place, the United States representative construed the "decision" in Security Council Resolution 461 (1979) "to adopt effective measures" as a decision binding the members of the organisation under the terms of Article 25 of the Charter[16] placing the Soviet Union (and presumably the Democratic Republic of Germany) in the position of violating the Charter. But it is not clear that members of the organisation in their capacity as members of the Security Council are bound to regard Security Council "decisions to decide" as immutable. Furthermore, reasonable differences of opinion may exist as to whether the embargo measures proposed by the United States would have been "effective" to help end the crisis. Many observers at the time were predicting that the passage of time and the evolution of Iran's political leadership would be necessary before the hostages could realistically be expected to be released, and that confrontational approaches and embargoes were more likely to feed Iran's sense of martyrdom and mission, thus prolonging the crisis.[17] Given the intricate politics of Iran and the high level of emotion there, coupled with the history of the Persian Gulf States, the industrial world's intense interest in its resources, and the strategic position of Iran, it is not at all clear that an embargo called by the Security Council would have been effectively carried out or, if carried out, would have significantly altered the political situation in any way to the advantage of the hostages or the United States.

The United States apparently interpreted the Soviet veto as signalling the end of any help from the Security Council. Precisely why this sweeping conclusion was reached cannot be told from the outside; presumably the position of the Soviet Union was made clear to the United States in corridor discussions never made public. In any event, while the case between the United States and Iran was being further considered by the International Court, the Secretary-General of the United Nations, Kurt Waldheim, acted. On February 20, 1980, he announced the establishment of a five-member Commission of Inquiry to visit Iran, hear the Iranian grievances, and attempt to facilitate an early resolution of the

---

[16] Art. 25: "The Members of the United Nations agree to accept and carry out the decisions of the Security Council in accordance with the present Charter."

[17] One example that comes readily to hand is Rubin, How International Law Bolsters the US Hand, in *Christian Science Monitor*, January 21, 1980, p. 23. It was common gossip among American international lawyers discussing the crisis at the time that it had taken over a year of patience in 1948–49 to secure the safe release by the People's Republic of China of Angus Ward, the American Consul General in Mukden, and his staff whose immunities were violated by the Communist authorities as they swept to victory; the politics had obvious similarities to the Iranian hostages situation, and obvious differences. 7 Whiteman, *Digest of International Law* 741 (1970). The crew of the *Pueblo* was held for 11 months by the authorities of North Korea in 1968.

crisis.[18] It soon became clear that the Iranian authorities intended the Commission to be used as a conduit for publishing Iran's grievances, but that the relationship between the activities of the Commission and the release of the hostages was considered by the Iranian authorities to be a matter within their own discretion. Apparently feeling that the hostages were being used as a guarantee of favourable bias towards Iran, and that this situation was incompatible with the neutral position of the Secretary-General and with the integrity of the members of the Commission, the Commissioners left Iran on March 11 saying that it "is not in a position to prepare its report." Its activities were suspended.[19] In mid-May, after a disastrous United States attempt at a rescue mission, and just as the International Court of Justice was completing its work on the case, Adib Daoudy, one of the Commissioners, visited Iran to discuss the possibility of reviving the Commission. Nothing seems to have come of this effort.[20]

(c) *The International Court of Justice: The decision to bring the case*

During the years Jimmy Carter was President of the United States, the post of senior law officer of the Department of State, an official with the rank of Assistant Secretary of State but with the title "Legal Adviser to the Department of State," was filled by two successive incumbents neither of whom had any prior training, experience or manifest interest in international law.[21] Thus, while the notion of using the pressure of a court decision to help bring the Government of Iran to recognise the enormity of its action might well have occurred to some lawyers within the Department of State, the idea was apparently not seriously considered at a policy-making level during the early days of the crisis. I was personally drawn into the situation in the late afternoon of November 13, 1979, when a former student then on the professional staff of a Senate Committee telephoned to ask if I thought it would be worthwhile to press the notion, and if so, whether I would help him and two colleagues gain access to the people in the Department of State who should consider it. What follows is a personal account based on diaries kept at the time of how the decision was made.

On receiving the call, I checked *Treaties in Force* and the texts of the principal documents on which United States and Iranian submissions to

---

[18] 17(3) *U.N. Chronicle* 16 (1980). The members of the Commission were Andres Aguilar (Venezuela), Mohamed Bedjaoui (Algeria), Hector Wilfred Jayewardena (Sri Lanka), Louis-Edmond Pettiti (France) and Adib Daoudy (Syrian Arab Republic).

[19] 17(4) *U.N. Chronicle* 5–8 (1980).

[20] 17(6) *U.N. Chronicle* 16 (1980). The failed rescue mission had taken place on April 24–25, 1980 (see section (e) below); Daoudy's trip was announced on May 17; he arrived in Iran on May 24, the same day the International Court of Justice announced its judgment (see below).

[21] This situation was well known to America's allies and a subject of gossip among international lawyers generally in the United States. It has not frequently been adverted to publicly.

the jurisdiction of the Court would have to rest.[22] I then checked with my colleague, Professor Leo Gross, who made the same preliminary investigations I had, and we discussed the likelihood that the Court would consider this an appropriate case for "provisional measures" under Article 41 of the Statute of the International Court of Justice, thus helping in the immediate problem of mobilising world opinion quickly to end the crisis, rather than delaying its resolution. We agreed that the idea was worth pursuing.

I spent most of the next two days on the telephone discovering that nobody at the decision-making levels in State Department was in fact seriously considering taking the case to the Court.[23] By noon on Thursday, November 15, through the good offices of Theodore L. Eliot, Jr., The Dean of Fletcher School and former American Ambassador to Afghanistan, I was able to speak with Ambassador Henry Precht, the Chairman of the Iranian Task Force. His first reaction was to ask what good it would do to take Iran to the Court, since the Ayatollah was unlikely to be moved by anything the International Court of Justice

---

[22] The terms of the United States general submission under Art. 36(2) of the Statute of the International Court of Justice contain a reservation available as a matter of reciprocity to any respondent in a case brought by the United States under which Iran, even if it had made an unqualified submission to the Court under Art. 36(2), would have been able to deny effectively the Court's jurisdiction. The literature on this so-called Connally Amendment is voluminous. Those interested might start with Gross, "Bulgaria Invokes the Connally Amendment," 56 A.J.I.L. 357 (1962). For purposes of taking a case involving diplomatic and consular imunities to the International Court of Justice, the submissions to the Court of both Iran and the United States are special submissions contained in the Optional Protocol concerning the Compulsory Settlement of Disputes, 500 U.N.T.S. 241, accompanying the 1961 Vienna Convention on Diplomatic Relations cited in note 1, above, and the Optional Protocol concerning the Compulsory Settlement of Disputes, 596 U.N.T.S. 487, accompanying the 1963 Vienna Convention on Consular Relations cited in note 1, above. A third basis for jursidiction applicable to the Iranian "arrest" of non-diplomatic or consular personnel is the submission to the International Court of Justice contained in the Treaty of Amity, Economic Relations, and Consular Rights between the United States and Iran, signed August 15, 1955, 284 U.N.T.S 93. In its Memorial to the International Court of Justice of January 1980, the United States also cites Art. 13, para. 1, of the 1973 Convention on the Prevention and Punishment of Crimes Against Internationally Protected Persons, 28 U.S.T. 1975, T.I.A.S. 8532. Since this Convention provides for jurisdiction in the International Court of Justice only after six months' time have elapsed without the parties being able to agree on arbitration procedures, the relevance of that Convention is not apparent.

[23] Many people in State Department will undoubtedly disagree; indeed one of them on November 27, two days before the case was publicly brought, told me that he had thought of it first and that my activities had been unnecessary. Since I have never been concerned with claiming credit for originality, indeed throughout the period insisted that I was a mere conduit for an initiative that had been begun by my former student and his friends, this adversary approach to policy as to which we in fact agreed I find a bit strange. Be that as it may, I know that as of the time I was contacting the appropriate people in the Legal Adviser's Office and State Department's Iranian Task Force the idea was treated as original, and I know from two quite separate sources that it was mis-called "the Rubin proposal" at levels well above the bureaucratic levels that later claimed originality. It was no secret that during the Carter years, ideas originating outside of the bureaucracy were frequently given more attention than ideas originating within it and this prejudice had nothing to do with the merits of particular ideas.

might have to say. The question was not unexpected, and the answer was the one any international lawyer would have given: The judgment if favourable would enable the United States to present the case to the Security Council and, if appropriate, to the General Assembly and any other forum with political influence in Iran, as a basis for exercising their influence without appearing to side with the United States in a political confrontation with Iran; that a favourable judgment would also turn aside the confrontational posture assumed by Iran and make it possible for the United States to refuse to discuss the return of the Shah or any other American concessions as *quid pro quo* for the release of the hostages. I referred him to one or two of the State Department lawyers who I knew were able to advise him competently on matters relating to the enforcement pattern of international law, as distinguished from giving mere technical advice in a confrontational mode. He seemed unhappy with this last suggestion. The next day, my former student called to say that he and his friends had been invited by Ambassador Precht to present a rough brief on the implications of presenting the case to the Court; much jubilation was expressed by the former student, and I pressed on him much, probably unheard, advice as to the "interim measures" point and other technicalities.

It had now become apparent that the problem would not be the legal problem of formulating the best case, but the political one of convincing the responsible officials in the Department of State and the White House that it was in the interest of the United States to present it. One important channel for presenting policy arguments that is available to academics with no direct line to policy channels is the letters column of the *New York Times*.[24] By coincidence, the editorial writer for the *New York Times* who was seized of the Iranian hostages crisis, Karl Meyer, had served a term as Adjunct Professor at The Fletcher School of Law and Diplomacy, which sponsors the Edward R. Murrow Center of Public Diplomacy and maintains close relations with media. On November 15 the Director of the Center, Professor Hewson Ryan, a former Ambassador and Deputy Assistant Secretary of State himself, told me that Meyer had telephoned to ask about the hostages crisis, and suggested I call him back. I did, and could not resist suggesting to him the absurdity of the State Department not having an international lawyer on the Iran Task Force. He replied that in an emergency one does not like to clutter up proceedings with fringe experts. I responded, in some heat I am afraid, that "When you, personally, are in a crisis or emergency, who is the very first person you call?" There was a pause, a

---

[24] Discretion whether or not to print letters lies, of course, with the *New York Times*; it is in part because that discretion is so well exercised that publication in the *Times* letters column has become a significant policy channel. I have no special influence on that discretion. Other national channels for academics to find quick influence include guest columns in the *Wall Street Journal* and the *Christian Science Monitor*. The process is fundamentally capricious.

gentle laugh, and Meyer replied, "Good point." I then pressed too hard about the staff structure, to which he finally responded, "Inshallah"—by the will of God. It was then my turn to laugh: end of conversation. The next morning Meyer called to ask a technical question of treaty interpretation; it turned out that he was looking at the wrong treaty,[25] a problem that was quickly straightened out.

The next few days were spent pulling whatever strings I could find to bring the advantages of world court action to the attention of those making policy, and included circuitous channels whose final destinations cannot be checked. There were also one or two television interviews as the local stations stretched their normal criteria to include academics among the instant experts presented to an unsuspecting and non-discriminating multitude.

On November 20 Karl Meyer's editorial appeared in the *New York Times*. But instead of urging the United States to bring Iran to the International Court of Justice, it suggested that Iran bring the United States there for a judicial determination of American culpability for the Shah's alleged evils. This garbled suggestion seemed so badly attuned to any reality that in some excitement I wrote a letter to the *New York Times* myself hoping to refocus the discussion that seemed to have gone wildly astray.

On the same day, November 20, Senator Daniel Patrick Moynihan, a graduate of The Fletcher School who had been in direct contact with Professor Gross about the hostages situation, gave a speech on the Senate floor urging that the United States take the hostages situation to the International Court of Justice.[26] While Professor Gross was convinced that the bureaucracy in the State Department was unmovable, he had concluded that pressure from Moynihan might have direct effects in the White House. I was pretty well convinced that the White House was hopelessly uninterested in the range of pressures that could be placed on Iran if the legal measures were carried through, and resolved to continue to press through the bureaucracy. Accordingly, I circulated my letter to the *New York Times* (which never printed it) as widely as I could. Since it lays out the full scope of my reasoning, appears to have in fact had some influence, and is as concise as I could make it, it is reproduced here in full, without correcting the awkward phrasings and hyperbole resulting from haste and passion:

---

[25] Since the matter was cleared up in just a few minutes, and minor errors by non-lawyers in such matters are not significant, I did not note which treaty he was looking at. Only later did it occur to me that he might have been referred to an inapplicable treaty either by somebody in the State Department who did not want the *New York Times* to publish an editorial about taking the case to the International Court of Justice, or that the citation might have been to the 1973 Convention on the Prevention and Punishment of Crimes Against Internationally Protected Persons, cited in note 22, above. In either case, it points up the delicacy of Meyer's position and the wisdom of his never taking anybody's word on anything.

[26] Congressional Record—Senate, S/17148 (November 20, 1979).

"Dear Times Editor:

"In your editorial of November 20, 1979, you suggest that if the Ayatollah considers American actions in Iran to have violated international law, he should take his case to the International Court of Justice. It is true that under the terms of the Optional Protocol to the Vienna Convention of 1961 Iran could have done so, but it is obviously in the current Iranian Government's interest not to, since its position is stronger internationally if it interprets its violation of the American Embassy in Teheran to be part of a mix of bilateral issues involving also America's role in supporting the Shah and his apparently corrupt régime. But for more than two weeks it has been in the interest of the government of the *United States* to take the issue of the Embassy hostages to the court. The real question is why *we* have not done so. The court even has the legal power to grant interim measures of relief, and can act very quickly when asked to.

"Of course, it is doubtful that the Ayatollah would obey a court order for the immediate release of the hostages, but that is hardly a reason for not trying to add possibly effective legal pressures to the futile economic pressures and impracticable military pressures we seem to consider so seriously. Moreover, the terms of the court's jurisdiction in the case under the Optional Protocol of 1961 restricts its focus to the issue of diplomatic issues; the extraneous concerns over the Shah and his money would be severed from the case thus adding clarity to the American position and putting the safety of the hostages above the other issues in the eyes of the world. Moreover, if we are to claim compensation for the violations of our Embassy out of frozen Iranian assets in this country, to avoid the appearance of an American economic confrontation with Iran, a country with which many will sympathize or attempt to placate in any bilateral confrontation with the United States, it would obviously be wise to have the pronouncements of the International Court of Justice to support our action. And that applies to military options also, if any exist; it would help immeasurably to secure the sympathetic understanding of the countries over which our aircraft must fly, among others, if any such action were seen as the upholding of legal rights of importance to the entire international community, and not just a bilateral quarrel between the United States and Iran. Also, the International Court of Justice is a high platform addressing intellectuals and statesmen all over the world. Wouldn't it help to mount the kinds of pressures most likely to influence the government in Iran if the issues were raised out of the gutter and language of martyrdom into which the Ayatollah for his own political reasons has put them? And wouldn't it be useful in the longer run for the United States to appear in the forefront of all countries concerned with international law and procedures for us to be seen using them, instead of using only economic or military options? And, finally, if the result of the incident is to force the United States to face the need to avoid future crises by withdrawing our diplomats from such exposed posts as Afghanistan as well as Iran, it would seem obvious that a decision of the International Court of Justice would help make that withdrawal seem a statesmanlike upholding of the principles of diplomatic intercourse and not a retreat before the kind of mindless fanaticism that seems heroic to the would-be martyrs of some political movements.

"This hardly exhausts the list of advantages, and I see no disadvantages to the United States bringing the case before the International Court of Justice, even if we lose there—a loss that would bring about a revolution in diplomacy that could not be avoided by pretending the law has remained as codified in the Vienna Convention. The only serious question remaining is why there is no international lawyer on the State Department Task Group handling the crisis in Iran, and why both Carter appointments to the position of senior Legal Adviser to the State Department, approved by the Senate, have been lawyers with neither training, experience or any manifest interest in international law."

The next day, November 21, I learned that the reason Karl Meyer had reversed the parties in his *New York Times* editorial was a request to that effect from a Deputy Legal Adviser in the State Department who felt that too much pressure on our policy-makers would have a reverse effect. Fuming over this evidence that national policy issues were decided as a matter of pique rather than sense, I wrote another letter to the *New York Times* (never published and too focused on headlines of the day under which various military options were discussed to be worth preserving) pointing out that continued delay gave Iran time to withdraw its adherence to the various documents under which the International Court of Justice could claim jurisdiction in the case and thus jeopardised one of our potentially strongest political tools. By evening I had worked off the frustration, mailed the letter (sending a few copies elsewhere), and relapsed into anguished frustration.

On Monday, November 26, 1979, I was at the Naval War College in Newport, Rhode Island, to participate in a two-day conference on the law of armed conflict. The conference participants included several eminent academics and officials of the Department of State. I urged the case for taking Iran to the International Court of Justice in the corridors to a mixed reaction. The objection that came most cogently from academics and officials alike was a feeling that military operations, if successful, would not only free the hostages but teach a needed "lesson" to the Iranian leaders responsible for the outrage. At dinner with Leslie Green[27] and George Aldrich,[28] among others, these ideas were explored

---

[27] Professor L. C. Green is University Professor at the University of Alberta in Canada and former Dean of the Faculty of Law at the University of Singapore.

[28] Ambassador George H. Aldrich was the head of the United States delegation to the international conference that drew up the texts related to armed conflict that were the subject of the Newport Conference. He had earlier served as Deputy Legal Adviser to the Department of State.

at repetitive length; I thought my answers were responsive in pointing out the instability such a "lesson" would lead to in such a volatile area and that military action would not be ruled out if the legal groundwork were laid first, but that premature military action, even if successful, would result in a weaker legal framework for future United States investment and political influence in the area. But I was quite sure that we parted in disagreement.

Concluding that with lawyers of this eminence so doubtful of the legal or political wisdom of taking the case to the International Court of Justice, and seeming to prefer what I regarded as short-sighted and probably futile military action, the chances of the non-lawyers in Washington opting for the quieter and surer procedure were dim, I spent most of the next day lobbying with whoever would listen and generally being unpleasant. At about 4.30 p.m. the word was passed that Judge Richard R. Baxter, who had been scheduled to address the conference, had been summoned to The Hague. It was the unanimous surmise that the decision had in fact been made to take the case to Court. There was a small party at Ambassador Aldrich's room at which we discussed the implications of the decision, but nothing new was said. The next day, Wednesday, February 28, back in Boston, it turned out that the Iranian Foreign Minister, Bani-Sadr, had been relieved of his portfolio[29] and in his speech that night President Carter mentioned international law but did not announce taking the case to the Court.

On Thursday, November 29, my students greeted me at midday with the news that our case had just been filed. All afternoon and the next day there were telephone calls of congratulations, a couple of interviews on local television, and other excitement. I called my former student in Washington to congratulate him and share the euphoria. Over the next several weeks a number of well-placed acquaintances quietly congratulated me and made it clear that in their views my efforts were very significant in the final balance of influence; others, particularly in the middle levels of the bureaucracy, quietly told me that I had had nothing to do with anything, that the decision was made in the normal bureaucratic mix. What a strange government we have, and what a strange profession to be an international lawyer.

(d) *The International Court of Justice: the progress of the case*

The United States Application of November 29, 1979, was accompanied by a formal request that the Court indicate provisional measures of protection to be taken promptly by Iran. The five specific measures sought included the immediate release of all the hostages, return of the diplomatic premises in Teheran to the control of the United States; full freedom of movement and protection of all persons "attached

---

[29] See note 7, above.

to" the United States Embassy and Consulate; no trial of any hostage; and "That the Government of Iran ensure that no action is taken which might prejudice the rights of the United States in respect of the carrying out of any decision which the Court may render on the merits. . . . "[30] The next day, the Registrar of the Court, on instructions from the President of the Court, Sir Humphrey Waldock, in a telegram to the United States and to Iran advised the two States that the matter was *sub judice* and that under the rules of the Court relating to interim protection both parties should "act in such a way as will enable any order the Court may make on the request for provisional measures to have its appropriate effects."[31] Monday, December 10, 1979 was set as the date for the parties to present their observations on the request for interim measures.[32]

At the hearing on that day, the Government of Iran did not appear. The United States was represented by Attorney-General Benjamin Civiletti and Mr. Roberts B. Owen, the State Department Legal Adviser. They were accompanied by Stephen M. Schwebel, a Deputy Legal Adviser, as Counsel, and Mr. David H. Small, an Assistant Legal Adviser to the Department of State.[33]

On December 15, scarcely two weeks since the request for provisional measures was filed, the Court produced its Order.[34] It was unanimous and met all the United States positions. Moreover, envisaging the possible refusal or political inability of Iran to release the hostages and return the premises to American control, the Order went further: "[P]ending the Court's final decision in the case . . . : . . . The Government of the United States of America and the Government of the Islamic Republic of Iran should not take any action and should ensure that no action is taken which may aggravate the tension between the two countries or render the existing dispute more difficult of solution."[35]

Pursuant to the Court's procedural Orders, the United States filed its formal Memorial in January 1980, and presented oral argument on

---

[30] International Court of Justice, Communiqué No. 79/3 of November 29, 1979.

[31] This was apparently intended to set a legal bar to Iran's dispersing the hostages or placing them into Iranian legal procedures that would have delayed their repatriation under order of the Court.

[32] International Court of Justice, Communiqué No. 79/4 of November 30, 1979.

[33] International Court of Justice, Communiqué No. 79/6 of December 14, 1979. Mr. Schwebel has since been elected Judge on the International Court of Justice.

[34] International Court of Justice, Communiqué No. 79/7 of December 15, 1979.

[35] This awkward use of the subjunctive, "should," and avoidance of any language of direction seems to betray an apprehension on the part of at least some of the judges that such an Order was beyond the authority of the Court. It was, after all, not the granting of anything that had been requested by either party. No exception was taken by either party, and the proceedings continued on the apparent assumption that *both* parties were now legally required to avoid any action which might aggravate the tension between them even if Iran violated its obligation under other parts of the Order to release the hostages and premises. There are some other possible inconsistencies between the terms of the request by the United States and the actual Order issued by the Court, but they seem more of form than of substance.

March 18, 19 and 20, 1980. Iran did not send a representative to the hearings. At the close, the Court indicated that its next public action would be to announce the date it would deliver judgment.[36]

(e) *The attempted rescue mission of April 24–25, 1980*

At the annual meeting of the American Society of International Law, April 17–19, 1980, nothing but praise was heard with regard to the decision to take the case to the International Court of Justice. There was an undercurrent of rumour about possible military action, but it seemed to be assumed that if any such action were planned, it would come in a few weeks, after the Court had pronounced judgment, and that it would be based legally on the justifiability of self-help action to support the judgment, thus avoiding a return to the confrontational position Iran seemed to prefer. In the corridors it was suggested that whatever force was used (the speculation centred on possibly seizing a strategic Iranian-claimed island in the Persian Gulf or instituting a selective blockade of Iranian shipping) should be immediately reported to the Security Council and support sought under Article 94(2) of the United Nations Charter, which says: "If any party to a case fails to perform the obligations incumbent upon it under a judgment rendered by the Court, the other party may have recourse to the Security Council. . . . " In light of the Order for provisional measures, nobody seemed to express any

---

[36] International Court of Justice, Communiqué No. 80/3 of March 20, 1980. Mr. Owen, the Legal Adviser, appeared as Agent for the United States with Mr. Schwebel as Deputy-Agent and Counsel. Another Deputy-Agent, Mr. Thomas J. Dunnigan, Chargé d'affaires a.i. at the United States Embassy in The Hague, is also listed as representing the United States, and two State Department lawyers and the Second Secretary of the American Embassy as Advisers appeared. Only Mr. Owen and Mr. Schwebel spoke for the United States.

The legal situation was apparently not understood in the United States outside of the Legal Adviser's office. In his message to the Congress reporting a new Executive Order intended to tighten the freeze of Iranian assets in the United States on April 7, 1980 (see section II below), thus during this period between the issuance of its interim Order and its Judgment, one of the bases for the new action was that "Iran has ignored or rebuffed a decision by the International Court of Justice." 16(15) *Weekly Compilation of Presidential Documents* 614 (1980), para. 2. But an interim Order is not usually considered a "decision" within the sense of Art. 94(1) of the U.N. Charter, and even if it were, the provisions in Art. 94(2) triggering enforcement action by the Security Council depend on the prior rendering of a "judgment." The American view thus expressed, that failure to obey an interim Order of the Court amounts to ignoring a "decision" in the sense of Art. 94(1), seems extreme. Indeed, since only the U.N. itself has the legal authority to determine how the Charter should be interpreted as it relates to the coordination of the judicial arm of the organisation with its members and political arms, the American auto-interpretation might even be regarded by some as contemptuous of the organization as a whole. If the word "decision" was chosen in disregard of the Charter language and the normal usage of the Court, it is difficult to understand just how the United States views the function of the Court in this case, which was, after all, brought by the United States. It might be supposed that by April 7, 1980, the United States had abandoned the legal process and determined to return the situation to the confrontational mode the legal process had been intended to avoid. The reasons for such a shift in policy, if it was indeed a shift consciously made, cannot be determined, but its results became clear within a few weeks.

doubt that the final judgment would be wholly favourable to the United States.

The United States instead attempted to rescue the hostages directly by sending a small military force into Iran on April 24. The attempt failed; eight American military persons were killed, one large transport airplane and one helicopter were destroyed by accident and then another helicopter was destroyed in haste by design as the force pulled back; secret documents were left behind.[37] It turned out that the entire mission was undertaken against the advice of the Secretary of State, Cyrus R. Vance, who resigned, his credibility as the principal spokesman and formulator of United States foreign policy destroyed within the hot-house world of Washington, if not world-wide. As further details were exposed bit by bit in the American Press, and military analyses by friendly experts began to be published, the practical absurdity of the entire conception became apparent.

From a legist's point of view, the military ineptness of the desert *débâcle* was irrelevant. In the short range, the question was what would be the impact of the attempt on the posture of the United States before the International Court of Justice, whose subjunctive direction to both parties to refrain from any action which might aggravate the tension had been violated. Even if technically it were possible to argue that this direction was not sufficiently forceful legally to forbid a rescue mission, as a matter of general legal procedure the disregard of a Court's wishes while a case is *sub judice* must place the United States in a strange position. The possibility seems to have been ignored that the mission would either fail or might well, if successful, create political chaos in Iran and the Gulf region generally as friendly governments in the Arab and Muslim world would be forced by Arab chauvinism and xenophobia to dissociate themselves from American interests, and our European allies and Japan would be forced in the interest of secure oil supplies to follow suit. Thus, making the attempt as a practical matter foreclosed for a while at least the strongest hope the United States had for a peaceful resolution of the crisis: recourse to the Security Council for it (not the United States) to act under Article 94(2) of the Charter and, ultimately, action by the General Assembly to support the Court and the integrity of the Charter. Article 94(1) of the Charter requires each member of the United Nations, including Iran, "to comply with the decision of the International Court of Justice in any case to which it is a party." Since the Order of provisional measures was not yet a "decision," and the judgment, which would be a "decision," was expected momentarily, the

---

[37] The first official United States explanation and statement of its version of the facts is U.S. Department of State, "Hostage Rescue Attempt in Iran," *Current Policy No. 170* (April 25, 1980). Further details dribbled out and President Carter spoke on television about it on April 29, 1980.

rescue mission amounted to the United States gambling on a military success that would in the longer run prove disastrous, or a failure that would in the short run remove from the hands of the United States the strongest tool it had to bring world pressure on Iran to release the hostages.

Furthermore, the display by the United States of what many would certainly regard as contempt for the peaceful settlement procedures of the United Nations would be expected to undercut the organisation and the procedures of the law. The result would likely be to diminish the power of the organisation and the normal political enforcement pressures of the law to bring about the kind of world process on which the United States, above all nations, relies for a stable investment climate and personal security against terrorism and the adventurous military activities of various countries. Thus from the legist's point of view the mere attempt was bound to lead, at best, to mitigated disaster for United States longer-range interests whatever its degree of immediate success in releasing the hostages. The best that could be hoped for was what in fact happened: a fiasco removing the "military option" from the table for a while.[38]

The United States reported its military adventure to the United Nations Security Council on April 25, 1980, arguing that it was justified under Article 51 of the United Nations Charter as "self-defence" and construing the occupation of the Embassy in Teheran as the "armed attack" against the United States necessary as the condition contained in Article 51 for the applicability of the law of self-defence.[39] The Security Council did not respond in any way to this letter.

The International Court of Justice produced its judgment on May 24, 1980.[40] It was unanimous in affirming the legal obligation of Iran immediately to take all steps necessary to redress the situation, specifying the steps already ordered as provisional measures. As to the failed rescue mission, all the judges except Judges Morozov and Tarazi agreed that the mission was "of a kind calculated to undermine respect for the judicial process in international relations." Without actually saying that the Order of December 15, 1979, legally forbade the use of force, the main opinion went on to "recall" that the Order "had indicated that no action was to be taken by either party which might aggravate the tension between the two countries." Nonetheless, 13 of the 15 judges concluded that the question of the legality of that operation was not before the Court, and that even if it had been illegal, that subsequent illegality had

---

[38] I wrote a highly condensed version of this analysis on April 29, 1980. It was published in the *New York Times*, May 12, 1980, p. A18.

[39] S/13908, transmitting the statement by President Carter in *op. cit.*, note 36, above.

[40] *United States Diplomatic and Consular Staff in Tehran, Judgment, I.C.J. Reports 1980*, p. 3.

no bearing on the legality of the conduct of the Iranian Government over six months earlier.[41]

As to the more general questions regarding Iranian obligations owed to the United States directly, including the possibility of reparations, the Court found that such obligations existed and reserved for subsequent procedure in the case the question of reparations should the parties fail to agree between themselves. But Judges Morozov and Tarazi dissented and Judge Lachs expressed serious concern that the Court seemed to be ignoring many bilateral issues which clouded the parties' ability to negotiate out their differences, urging that bilateral negotiation perhaps under third-party conciliation would be the wisest course, not recourse to judicial pronouncements on issues fundamentally obscured by history and emotion.

Judge Tarazi, in his dissent, bluntly stated that he was not convinced that there was any legal justification for the rescue mission; that the stable occupation of the American Embassy compound in Teheran for six months was hardly an "armed attack" justifying self-defence measures under Article 51 of the Charter. He also viewed American unilateral action to freeze the assets of the Government of Iran in the United States and President Carter's threat to use them to pay American claims[42] as "an encroachment on the functions of the Court" and a confusion between the proper scope of municipal law and international law.[43]

Judge Morozov seemed to go even further, apparently viewing any United States action outside the United Nations framework as at least potentially illegal and giving rise to a right of reparation in Iran. He made it clear that without excusing Iran its violations (and he did concur in the terms of the *dispositif* directing Iran to release the hostages) that the United States appeared to have committed many violations of international law in its handling of the crisis, that the rescue mission was wholly unjustifiable under the rubric of self-defence, and that he would not concur in those parts of the judgment and those paragraphs of the *dispositif* that seemed to hold Iran overall more culpable or to owe more reparation than the United States could be argued to owe to Iran.[44]

---

[41] *Ibid.* pp. 44–45.
[42] See Part II below.
[43] *Ibid.* pp. 65–66.
[44] *Ibid.* pp. 51 *et seq.*, esp. pp. 54–57. Soviet military forces were active in Afghanistan and the Soviet Union had been roundly condemned for that military action by the General Assembly in its Resolution ES–6/2 of January 14, 1980. Morozov appeared careful to base his condemnation of United States action in Iran on grounds that could not be considered to undermine the Soviet rationale for its action in Afghanistan. To the outsider, a logic that seems to justify Soviet military action on the ground of collective security against an external enemy that cannot be shown to exist in fact, and to condemn United States military action aimed (however foolishly) at alleviating a situation brought about by a patently illegal use of force by the State whose territory was being invaded, seems a bit unreal. But such is the world of law and the United Nations Charter at this time. There is, of course, some underlying truth to the Morozov position if one is

One implication of the position taken by Judges Morozov and Tarazi seems important to address here: the view that steps taken parallel to judicial recourse to create pressure for settlement, steps that would be possibly legitimate self-help or retorsion in the absence of recourse to the Court such as freezing foreign assets, are somehow inconsistent with attempts at judicial settlement. The underlying apprehension that such parallel recourse is forbidden by the legal order might well reflect the conception of the role of the public authority acting through a judicial aspect in some municipal law systems, but it is hard to understand how the analogy applies to the international legal order. This is not the place to explore its implications further, but it seems clear that in the real world today, if such a position were adopted by the International Court of Justice it would end recourse to the Court by all States with other leverage to apply. It also seems inconsistent with the sensible position taken by Judge Lachs that in the long run only negotiations between the States directly concerned can really resolve complex disputes; negotiation with neither side permitted to apply those pressures which reflect the relative economic, political and public relations powers of the States involved must result in an artificial evaluation of the realities of power and interest truly affected by the negotiation. No State would enter into negotiations on such terms unless as part of a pre-negotiated agreement which itself reflected the pressures on each State which the real world creates. It seems fortunate that this interesting approach was not shared by 13 of the 15 judges sitting. It also points up the need for a deeper analysis than yet exists of the relationship between judicial settlement and the overall legal order.

II—THE EXTRAJUDICIAL AND EXTRAORGANISATIONAL RECOURSE

Judges Morozov and Tarazi apparently regarded United States counteraction to the Iranian taking of hostages as possibly illegal. It is difficult to see why in principle self-help should be forbidden by general

---

prepared to accept as valid the doubtful assertions of fact made by the Soviet Union in connection with the situation in Afghanistan. It is not necessary to concur in the Soviet position to see the weaknesses in the United States position; a rescue mission undertaken immediately might more convincingly have been considered to fit the traditional "self-defence" mould, or the rather more flexible Art. 51 interpretation of "self-defence," but absent the factors of immediacy and the unavailability of other recourse, it is hard to justify the United States action in April. The only issue separating Morozov and Tarazi from the rest of the Court on this was the relevance of the United States rescue mission to the case before the Court—the United States complaint regarding the Iranian seizure of the hostages and Embassy compound. The majority did not think the United States action relevant, and therefore went no further than to express doubts as to its legality. In the circumstances, the mere expression of doubt as to an action declared to be irrelevant, implies condemnation. But that condemnation rested on the apparent disregard of the judicial process and the Order of the Court, not on the theoretical reach of the international law of self-defence.

international law, or be regarded as necessarily inconsistent with other legal recourse. But there is no doubt that self-help action complicates the pattern of legal response when third parties become involved, and might be excessive, otherwise inappropriate, or even illegal. It should be borne in mind throughout the following discussion that while the Iranian seizure of American hostages shocked the world and a consensus quickly formed that whether legal or not it should be stopped, and that after the judgment of the International Court of Justice had been issued there could be no doubt that within the world of the United Nations and all its members the Iranian continued detention of the hostages was illegal, until that time United States action was based on its own interpretation of the law and facts. It cannot be presumed that United States actions viewed in quietness and with detachment were justifiable.

Under United States municipal law as currently interpreted, the President has the authority to declare a national emergency to deal with "an unusual and extraordinary threat, which has its source in whole or substantial part outside the United States, to the national security, foreign policy, or economy of the United States."[45] President Carter made such a declaration on November 14, 1979. While the declaration follows the statutory language, it sets forth no facts to indicate why the declaration was made: whether it was based on the seizure of the hostages and Embassy compound 10 days before, the rumoured imminent transfer of major Iranian bank accounts from the control of American banks, or any other facts. It does, in the most sweeping terms, "order blocked all property and interests in property of the Government of Iran, its instrumentalities and controlled entities and the Central Bank of Iran which are or become subject to the jurisdiction of the United States or which are in or come within the possession or control of persons subject to the jurisdiction of the United States."[46] In his message to the Congress reporting on this action, President Carter referred merely to "recent events in Iran and the recent actions of the Government of Iran" which,

---

[45] The National Emergencies Act, 50 U.S. Code sec. 1601 *et seq.*, authorises the President to set "national emergency" procedures in motion when other acts of the Congress authorise the exercise of special of extraordinary power in a period of national emergency. The International Emergency Economic Powers Act, 50 U.S. Code sec. 1701 *et seq.*, authorises the exercise of designated powers not normally exercisable by the President if he first declares a national emergency with respect to "an unusual and extraordinary threat" as set out in the text above.

[46] Executive Order 12170, *Federal Register* 65729 (1979); 15 *Weekly Compilation of Presidential Documents* 2117 (1979). In addition to this Order, the President under other legislative authority embargoed American imports of petroleum and petroleum products from Iran (Proclamation 4702; Federal Register 65581 of November 12, 1979) and delegated authority to the Secretary of State and Attorney-General to tighten the controls on Iranian nationals admitted temporarily to the United States (Executive Order 12172 of November 26, 1979; 44 Federal Register 67947). It is not proposed in this place to analyse these harassing gestures or specify other essentially symbolic and public-relations measures of the United States growing out of the hostages crisis.

he asserted, "put at grave risk the personal safety of United States citizens and the lawful claims of United States citizens and entities against the Government of Iran." "Blocking property and property interests of the Government of Iran, its instrumentalities and controlled entities and the Central Bank of Iran will enable the United States to assure that these resources will be available to satisfy lawful claims of citizens and entities of the United States against the Government of Iran."[47]

The Executive Order was legally implemented by Iranian Assets Control Regulations issued by the Department of the Treasury.[48] The basic rule of those Regulations was: "No property subject to the jurisdiction of the United States or which is in the possession of or control of persons subject to the jurisdiction of the United States in which on or after [November 14, 1979] Iran has any interest of any nature whatsoever may be transferred, paid, exported, withdrawn or otherwise dealt in except as authorized."[49] "Iran" is defined in the Regulations to include: "(1) The state and the Government of Iran as well as any political subdivisions, agency, or instrumentality thereof ... ; (2) Any partnership, association, corporation, or other organization substantially owned or controlled by any of the foregoing; (3) Any person ... acting or purporting to act directly or indirectly on behalf of any of the foregoing ... and (5) Any other person or organization determined by the Secretary of the Treasury. . . . "[50] "Property" is defined to include: "[m]oney, checks, drafts, bullion, bank deposits, ... debts, ... obligations, notes, debentures, stocks, bonds ... and any other property, real, personal, or mixed, tangible or intangible, or interest or interests therein, present, future or contingent."[51] The term "person subject to the jurisdiction of the United States" was defined to include: "(a) Any person wheresoever located who is a citizen or resident of the United States; (b) Any person actually within the United States; (c) Any corporation organized under the laws of the United States or of any state ... of the United States; and (d) any partnership, association, corporation, or other organization wheresoever organized or doing business which is owned or controlled by persons specified in paragraphs (a), (b), or (c) of this section."[52]

There are some exceptions to the basic rule to permit payments into blocked accounts, transfers between blocked accounts, and the segrega-

[47] 15 *Weekly Compilation of Presidential Documents* 2118 (1979).
[48] 44 *Fed. Reg.* (No. 222) 65956–65958 (November 15, 1979); photographically reproduced in 18(6) I.L.M. 1549–1556 (1979) 31 *Code of Federal Regulations* Pt. 535 (1979).
[49] *Ibid.* sec. 535.201(a).
[50] *Ibid.* sec. 535.301.
[51] *Ibid.* sec. 535.311.
[52] *Ibid.* sec. 535.329.

tion of moneys owed by Iran to American creditors, but in general no payments were permitted out of any blocked account.[53]

The result of this freezing of Iranian assets to the extent the United States could assert jurisdiction to do so was to raise a host of questions and problems. One fundamental problem of immediate concern to the United States banking industry was the impact of the freeze on the willingness of foreign governments, particularly the newly rich Arab States' governments, to deposit money and bullion in United States banks. The full impact of the freeze order on foreign governments seeking channels for their overseas accounts will not be apparent for many years, since careful investors move their money slowly and there are few alternatives at this time to the American banking facilities in New York as a supplement to English, Swiss and other banks handling investments in the United States.

A second problem complicating the situation was the impact on our allies of the freeze order, as extended via American investors and managers to foreign corporations and banks doing business wholly outside the United States. In the face of similar American Regulations directed against the People's Republic of China, France had actually in 1965 placed the French subsidiary of an American Corporation under a temporary administrator to relieve the Corporation of the American restraints, which were regarded as an attempt to export American foreign and commercial policy to France.[54] Now, without implying that France or any other country was not wholly on the side of the United States in seeking the quick and safe release of the hostages in Iran, it is

---

[53] *Ibid.* secs. 535.508, 535.904 (added to the basic Regulation on November 16, 1979); 535.415 (added on November 23, 1979). Two other Executive Orders added a super-structure to this scheme and should be noted, although it is impossible in this place to analyze all the Executive Branch actions pertinent to a full understanding of the freeze regulations and their effects. Executive Order 12205 of April 7, 1980, prohibited the transfer to Iran by persons subject to American jurisdiction of commodities except for food and medicines and other items intended to be used to relieve human suffering, and prohibited "Failing to act in a businesslike manner in exercising any rights when payments due on existing credits or loans are not made in a timely manner." Executive Order 12205 sec. 1–101(*d*)(iv), in 16(15) *Weekly Compilation of Presidential Documents* 612 (1980). Executive Order 12211 of April 17, 1980, made minor amendments to this Order of which the most important seems to be the prohibition of imports into the United States from Iran of any goods or services other than materials for news dissemination. Oddly, part of the rationale for that new prohibition appears to have been a declaration of national emergency with respect to "the Soviet invasion of Afghanistan," which had occurred some months before and does not seem relevant to the actions actually involved in the Executive Order. See 16(16) *Weekly Compilation of Presidential Documents* 714 (1980), sec. 1–102. The Declaration of a National Emergency is on p. 715.

[54] *Fruehauf Corporation* v. *Massardy*, Court of Appeals, Paris, May 22, 1965; [1965] Gazette du Palais II, Jur.86. The case is neatly summarised in Steiner and Vagts, *Transnational Legal Problems* (2nd ed.) 1225–1226 (1976). The United States took account of this situation with regard to non-banking foreign institutions by exempting them from the prohibitions of Executive Order 12205 of April 7, 1980, cited in note 53 above, sec. 1–102. Banks organised abroad by persons "subject to the jurisdiction of the United States" as interpreted by the United States remained subject to the whole range of prohibitions making up the freeze on Iranian transactions to the degree the American persons could control them.

more than possible that dormant apprehensions regarding the American use of foreign corporations to help implement United States policy in disregard of the interests of the States of incorporation (which were not even consulted) were awakened by the sweeping terms of the freeze order. Certainly it would henceforth be in the interests of countries in which American-based firms sought to invest to reconsider the terms under which they were willing to accept that investment, and United States participation in foreign banking and joint ventures would become an object of some official and unofficial scrutiny.

But there was a more immediate implication to the American freeze order that came to dominate the scene. American and foreign creditors of "Iran" (as so broadly defined in the Regulations), despite the President's message to Congress saying that one reason for the Order was to assure the availability of Iranian resources to pay lawful American claims, could not be paid out of the Iranian bank accounts under the Regulations as the debts became due. Thus, although there might be no doubt as to the existence of the debts, the amounts due, or the eagerness of Iran to pay its debts to private American (or foreign) creditors, in many cases, alleged to amount to billions of dollars,[55] a class of new claimants was created whose legal recourse would normally have been to Iranian courts, possibly American courts, and ultimately to some international claims procedure. Thus United States freeze Regulations, by apparently requiring suit in United States courts under the terms of Executive Order 12205 of April 7, 1980,[56] and by not allowing for any procedure to hear American creditors and pay their claims out of the Iranian assets by American administrative or judicial action, had placed the United States in a position in which even the rescission of the freeze Regulations could not return relations between Iran and the United States to the position they were in before the hostages were seized. The release of the hostages would have to involve either a continuance of the freeze until a claims procedure could be negotiated with Iran, or, if accompanied by an immediate release of the Iranian assets, presumably to be immediately withdrawn by Iran from American banks, would potentially cost American (and foreign) creditors of Iran large sums until some claims procedure could in the distant future be negotiated.

In the circumstances, the obvious tactic by the United States to minimise the effect of its own Regulations on its own people who were creditors of Iran, would seem to have been to attempt to separate the two issues: hostages and claims. The legal mechanism for such a separation was right at hand. As noted above, the recourse contained in the United Nations Charter for failure of a party to a case before the Inter-

---

[55] The total figures have not been reliably reported; it has been in the interests of the claimants to exaggerate their claims both as to amount and as to legal substance.

[56] Quoted in note 53, above.

national Court of Justice to comply with a judgment of the Court can be for the other party to take the situation under Article 94(2) of the Charter to the Security Council. The part of the judgment relating to the release of the hostages was peremptory and unanimous. Failure of the Security Council to do all within its power to further isolate Iran and thus take measures to give effect to the judgment would have been, if not unthinkable, at least a serious matter in which the United States would have had all right both legally and morally. Moreover, referring the situation to the Security Council now with the focus on the integrity of the United Nations Charter and the sanctity of judgments of the International Court of Justice would have opened a path through which Iran, as its internal politics began to change and the release of the hostages became important to those in power, would have been able to avoid a difficult negotiation with the United States and the appearance of backing down to United States pressures. It could have handed the hostages over to the Secretary-General or the Security Council as a discharge of its obligations as a party to the case and a gesture of respect to the International Court of Justice.[57] The negotiation over the claims could have been conditioned by the United States on the release of the hostages.

An even more powerful position might well have been taken by the United States agreeing that if the hostages were released the claims situation would be submitted to the International Court of Justice as part of the Court's disposition of the reparations aspect of the case. The Court had already decided by a vote of 14 to one in May 1980 that "the form and amount of such reparation, failing agreement between the Parties, should be settled by the Court," and reserved for that purpose "the subsequent procedure in the case."[58] Since none of the money was by any rationale American, the United States had nothing to lose by such a commitment except perhaps some harsh words by the Court about the freeze order being disproportionately rigid. Bearing in mind the circumstances in November 1979, the absolute illegality of the Iranian hostage seizure already pronounced by the Court, and the ultimate willingness of the United States to come to terms regarding the claims, even that risk seems negligible. And taking the claims aspect of the case to the Court, adding to it the direct United States claim against Iran for the taking of the hostages, and providing for the Court to determine the entire disposition of the claims, both public and private, in one judgment, would have enabled the United States and Iran to step back from their confrontational postures and each could satisfy its internal

---

[57] This suggestion, repeatedly made earlier, was elaborated at some length in a memorandum written in December 1980, when the newspapers were reporting the imminent breakdown of the negotiations between the United States and Iran over the claims issue. The memorandum was published as Rubin, "The Hostages: International Law to the Rescue," *Christian Science Monitor*, January 9, 1981, p. 22.

[58] *Op. cit.* in note 40, above, p. 46, para. 6 of the *dispositif*.

constituents that whatever occurred that was unsatisfactory was the fault of third parties against whom no further recourse was possible. If peace in the Middle East and an eventual reconciliation of both sides were considered desirable, then this way of avoiding the recriminations that must accompany any direct settlement in which some interests are compromised was the obvious course.[59]

There was another, and more complicated reason for the United States to seek a different way to resolve the crisis from direct negotiations in which the release of the hostages and the settlement of claims resulting from the freeze order were mixed. Under the Foreign Sovereign Immunites Act of 1976[60] a second State is not immune from a private suit in United States courts "in any case . . . in which the action is based . . . upon an act outside the territory of the United States in connection with a commercial activity of the foreign state elsewhere and that act causes a direct effect in the United States."[61] In a case focusing on the distinction between a "commercial" refusal to pay a contract debt and an "act of State" just before the Act was passed, the Supreme Court by a very narrow majority held that failure to pay a contract debt was "commercial" even though it was clear that under the law of the *situs* of the debt it was obvious that the creditor could have no hope of a recovery.[62] Since the majority was split, narrow, and its opinion unsatisfactorily reasoned, no opinion can be sensibly offered as to the ultimate chances of success in suits filed by the American (and foreign) claimants. That uncertainty surrounding the word "commercial"

---

[59] The International Court of Justice has the legal authority to determine "the nature or extent of the reparation to be made for the breach of an international obligation" under Art. 36(2)(*d*) of the Statute of the Court, annexed to the Charter of the United Nations. See United Nations Charter, Art. 92. Since the Court's purview was in the hostages case restricted to issues within the narrow terms of documents cited in note 22, above, it would have been necessary for both parties to agree on a supplemental submission. In light of the much more elaborate provisions negotiated in January 1981 between Iran and the United States, and involving several reluctant third parties, it is hard to see why this simpler procedure was not tried.

[60] 28 U.S. Code secs. 1330, 1332, 1391, 1441, 1602–1611.

[61] *Ibid.* sec. 1605(a) . . . (2).

[62] *Alfred Dunhill of London, Inc.* v. *The Republic of Cuba et al.*, 425 U.S. 682 (1976). Sovereign immunity was not as such an issue in the case since, for complex reasons arising out of the specific facts of the case, Cuba appeared initially as a party plaintiff, waiving sovereign immunity for purposes of the case. The three judges joining in the "majority" opinion concluded that: "For all the reasons which led the Executive Branch to adopt the restrictive theory of sovereign immunity, we hold that the mere assertion of sovereignty as a defense to a claim arising out of purely commercial acts by a foreign sovereign is no more effective if given the label 'Act of State' than if it is given the label 'sovereign immunity.' " Two judges concurring separately in very short opinions joined in the conclusion of the three, but one of them pointedly refrained from endorsing this particular language. Four judges dissented specifically on this point. Since there is much in the logic of the "majority" that is of questionable persuasiveness, although this is not the place for further analysis, it may be concluded that the American law is not clear. But claimants against Iran basing their claims on Iran's failure (for whatever reason) to pay its contract debts do have a Supreme Court precedent that appears to support their position. Given the amount of money involved, it is absurd to imagine that they would not pursue their American remedies in what they would imagine to be a friendly court.

extends to jurisdictional questions under the 1976 Act. It is possible that
the Supreme Court would hold the transactions in question caused no
"direct effect in the United States" within the sense of the Act, and
uphold Iranian pleas of sovereign immunity despite the Act. But such a
result would deprive American multinational corporations of most of the
advantages they expected to gain from passage of the Act, and it can be
expected to be fought vigorously in the courts. A legal battle concerning this much money and principle can be expected to take years.
Moreover, it is highly doubtful that the Executive Branch of the Government, without the support of the Senate in a Treaty, or the support of the
entire Congress exercising its power to regulate foreign commerce, has
the legal authority under the American Constitution to deprive the
claimants of their day (actually, probably years) in court whatever the
likely ultimate outcome of the litigation. A detailed analysis of the Constitutional problems is out of place in this paper, but it may be
noteworthy that in the major precedent for settling the claims of
Americans against a foreign State by so-called Executive Agreement
unsupported by Treaty or legislation, the Litvinov Assignment of 1933,
the Constitutional authority of the President was found by a majority of
a split Supreme Court to lie in his power to "recognise" foreign governments, which was held to be implicit in his undoubted power to send and
receive foreign ambassadors.[63] Those underpinnings are simply not present in the Iran situation where the United States recognised the Iranian
Government (with which it eventually negotiated the agreement resulting
in the release of the hostages and a claims procedure) throughout the
entire period.

It must have been obvious to anybody with a background in international law and American Constitutional law that direct negotiation
with Iran over the claims would involve delays and serious legal
difficulties. Since no release of the hostages could be expected until the
authorities in Iran found it in their interest to release the hostages
regardless of the claims situation, and the claims situation was complex
and possibly a major point of further contention, it was in the interest of
the United States to separate the two issues as far as possible. Instead,
the United States did nothing.

Finally, in October 1980, the internal political pressures in Iran, a
military invasion of disputed territory by Iraq in late September, and the
Iranian leadership's evaluation of the internal pressures on the Carter
Administration in the United States, combined to make Iran willing to
risk a negotiation with the United States through the intermediacy of
Algeria; Iran would exchange the hostages for an arrangement on proce-

---

[63] *U.S.* v. *Pink*, 315 U.S. 203 (1942). Four judges joined in the "majority" opinion written by
Justice Douglas; Justice Frankfurter wrote a separate concurrence, Justices Stone and Roberts
dissented and two Justices took no part in the decision.

dures that would lead to a settlement of the American private claims arising out of the American freeze order, and the return to Iran of a portion of its frozen assets. The deal was completed in the last days of the Carter Administration, and implementation begun with the transfer of some of the Iranian funds to the Bank of England on January 20, 1981, the day President Reagan took office. Following a few hours' further delay, the hostages were released by Iran a few minutes after the change of Administration in the United States in what seems to have been a final gesture of contempt for President Carter.

The arrangement to settle the claims involves much more than the legal problems in the United States indicated above, and the ability of the United States to meet its apparent commitment to Iran without Senatorial or Congressional support is in serious question. But a discussion of the full range of legal and political problems the final arrangement poses to the United States is beyond the scope of this article.[64]

CONCLUSIONS

On learning of the conclusion of an Agreement that, however brittle, would result in the immediate release of the hostages I felt as if I had been through a race on country roads in a small car driven by an expert

---

[64] The major documents involved in the release and claims Agreement are reproduced photographically in 20(1) I.L.M. 223–240, 282–293 (1981). The problems created by the freeze order and the Foreign Sovereign Immunities Act of 1976 are illustrated by the Opinion and Order of September 26, 1980, in which Judge Kevin Thomas Duffy of the United States [Federal] District Court for the Southern District of New York found that the Act authorised him to apply the normal rules relating to prejudgment attachment independently of the freeze regulations, denied the Iranian motions to vacate the cases, denied the request of the United States for an indefinite stay in the proceedings, and issued orders of attachment sufficient to secure the claims of plaintiffs against various Iranian defendants in 96 separate actions. 19(5) I.L.M. 1298–1329 (1980). Immediately on the conclusion of the hostage release, on January 20, 1981, the United States filed a *Statement of Interest* in the same court asking that the prejudgment attachment orders be vacated. 20(1) I.L.M. 171–185 (1981). As this is written (April 1981) it is not clear what effect this and other actions by the Executive Branch of the United States Government will have; whether the United States Executive Branch overstepped its authority under the Constitution and common law in apparently committing the United States to the claims procedure contained in the release Agreement and whether, if so, a way can be found within the United States to secure whatever cooperation of the claimants or the courts or the Congress may be necessary to enable the United States to perform its undertakings.

Shortly after the main outlines of the Agreement were indicated in the press, letters and guest columns began appearing in the major American papers suggesting that the entire Agreement was "void" under the general international law codified in Art. 52 of the 1969 Vienna Convention on the Law of Treaties, U.N. Doc. A/CONF. 39/27 at p. 289, reprinted in 8 I.L.M. 679 (1969). That article relates to treaties whose "conclusion has been procured by the threat or use of force in violation of the principles of international law embodied in the Charter of the United Nations." Since it is not at all clear that the undoubted delict of Iran in seizing the hostages was also a use of force in violation of the "principles" of the Charter, which are explicitly set out in Art. 2 of the Charter and do not seem to apply to this case, the argument seems weak. Moreover, it is hardly logical to classify an agreement aimed at returning the situation to what it was before the delict occurred as "coerced" or "procured" by the delict itself. It could as well be argued that the Agreement was "coerced" or "procured" by the United States failing to confine its reaction

racing driver who had broken his eyeglasses at the start and was dead drunk throughout. We won the race, but at the cost of the car itself, which seemed about to fall apart, and of all confidence in the driver. While a rational argument could be made to support United States policy in admitting the Shah for medical treatment in disregard of the probable reaction in Iran in October 1979, and other early decisions can be criticised only with the certainty of hindsight, there can be no doubt that what passed for calm and mature handling of the crisis in its later stages was even worse and no hindsight is necessary to support the judgment of the American people on election day in November 1980.

Lawyers in the Department of State competent to place the crisis into orderly perspective were apparently not consulted on the major questions of policy. The decision to take the case to the International Court of Justice was taken apparently reluctantly. The United Nations procedures for enforcing world court judgments by political pressures were never attempted. The freeze Regulations, apparently useful and effective to bring Iran into serious negotiations to end the crisis, unnecessarily created claims and complications that seem to have had no purpose other than to transform unsecured Iranian debts into secured debts for the benefit of creditors. The aborted rescue mission risked, even if successful, creating a political situation in the Middle East in which the Western world's oil supplies would have been seriously jeopardised. The failure to seek the orderly remedies the law provides prolonged the crisis

---

to the peaceful settlement modes mentioned in Art. 33 of the Charter. Both arguments seem absurd. Moreover, even if the Agreement is void, the legal result of such a holding would be to end the parts of it that created obligations in the Bank of England to hold some of the money pending action of the tribunal set up by the Agreement to hear and evaluate the various claims. The money would probably have to be returned immediately to Iran, its undisputed source, and not the United States banks, which had no claim at all to the money other than as places in which Iran had at one time in the distant past deposited it under normal banking arrangements. It is hard to see how such a step could help anybody in the United States. The Reagan Administration on February 18, 1981, announced that it would honour the Agreement.

There are many questions of law impossible to analyse here, such as the possibility that the Iranian defaults, having been caused by the freeze Regulations of the United States and not any refusal by Iran to issue the appropriate payment orders, are properly claims against the United States, not against Iran. And to the extent any claims based on alleged contract breaches by Iran involve contracts with arbitration, choice of law, "distraint of princes" or other terms that affect the allocation of insurable risks and ultimate liability for breach, each contract would have to be examined before any opinion on the ultimate validity of the claims based on its alleged breach by Iran could properly be offered. For current purposes it is necessary merely to point out that all these problems were obstacles to resolution of the hostages crisis at the earliest moment, and that the freeze on Iranian assets could have been imposed by the United States without forcing American claimants to forego collecting their claims as they fell due. Indeed, a procedure to permit claims to be paid out of the frozen assets on presentation of appropriate evidence, and providing Iran with an opportunity to defend its assets from unjustified claims, would seem to have been feasible. The spectacle of a diminishing bank balance might well have encouraged Iran to settle the crisis sooner than the contemplation of frozen assets that Iranian leaders imagined would all be returned as soon as the hostages were freed. In any case, nothing suggested here would have foreclosed eventually moving to the rigid position actually taken by the United States, with all its complexities, if the milder approaches had failed.

past the time at which it became important to the groups ruling Iran to release the hostages, and the intrusion of the claims issue into the final negotiation made it necessary to wait until the Iranian authorities could be satisfied that the substantial risks and delays they faced in seeking the return of their money were less important to them than the release of the hostages. The final Agreement appears to have created Constitutional problems in the United States which were clearly foreseeable, and the Agreement itself may be unenforceable there, with a concomitant loss of American credibility in all complex negotiations. Involving third States, like Algeria and the United Kingdom, in an Agreement placing Iran and the United States unnecessarily in a confrontational position, rather than using international organisations to avoid confrontations, is a signal to the entire world of the cost of friendship with the United States. The stability of the Middle East, which could have been improved by pulling Iran back into the world of institutional pressures and rational decision-making, has been further undermined by accepting the confrontational mode, which makes it difficult for friendly Powers in the Middle East to support the initiatives of the United States and its allies there.

The ostensibly happy ending of January 20, 1981, conceals a potential tragedy which the electoral defeat of President Carter may have mitigated to some extent, since he can be personally blamed for the actions of his incompetent Administration, but cannot be overlooked. The disinterest in sound legal advice at policy councils in a United States administration must be reckoned as a cost the entire world must pay for American democracy. It is that cost, at least as much as any military weakness, which seems responsible for the decline of United States prestige in the world. It may be hoped that the Reagan Administration and its successors learn from the mishandling of the hostages crisis the importance of including competent legal advice in the highest levels of government, and that the Senate, which has a constitutional obligation to "advise and consent" to the appointment of officials of the rank of Legal Adviser to the Department of State, will discharge that obligation with considerably more care than has been its recent practice.

THE JUDICIAL CORPS
OF THE INTERNATIONAL
COURT OF JUSTICE

By

GEORG SCHWARZENBERGER

Two considerations suggest a change in emphasis in the study of the judicial personnel of international institutions such as the International Court of Justice from their individual members to the judicial corps as a whole[1]:

(1) the permanent, that is, indefinite character of the existence of a judicial corps as compared with the more transient character of individual membership, in the case of judges of the International Court of Justice averaging out at one full nine-years term of office, and

(2) the proved ability of Courts such as the Permanent Court of International Justice, the International Court of Justice, the Court of Justice of the European Communities and the European Court of Human Rights to absorb individual idiosyncracies.

It is proposed to explore the subject under three heads: the judicial image portrayed in the Statute of the International Court of Justice, the recruitment and renewal of the Court's judicial corps, and the impact of the dialectics of world affairs.

I—THE JUDICIAL IMAGE

The international judge envisaged in the Statutes of the Permanent Court of International Justice and the International Court of Justice has to comply with seven requisites. He is to be internationally-minded, independent, disinterested, impartial, conscientious, competent and of high moral character.[2]

(1) *The internationally-minded judge*

The expectation of an international outlook on the part of members of the Court is implied in a number of the other requisites. In an inter-

---

[1] On the Court in general and background literature, see Schwarzenberger-Brown, *Manual of International Law* (Professional Books, 6th ed., 2nd impression—1978), pp. 194 and 490 *et seq.*, and, on questions related to this paper, for instance, S. Rosenne, *The Law and Practice of the International Court* (1965—Chap. V: The Personnel of the Court) and the perceptive study by L. V. Prott, *The Latent Power of Culture and the International Judge* (1979—useful interdisciplinary bibliography).

[2] Art. 2 *et seq.*, Statute, International Court of Justice (I.C.J.—*Acts and Documents* Nr. 4 (1978), pp. 61 *et seq.*) and Arts. 1 *et seq.*, Rules of Court (*ibid.* pp. 93 *et seq.*).

national dispute, it would be difficult to imagine an independent, disinterested and impartial judge who was not internationally-minded.

The requirement is also implicit in the injunction to the electors that the judges are to be elected "regardless of nationality." This involves the possibility that more than one national of a particular State will be elected. In order to avoid this contingency, it had been provided in the Statute of the Permanent Court of International Justice that, in this eventuality, the elder of the two should be considered to be elected. In the 1945 revision of the Statute, an express prohibition to have on the Court more than one national of the same State has been added. As before, any necessary adjustment is to be made by reference to the seniority principle. Issues of dual nationality are to be resolved by reference to the principle of effective nationality.

As with the Permanent Court of International Justice in the League of Nations era, each of the greater Powers in the guise of the permanent members of the United Nations Security Council expects to have always a judge of its nationality on the Court. The prescience with which the General Assembly and the Security Council—like their predecessors in the League of Nations—have been able to fulfil these expectations in votes in which they are supposed to disregard the nationality of any candidate verges on the miraculous.

(2) *The independent judge*

The first question is: independence from whom? In the Court's Statute, guidance is offered by the list of judicial incompatibilities. Any of these prohibited involvements may not only affect a judge's disinterestedness and impartiality but also create unacceptable dependencies. More explicit guidance is offered on civil servants in the United Nations Charter of which the Statute forms an integral part. The Secretary-General and the other members of the Secretariat are not to seek or receive instructions from any government or any other authority external to the United Nations, and each member of the United Nations undertakes not to seek to influence the members of the United Nations civil service in the discharge of their responsibilities.

If so far-reaching a degree of autonomy is due to the administrative services of the United Nations, it must constitute the rock-bottom minimum for its judicial sector. Yet this is hardly the real difficulty. It arises from the possibility of unverifiable self-co-ordination. The draftsmen of the 1945 Statute, like their 1920 predecessors, thought it unnecessary or inadvisable to face this more insidious threat to judicial independence or, perhaps, it did not occur to them.

(3) *The disinterested judge*

Like independence and impartiality, judicial disinterestedness is implied in the list of incompatibilities set out in the Court's Statute.

As with independence and impartiality, difficulties may arise below the surface of judicial correctness. Three types of case come to mind: (1) cases in which the government of a third State would prefer to leave particular issues undecided; (2) cases in which a judge is aware of the possibility that he may prejudge, in effect, another case that, at the time, is not before the Court; (3) cases in which, for the time being, the government of a third State would wish to avoid crystallisation of the substantive law.

(4) *The impartial judge*

Experience has proved independence and disinterestedness to be well-tried mainstays of judicial impartiality. The promise in open court to exercise his powers impartially is the first of the two solemn undertakings demanded from a judge before taking up his judicial duties.

Again, the real problems are masked partiality and commitment. In their least detectable forms, they may surface in, to all appearances, technical decisions on admissibility, jurisdiction or procedure. Even votes which, at first sight, appear "against interest" may deserve second thoughts.

(5) *The conscientious judge*

Under the Court's Statute, the second of the solemn undertakings a new judge has to give is conscientious discharge of his duties. Since, on the duty of attendance, the Statute of the Permanent Court of International Justice was stiffened, conscientious discharge of judicial duties means, in the first place, that every judge holds himself permanently at the Court's disposal. Exceptions to the rule are exhaustively enumerated in the Statute: absence during judicial vacations, leave of absence and prevention from attendance in Court by illness or for other reasons duly explained to the Court's President.

Apart from participation in sittings of the Court—open, closed and internal—conscientious and, under the Rules of Court, faithful fulfilment of a judge's duties includes a variety of judicial and administrative tasks: for instance, the study of frequently voluminous pleadings and corresponding material in advisory proceedings, participation in deliberations on, and drafting of, decisions to be made, and the duties involved in membership of Chambers and committees of the Court.

Leaving aside the onerous implications of the presumption of *jura novit curia*, conscientiousness, no less than professional self-respect, implies the duty of acquiring and maintaining expertise in international law becoming to a member of the highest judicial organ of the United Nations, as well as linguistic proficiency in, at least, the Court's two working languages. Thus, even while the Court may be condemned to frustrating periods of "free-wheeling," the time-table of the judge conscientious may be crowded.

(6) *The competent judge*

Alternative qualifications for members of the Court are those required in the respective countries of the judges for appointment to the highest judicial offices and those of a jurisconsult of recognised competence in international law. The first of the two alternative qualifications is to ensure a modicum of legal training and knowledge, if not necessarily in international law. The second is to make possible the nomination and election of international lawyers who may lack formal qualifications for appointment to high judicial office in a system of domestic law.

While the first of these qualifications may not be unduly exacting, the second is as subjective as the evaluation to be made in Article 38 of the Court's Statute of the most highly qualified publicists of the various nations. Beyond this, it becomes increasingly questionable whether electors still mean the same thing when they bear in mind the international law that is taken for granted in Article 2 of the Court's Statute and prescribed in greater detail in Article 38 as the law to be applied by the Court.

(7) *The moral judge*

In 1921, the meanings attached in the Statute of the Permanent Court of International Justice to terms such as "persons of high moral character" and "honourable" performance of the judicial office were reasonably clear. They were based on ethical concepts common to "the main forms of civilisation and the principal legal systems of the world."[3]

In 1945, a negative consensus probably still existed on the barbarous character of the political systems of the enemies of the United Nations at war and their worst offenders in high office, including their most prominent lawyers. Yet, even then, tyrannical oppression and neo-barbarism were not limited to one side and, subsequently, have spread far and wide.

Unavoidably, two questions arise. *First*, is it possible to accept at their face value implied assurances of the high moral character of candidates from nominating organs in notoriously oppressive systems? *Secondly*, what credibility attaches to the solemn declaration made by a judge with this type of background and pressures on his independence that he will honourably carry out his judicial duties?

(8) *Lex imperfecta?*

What happens if, at the time of nomination or election, a candidate manifestly lacks one or more of the "required conditions"[4] under the

---

[3] Art. 9, Statutes, Permanent Court of International Justice (P.C.I.J.) and I.C.J. (*ibid.*, pp. 64–65).

[4] Art. 18, Statute, I.C.J. (*ibid.* p. 67).

Statute? The responsibility may have to be left to the nominating and electoral organs, in reliance on their ability and willingness to discharge their own functions in good faith. To reason in this way would be comparable to the finality of the admission of new members of the United Nations irrespective of whether they fulfil the conditions for admission laid down in the United Nations Charter.

During the judge's tenure of office, a different régime applies. In the interest of the Court's judicial autonomy and the independence of the individual judges, investigation and dismissal of judges is left entirely with the Court. To obtain a dismissal, it is necessary that, "in the unanimous opinion of the other members," the judge under investigation "has ceased to fulfil the required conditions."

Article 18 of the Court's Statute raises three questions of interpretation: (1) May the Court concern itself only with facts which relate to the period *after* a judge's election? Circumstances can be readily imagined in which, in good faith and protection of its own standing, the Court should not have to treat the election date as an absolute bar to investigation. (2) What are the requisite conditions? They appear to cover all the seven conditions enumerated in the Statute which relate to candidates "individually."[5] (3) Is the unanimity required that of all the other ordinary judges in office or only that of the members present at the meetings of the Court convened for the purpose?

In accordance with the unambiguous language of the Statute and in the interest of the security of tenure of the judge under investigation, a strict interpretation of the Statute on this point appears advisable. It is significant that, in the 1978 version of Article 6 of the Rules of Court, the previous reference to the unanimity of the members *present* at the further meeting in the absence of the judge investigated has been deleted, and an express reference has been added to the requirement that each member of the Court has to state his opinion. Another new Rule is also relevant: it is now expressly stated that the Court's quorum of nine under the Statute applies to all meetings of the Court.

The dismissal procedure under the Rules of Court provides elaborate guarantees for a fair hearing of the judge under investigation. Formal notification of the Court's decision has to be made by the Court's Registrar to the Secretary-General of the United Nations, and this notification makes the judgeship vacant. In the sense that the Court alone has control over its members during their tenure of office and the duty to watch over the maintenance of their judicial standards, the Court may justly claim to be the exclusive guardian of its own judicial integrity.

---

[5] Art. 9, Statute, I.C.J. (*ibid.* p. 63).

II—RECRUITMENT AND RENEWAL
OF THE JUDICIAL CORPS

On the nomination and election of candidates for judgeships in the International Court of Justice, noteworthy discrepancies exist between the Court's Statute and the actual practice of the United Nations.

In relation to candidates from the two super-Powers, all that matters is nomination. The rest is ritual. The electorates—the General Assembly and the Security Council—are more critical towards candidates on lower rungs of the world power ladder.

(1) *Nominations*

The nomination system in the Court's Statute is intended to serve three potentially conflicting objects: to select candidates who fulfil the personal requirements of the Court's Statute and are in a "position"[6] to accept the duties of members of the Court; to secure that no government has influence on the choice of candidates or, at least, avoid overt government-direction of nominations, and to ensure a minimum of respect for the ideals and ideologies embodied in the Court's Statute.

Nominating organs.   In their capacity as members of the various national nominating organs, the names on the panel of arbitrators in the Hague Peace System[7] spring to life. Under Hague Conventions I of 1899 and 1907, the maximum number of members of the Permanent Court of Arbitration appointed by each party is four. There is no fixed minimal number. Thus, a national group may consist of a sole member.

Parties to the Court's Statute who are not parties to Hague Conventions I of 1899 or 1907 are to form national groups of their own with members of corresponding standing. Increasingly, this has become the position of the majority of the members of the United Nations.

The Statute does not preclude nomination by members of national groups of any of their own members. A high proportion of members of the Court of the nationalities of parties to Hague Conventions I of 1899 or 1907 were in this position at the time of their election. In the Court's practice, judges may continue to hold these appointments during their tenure of office. Thus, these national groups have come to fulfil also typical control-functions of oligarchic in-groups.

The nominating process.   Before making nominations, national groups are recommended to consult a variety of legal bodies in their countries. Yet this is only an exhortatory rule, and consultation does not necessarily mean acceptance of advice offered.

If national groups take their task seriously, they have to do better than assure themselves of the judicial qualifications of their candidates.

---

[6] Art. 5(1), Statute, I.C.J. (*ibid.* p. 63).
[7] See this *Year Book*, Vol. 34 (1980), pp. 335 *et seq.*

To be able to state that their nominees are "in a position to accept the duties of members of the Court,"[8] they may be expected to ascertain at least whether their candidates are willing to stand. It may also be thought that the language used suggests some assurance on the ability, physical and mental, as distinct from mere willingness, of candidates to fulfil their judicial duties.

The maximum number of nominees by each national group for any election is four, no more than two of whom shall be of the group's nationality. Moreover, in no case may the number of candidates nominated by a national group be more than double the number of seats to be filled.

With a membership of the United Nations of over 150 members and three non-member parties to the Statute, any of the regular triennial elections of five members of the Court could lead, in the abstract, to the nomination of over 600 candidates.

In practice, informal contacts between national groups, foreign ministries, permanent delegations to the United Nations, the chairmen of the "regional" groups of the General Assembly and others active in the process of election-management assist in keeping the number of actual nominations on a relatively low level.

Such understandings may also lead to questionable forms of cutting corners. In a strict interpretation and application of the Statute, nominations must reach the United Nations Secretariat "within a given time,"[9] stated in the Secretary-General's invitation to the national groups and equal for all. Moreover, on receipt of the nominations, they should be considered to be irrevocable.

In practice, these invitations appear to be sent to the members of the national groups through the foreign ministries involved; late nominations are accepted; nominations are withdrawn even during elections in progress, and such withdrawals are frequently announced by members of delegations who purport to act on behalf of their national groups or individual candidates.[10] Occasionally, nomination- and election-management surpasses itself. In the 1972 elections, "the number of effective candidates was so small as to offer virtually no choice. The candidates elected themselves."[11]

(2) *Elections*

The principal rules on the election of judges, and a notable discontinuity in the interpretation of the Statutes of the Permanent Court

---

[8] Art. 5(1), Statute, I.C.J. (*ibid.* p. 63).

[9] Art. 5(1), Statute, I.C.J. (*ibid.* p. 63).

[10] See S. Rosenne, *Election of Members*, etc. (70 *American Journal of International Law* (A.J.I.L.—1976), pp. 545 *et seq.*).

[11] Sir Gerald Fitzmaurice in L. Gross (ed.), *The Future of the International Court of Justice* (1976), Vol. II, p. 493, note 35.

of International Justice and the International Court of Justice may claim more than technical interest.

Principal rules.   Four principal rules in the Court's Statute govern the election of members of the Court:

(1) Five members of the Court are elected or re-elected in *triennial* elections, held by the General Assembly and the Security Council of the United Nations.

(2) In the case of a vacancy by resignation, death or dismissal of a member of the Court, a *supplementary* election is held to fill the vacancy for the remainder of the predecessor's term.

(3) The General Assembly and the Security Council proceed "independently of one another." While, usually, the elections in the two organs take place simultaneously, there are to be no official contacts between them on election matters other than in the case of a deadlock.

(4) Candidates require an "absolute majority of votes" in each of the two electoral organs. This implies—but is also stated expressly—an exception to the veto-power of permanent members of the Security Council in the United Nations Charter.

The meaning of absolute majority of votes.   The meaning of "an absolute majority of votes" (in the original French text: "*la majorité absolue des voix*")[12] will become clearer in the wider context of two directly relevant voting systems:

(1) According to Voting System One, the choice is between *simple* and *qualified* majority: *simple* majority means one more than half of the actual voters or valid votes, and *qualified* majority means a larger majority than one-half.

(2) According to Voting System Two, the choice is between *relative* and *absolute* majority: *relative* majority means more voters or votes for one candidate or proposal than for any other, but not necessarily an overall majority as under (1). *Absolute* majority means more than one-half of voters or votes. In English usage, this may be determined by reference to *actual* voters (or *valid* votes) *or* by reference to all *potential* voters, irrespective of whether they actually voted (or by reference to all potential votes), irrespective of whether any of them were validly cast.

Continental usage does not appear to include potential voters or votes in an absolute majority. As the English text is merely a translation from the French text and compatible with both versions, it is the French version and its linguistic usage which ought to prevail, and this was what happened in a constant League practice.

---

[12] Art. 10(1), Statute, I.C.J. (*loc. cit.* above, note 2, pp. 64–65).

On the possibilities of two different interpretations of these words, see H. Kelsen, *The Law of the United Nations* (1950), pp. 188–189, the impressive piece of research by A. W. Rudzinski on *Election Procedure in the United Nations* (53 A.J.I.L. (1959), pp. 81 *et seq.*), and *contra*, W. N. Hogan (59 *ibid.* (1965), pp. 908 *et seq.*).

Right from 1946 onwards, the United Nations showed an unwavering preference for the other interpretation—possible under English usage—and determined absolute majority of votes by reference to all potential voters.

Ratio legis. The *original* composition of the League Council—five permanent members and four non-permanent members, the latter elected by the League Assembly—provides a clue to the unusual formulation of the voting rule on the election of judges in the Statute of the Permanent Court of International Justice.

The object was to secure permanent "representation" of the five Principal Allied and Associated Powers in the Court. With five out of nine votes, the permanent members had an absolute majority in the French usage of the term and, so long as they were united, they could block any other candidate if their common oligarchic interests were at risk.

With an original membership of 11, the special interests of the five permanent members in the Security Council of the United Nations were more effectively masked. If all permanent members were represented at an election, the majority required would be six, whichever interpretation of absolute majority of votes was adopted. Thus, the permanent members would require but one additional vote from a non-permanent member of the Security Council. Since the increase in the membership of the Security Council to 15 members in 1965, the requisite majority is eight, and candidates of permanent members need three votes from non-permanent members of the Council to obtain a majority.

The mystery of discontinuity. Granting the freedom of the United Nations to adopt any voting practice of its own compatible with the Court's Statute, the question remains why, on the subject of an unaltered provision in the Court's Statute, the two electoral organs of the United Nations should have desired this break in continuity with their predecessors.

The preparatory material is not conclusive. Similarly, in 1946 and after, enough representatives were available in both electoral organs who had been familiar with the election practices in the League era. Thus, ignorance of League practice under Article 10(1) in both Statutes can be excluded. None other symbolised this continuity more vividly in the First General Assembly than the senior delegate of El Salvador: the last President of the Permanent Court of International Justice and soon to become the first President of the International Court of Justice.

What is certain is that the practice was started by a series of presidential ad hoc rulings, acceptable to both electoral organs. The parallelism in the briefings of each of these organs by their Presidents suggests a common source, possibly the London emergency Secretariat of the United Nations. In any case, after a short while, the Secretariat emphasised in its memoranda for the benefit of the Presidents of the General Assembly and the Security Council the practice previously adopted, and soon this was claimed to be a consistent practice.

What is also reasonably clear is that, without strong interests in the two electoral organs pulling in the same direction, the discontinuity in the interpretation of Article 10(1) of the Court's Statute could not have consolidated so smoothly into accepted practice.

In the absence of more solid evidence, the *cui bono?* question must be put. It cannot lead further than to a possible working hypothesis. Yet, it does assist in identifying a variety of beneficiaries from the changed interpretation of Article 10(1) of the Court's Statute: successive Presidents of the General Assembly and the Security Council who would appreciate a rule calculable in advance and, after some lapse of time, the standard argument that this was how it had been done before. Similarly, the leaders and election-managers of the more powerful voting coalitions would find that the stiffer rule suited their books. A rule which, in effect, transformed a simple majority into a qualified one (in the terminology of Voting System One[13]) could but assist in reducing the number of "effective" candidates.

In this context, the common-sense truth that, whenever a particular voting rule favours one group, it inevitably discriminates against another, deserves to be recalled.[14] This explains why, at least in this sphere, the siren calls of practitioners of the art and an ideologically tinged pragmatism—*quieta non movere* or, in the vernacular, "let sleeping dogs lie"—have to be met with Odyssean resistance.

(3) *The request that was never made*

On the level of auto-interpretation, several interpretations of Article 10(1) of the Court's Statute are possible yet, in proceedings conceived as essentially adversary, only one of these interpretations tends to be equated with the true intention of the parties. Thus, it may be asked why, before accepting a radically different interpretation of a provision that was literally borrowed from the old Statute, it was thought unnecessary to seek guidance from the Court about to come into operation.

Comparable cases. In relation to a similar term—"by the vote of an absolute majority" in Article 12(1) of the Court's Statute, inserted at the San Francisco Conference to avoid any doubt on the non-applicability of the veto—the possibility of an Advisory Opinion was considered in 1946 but rejected. Similarly, an Advisory Opinion was under discussion on a more trivial question: the lawfulness under Article 11 of the Court's

---

[13] See above, text to note 12.
[14] Judge Sir Hersch Lauterpacht (S.O.), *Voting Procedure, I.C.J. Reports 1955*, p. 108.

Statute of holding more than one ballot for the election of judges at any one meeting of the General Assembly or the Security Council.[15]

On the second of these issues, there had also been a settled League practice, and it had been in favour of the possibility of several ballots at any one meeting. On grounds of economy of time—so as to hasten joint conferences of representatives of the General Assembly and the Security Council under Article 12 of the Court's Statute—the President of the First General Assembly ruled that only one ballot could be held at any one meeting. He was challenged on this by the Senior Delegate of El Salvador[16] but, backed by a majority in the General Assembly, the President carried the day. Before long, he was overruled with a vengeance: by additions to their Rules of Procedure, the General Assembly and the Security Council decided to apply Article 11 in accordance with the practice that had proved itself in the League of Nations.

Hypothetical questions. Were the Court to be asked for an Advisory Opinion on the meaning of "absolute majority of votes" in Article 10(1) of the Court's Statute, three major problems would arise:

(1) At least by implication, the Court might have to advise on the legality of all previous elections of members of the Court, including those of the sitting members. Even leaving aside the *nemo judex in sua causa* maxim, would any member of the Court be able to act without infringing the prohibitions in the Court's Statute regarding disqualifications on the ground of direct personal interest?

(2) If the Court decided to deal with the substance of the request, would it be fair to expect from the Court advice that might severely prejudice the authority of all previous findings of the Court and might have to be accompanied by the collective resignation of all sitting members of the Court?

(3) If, on the line of least resistance and in accordance with what might be expected from a "co-operative" Court,[17] the Court found on any ground that all previous elections were unchallengeable, and the interpretation of Article 10(1) of the Court's Statute in United Nations practice was in conformity with the intentions of the Parties (if not those to the Statute of the Permanent Court of Justice, then at least those to the Statute of the International Court of Justice), what would be the credibility of such advice?

---

[15] See the Report of Subcommittee IV/1/C to Committee IV/1 (U.S. Dept. of State, *The United Nations Conference on International Organisation* (1946), p. 851), and, on the issue relating to Art. 11 of the Court's Statute, the different accounts in *United Nations Year Book 1946–47*, p. 62, and *Répertoire of the Practice of the Security Council 1946–51*, p. 320, note 64.

[16] See above under heading (2) (sub-heading: *The mystery of discontinuity*).

[17] Judge Padilla Nervo (D.O.) in the *South West Africa Cases (Second Phase—1966), I.C.J. Reports 1966*, p. 468.

Resolving the conundrum. The political and administrative organs of the United Nations may compliment themselves on having saved the Court from a major embarrassment by masterly inactivity. They may even consider that what in 1946 may have been an error has been transformed, by the passage of time, into the "law recognised by the United Nations" and, in any case, has been redeemed by the last resort of bad law: *communis error facit jus.*

Yet, in the unlikely case that the collective conscience of the General Assembly and the Security Council should rebel at this late stage, as did at least one sensitive delegate,[18] a simple remedy exists: return to the earlier interpretation of Article 10(1) of the Court's Statute. In doing so, the electoral organs would free the Court from the necessity of living with what, on balance, appears to have been at best an error—if not one of the Court's making. Though belatedly, they would also pay due respect to the quasi-constitutional law of the United Nations of which, as appears advisable to re-emphasise, the Court's Statute forms an integral part.

III—THE JUDICIAL CORPS
IN THE DYNAMICS OF WORLD AFFAIRS

The impact on the Court of the dynamics in post-1945 world society will be considered from eight angles: expanding constituencies, entrenched positions, tests of composition, triennial elections, tentative challenges and responses, the redistribution of judgeships, impact of the *South West Africa (Namibia)* crisis, and, finally, judicial consensus, conformity and credibility in adversity.

(1) *Expanding constituencies*

The atomisation of the Western salt-water empires into a multitude of "sovereign and equal" members of the United Nations has led to a corresponding expansion of the General Assembly and to the enlargement of the Security Council by just under one-third.

Arithmetical aspects. The effects of the growth of the Security Council since 1965 from 11 to 15 members on the Council as an electoral organ have been twofold: the majority of non-permanent over permanent members of the Council has been increased from one to five, and the absolute majority required by each candidate from six to eight.

The triplication of the membership of the United Nations and, consequently, the General Assembly, augmented by a small number of non-member parties to the Court's Statute, has dramatically increased the

---

[18] The Netherlands Delegate at the 567th meeting of the Security Council (December 6, 1951), as quoted by Rudzinski, *loc. cit.*, above, note 12, p. 86.

absolute majority required by candidates for election to the Court. In Hegel's terminology, it has transformed quantity into quality:

General Assembly:

Absolute Majorities Required

Year	Absolute Majority	Members	Year	Absolute Majority	Members
1946 [a]	26	50	1966 [f]	63	125
1948 [b][c]	30	59	1969 [f]	65	129
1951 [d]	32	62	1972 [f]	68	135
1954 [e]	33	64	1975 [f]	74	147
1957 [f]	43	85	1978 [f]	78	154
1960 [f]	52	102	1981 [f]	80	159
1963 [f]	58	115			

(Table based on U.N.Y.B. and I.C.J.Y.B. (Ch. 3))

(a) Initial general election of *all* 15 judges. Their terms of office expired by lot after three, six or nine years (Article 13(1) and (2), Statute, I.C.J. (*loc. cit.*) above, note 2, pp. 65–67).
(b) First of subsequent triennial general elections of five judges.
(c) Including Switzerland.
(d) Including Lichtenstein and Switzerland.
(e) Including Japan, Lichtenstein, San Marino and Switzerland.
(f) Including Lichtenstein, San Marino and Switzerland.

Psephological aspects. If, although in a non-judicial capacity, a Vice-President of the Court discloses that, according to his own—extensive and varied—inside knowledge, elections to the Court involve "a good deal of horsetrading at the best of times,"[19] such practices call for examination.

The simile employed by Judge Elias describes pointedly a typical market situation in agricultural communities: the horse-fair. Through the ages, this periodic event has created a common denominator in market prices for anything that goes, has become proverbial for sharp practices and has suggested the rule of *caveat emptor.* Translated into electioneering, the existence of a vote-market makes possible acquisition of a maximal number of votes in a rationally calculable manner and with minimal waste of time and effort. As a rule, the "consideration" required for votes is determined in terms of "favours," depending on circumstances. Exceptional scarcity in marginal cases explains surcharges in cases of special needs, including that of prestige votes. As

[19] T. O. Elias in Mosler, H., and Bernhardt, R. (eds.), *Judicial Settlement of International Disputes* (1974), p. 27, and *New Horizons in International Law* (1979), p. 78.

with other markets, the international vote-markets have their own contact-points, agents and middle-men. It may also be recalled that a good deal of this happens only "at the best of times."[20] Until a writer with Graham Greene's sardonic humour portrays what happens at the worst of times, this intriguing facet of the matter may be left to the reader's own investigative skills.

Normative aspects. In terms of society (and, perhaps, situation) ethics, the Pharisee who passes through the corridors of the United Nations would be justified in closing his mind to the existence of any normative problems in these "facts" of institutionalised international life. Yet, in terms of community ethics, and even contemporary international law, such problems do arise.

In any highly integrated community, vote-trading in any form is likely to be incompatible with commonly accepted standards of morality and law and stigmatised as a corrupt practice. Thus, at least the question arises whether election practices on the "horse-trading" level contravene the general principles of law recognised by civilised nations.

De lege ferenda, a series of options presents itself. They range from possibilities of coping with objectionable practices by changes in the rules of procedure of the electoral organs via election committees of these two organs to a full-dress election court, with powers of disqualifying offenders from voting and standing as candidates in any future elections of the organisation concerned or, at least, elections relating to the Court.

Considering the improbability of even more modest changes in the Court's Statute ever surfacing to *lex lata*,[21] the chances for any effective change in vote-trading practices in relation to the Court appear remote. Thus, the conscientious judge envisaged by the Statute appears to be condemned to live with his own brand of original sin.

(2) *Entrenched positions*

As in the post-1919 period with the Permanent Court of International Justice, the greater Powers of the post-1945 era have worked on the assumption of permanent "representation" in the Court.

The greater Powers, disguised as the permanent members of the Security Council, have taken it largely for granted that, in elections to the Court, the General Assembly and the Security Council of the United Nations would go almost automatically through the required motions; that they would take hints on preferred and "other" candidates of the nationalities of the permanent members, and that greater-Power

---

[20] *Loc. cit.*, above, note 19.
[21] On the long-drawn-out process and failure in 1976 of amendments (proposed by the Court) to Art. 22 of the Court's Statute on the Court's seat and consequential amendments to Arts. 23 and 28, see, for instance, I.C.J.Y.B. 1976–77, p. 113.

"representation" should not depend on submission by any of these Powers to the Court's automatic jurisdiction or evidence other than their own—past or continuing—pre-eminence in the hierarchy of power.

The equilibrium reached so far in the conflict between statics and dynamics in elections to the Court will emerge most sharply from the voting records in favour of preferred candidates from the two most pronounced oligarchic Powers in contemporary world society: the United States and the Soviet Union.

Voting Records
of Preferred U.S.A. and U.S.S.R. Candidates

Year of election	Absolute Majority required	Votes Obtained U.S.A.	Votes Obtained U.S.S.R.	Absolute Majority required	Votes Obtained U.S.A.	Votes Obtained U.S.S.R
	General Assembly			**Security Council**		
1946	26	32	34	6	8	11
1951	32	43	41	6	11	9
1953	32	—	52 [a]	6	—	9 [a]
1960	52	77	62	6	11	9
1969	62	88	81	8	12	11
1978	77	103	92	8	9	9
1981	79	122	—	8	15 [b]	—

(a) Supplementary election of a U.S.S.R. judge, owing to resignation of his U.S.S.R. predecessor.
(b) Supplementary election of a U.S.A. judge, owing to death of his U.S.A. predecessor.

It becomes evident from the above Table that, even during the first Cold War, the United States protected the oligarchic claim of the Soviet Union to permanent "representation" in the Court. Similarly, until the Court's South West Africa crisis,[22] the Soviet Union refrained from challenging resolutely Taiwan's claim that her preferred candidate "represented" China.

A comparison of the votes cast in the two electoral organs for pre-ferred and non-preferred candidates of the nationalities of the super-Powers is also instructive. The low-vote ignominies inflicted in one or both electoral organs on non-preferred candidates of the super-Powers raise wider questions of international morality and decency. In this con-text, it suffices to point out the evidence, which the discrepancies in the votes for preferred and non-preferred candidates of the two Powers fur-nish: they prove the efficiency of the election-managements of the super-

---

[22] See below under heading (7).

Powers and the, at most, marginal relevance of the personal qualifications of their preferred candidate.

It is primarily for purposes of insurance and prestige votes that the election-managers of the super-Powers are likely to heed the advice, significantly limited in its addressees, on the need for greater constituency-mindedness: "Western European candidates in the future would stand a far better chance of being elected if they had or were thought to have liberal or progressive views *vis-à-vis* the problems of the Third World."[23]

(3) *Tests of the court's composition*

The Court's Statute provides its own tests for the Court's composition.

The statutory rules.   The electors are enjoined to bear in mind at every election not only the personal qualifications required from candidates but also the composition of the Court as a whole. At all times, they are to assure representation in the Court of the main forms of civilisation and of the world's principal legal systems. While the electors are to disregard the nationality of candidates, they are to take into account the association of candidates with particular civilisations and legal systems.

As with other rules of constitutional and quasi-constitutional law, compliance with this electoral duty under Article 9 of the Court's Statute is essentially a matter of the law-abidingness and integrity of the electors. Also, there must be wide agreement to disagree on what, at any time, are the main forms of civilisation and principal legal systems.

Article 9 is addressed to the electoral organs. It is not an invitation to individual judges to consider themselves as representatives in the Court of any particular legal system. Whatever their legal *formation* or association, their duty is, to the best of their ability, to apply international law as Article 38 of the Court's Statute bids them to do.

Simplifications and over-simplifications.   In the practice of the United Nations, a marked tendency is noticeable to identify the tests laid down in the Statute with other tests, developed for purposes of electing members of political organs.

In the context of collective security, "equitable geographical distribution" of the non-permanent members of the Security Council is a relevant consideration and has found its place in the United Nations Charter.[24] To extend this test to elections for other organs in which the electors are left a free hand is a sensible rationalisation and limitation of bargaining unlimited. Yet to apply this test to the election of members of the Court means disregarding prescribed tests for rules of thumb of supposedly "regional" or "continental" representation, admittedly handier for purposes of vote-trafficking across the board.

---

[23] Judge Elias, *loc. cit.*, above, note 19 (1979), p. 78.
[24] Art. 23(1), U.N. Charter.

(4) *Triennial elections*

The parties to the original and revised Statute of the Permanent Court of International Justice worked on the assumption of a reasonably homogeneous electorate. Thus, they took but a small risk in deciding in favour of simultaneous election of all judges at nine-year intervals.

More than half of the candidates elected in 1930 were new faces. Yet, their social, educational and professional background differed little from that of their predecessors: urbane upper-middle class lawyers and higher civil servants in the Anglo-Saxon or French mould, with a sound working knowledge of international law or other international experiences.

In 1945, it was considered preferable to switch over to triennial elections of five of the Court's fifteen members. As before, responsibility for the choice of candidates with the necessary qualification was left with the nominating and electoral organs. What neither system of election was designed to cope with was any appreciable increase in outside pressure on the Court or individual members.

On the inside evidence of a member of the Court, drawing on 13 years' "intimate experience" from 1960 to 1973, the destabilising effects of the triennial elections are more severe than may be thought. They are intensified by unpredictable needs for supplementary elections and the minority position of international-law specialists in the Court. Thus, the task of integrating new members and maintaining continuity in the Court's judicial practice has become more arduous.[25]

In Sir Gerald Fitzmaurice's uncontradicted opinion—supported, as he avers, by other "recent or contemporary" members of the Court—the frequency of elections to the Court has "even more sinister implications." They "afford occasions on which various political pressures can be brought to bear on the Court and its members." "What is still worse," it becomes possible for the Court "to be constituted—or reconstituted—with a direct view to a particular case then before it, or some phase of which still has to be adjudicated upon". In conclusion, Sir Gerald affirms that his strictures do not relate to "merely theoretical or hypothetical possibilities."[26]

Whether greater emphasis on the international-law qualifications of the members of the Court—and what kind of international law is assumed?—would be more than a cosmetic remedy may be doubted.

(5) *Tentative challenges and responses*

From the early days of the Court onwards, there were signs of discontent with the Court's pronounced Western composition and pained reactions to these rumblings of unrest.

---

[25] Institute of International Law (I.D.I.), *Livre du Centenaire* (1973), pp. 288 *et seq.*
[26] *Ibid.* p. 289.

Challenges.   Superficially, the first triennial elections held in 1948 were reassuring for the beneficiaries of the post-1946 judicial status quo. All five retiring judges stood for re-election and were duly re-elected.

Behind the scenes, the election figures gave rise to justified anxieties. To achieve the end-result, seven ballots were required in the General Assembly, and eight in the Security Council. The absolute majority of six votes in the Security Council at one of these ballots in favour of Sir Benegal Rau (India) served notice of an unsatisfied claim from a legal system which served the world's second-largest population and could offer a presentable candidate of its own.

At the 1951 triennial elections, Sir Benegal Rau obtained absolute majorities in both electoral organs ahead of two sitting judges from the Western half of the Continent. Thus, only one more seat was to be filled and, in the ensuing contest, Judge Klaestad (Norway) prevailed over Judge de Visscher (Belgium).

In terms of legal systems, Anglo-Indian Law had triumphed in these two elections over Western-oriented Continental Law which, in addition to its Latin-Law representation, was reduced to representation by Scandinavian Law.

An indirect response.   In the West, Charles de Visscher's defeat was not only widely regarded as an affront to a distinguished international lawyer but also as a threat to the continued representation of other legal systems on the existing footing. Thus, Judge Guerrero, a former President of both Courts and, currently, Vice-President of the International Court of Justice, went into action. He chose as his battle ground the Siena Session of the Institute of International Law (1952) and persuaded the Institute's first plenary meeting, attended by a considerable number of members of the old and new Courts, to consider the Court's composition.

In Judge Guerrero's oral communication, the almost instant Report of the Guerrero Commission, and the Resolution adopted, two failings of the 1951 elections to the Court were castigated: the insufficient attention paid by the electoral organs to the relative personal merits of the candidates, in contravention of Article 2 of the Court's Statute, and the informal—and no less reprehensible—contacts between the two electoral organs in breach of Article 8 of the Court's Statute.

The Institute's Resolution was forwarded to the Secretary-General of the United Nations. Beyond the usual routine acknowledgement, nothing happened. Even the Institute's modest recommendations of formal separation, as far as possible, of elections to the Court from those to political United Nations organs and inscription of elections to the Court as the first item on the agenda after the closure of the initial General Debate were ignored.

Judge Guerrero (deceased 1958) was at least spared the performance by a Peruvian delegate during the 1960 triennial elections who ventured to flout openly the rule of isolation of the two electoral organs from each other. In these elections, a former President of Peru was a candidate. Knowledge that he had achieved the requisite absolute majority in the Security Council was likely to improve his chances in the General Assembly. Thus, when, with minimal delay,[27] the success of the Peruvian candidate in the Security Council had been communicated to the Peruvian delegate, he decided to impart this news forthwith to the General Assembly. He did so by intervention on a point of order. With only the mildest of rebukes from the Chair, he got away with his insouciance. With, or in spite of, this assistance, the Peruvian candidate—a future President of the Court—was elected.

Perhaps, the indirect response by individual members of the Court to the challenge of the 1951 elections was also intended to provide support from the side-lines for Charles de Visscher's re-election in 1954. If so, the negative result of this effort confirmed that declarations of professional solidarity were a poor second best for votes given by government-delegates to others when and where it mattered.

In due course, the enlarged Guerrero Commission produced a report as wise as anything from Max Huber's pen. It became the prototype for a series of—unimplemented—projects on the reform of the Court's Statute.[28] Perhaps the most valuable effect of the Institute's intervention was that it provided an early opportunity to put on record the pragmatic disregard by the electoral organs of the "constitutional principle" embodied in Article 2 of the Court's Statute.[29]

A direct response. The seats most at risk from the increase in the membership of the United Nations since 1955 were some of the four held by Latin American judges.

In the Permanent Court of International Justice, the representation of the Latin American legal system had increased from an initial two to three judges and, in the International Court of Justice, their share had expanded right from 1946 onwards to just under one-quarter of the Court's members. Thus, it was not surprising that, in 1956, six Latin American governments, including El Salvador, and Spain joined in proposing to the United Nations General Assembly consideration of an increase in the Court's membership. In view of the likely negative effects of any drastic increase in numbers on the Court's collegiate character, the Institute of International Law had dismissed already in 1954 any proposals for increases in the Court's membership beyond 18 members. Unlike proposals for the increase in the membership of the political organs of the United Nations, those relating to increases in the Court's

---

[27] Ten minutes (according to Rosenne, *loc. cit.*, above, note 1, Vol. II, p. 930).

[28] See Gross, *loc. cit.*, above, note 11, Mosler-Bernhardt, *loc. cit.*, above, note 19, and L. V. Prott, *The Future of the International Court of Justice*, this *Year Book*, Vol. 33 (1979), pp. 284 *et seq.*

[29] Judge Guerrero (45 (I) I.D.I.L. (1954)), p. 519.

membership fell on stony ground and, in 1959, were quietly dropped. Whatever adjustments were to be made had to come from one or more of *beati possidentes*.

(6) *The redistribution of judgeships*

The scale of the redistribution of seats in the International Court of Justice that has taken place becomes evident from a comparison of the composition of its judicial corps in 1946 with the changes since the triennial elections of 1966.[30]

The test applied. In addition to the individual qualities expected from candidates, the electoral organs are charged with applying two overall tests: representation in the Court of the world's principal legal systems and of the main forms of civilisation.[31]

In the abstract, it may be difficult to determine the identity of the world's principal legal systems. For the purposes of this evaluation, it must suffice to include—individually or in groups of related legal systems—all those legal systems which, at least once, have succeeded in sending judges to the Court.

Within limits, a liberal application of the principal-legal-systems test will also provide at least indirect evidence of the application by the electoral organs of the main-forms-of-civilisation test.

Tests rejected. A number of tests appear to be less suited for our task than those chosen in the Court's Statute:

The test of *regional* representation suffers from the elusiveness of the term "region." However defined, most regions appear to be interconnected. Thus, the regional test is liable to be applied with considerable subjectivity and prone to pragmatic abuse. If, for instance, each portion of a divided country with a common ethnic, historical and cultural heritage is allocated to a different region, the description of some countries as west- or east-European States may be unduly escapist.

Similarly, *continental* representation implies a geographical certainty which is less manifest in the case of some continents than others. Moreover, some countries happen to be straddled across two continents and, for normative purposes, the description as a continent of the smallest of the world's continents is perhaps less relevant than its Common-Law connection.

Understandably, the terminology of regional and continental representation is attractive for purposes of election-management in the United Nations. Thus, the reference in the United Nations Charter to equitable geographical distribution as a factor relevant to the election of non-permanent members of the Security Council has been extended to

---

[30] *Cf.* I.C.J.Y.B. 1946–47 and 1966–67 *et seq.* (Chap. 1) and the Table below.
[31] Art. 9, Statute, I.C.J. (*loc. cit.*, above, note 2, pp. 63–65).

elections for other political organs. Further extension to the Court of these pseudo-geographic tests would ease still further the tasks of across-the-board bargaining in contravention of the Court's Statute.

It has also been suggested that representation in the Court should be related to submission to the Court's automatic jurisdiction. Yet such declarations may be qualified by far-reaching or derisory reservations and, in any case, this and similar tests are relevant only *de lege ferenda*.

The principal-legal-systems test in operation. In accordance with the Court's Statute, *de facto* claims by Powers to permanent representation of their legal systems in the Court are ignored for purposes of the Table that follows, and, as with other sovereign and equal members of the United Nations, judges of the nationalities of permanent members of the Security Council are allocated to their respective legal systems.

Comments on the Table. Five comments may assist in analysing the Table:

(1) If and when China should claim representation of its legal system in the Court, some other legal system would have to be the loser. This possibility permits instructive psephological forecasts.

(2) It deserves emphasising that the switch from the BENELUX legal system to the Anglo-Indian legal system in the 1951 elections[32] occurred long before the West lost its preponderance in the electoral organs of the United Nations.

(3) When, from 1964 onwards, the representation of the Latin American legal system in the Court was reduced by half, this situation led to an incipient practice of rotation between members of the Latin American Law group in the Court. Other groups of related legal systems may ignore this self-denying ordinance at their peril.

(4) The Table suggests a smoother progression to universalisation of the Court's membership than actually happened. This potentially mis-leading impression will call for correction.[33]

(5) In view of the sharpening divisions in an increasingly heterogeneous world society, the triennial system of elections to the Court may perhaps claim in its favour that it slows down processes of change and eases the Court's task of absorbing *homines novos*.

(7) *The South West Africa (Namibia) issue*

It was the South West Africa (Namibia) issue, with *apartheid* at large in the background, that gave a sharp edge to the quest for redistribution of seats in the Court.

The voting figures in the two Phases of the *South West Africa Cases* show the deep split on the issue in the Court from the early 1960s

---

[32] See above under heading II (5).

[33] See below under heading (7).

Representation of Principal Legal Systems

Year — July after election	Common Law	Latin Law	Latin Am. Law	BENELUX Law (F.R.G.)	Scand. Law	German Law	Greek Law	Yug. Law	Polish Law	Russian Law	Anglo-Afr. Law	Franco-Afr. Law	Islamic Law	Indian Law	Chin. Law	Jap. Law	Philipp. Law
1946	3	1	4	1	1	—	—	1	1	1	—	—	1	—	1	—	—
1949	3	1	4	1	1	—	—	1	1	1	—	—	1	—	1	—	—
1952	3	1	4	—	1	—	—	1	1	1	—	—	1	1	1	—	—
1955	3	1	4	—	1	—	—	1	1	1	—	—	2	—	1	—	—
1958	3	1	4	—	1	—	1	—	1	1	—	—	2	—	1	1	—
1961	3	2	4	—	—	—	1	—	1	1	—	—	1	—	1	1	—
1964	3	2	2	—	—	—	1	—	1	1	—	1	2	—	1	1	—
1967	2	2	2	—	1	—	—	—	1	1	1	1	2	—	—	1	1
1970	2	2	2	—	1	—	—	—	1	1	1	2	2	—	—	—	1
1973	2	2	2	—	1	—	—	—	1	1	1	2	1	1	—	—	1
1976	2	2	2	—	—	1	—	—	1	1	1	2	1	1	—	1	—
1979	2	2	2	—	—	1	—	—	1	1	1	1	2	1	—	1	—

Figures based on I.C.J.Y.B. 1946–47 et seq. (Chapter 1)

onwards: eight to seven in favour of the Court's jurisdiction (1962), and—with the help of "acts of God" and men, including the President's casting vote—transformation in 1966 of the former minority into a majority of also eight to seven.

Time-scale and character of the crisis. The Court's crisis, open to various interpretations—as a transformation of the Court into a co-operative court, a process of rejuvenation and purge—was prolonged.

As is indicated by the voting figures in the First Phase of the *South West Africa Cases* (1962), a considerable division on the wider issue in the Court already existed when, in 1960, the Ethiopian and Liberian Applications were submitted to the Court.

The 1966 triennial election, following in the wake of the Court's judgment in the Second Phase of the *South West Africa Cases*, was neither the beginning nor the end but the climax of this long-drawn-out malaise.

With triennial elections for only one-third of the members of the judicial corps, the Court's purge was necessarily a slow-motion picture that would last, at least, until 1972 and even longer in relation to sitting judges whose term expired later. Yet, some of the reactions were more instantaneous: the rejection of "one of the most highly qualified jurists who ever stood for election to the Court,"[34] a pointed change-over in the representation of the Polish legal system, and the election of an additional judge from Black Africa.

As with other purges, what mattered most was not so much its quantitative aspect as the shock-effect on the surviving members of the judicial corps, their chances of being re-elected and the selection of future candidates by nominating groups short of votes.

The *Namibia* case (1971) proved the success of the tactics applied. On the decisive first of the Court's three answers, the vote was 13 against 2 in favour of the illegality of the continued presence of South Africa in Namibia and her duty to withdraw immediately her administration from Namibia. It was only on two consequential issues that two members of the majority were prepared to join the hard-line dissidents. If anything was surprising, it was the re-election of Judge Gros, and with a resounding number of votes.

The lengths to which the Court was prepared to go were made manifest by two of the most questionable features of the *Namibia* case:

(1) In common knowledge, the request made by the Security Council was hardly a bona fide attempt by the Security Council to obtain legal guidance from the Court. Its object was to obtain a *de facto* revision of the Court's 1966 judgment and the Court's endorsement in advance of any more militant action that might recommend itself to the political organs of the United Nations. In other words, the request was a blatant abuse of procedure. Yet, the last course of action the Court was pre-

---

[34] P. C. Jessup, 71 A.J.I.L. (1977), p. 794.

pared to adopt was to meet this challenge to its independence and dignity by exercising in the negative its discretionary power to render the Opinion requested.

(2) Given that the 1970–71 proceedings were a *de facto* continuation of the previous contentious proceedings, South Africa was at least entitled to a judge ad hoc. Yet, her request to this effect was rejected by 10 to 5 votes. On this point, Judge Dillard joined the four other dissenters.

What happened during this period of the Court's "reconstruction" in connection with the election of its judicial officers is no less instructive. These elections take place by secret ballot. Coincidentally or otherwise, all judges serving as Presidents or Vice-Presidents of the Court between 1967 and 1976 had voted (if in a position to do so) on South West Africa (Namibia) issues in the "correct" manner. It took until 1978 to consolidate further readjustments, including closer contacts of the Court with the political organs of the United Nations (initiated in 1967) and completion of the revision of the Court's own Rules with what, in this context, is most relevant: greater emphasis on judicial leadership.

Factors of exacerbation.   The divisiveness of the South West Africa (Namibia) issue in relation to, and in, the Court was heightened by a number of debatable moves:

(1) The artificiality of pressing the issue in the form of contentious proceedings between Ethiopia and Liberia as Applicants and South Africa as the Defendant under a jurisdiction clause, based on the 1920 League Mandate of South West Africa;

(2) the transformation of the Court's minority into a majority by a double presidential intervention: Judge Sir Muhammad Zafrulla Khan's "withdrawal" from the case and the exercise of the presidential casting vote[35];

(3) the failure of the 1966 majority to give an opportunity to the parties to be heard on the Court's ruling, denying the Applicant's *jus standi*;

(4) the manner in which the request leading to the 1971 Advisory Opinion was engineered;

(5) the denial to South Africa of a judge ad hoc in the proceedings leading to the 1971 Opinion.

On each of these counts, those negatively affected considered that formal devices were abused for metalegal ends, and that equity was neither done nor seen to be done. Rationalisations and justifications under each of the five heads are possible. Yet, it would be difficult to imagine that international judges such as Max Huber, Cecil Hurst or Manley

---

[35] See, further, this *Year Book*, Vol. 27 (1973), pp. 437 *et seq.*, and also Sir Percy Spender (the Court's then President), *The Office of the President of the International Court*, 1 *Australian Yearbook of International Law* (1965), pp. 14 *et seq.*

O. Hudson would have associated themselves with any of the judicial acts involved.

(8) *Judicial consensus, conformity and credibility in adversity*

In a corps limited to 15 members, the sequence of triennial and supplementary elections over more than 30 years alone tends to lead to substantial changes in composition.

Factors such as the Court's universalisation, the erosion of judicial emoluments by inflation, deterioration of the Court's international environment and changes in the professional *formation* of the Court's members are likely to condition further the character of this judicial corps.

The Court's universalisation. In the disarming view of Judge Elias, one of the results of the *South West Africa Cases* and the Court's accelerated universalisation may be a decline in "candidates with real competence in international law" and "professional integrity."[36]

Insofar as a greater risk of lesser competence stems from increased representation of legal systems which, so far, are un- or under-represented in the Court, any lesser acquaintance with international law may not be as significant as Judge Elias fears. In the past, the Court has absorbed reasonably well recruits who, only during their terms of office, approximated more closely to the ideal of *jura novit curia.* Conversely, the benefits which a universalist Court can derive from fuller representation in the Court of the world's chief legal systems and forms of civilisation—as prescribed in its Statute—are considerable.

The doubts Judge Elias expresses on the subject of professional integrity, covering the whole gamut of judicial independence, disinterestedness and impartiality, raise a more serious issue. Yet, in an increasingly "dangerous age,"[37] the main threats appear to arise from quarters more solidly entrenched in the United Nations than even "third-world" governments.

Effects of monetary inflation. The erosion of judicial emoluments through inflation is also thought to discourage some otherwise eligible candidates. If this were so, it might be a blessing in disguise.

Moreover, in the past, the primary reason for policies of generous judicial remuneration was that economic independence would promote judicial independence and integrity. In view of the different character of the most serious threats to judicial independence and integrity in our time, extended tenure of judicial office and, for judges who prefer to end their days in at least relative tranquillity outside their home countries,

---

[36] *Loc. cit.*, above, note 19 (1979), p. 78.
[37] With acknowledgements to the title of the paper by M. Lachs, *On the Importance of International Law in a Dangerous Age*, 1 Polish Y.B.I.L. (1966–67).

offers of permanent residence in countries with less oppressive régimes might constitute greater attractions than even indexed remuneration.

A deteriorating environment. Compared with the international environment of the Permanent Court of International Justice, that of the International Court of Justice is probably even less stable and auspicious. Correspondingly, the chances of its members to equal the great among the judges of the Permanent Court of International Justice are receding.

Six features of this daunting environment directly affect—and all negatively—the Court's radius of positive action in its allocated field:

(1) The shortage of general peace settlements which, like those of 1919–23, provide for automatic submission to the Court of a wide variety of disputes.

(2) The depressing effect of the weaknesses of a world quasi-order based on fear of coextermination.

(3) The make-believe element in international affairs, with the contradictions between a highly stratified world society and the ideologies embodied in the constituting instruments of its consensual superstructures.

(4) The discrepancies between the object-role of in-between areas on the level of super-Power politics and the claims of nuclear non-Powers to be treated as sovereign and equal States on confederate levels in and outside the United Nations.

(5) The phenomenon of small-Power lawlessness with impunity, spreading opportunism and hesitation of greater Powers to enforce their rights for fear of major confrontations, and a corresponding loss in credibility of international law, morality and institutions.

(6) Growing preference for pragmatic ad hoc solutions, reached under the direct control of the parties concerned.

Judicial credibility in adversity.   The judge conscientious, postulated in the Court's Statute, may well wonder how, in contemporary world society, he can ever hope to emulate the judges of the previous inter-war period.

Admittedly, in present-day conditions, the path to greatness of a judge who desires to attain pre-eminence by what he *does* is harder than it was for earlier generations. Yet, nobody can deprive him of his opportunities of making it crystal-clear what he is *not* prepared to do.

On any occasion which calls for his co-operation in the Court, he remains free to apply at least five tests which, to judge by the Court's practice, do not appear to relate to entirely hypothetical situations:

(1) Is the judicial act envisaged fair and likely to be considered to be so by reasonable onlookers?

(2) Is, to the best of his powers of self-analysis, his own attitude to judicial acts motivated by any but intrinsically relevant considerations?

(3) Is he reasonably sure that an organisational, jurisdictional or procedural decision contemplated is equitable and does not constitute an abuse of a formal device for undisclosed ends?

(4) Is he willing, at least for the benefit of his fellow-members of the Bench, to state articulately in any particular case the major premises of his choice between potentially relevant rules of international law and assure himself that this choice does not rest on undisclosed preferences of a metalegal character?

(5) Is he willing, in each and every case, to make strict compliance with his particular *jus cogens*—that is, the Court's Statute, and especially Article 38—his overriding obligation?

If the judge conscientious in adversity can answer in the affirmative these not unduly hard questions in the crucial area of confidence, his judicial credibility is assured, and he need not fear comparison with international judges of a less inauspicious age.

INDEX

269